The Ruin of All Witches

The Ruin of All Witches

Life and Death in the New World

MALCOLM GASKILL

ALLEN LANE
an imprint of
PENGUIN BOOKS

ALLEN LANE

UK | USA | Canada | Ireland | Australia
India | New Zealand | South Africa

Penguin Books is part of the Penguin Random House group of companies
whose addresses can be found at global.penguinrandomhouse.com

Penguin
Random House
UK

First published in Great Britain by Allen Lane 2021

002

Copyright © Malcolm Gaskill, 2021

Endpapers: Interrogation of Hugh and Mary Parsons, March 1651, where at the end of the first paragraph
is written in William Pynchon's hand: 'this expression of y[ou]r anger was bec[ause] she wished
the ruine of all witches' – part of a question addressed to Hugh about his wife. New York Public Library,
Mss Col. 1900, William Pynchon's Deposition Book, 1650–51 ('Testimony against Hugh Parsons,
charged with witchcraft'), ff. 18v–19r.

The moral right of the author has been asserted

Set in 12/14.75 pt Dante MT Std
Typeset by Jouve (UK), Milton Keynes
Printed and bound in Great Britain by Clays Ltd, Elcograf S.p.A.

The authorized representative in the EEA is Penguin Random House Ireland,
Morrison Chambers, 32 Nassau Street, Dublin D02 YH68

A CIP catalogue record for this book is available from the British Library

ISBN: 978–0–241–41338–8

For Sheena Peirse
Who makes all things possible

Always and everywhere, human beings have felt the radical inadequacy of their personal existence, the misery of being their insulated selves and not something else, something wider.

Aldous Huxley, *The Devils of Loudun* (1952), appendix

A house, a city, a kingdom, divided against itself cannot stand . . . Therefore if division do inevitably bring destruction to a kingdom, to a city, how shall one poor family divided subsist without destruction?

Robert Burnam, *A Remonstrance*, 1645 – the year Hugh Parsons and Mary Lewis were married in New England

One reason why she doth suspect you to be a witch is because you cannot abide that anything should be spoken against witches . . . this expression of your anger was because she wished the ruin of all witches.

William Pynchon, interrogating Hugh Parsons about his wife Mary, 1651 – the year their marriage ended

Contents

Author's Note

The dates of the Old Style Julian calendar, whereby the New Year began on 25 March, have been changed to New Style so that the year starts on 1 January.

Sums of money are given as pounds, shillings and pence (£, s, d). There were twelve pence to a shilling and twenty shillings to a pound. In New England, where silver was scarce, other forms of currency were used, including bushels of corn and Native American wampum – blue-and-white polished shells, pierced and strung on long cords.

Spellings and punctuation in quotations have been modernized, contractions expanded and names standardized. As in Old England, people addressed each other as 'Goodman', 'Goodwife' (or 'Goody') and 'Widow'. The gentry were 'Mister' and 'Mistress'.

New England in the 1650s

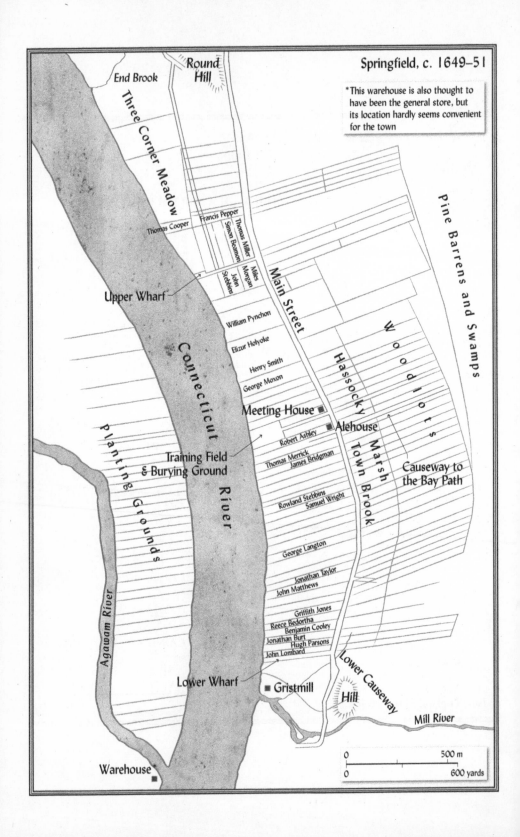

Springfield, c. 1649–51

*This warehouse is also thought to have been the general store, but its location hardly seems convenient for the town

Round Hill

End Brook

Three Corner Meadow

Pine Barrens and Swamps

Thomas Cooper
Francis Pepper
Thomas Miller
Simon Beamon
Miles Morgan
John Stebbins

Main Street

Upper Wharf

Connecticut River

Woodlots

William Pynchon

Elizur Holyoke

Henry Smith

George Moxon

Hassocky Marsh

Meeting House ■

■ Alehouse

Robert Ashley

Training Field & Burying Ground

Thomas Merrick
James Bridgman

Town Brook

Causeway to the Bay Path

Planting Grounds

Rowland Stebbins
Samuel Wright

George Langton

Jonathan Taylor
John Matthews

Griffith Jones
Reece Bedortha
Benjamin Cooley
Jonathan Burt
Hugh Parsons
John Lombard

Agawam River

Lower Wharf

■ Gristmill

Hill

Lower Causeway

Mill River

Warehouse ■

| 0 | | 500 m |
| 0 | | 600 yards |

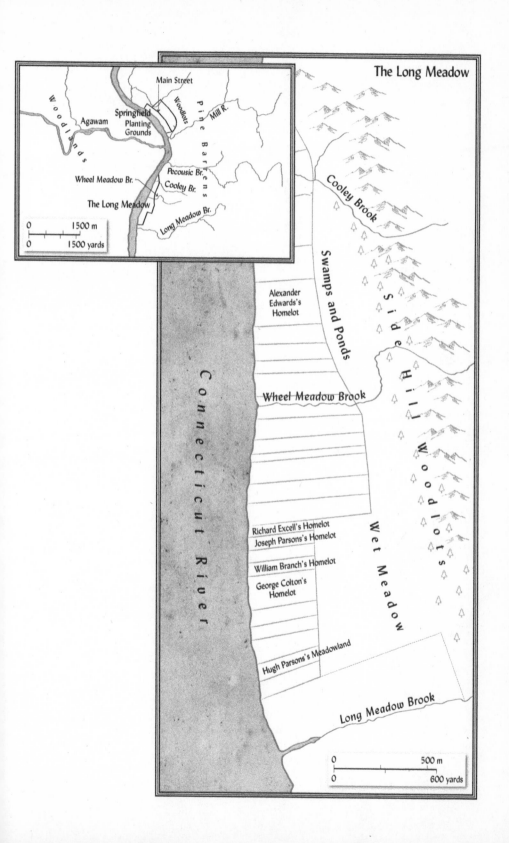

The Long Meadow

Main Street

Woodlots

Pine Barrens

Mill R.

Springfield
Planting
Grounds

Agawam

Woodlands

Wheel Meadow Br.

Pecousic Br.

Cooley Br.

The Long Meadow

Long Meadow Br.

0   1500 m
0   1500 yards

Cooley Brook

Swamps and Ponds

Side Hill Woodlots

Alexander
Edwards's
Homelot

Wheel Meadow Brook

Connecticut River

Wet Meadow

Richard Excell's Homelot

Joseph Parsons's Homelot

William Branch's Homelot

George Colton's
Homelot

Hugh Parsons's Meadowland

Long Meadow Brook

0   500 m
0   600 yards

Principal Characters

Hugh Parsons, *a turbulent English brickmaker and jack-of-all-trades, in his thirties.*

Mary Parsons (formerly Lewis), *a maidservant from Wales, Hugh's wife (m. 1645).*

Hannah (b. 1646), Samuel (b. 1648) and Joshua Parsons (b. 1650), *their children.*

William Pynchon, *founder of Springfield, fur trader, magistrate and amateur theologian.*

Anne Smith, *Pynchon's daughter, mother of many daughters, confidante to Mary Parsons.*

Henry Smith, *her husband (and Pynchon's stepson), town clerk and sometime deputy magistrate.*

Margaret (b. 1646) and Sarah (b. 1647), *the Smiths' daughters, who perished in June 1648.*

George Moxon, *minister, whose daughters Martha and Rebecca were possessed or bewitched.*

Thomas Merrick, *a Welshman, town constable.*

Sarah Merrick, *Thomas's wife, implicated as a witch.*

Mercy Marshfield, *a widow of dubious reputation, who fled Windsor to resettle in Springfield.*

Sarah Miller, *wife of unlucky sawyer Thomas Miller and Widow Marshfield's daughter, who suffered fits and saw terrifying apparitions.*

John Stebbins, *whose wife Anne also had fits, and on whose homelot the witches met in secret.*

Mary Bliss Parsons (no relation), *who was troubled by spirits and roamed the meadow at night.*

Anthony Dorchester, *a poor, ambitious man and his ailing wife Sarah, Hugh Parsons's lodgers.*

John Lombard, *a herdsman from Somerset, the Parsonses' next-door neighbour, whose borrowed trowel mysteriously vanished.*

Blanche Bedortha, *a Welsh housewife, married to Reece, a carter, terrified of Hugh during her pregnancy.*

Pentecost Matthews, *also Welsh, wife of John, and first to notice Mary's witch obsession.*

William Branch, *the town barber, who was disturbed in the night and fell strangely lame.*

Griffith Jones, *a Welsh tanner, tricked at home by witchery.*

Thomas Cooper, *a Warwickshire carpenter, who heard Mary Parsons's shocking confession.*

George Colton, *William Pynchon's quartermaster, a principal witness against Hugh Parsons.*

Benjamin Cooley, *a weaver, Colton's brother-in-law, next-door neighbour to the Bedorthas.*

George and Hannah Langton, *who were convinced their steamed meat pudding was bewitched.*

Simon Beamon, *cobbler and servant to William Pynchon, prey to Hugh Parsons's impatience.*

Alexander Edwards, *who had known Mary in Wales, and whose cow gave abnormal milk.*

Jonathan Taylor, *a young married labourer, menaced in his bed by demonic serpents.*

Introduction

This is a true story about witchcraft in mid-seventeenth-century New England. At this time none of its colonies – New Hampshire, Plymouth, Massachusetts, Rhode Island and Connecticut, sited along America's east coast – was over thirty years old. Each was still finding its way in a new world. Unlike the icy shores of Newfoundland and Maine or the tropics of Virginia and the Caribbean, New England resembled the old, with hills and plains, forests and rivers. For much of the year the climate was mild – well suited to English bodies, colonists felt. Farmsteads produced cattle and corn. There were busy ports at Boston and Salem, and trade flourished. Yet life was fraught with peril. Settlers were far from home, assailed by sharp winters and sweltering summers and hemmed in by wilderness. By day a labourer could pretend he was still tending wheat in Kent or herding sheep in Wiltshire; but the illusion was easily dispelled, especially after sunset. Old World folktales where travellers were stalked by evil became reality, trapping colonists in nightmares of echoing isolation and heart-thumping panic. In these moments, New England, for all its hopeful beginnings, meant only the skin-prickle of being watched, the twisting grip of a curse and the terrors of the dark.

The setting for this story is a remote community in Massachusetts, a hundred miles west of Boston, named Springfield. There, on the border between what they saw as civility and barbarism, Springfield's pioneers laboured to cultivate both land and a new way of living together, only too aware of how closely their fragile world was overseen by God and existed at his mercy. They contended with waves of epidemics, severe flooding and constant tension with the Native Americans they called 'Indians', whose possessions they appropriated. They also clashed with Dutch traders into whose territory they strayed, and with English planters further down the

Connecticut River valley. Mostly, however, they clashed with their own neighbours, competing furiously for material advantage: farmland, livestock, wealth and power. Whenever this fury subsided, consciences were apt to be pricked, guilt bubbling up in private thoughts, and in dreams where colonists saw their own self-serving desires wrestling with those of their enemies. But still they didn't yield; nor did they show remorse. Instead, conflicting emotions were batted away, projected onto a diabolic 'other' – onto witches – and thus assuaged.

Springfield's disquiet settled with lethal ferocity on a labouring couple, Hugh and Mary Parsons, whose ailing marriage epitomized deeper currents of animosity in the town. He was moody, taciturn, avaricious; she depressive and delusional, perhaps suffering from paranoid schizophrenia or postpartum psychosis. Years of quarrelling, gossiping and bitten-back suspicions among neighbours – suspicions festering even between husband and wife – accumulated until a tipping point was reached in the winter of 1650–51. Springfield's community could no longer bear the presence of witches. For the Parsons family the outcome was catastrophic.

All but forgotten now, the troubled lives of Hugh and Mary, interlaced with that of Springfield's overlord William Pynchon, were shaped by and reflect an age of upheaval and transformation. Only rarely do historians find such a fine-grained microcosm of change, a grand narrative told through the ordinary courses of daily life. For the birth of Springfield, like the colonization of America as a whole, belonged to an age of transition between medieval and modern ways of seeing the world: magic shading into science, tradition displaced by innovation, communities eroded by a more strident individualism. Ancient wisdom about everything from planetary motion to human physiology was being questioned, and new technologies deployed, notably in the production of print. Even humble people learned to read and became consumers of cheap spiritual and sensational literature. Commonplaces about the relationship between God and man were picked apart, and new religious orthodoxies were enforced by nation states using the law as a formidable instrument of government. Nations strove for global pre-eminence, searching the oceans for commodities and land.

For all that, the birth pangs of this new order were both intense and protracted. Hardship, bloodshed and persecution blighted the whole century, and change was hesitant, often subtle. Lives adhered to the rhythms of the past, and the same old beliefs, with little sense of the underlying alteration of the world. Even colonists, once settled, swapped the drama of migration for routine: felling trees, pushing ploughs, making homes, feeding children.

Most characters in this book were low-born migrants from England and Wales. By the 1630s the British Isles were drifting into political crisis, due mainly to Charles I's absolutist 'personal rule', which in the following decade erupted into rebellion and civil war. Enmity between crown and parliament over how the nation should be governed, and by whom, divided families and communities. Conflict was fuelled by economic strife. England's population had doubled in a century, causing widespread poverty, hunger and dependence on charity. Young men struggled to set up their own households, and tenants were evicted to make estates more profitable in an era of soaring inflation. Crime and vagrancy escalated, and hungry people rioted; hundreds went to the gallows. Communities tried to help their poor, but families who themselves were hard up did so grudgingly. Sermons from the pulpit and ballads sung in alehouses lamented the passing of happier times.

Religion, too, was a source of bitter conflict. During the long ordeal of Europe's Protestant Reformation and Counter-Reformations, every point of doctrine was debated – and no longer just by academic churchmen, but by ordinary people, for whom finding the true road to salvation was a matter of eternal life or death. Sacred devotions, furthermore, had become a touchstone for secular allegiance: to a suspicious political establishment freethinking meant sedition, dissent was construed as treason. Passions raged as reformers smashed 'idolatrous' art, and Catholic and Protestants alike burned 'heretical' books. In Britain, Charles I was detested not just as a tyrant but also for restoring ornamentation to parish churches, whose interiors, like the liturgy, had been simplified in the first wave of the Reformation. Protestant idealists, derided by their enemies as 'puritans', who already craved a further cleansing of religion, were horrified by what they saw as Catholic backsliding and set their faces against Charles's regime. Conversely, the crown censured puritan ministers for neglecting official ceremonies (which these ministers saw as superstitious, idolatrous even), and for preaching that the one true law was the word of God, Christ the one perfect monarch. For the duration of earthly life, though, the authority of kings and bishops prevailed. Puritans were gaoled or put to death. But there was one alternative left to them: to flee to the tolerant haven of New England, there to build a new life ordered by their faith.

Land in England was scarce. Across the Atlantic, however, it was there for the taking, and might enrich the English state and reduce the burden of relieving the poor if labouring families were settled there. This prospect attracted paupers desperate to raise a family and puritans craving freedom of conscience alike. In the seventeenth century 350,000 Britons sailed to America, 25,000 of them to New England, mainly in the 1630s during the 'great migration' to Massachusetts Bay. The prize was both glittering and attainable, and emigrants felt as if they were acting out a fantasy of prosperity and fulfilment. Many, too, were motivated by sheer desire rather than desperation and gambled comfortable lives in the old country for self-advancement in the new. The risks were huge. Some dreams came true; others perished on rocky shores and barren soils. Thousands of migrants slunk home: either because they had failed or to fight in the civil war between royalists and parliamentarians, which broke out in 1642 and would lead, momentously, to the first and only republic in England's history – and a brief feeling among puritans that they had prevailed against the forces of Antichrist. More stayed in America, measuring out their days in contentment or despair.

Life in New England was dominated by piety and toil. It was an existence colonists stoically accepted; they had, after all, gone there to carve out new lives. Beneath the surface of most settlements, however, coursed dark currents of wrath. The mid-1630s were mired in controversy, as the intransigence of godly magistrates and ministers widened sectarian fault lines in puritanism that had existed long before anyone went to America. A shared commitment to bring change to the established Church of England, whose head was the English king, had never been enough to unite puritans. The question was what to change and how, and on these points there could be no agreement. Separatists and Independents cut ties with the English church, favouring self-governing congregations; Presbyterians preferred a national puritan church. And there were many shades of opinion besides – dizzying, fraught and, in the end, irreconcilable. Before the Reformation, religion had been a Catholic monopoly; now it was a free market, swarming with different Protestant interpretations – including of the Holy Trinity, and the identity of God and Christ – which governments on both sides of the Atlantic refused to tolerate.

In New England, challenges to religious orthodoxy were also challenges to political authority, and nobody was more sensitive to such defiance than Boston's governors: in their rhetoric and law, religious dissenters were defined as devilish heretics. The government in London, however, upon hearing of this ferment, cared only that a colonial scion was pulling away from its stock. The puritans' vision of New England as a 'city on a hill' was supposed to be an exemplar for the English church to which – in theory – they still belonged. Yet by 1640, if not earlier, Massachusetts Bay Colony was behaving like a free state, imposing its own orthodoxy on colonists, many of whom were either not puritans or, at the other end of the spectrum, held views more extreme than their governors. Old England tried to assert its control over the New – but it was 3,000 miles away across the Atlantic and animated by a fierce independent spirit that was difficult, ultimately impossible, to suppress.

In New England's communities, as between continents, there was no end of strife. Nor was religion the only bone of contention. Yearning to improve themselves in the New World, ambitious settlers locked horns and made gains in the acquisition of estates and property at each other's expense. Puritan idealists who had predicted that charity between neighbours, which was waning in England, would be revived in America were proved wrong. Local quarrels were to an extent contained by litigation and arbitration but could also burst into violent rage. Passions were thought to emanate from without and within, volatile souls inflamed by heavenly or demonic forces. And at the crossroads of the human and the cosmic, at the core of local society, lurked the mundane evil of the witch.

Witchcraft was not some wild superstition but a serious expression of disorder embedded in politics, religion and law. Witches were believed to invert every cherished ideal, from obeying one's superiors to familial love. They were traitors and murderers, bad subjects and neighbours, delighting in spite and mayhem. Like other horror crimes, such as sodomy and infanticide, witchcraft represented the polar opposite of goodness and godliness, especially when, as in the mid-seventeenth century, such virtues felt gravely threatened. Although there had been witch-hunts in medieval Europe, and the belief in diabolism endured after the last execution in the eighteenth century, the so-called 'witch craze' occurred mainly between the mid-sixteenth and mid-seventeenth centuries, when every aspect of political, religious and economic existence was in turmoil throughout the Western world. Witches were tangible symbols of this chaos. Every witchcraft accusation, from muttered suspicions through to the theatrics of the courtroom, was driven by the malice imputed to witches and the zeal of accusers to annihilate them. Yet the need to be rid of witches, however pressing, was frustrated by doubts about legal evidence: could witness testimony be relied upon to put a suspect to death for such a secret misdeed, shrouded in hellish darkness?

The entwined tales of Parsons and Pynchon signify intellectual friction between old and new habits of thought, and political and religious friction within New England as well as between colony and motherland. Should truth depend more on proof than precept, on seeing rather than believing? Such questions, raised in situations where life and death hung in the balance, reveal stirrings of a shift from an enchanted world towards a world of enlightenment in which demons and spectres vanished in the bright light of reason; and witches and heretics – for heresy is another thread of this story – no longer threatened the temporal dominion of God, the integrity of the state or the common peace.

But this disenchantment wouldn't be complete in their lifetimes; even forty years later, witchcraft still had the power to divide and wound communities in New England, as it did throughout Europe and the British Isles. For what happened at Springfield was both America's first witch-panic and an overture for Salem, America's last. The infamous witch-trials of 1692 would be similarly rooted not in pre-modern hysteria or the madness of crowds, but in reckless ambition and simple failings of compassion towards others. Whatever the rewards of such conduct, selfish hearts were beset by profound unease. In the precarious frontier town of Springfield, this manifested as anger and aggression, and was experienced by people like Hugh and Mary Parsons, William Pynchon and their neighbours as deadly hostility and terror.

1.   A Voice That Said 'Death'

Once, beside a great river at the edge of a forest, there stood a small
town. Time has erased its every trace, but we can imagine it, quiet
and still, settled under a pall of late winter darkness. A man is hurrying home along the main street, to his left a trickling brook and a
fathomless bank of trees, to his right a curve of clapboard houses
with steep roofs and leaded windows. Down the narrow lanes
between homesteads he glimpses the moonlit river, in spate from the
thaw. The air is ice-sharp, tinged with smoke and resin, the only
sounds the rush of water, the muffled bellows of cattle and the distant cry of a wolf. It feels like the edge of the world, and to those who
have settled here it is. Beyond the mountains to the west lie uncharted
lands, as mysterious as the heavens, inhabited by people of an
unknown, perhaps hostile, disposition.

It is February 1651. The man's name is Jonathan Taylor, and he
has had an unsettling day, which is not over yet. Arriving home,
Taylor lifts the door latch, treading softly to avoid waking his wife,
who is eight months pregnant, and their infant girl beside her. They
have lived in the young plantation of Springfield for two years,
labouring to make something of themselves in this new land. The
family sleeps downstairs in one bed near the glowing hearth, which
flickers shadows round the low-ceilinged room. Taylor undresses,
slips between the coarse sheets. He closes his eyes. But then he's
awake, the room suffused with light. He sits up rigid with fear, sens-
ing movement on the floor. He forces himself to look. Three snakes
are slithering towards him. He glances at his wife but doesn't rouse
her, afraid the shock will hurt their unborn child. Nor does he want
his daughter to see.[1]

The smallest snake, black with yellow stripes, slides up the side of
the bed. Taylor strikes it off, but it returns. Again he lashes out.

Heart pounding, he shrinks back against the bolster. Daring to raise his head again, he meets the snake's beady eye. With a flick of its jaws, the creature sinks its fangs into Taylor's forehead. The pain is excruciating, but Taylor is too petrified to move. In the deep voice of a man – a voice he recognizes – the snake breathes the word 'death'. Trembling, Taylor splutters that no man ever died from such a bite. Then, the room snaps back to darkness, and the snakes are gone. Taylor's tremors wake his wife. Unable to calm him, she asks if he's cold and whether she should warm his clothes. He replies that he's hot and sick and falls back on the bed, shaking and sweating. All that Thursday night he writhes feverishly, his mind a confusion of images. But in the morning Taylor is clear about one thing. He knows who to blame for his torment: the brickmaker, Hugh Parsons.

Jonathan Taylor is not alone in suspecting Parsons. Two days ago, on Wednesday, the constable arrested Hugh's wife Mary as a witch – the first that Springfield has known. Once, witches were unheard of in New England, but recently a plague of accusations has infected the colony. Back across the Atlantic, Old England has also been scourged by witch-panics, reports of which arrive by letter and word of mouth. Stories that by day are food for gossip, after dark fuel nightmares. Colonists fear God but also the devil and believe that witches can send beast-like demons to hurt them. Such thoughts were always present, but now witchcraft has become real among the settlements of the Connecticut valley, lonely outposts of piety and trade, of which Springfield is the most northerly. Meanwhile, rumours of heresy dog the town's all-powerful governor, William Pynchon. These days, anything seems possible.

Hugh Parsons is a working man in his thirties, who says little but radiates discontent. He left England several years ago, and has spent the last six in Springfield, at odds with the world. After Mary's arrest, he tossed and turned through Wednesday night – worrying for her sake, perhaps, but also for himself. The following morning Hugh came looking for the constable, a Welshman named Thomas Merrick, eager to know what was happening. The constable wasn't around; Jonathan Taylor, labouring in Merrick's barn, was. Hugh asked Taylor if he knew who had pointed the finger at his wife. Taylor replied tersely that he – Hugh – would know soon enough. Just then Merrick appeared, marching Mary to the house of William Pynchon, who was also Springfield's magistrate, for questioning. Hugh did nothing. Strangely calm, he sat in the barn until dusk, waiting until Taylor had finished, then, as Taylor went up to Merrick's house, followed him. The constable was still not back, but his wife said the two men could help themselves to beer. Taylor went down to the cellar, but the barrel plug was so stiff it hurt to twist it. When Sarah Merrick tried, it came out easily. 'What are you, a witch?' quipped Taylor: a risky joke. Back upstairs, Goody Merrick made light of it all and was sorry about Taylor's sore hand, which she showed to Parsons. He said nothing, convinced that Taylor's joke was on him. The two men then went to their homes, Taylor scarcely imagining what lay ahead that night.

The next day – Friday – Taylor complains of what he described as 'fits' racing through his body. His panicked wife summons their neighbours. What if Jonathan were to die? She has a child of seventeen months and another in the womb. Angry and afraid, the townsfolk go to Pynchon and demand that Hugh Parsons be arrested. After all, others in the community have recently suffered at the hands of witches. Two years ago the town barber was traumatized in bed at night by a fiery apparition of a boy, for which he now blames Parsons.[2] The saturnine brickmaker is seized and bound with chains. Pynchon investigates, determined to restore peace, yet aware that he, too, is a fountain of dissension. From every corner of the town come disturbing tales and outbursts of anger and anguish. Hugh and Mary Parsons can only wait, thinking about the calamitous last few years and wondering what will become of them.

William Pynchon, the figure who presided over Springfield, was sixty years old. He had travelled far, taken huge risks and weathered storms, metaphorical and real. New England had proved a gruelling ordeal. His wife had died; his boat had been swept away; other townships had censured him. With courage girded by a strong faith, he had journeyed far into the wilderness to trade with the Indians, standing his ground in tense, halting exchanges. Life was unpredictable, and there were few people he could trust. Pynchon had been stalked by war, hunger and pestilence. But he had never experienced anything like the events of winter 1650–51: strange accidents blamed on the Parsons household, their neighbours swooning and convulsing, eerie sounds and apparitions, and throughout Springfield a pervasive mood of dread.[3]

Pynchon was head to foot an English country gentleman: austere and determined with a godly passion for rectitude. He was a natural entrepreneur whose gaze took in the entire world, or as much of it as he might reach with a scheme. Calculating yet candid in negotiations, he spoke plainly and never flattered to deceive. He had no need to be loved; God's love was sufficient. To him, as to all migrant puritans, New England meant religious freedom and bringing the gospel to the natives, both of which would come from populating virgin land with hard-working Christians: prosperity and piety were companionable virtues.[4] Pynchon was also a theologian, steeped in classical wisdom, including restraint of the tongue: he knew when to speak, and then with economy and precision. He lacked the rhetorical discipline of an Oxford or a Cambridge education, which made him self-conscious and cranky, yet also preserved in him a certain independence of thought.[5] He read prodigiously and took pains with his writing, craving to be understood. Even his letters went through drafts, full of crossings-out and substitutions in his crabbed hand, the lines bunched to save paper.[6] But Pynchon had never flinched or faltered – yet.

The town he founded fifteen years earlier stood at the furthest western limits of New England, high in the Connecticut valley. Unlike so many other plantations, Springfield had not grown out of a puritan congregation transplanted from England to the American wilderness. It was born of capitalist enterprise, godly yet commercial and confident. Nonetheless, it still comprised fewer than fifty households – a limit set by Pynchon to maintain coherence – on a plateau two-and-a-half miles by one third. The homelots – house, barn and garden – formed parallel ribbons between the river and the main street. On the opposite bank of the river, to the west, lay planting grounds, and to the east, across the street and 'hassocky marsh' – named for its clumps of grass – lay upland woodlots, thick with maple, elm, birch, oak and pine. Every family was thereby provided with food, fuel and shelter. Streams meandered down the hillside, feeding fresh water into a brook beside the main street. At the top of a sharp bluff lay the unmanageable 'pine barrens' and, beyond, the long 'Bay Path' to Boston, a hundred miles east.[7] Indians, the people whose land this had been since time immemorial, were employed as messengers and carriers; but mostly their dealings with the English were limited to farming and trade; and watching, as their ancestral homeland was transformed.

The greatest transformation lay in the town's north end, where the principal inhabitants lived. This was the heart of Springfield's civic life, centred on a main square. There was no grandeur to it, and it flooded when the marshes were saturated. The only prominent building on the square was the meeting house, forty feet long, faced in clapboard, its gable ends topped with turrets, one for a bell – a recent acquisition – the other a lookout post. All meetings were held there.[8] From the square, a lane led down to the field where, once a month, Hugh Parsons and his fellow militiamen trained with muskets and arrow-proof corselets. There, too, lay the burying ground, a two-acre plot rapidly filling up, for these were days of raging infection – of smallpox and other diseases. Many children and babies had died: Springfield's long-standing minister, George Moxon, offered reassurance about salvation and helped the bereaved master their grief.[9] Besides Moxon, William Pynchon's staunchest supporter was his stepson Henry Smith, who, as husband to Pynchon's daughter Anne, was also his son-in-law: this was a close-knit community, in more ways than one. Smith, the town clerk, had signed its founding covenant in 1636; Moxon arrived the following year.[10] Pynchon was also close to his other son-in-law, Elizur Holyoke, whose father was a friend at the port of Lynn, between Boston and Salem. The estates of these men covered an area ten times the size of the holdings of other townsmen, many of whom rented land, houses, livestock or all three from Pynchon.[11] Moxon's house had bedrooms, a study, a south-facing porch, and – a real luxury – carpets. Pynchon's, by contrast, was plain yet spacious and imposing. Together these four neighbours – Pynchon, Holyoke, Smith and Moxon – were the hub of power in Springfield.[12]

Authority devolved to householders, who chose 'selectmen' to regulate highways, bridges, fences and ditches.[13] In this, they resembled vestrymen in English parishes, a quasi-republican model of governance that Pynchon knew well.[14] But the selectmen also oversaw land distribution, any plantation's most sensitive issue. Springfield abided by the Massachusetts law code, but like many settlements remote from Boston was largely autonomous. Ultimately, this was Pynchon's town, at his command. His main reason for sharing power at all was to avoid the friction between magistrates and freemen endemic in other townships.[15] And Springfield's magistrate was, of course, Pynchon himself. His duties, stipulated by the General Court at Boston, included taking testimonies and hearing suits for slander, debt and breach of contract. He also saw himself as a mediator, a counsellor – a 'commissioner of the peace', as much as a justice of the peace. Pynchon was in everyone's life, like a lord of the manor from the Old World.[16] Even the ties of patronage and clientage were similar. Men like Hugh Parsons sustained the customary illusion of independence, pretending to work for themselves when in fact they all worked for Pynchon. No other hierarchy in New England was quite like this – nor any town so industrious. Few Springfield folk would have admitted it, but burning ambition, made possible by Pynchon's power yet also constrained by it, undermined community and piety. The worst sin, apart from murder or witchcraft, was idleness.[17]

From March to September the working day lasted between ten and sixteen hours, 4.30 a.m. to 8.30 p.m. Shadows marked time: at noon a man could step on his own head. Fieldwork was paid at 20d per day in summer, 16d for shorter winter days: twice the rate in England, which had a surfeit of workers. There was no clear division of labour. Men might be artisans and farmers, like Hugh Parsons, and still do jobs for Pynchon. They toiled in enervating heat and bone-chilling cold, felling timber, excavating stumps, sawing planks, splitting shingles, breaking rocks, digging drains, diverting streams, shoring banks, building bridges and laying causeways. They mowed meadows, stacked hay and boxed pine trees for pitch and resin. They tended cattle and sheep, netted pigeons and caught fish on deerskin lines, as the Indians had taught them.[18] As well as wheat, barley, oats flax and hemp, they grew 'Indian corn' or maize, despite a sense that it was unwholesome. They learned the Indian tricks of planting when white oak leaves were as big as a mouse's ear; using fish as fertilizer (dogs' paws were tied to their collars to stop them digging it up); and growing pumpkins, squashes and beans between the tall stems.[19] At the end of the six-day week, labourers rested aching muscles and rubbed grease into cracked hands. The Sabbath, kept holy by law, began at sunset on Saturday and ended the following night – though Pynchon, preferring the 'natural Sabbath', hated people using Sunday evenings for games or 'the servile works of their particular callings'.[20]

At home, men made furniture, whetted saws and axes, twisted rope and sewed sacks. They chopped firewood, repaired roofs, daubed walls, pruned trees, trimmed hedges, cleared paths, scoured ditches and maintained fences that were (so the saying went) 'hog-tight, horse-high, and bull-strong'. Hugh Parsons did all these things. Pigs were slaughtered under a waning moon to prevent – or so it was believed – the pork swelling in the barrel. Nothing was wasted: the offal eaten at once, intestines stuffed with fat and blood for sausages, bacon smoked from the chimney lugpole; bladders were receptacles for lard. Wives like Mary Parsons made hog's-hair twine for sewing buckskins. They also tended orchards and helped with the harvest, threshing and winnowing, and made hay; in the process, they too suffered from sunburn and chilblains, back pain and sprains. They foraged for herbs and nuts; grew carrots, cabbages and turnips; fed hens and geese; and milked goats and cows. Household chores were just as arduous. Laundry was heavy lifting, and caring for children went on all day, as did cooking: stewing, baking, roasting, frying, pickling, brewing. Women spun hemp and flax, knitted stockings and gloves and carded wool; they sewed and patched and darned. As much as possible was done together outdoors: husking maize or stitching quilts or berrying, while sharing stories and news – the more fanciful and grotesque, the better for relieving the tedium of repetitious tasks. Relations between women were cordial but easily curdled by conduct deemed 'froward', the opposite of 'toward': facing away, selfish, harmful to the community.[21]

Some families in the valley had only recently left the riverside burrows they had dug upon arrival in Connecticut. But Pynchon's leadership meant everyone in Springfield had always had a timber-framed house with a roof sharply angled against heavy snow, some with lean-tos at the rear. There were two downstairs rooms: a hall, where the hearth was, and a smaller parlour to one side. Cellars for cool storage, rare in Old England, were lined in planks with floors of sandstone hauled from the river. Low-beamed rooms were dingy and cluttered, rank with woodsmoke and the stale odours of cooking. Windows were few, small, and covered by shutters or canvas if glass was unavailable – which it often was, costing a day's wages for a single imported pane. But unventilated stuffiness scarcely mattered: 'fresh' air was often bad air – *mal aria* – especially near insect-infested marshes. Houses were places to be warm and safe, especially after dark, when every home became a redoubt, battened and bolted. Those inside were attuned to the night's crackling silence, alert to the approach of intruders, human and animal, and the insinuation of evil spirits.[22]

The comfort of daylight was eked out with puffed-up embers, tallow candles and pine slivers, rich in turpentine and pitch, burning brightly in clay dishes.[23] Labouring couples like Hugh and Mary Parsons went to bed as soon as their chores were done. The best bed was usually in the hall, near the fire, sometimes behind a wooden screen, or in the parlour, which might have its own, smaller fireplace.[24] Most workers, exhausted, fell asleep at once; others lay awake listening to rodents scratching in the eaves and rafters. Occasionally snakes slithered in. For every home had its weak points: windows, doors and chimneys open to the sky. Demons, too, crossed boundaries. Households were imagined as models of the state, and vice versa; and bodies and homes similarly corresponded: the hearth as the heart, the rooms like limbs, the windows eyes.[25] Preachers likened souls to castles, unlocked by wicked thoughts to let in diabolic enemies without a fight.[26]

Dreams extended a real world of danger into an imaginary one. The minds of sleeping colonists were transported to a place where the wilderness met the invisible realm and received supernatural revelations encoded as symbols of civility and savagery: angels and serpents, Christians and heathens. Here, the devil turned fantasy into fact and made witches of the weak by convincing them they had acquired his power.[27] Everything was polarized between good and bad, day and night. As one New Englander declared: 'I saw my hellish, devilish nature opposite to God and goodness, between light and darkness.' Satan was not God's equal adversary – the idea was heretical – but more like a pet ape on a long chain, bestial yet restrained, and judiciously used by God to tempt sinners. The Calvinist doctrine of predestination held that some souls, the elect, were destined to rule as 'Saints' at the millennium, and the rest, the reprobate, were irredeemably damned. Yet even the elect needed to find their inner grace through contemplation and by avoiding sin. Not that this was easy: humans were frail, whereas demons were cunning and relentless.[28]

Protestants, among whom puritans were the most zealous, stripped the material trappings of Catholicism – icons, rosaries, rituals – from Christian devotion, leaving only the spiritual essentials. Yet, like dreams, the imagination dealt in images not ideas. The heart may have *sensed* Satan's presence, but the mind's eye *saw* him: his ravening glare and beckoning finger. Witches went further, reifying evil in human form – usually, but not exclusively, as women.

New Englanders, like all people of the age, venerated motherhood, a virtue witches negated.[29] Disguised as amiable wives and neighbours by day, witches were nocturnal monsters, who, like demons, crept into homes or sent envoys shaped like mice, birds and snakes. Fear of witchcraft settled along boundaries, including the line separating body and soul.[30] Colonists sought to protect themselves with prayer, and their thresholds with charms: magical symbols carved into posts and beams, iron knives tucked in roof thatch, horse-shoes and bunches of bay hung over doorways. A victim's urine, in which the witch's essence was said to linger, was boiled in stone bottles to torment the witch. Bewitched food and livestock were burned to the same end. An egg swirled in water, and a sieve pivoted between shear-blades, were also used to identify witches.[31]

Puritans detested such magic, but it was so engrained even they were not immune to it, especially at times of crisis. Though they were loath to admit it, spells were not unlike prayers, at least in purpose, and consonant with a way of seeing that understood the world as teeming with supernatural entities. Protestants knew the age of miracles had passed, yet they continued to interpret comets, eclipses, storms, plagues and birth deformities as expressions of heavenly anger.[32] Living in New England heightened the paradox. This wild, godless world struck colonists as a natural breeding ground for witchcraft. One puritan lambasted native holy men as 'great witches, having fellowship with the old Serpent', drawing off his power to heal their sick. Indians were also said to use 'diabolic skill' to cause harm and to consort with 'infernal spirits'. But, again, puritans distanced themselves from indigenous 'superstition' because their own sense of the miraculous was, in essence, unnervingly similar. Conversely, a closeness between English and native beliefs absolved puritans from superstition – a predilection for demons, ghosts and witches – as if the godly might be forgiven for slipping into popish error in a pagan land. America's real witchcraft, as a pernicious crime to be stamped out, lay not among the Indians but in colonists themselves: a disease that they they imported from the old country to the new, seeded there and allowed to flourish.[33]

Springfield had not at first been obsessed with witches, whose agency was often too obscure to detect with certainty. Settlers knew they existed, but saw most misfortunes as natural or divine in origin. But from the later 1640s, as word of witch-trials overseas and in New England spread, the problems Springfield's people brought to William Pynchon were more often of a supernatural kind. George Moxon found his congregation increasingly anxious about the devil, which he felt damaged trust in God's mercy.[34] Suspected bewitchment and demonic possession were not, however, merely spiritual matters: they were matters of law. Pynchon habitually consulted Dalton's *Countrey Justice*, the English magistrate's handbook: its 1630 edition included advice from Richard Bernard, a godly clergyman in Old England, about the secret marks where witches supposedly fed their diabolic imps.[35] Most puritans had also read the eminent Calvinist theologian William Perkins, whose treatise on witchcraft stressed both its dangerous reality and, frustratingly, the scarcity of hard evidence for it. Other works took a similar line.[36] The Massachusetts legal code ranked witchcraft third in heinousness after blasphemy and idolatry, defining it as 'fellowship by covenant with a familiar spirit', but without guidance for proving it. Technically, like all felonies, witchcraft required two witnesses – but who ever actually witnessed this most secret of crimes?[37]

More than a year before Hugh and Mary's arrest, in the autumn of 1649, some Springfield farmers had told Pynchon a troubling tale.[38] They lived south of the town, across the surging Mill River, in an expanse of wetland: 'Masacksic', which colonists called 'the long meadow'.[39] This had been divided up for grazing, but some found it more convenient to build homes there, despite its being several miles from the meeting house. By nightfall it was also quieter and gloomier than anywhere in town. Mists crept across the marshes, and glowing lights had been seen, as elsewhere in New England, where witnesses described cascading sparks and flames darting like arrows.[40] One of these men, Joseph Parsons (unrelated to Hugh Parsons), believed that his wife was gripped by an unnatural power.

An early settler in Springfield, Joseph had married Mary Bliss in Hartford, thirty miles downriver, in November 1646, and a year later her widowed mother and four brothers followed her north. The Bliss family had emigrated from Devon in the 1630s, but Mary's father died in 1640, leaving her mother with ten children. Mary's marriage to Joseph Parsons brought fresh hope, especially after the arrival of two sons.[41] But when the youngest boy, just five months old, died in June 1649, Mary was seized by a distressing compulsion to leave the house at night, wandering the meadow in her shift, blind or by moonlight, in the company of a mysterious woman, whom neighbours saw but never identified. Joseph locked the front door and hid the key; but his wife always found it and was gone when he awoke. She had an uncanny ability, he said, to find any lost or hidden object and had been seen wading into the swamp, yet she'd always return dry as a bone. Joseph and his neighbours asked Pynchon for his reading of the matter. Pynchon merely expressed surprise: he 'could not tell what to say to it or what to think'.[42]

Pynchon's non-committal stance was not out of character. It was in his nature to observe 'holy silence', defined by the theologian William Perkins as reserving judgement about 'things which are secret in our neighbour'. Gradually, though, spreading suspicions of witchcraft, coupled with growing doubts about Pynchon's own position, made him more inclined to speak out, to discover the truth and re-establish order. History had shown that judicious governors tended to take witch-fears more seriously when their own equilibrium was threatened.[43] This is how it had been in Pynchon's home county of Essex, which had endured great hardship and religious strife, and more witch-trials than anywhere else in England.

William Pynchon was born in the village of Writtle, Essex, in October 1590, in the reign of Elizabeth I.[44] England's population was growing rapidly, and so too food prices: recent decades had seen smaller farmers squeezed out while larger ones made a killing. Poverty bred crime and unrest; magistrates responded with harsher punishments, ministers with exhortations to order. The Pynchons, respectable county gentry, clung to their status, especially in William's line of the family, which was poorer than the Pynchon heirs to the manor of Writtle. Falling rents and rising taxes closed like a vice on their fortunes. Had the local custom been primogeniture, all

John Pynchon's property would have passed to his eldest son, William. But it was not, and the estate had to be shared between eight children when John died in 1610. William Pynchon received land in a village five miles from Writtle, on the other side of the county town of Chelmsford. Its name, promisingly, was Springfield.[45]

Pynchon married Anne Andrew in 1618, and in the next decade they had four children. In these years, Essex suffered disastrous harvests: desperate people rioted; some were reduced to eating dogs.[46] Conditions deteriorated further with the Thirty Years' War, a pan-European conflict between Catholic and Protestant states, which broke out the year the Pynchons were married. England, as an island, was for now spared its sieges, massacres, epidemics and the witch-panics that ensued from polarized religious politics. The Church of England had for two generations attempted to steer a way between such extremes – though it dissatisfied both traditionalists, including Catholic recusants, and more radical Protestants, namely puritans. Yet the war in Europe hurt England in other ways: by disrupting trade it caused untold misery. Meanwhile, James I, the Scottish king who became king of England in 1603, continued to look for a middle way in religion, restraining both Catholics and puritans, for example by dismissing both sides' claims to superiority in exorcism. His disapproval of the execution of nine witches at Leicester in 1616 made judges cautious, though cases still came to court.[47] Two years later several women were examined about the deaths of two heirs of the earl of Rutland. One confessed that when Satan blew into her mouth, she exhaled a spirit to whom she surrendered her soul. Magistrates, wary of mistakes (and of royal disapprobation), suggested she had been dreaming, but she was adamant.[48] The death of James I in 1625 brought his son Charles to the throne. For a while, life went on much as it had always done in quiet places like Springfield, with its scatter of houses and medieval church. William Pynchon was a conscientious churchwarden, who used a bequest to repair and improve the church; when a desired spire proved too expensive, with typical pragmatism Pynchon adapted the designs. He also brought before the church court oath swearers, tipplers, gamblers, unlicensed victuallers and defaulters in the upkeep of bridges and roads.[49]

Beneath such mundane events, however, England was entering a period of dramatic upheaval, at the centre of which was religion. Pynchon was at heart a Protestant conformist, whose puritanism involved praying for further reform in the English church, not abandoning it like the Separatists who had emigrated on the *Mayflower* in 1620 and founded New Plymouth. And yet, with the persecution of puritans in the Stour valley, between Essex and Suffolk, and a return to decoration and ceremony in its churches – a 'beauty of holiness' that gratified King Charles, whose queen, Henrietta Maria, was Catholic, and who felt even more contempt for devil-fixated puritans than had his father – Pynchon's views gradually became more radical. By this point, he may even have shared the view of many puritans that episcopacy should be abolished, and bishops ejected as oppressive relics of the old Roman church. Even so, Pynchon was no doctrinaire Calvinist. The power of Christ's love, he felt, bridged the cruel predetermined divide between blessed and damned souls. Accordingly, the Crucifixion was not, Pynchon reasoned, an act of wrath by God; rather, it was a son's supreme act of obedience to his loving father. This was how Jesus atoned for Adam's disobedience, the root of original sin. Pynchon's thoughts turned often to the Epistle to the Hebrews, where Christ's voluntary sacrifice was 'the meritorious price of our redemption' – a phrase that resonated throughout his life.[50]

Pynchon considered writing a book about salvation. The idea that Jesus had been punished for burdening himself with humanity's sins, thus angering God, was, he thought, 'but a device of Satan', whose role in Christ's death had been underestimated. It wasn't a vengeful God who provoked Christ's tormentors, but the devil.[51] Some things in scripture, furthermore, seemed figurative, including Christ's descent into hell, a literal reading of which made God seem despotic. These ideas had fascinated Pynchon since he heard a sermon by Henry Smith, a Norfolk preacher (and namesake of Pynchon's future son-in-law).[52] He was also influenced by older theologians, such as

Hugh Broughton, who loathed the 'witchcraft of papistry' and believed Christ's soul had gone straight to heaven with only a slight detour to Hades, which, Broughton argued, was both heaven and hell, just as Britain comprised England and Scotland.[53]

By the end of the 1620s many puritans, oppressed more and more by the ecclesiastical authorities for their dissenting opinions, felt it was time to act, not merely to publish and preach. In 1629 Charles I dismissed parliament, which had curbed his power and ambitions, and began ruling by prerogative. In this, he was supported by the bishop of London, William Laud, an avid harasser of puritans. As England's religious politics grew more heated, puritans had a choice: stay and fight, or cross the Atlantic and build a new church in New England, a Promised Land for God's new Israelites. Puritans who dreamed of ending church government by bishops desired instead that Christ's chosen Saints – the elect – should form self-determining covenanted congregations. Such communities were already forming around charismatic preachers in England: men like Thomas Hooker, a firebrand minister in the Essex town of Chelmsford, near Springfield, whose sermons Pynchon heard. Hooker, who as a young man had exorcised demons from a possessed woman, despaired that so many of his fellow townsfolk were of 'the devil's camp'. But he persevered and spread godly wisdom at a school in Little Baddow, a stone's throw from Springfield, assisted by a devotee, John Eliot.[54]

Pynchon and Hooker had a friend in common, a Suffolk gentleman named John Winthrop. The puritan world of the Stour valley was a small one, busy with correspondence, meetings and 'gadding' to sermons. Like many puritans, Winthrop and Pynchon combined devotion and business nous, which they were eager to apply in the New World, where, according to the *Mayflower* pilgrim Edward Winslow, 'religion and profit jump together'. Winthrop's plans to emigrate were far advanced. He secured a royal patent for the Massachusetts Bay Company, a project he led with five others; there were also twenty associates, one of whom was Pynchon.[55] By now, such colonial ventures were not unusual. What was unusual was

Winthrop's daring plan to relocate his discreetly puritan company to New England, past the reach of the crown, which expected the foreign plantations it sanctioned to be governed from London. On 26 August 1629 Pynchon attended a meeting in the city of Cambridge, where the company 'weighed the greatness of the work' against likely 'difficulties and discouragements'. An agreement was signed – court order, contract and oath, all in one – which in faith, hope and charity would sustain Pynchon in his new life. Three days later he invested £25 in Winthrop's 'adventures', in return for a share of land and proceeds. Pynchon, like Winthrop, had set the costs and risks against the probable benefits – and, ultimately, saw his ailing finances as God's way of telling him to go.[56]

Pynchon went home to prepare his family and dispose of his property. Over the following months, Winthrop assembled a fleet of four ships, sourced livestock and everything from swords and shovels to butter and biscuits; several hundred passengers were recruited through letters and word of mouth, mainly from the south-east of England.[57] In March 1630 the Pynchons – William, Anne, their three daughters and young son – boarded the *Ambrose* at Southampton and waited for fair winds.[58] On the flagship, the *Arbella*, John Winthrop delivered a sermon in which he described the community they would build, a nostalgic vision of an English church built on Christian charity. Their 'city on a hill' would be a beacon, shining yet exposed – they could not hide if they failed – and full of danger, not least moral corruption, for the enterprise had to be commercially viable. On 7 April Winthrop signed a declaration of loyalty to England, from which they could only part with 'much sadness of heart, and many tears in our eyes', hoping to be remembered 'in our poor cottages in the wilderness'. The next day the *Arbella*, the *Ambrose* and the two other ships sailed down the English Channel and out into the Atlantic.[59]

The crossing took eight weeks: 'a long, troublesome and costly voyage', recalled one passenger, 'hindered with contrary winds . . . mists and tempests'. By the time the ships dropped anchor on 12 June, near a settlement called Salem, all the livestock was dead.

Salem had been founded some years earlier by an advance party but, as Winthrop's migrants discovered, it had fared badly: the town was just a few shacks along a muddy lane, short of everything except disease. The fleet moved down the coast and up a wide river to another primitive settlement, Charlestown. Those not sick with fever or scurvy built shelters, at night huddling by damp fires, listening to cicadas and mosquitoes, their fears taking shape in the forms of wolves, snakes and Indians. In August Pynchon attended the first Court of Assistants, an imitation of the governing councils of London livery companies. It was presided over by Winthrop, who believed that rampant mortality was purging the settlers' hearts of 'hardness and error'.[60] The following month, they crossed the river in search of springs, and settled at a place they called Boston, there to plant themselves as 'trees of righteousness'.[61]

Pynchon, however, settled seven miles south of Boston, erecting a house and barn at Squantum Neck near Dorchester, a township established by men from the west of England. Not long after, his wife Anne died. She was one of 200 who perished that year, it was said, for want of the good food and lodgings 'to which Englishmen are habituated at home'. With four children to care for, the youngest his five-year-old son John, Pynchon struggled through the autumn. Winter was dry with gentle frosts until Christmas Eve, when thick snow came from the north-west. Two days later the rivers froze, and farmers were forced to abandon livestock. By February 1631 the days grew warmer, but with violent storms, and sharp frosts at night; a boat in which Pynchon invested to trade along the Maine coast was wrecked at Cape Ann.[62] The following year he remarried, to Frances Sanford, a widow and 'grave matron of the church at Dorchester'.[63] The Pynchons and their children moved to Roxbury, a fledgling settlement inland between Dorchester and Boston, named after its punishingly rocky soils. There William Pynchon founded a church, and welcomed Thomas Weld – an Essex man from Terling, not far from old Springfield – and John Eliot, the former schoolmaster at Little Baddow, as its preachers. Pynchon speculated in land and dealt in furs; Eliot, though, was concerned to maintain the puritan balance between service to God as well as to Mammon.[64] In the summer of 1632 Weld wrote home that they were 'inwardly and outwardly, in spite of devils and storms, as cheerful as ever'. New England had a healthy climate and fertile land. 'I know no other place on the whole globe of the earth', he said, 'where I would be rather than here.'[65]

Meanwhile, at the Court of Assistants, Pynchon set prices and wages, issued defence orders and punished everything from letting pigs stray to selling guns to Indians. He served as treasurer to the Massachusetts Bay Company, prudently spending £560 17s 8d against receipts of £561 19s 19½d.[66] After the biting winter of 1632, when many died of fever, New England was afflicted by 'great swarms of strange flies up and down the country' – an omen, some feared, of greater mortality to come.[67] The following year, Pynchon went into business with John Winthrop, importing cloth from England in return for sea coal and beaver pelts. Pynchon became his own ideal merchant: experienced and confident, yet rigidly scrupulous. He took a new boat to the trading posts of Maine, where Indians brought furs, mostly in early winter, when beaver had grown thick coats. Pynchon purchased the skins, packed them in barrels and sent them to London, where the fur was made into felt for hats. But soon a scarcity of beaver, coupled with a desire to control the fur trade, led Pynchon's thoughts a hundred miles westward, where the forested valleys and capillaries of rivers and streams were the perfect habitat for beaver, otter, muskrat, marten, lynx and moose.[68] In September 1634, Pynchon sold his house and farmland at Squantum Neck, and with his family moved on again.[69]

Pynchon was not alone in imagining a better life to the west. Some, tired of Massachusetts, with its stony fields in need of constant manuring, had heard of rich soils along what the Indians called 'Quoneh-ti-cut' or 'long tidal river' – which godly colonists, self-styled modern Israelites, saw as their Nile.[70] By mid-decade, moreover, Boston, Dorchester and Roxbury were so overcrowded that, like teeming hives, as one puritan put it, they 'entertained thoughts of swarming . . . further into the country'.[71] Others decided to leave due to the harsh treatment of Antinomians at Boston. Antinomians were radicals who rejected the laws of man, including anything that smacked of salvation through good works, a Catholic doctrine, and took Calvinist predestination to such extremes they believed themselves exempt from the Ten Commandments. Antinomians claimed guidance by the Holy Spirit, but Winthrop and his deputies were convinced Satan deceived them. They were not therefore surprised when the Antinomian figurehead, Anne Hutchinson, miscarried: 'for as she had vented misshapen opinions, so she must bring forth deformed monsters'. Pynchon, a freethinker, was perturbed. 'The contention in the Bay grows hot and public', he warned, 'and what will be the issue the Lord knows.' The issue, it became clear, was greater prickliness towards, and more prosecutions for, dissent – a heterodoxy that Boston equated with heresy.[72]

Far from this fray, the Connecticut valley was dotted with marshes and woods, marbled with streams and bounded by distant misty mountains. It was wondrous, yet terrifying in solitude. The great river, which rose hundreds of miles away and fell hundreds of feet on its journey south, was unlike the English rivers, the Thames and Chelmer, of Pynchon's youth. In the summer of 1635 sixty Dorchester families drove cattle near to the highest navigable point and staked out a plantation: Windsor.[73] That autumn William Pynchon took two men in shallops to claim territory to the north, anticipating permission from the authorities at Roxbury. Pynchon knew that to corner the beaver market he must settle above Windsor, near the junction of the Connecticut and Agawam Rivers and the trail from the Bay. There he could trade directly with the Indians who came in elm-bark canoes from the hunting grounds of the Mohegans and the Woronokes at Woronoco, later Westfield, and store their furs at a warehouse just below the falls at Enfield. From there a sloop from Hartford could take the produce to the mouth of the Connecticut at Saybrook, to be transferred to a bigger ship bound for Boston.[74]

At this stage of its progress the river narrowed to 300 yards and flowed quickly. The explorers moored at a marshy plain, where they met Indians, who managed to tell them they were in Agawam, meaning 'low ground washed over by water'. On the other bank a small river the local Pocumtuck Indians called 'Usquaiok' – 'pure water from the hills' – gushed into the Connecticut, which Pynchon at once realized could power a mill. To stake their claim, the Englishmen built a shelter in a spot they called 'house meadow'. Pynchon returned to Roxbury for the winter of 1635–6, leaving his men in Agawam to tend to livestock. The weather was so bad it drove Windsor's settlers back to Dorchester until spring, when they returned in greater numbers, led by John Wareham, a minister from Somerset.[75] All this time, however, Pynchon's men remained at their posts in Agawam. In March 1636 Pynchon himself, still in Roxbury, ordered everything his new settlement would need, from cloth to telescopes, and urged John Winthrop Jr – son of the emigrants' leader and himself a colonial governor and speculator – to expedite delivery. Pynchon also sought the younger Winthrop's advice about how to start a plantation, he having established Saybrook the previous year, and before that Ipswich, a settlement north of Boston, named after the Suffolk port. Meanwhile, Pynchon was admitted to the church at Windsor, until such time as Agawam could gather its own church.[76]

Pynchon was back in Agawam by late April. Pack animals and livestock were driven along the Bay Path, and forty tons of household goods brought round the coast. On the 26th he attended the first General Court of Connecticut at Hartford, which comprised eight men, including himself and Henry Smith, the Norfolk minister to whom he owed his epiphany about Christ's Atonement, who had since settled in Wethersfield, five miles south of Hartford.[77] Early in May, Pynchon's company were permitted to develop their settlement however they chose, provided they obeyed the government at Boston. Within a fortnight, Pynchon had welcomed the first seven families at Agawam, and, weighing demand against resources, set a limit of fifty homes on ten-acre lots. The householders signed a covenant, agreeing to 'articles and orders to be observed and kept by us and our successors'. They decided to relocate to the east bank – reluctantly, as they would be boxed in by the river and the hassocky marsh. But the west side was too wet, and their livestock had eaten

the Indians' maize. Pynchon made a show of neighbourliness, ordering his settlers to deal fairly with the natives to 'avoid the least scruple
of intrusion'.[78] Beneath this, however, lay another assumption: that,
as a Jacobean diplomat once put it, it was 'lawful for a Christian to
take away anything from infidels'.[79]

Pynchon squared this ethical circle by persuading the Agawam
Indians, non-proprietorial hunter-gatherers, that they owned their
land – so he could buy it. The Agawam, however, had no frame of
reference for English law; besides which, in 1633–4 their community
had been devastated by a smallpox epidemic that had killed 12,000
Native Americans in the Connecticut valley. That July, speaking
through an interpreter from the Bay, Pynchon addressed represent-
atives of eighteen tribal bands, each ruled by a chieftain.[80] A deed
was signed – the Indians adding shaky monograms of bows and
arrows – leasing the English three parcels of land, five miles long,
mainly to the east; in return, the chieftains each received a coat,
a hatchet, a hoe, a knife and a fathom of wampum – the native
currency of polished shells – while Wrutherna, a local prince, was
given three coats. Natural rights would be inalienable, meaning the
Indians could continue to hunt on the land they had, in truth, signed
away for ever.[81]

The Englishmen spent the summer surveying their new territory,
using oaks and pines to mark boundaries. Trees were felled, boards
sawn, homes and barns raised, hay gathered for the coming winter.
Pynchon began importing sheep; his stepson Henry Smith (not the
minister), three daughters and their maidservant arrived by boat.
Indians exchanged furs for hoes, knives and axes – everything except
for guns, powder and shot, which they craved but the English
refused to provide.[82] Business was civil and brisk, the logic of supply-
and-demand a solvent for cultural difference. But then came winter,
full of 'disastrous difficulties' and 'grievous disappointments'. The
settlers' supplies remained ice-locked in the river. They packed up
and retreated through the snowy forests, abandoning their emaci-
ated livestock.[83]

Cattle fared poorly in the Connecticut valley. They had not taken to indigenous grasses, requiring the importation of English varieties. Until these arrived, they went hungry – as did the returning settlers in the autumn of 1637. A meagre harvest exacerbated shortages caused by war between the Pequot Indians and colonists across southern New England. By then, only twelve households remained in Agawam: the settlement was hanging by a thread. Pynchon recruited frantically. In Dorchester he found a minister, George Moxon, who had left Old England under a cloud owing to his dissenting religious views, and who arrived with his wife in Agawam that same autumn. Pynchon also sent letters downriver, searching for tradesmen and fieldhands. Windsor replied that they had barely enough labour for themselves and already relied on Indian allies to protect them against the Pequots; that year, its inhabitants had been forced to retreat inside the settlement's stockade.[84] Though he could spare no men, Pynchon lent the beleaguered Windsorians a shallop, while striving to grasp the tribal politics of these ravaged lands. His own settlers, terrified and malnourished, begged God to spare them. They heard stories of people carried off in the dark by Indians, stories that drifted like spores into nightmares, seeding neuroses of demonic predation.[85]

While the war lasted, and the Bay Path was too hazardous, grain from Massachusetts Bay was brought upriver at the inflated price of 45s per ton, but even this lifeline ceased in the winter of 1637–8 when the river froze again. Agawam's farmers fed reserves of malt and flour to starving pigs, and seedcorn to hens. Pynchon, who was down to his last half bushel of corn, was grieved to learn that some of the remaining families were thinking of giving up and going: soon there would be nobody left. The Indians were willing to sell maize, but only at a price that suited them, a principle Pynchon grudgingly respected.[86] The 'fair prices' of custom and tradition, already a nostalgic myth in Old England, simply did not apply in the New World. Necessity laid bare the frontier's free market, where a merchant could let his wares find their value.[87]

In January 1638 Agawam was submerged under waist-high snow. Roads were blocked, and it was impossible to put up fences ready for spring. Fingers were frostbitten. There was nothing to do but stay shuttered indoors and run down the log pile. Spring came late: even at the end of April it snowed for two hours, the flakes as big as shillings.[88] Once travel resumed, the General Court sent Pynchon to buy maize from the Indians at a set rate. He faced a dilemma. Pynchon knew that food, like redemption, had a 'meritorious price', and so struck a deal unfavourable to the English.[89] Summoned to the General Court to explain himself, he swore that he and Reverend Moxon had struggled to keep the price down *and* do their duty 'for the public good' by hurrying supplies to famished people. Others demurred. Thomas Hooker, the émigré from Chelmsford, now pastor at Hartford, accused Pynchon of wanting to 'have all the trade to himself . . . and so rack the country at his pleasure'. This, Hooker surmised, was Old World profiteering, which both men had known from dearth in Essex. Pynchon did not deign to reply. For puritans, the ethics of the market were based on the eighth commandment: Hooker, effectively, was accusing Pynchon of theft.[90]

Pynchon was so stung by this rebuke that by the early summer of 1638 he decided to transfer Agawam from the government of Connecticut to that of Massachusetts, a move of which the Massachusetts governor, John Winthrop Sr, was secretly supportive. This could be done with the stroke of a pen, as the settlement lay on the border with Connecticut; but it was deeply controversial. To mark the break, Pynchon started using a new name for Agawam: Springfield, in memory of his Essex home and befitting a plantation blessed with rivers, brooks, streams and springs. New England's commissioners were startled by Pynchon's declared intentions, not least because Winthrop had assured Thomas Hooker of Agawam's loyalty to Connecticut. Hooker, for his part, thought Pynchon's actions disobeyed God. He predicted unhappy consequences.[91]

They did not take long to materialize. One clear day in June, as men were mowing meadows and loading grass onto sledges, an earthquake struck New England. It began with a rumble like thunder; then the ground erupted, clattering plates and dishes off shelves and sending people running from the fields 'with ghastly terrified

looks'. In the newly named Springfield, the quake lasted four minutes. Puritans blamed divine judgement for sin, likewise when
several weeks of rain, hail and snow played havoc in autumn.[92] The
previously sweet impression of the Connecticut valley as a place of
'pretty plantations' had soured: now, it was equally associated with
war and famine. As Hooker told Winthrop that December, a popular verse went: 'Alas, do you think to go to Connecticut? Why do
you long to be undone?' That winter, the freeze was hard enough
for the river to be used as a road.[93]

Spring came late in 1639. Food stores rotted, and prices soared.
The charge that Pynchon had failed in his duty over the corn purchase rang in his ears.[94] Now, however, he answered to Winthrop,
who had appointed him as Springfield's magistrate, Boston being
too distant for justice to be administered there. He could now apply
everything he had learned at the Court of Assistants. Winthrop,
who agreed that ministers like Hooker had too big a hand in secular
affairs, believed that in Pynchon, the godly administrator, he had
found the perfect governor.[95] Pynchon now looked set to dominate
the region. With George Moxon at his side, he faced down other
valley towns, including Saybrook, whose fort he refused to subsid-
ize, on the somewhat spurious grounds that the river's mouth was
already guarded by a sandbank. Pynchon's swagger was also commercial. A corn monopoly, he felt, was inimical to 'the public good
and the liberty of free men'; but to him the fur trade was clearly
different, a distinction that would make him one of the richest men
in New England.[96]

The succession of bitter winters continued. Boston harbour froze
for five weeks. Beer was solid in barrels, then spoiled when it thawed.[97]
Seeking to assimilate, in divine terms, this extreme weather, in an icy
meeting house at Hartford Thomas Hooker breathed hellfire; at
Windsor, John Wareham urged his congregation to draw lessons from
suffering and stand firm against 'wicked men' and 'spiritual enemies'.
In Springfield, Reverend Moxon, as if emphasizing the difference
between the two communities, adopted the softer preaching style
favoured by Pynchon, offering the blessings of heaven to his cold,

frightened community. As tensions between Springfield and Windsor escalated, Moxon wrote to Roxbury and Boston denying that his town was inherently sinful.[98] Existence was stressful in these valley outposts, in a way that was hard to understand in Boston, impossible back in Old England. No one, wrote one of Saybrook's founders, 'can so well judge what it is to lay the foundation of plantations as those that have some hand in them'.[99]

In the months that followed, New England waited for news of the greater crisis brewing in the British Isles. Parliamentary collapse followed the end of Charles I's personal rule, anticipating rebellion against the crown. Back across the Atlantic, New England's communities felt more isolated than ever. Shipping was curtailed, migration dwindled and a trade depression loomed. By the spring of 1642 a farmer would be lucky to get £8 for a cow that once had fetched £22. The summer was cold and wet, and as the meagre harvest came in, rumours spread that Indians were about to launch a murderous attack. Prices plummeted through the autumn, while the scarcity of labour inflated wages, which then went unpaid. There were shortages of everything, including silver, but Indians refused to accept inferior English wampum, preferring pure white shells to blue.[100] Despite these woes, New England's preachers urged people to pity England more than themselves, for, said one, only 'witches and devils . . . rejoice in the misery that befalleth others'.[101]

In February 1643, as fears of Indian onslaught continued, fishing boats brought news of developments in Old England: now, with the country plunged into civil war, there was no hope of English help to resist the 'insolencies and outrages' of the natives.[102] Churches observed a day of fasting and prayer in sympathy for the motherland – yet, clearly, God was judging the whole North Atlantic world. One Sunday morning in March another earthquake struck, and by the end of April there was so little maize that families subsisted on clams and mussels. Charity, too, was scarce: John Winthrop lamented 'how little of a public spirit appeared in the country, but of self-love too much'. By summer, pigeons had eaten the young crops, fruit trees were stripped of bark and barns infested with mice. November brought rumours of 'a general design of the Indians to cut off the English'. Pynchon's trade seized up and, again, families deserted Springfield – half its original cohort.[103] Parliament's attempt to reassure the colonies about its 'great causes of religion and public liberty' had a marked impact. One in five New Englanders, puritans who identified royalists with the Antichrist, sailed home to join the parliamentary army. Others, desperate to make a living, departed for the West Indies. It seemed like the colony's population was steadily draining away.[104]

In 1645, after more than two years of struggle, New England was cheered by news that the war had turned in parliament's favour, and that Archbishop Laud, scourge of puritans, had been beheaded. The war, though, had unleashed strange energy. Old certainties had evaporated, new enthusiasms poured out: the world was turned upside down. On both sides of the Atlantic, conflict between puritan factions, brewing for many years, was as furious as the war between Protestants and Catholics. Opponents charged each other with diabolic allegiance, and freethinkers were denounced as heretics, which in Massachusetts was a crime akin to idolatry and witchcraft. This religious and political upheaval left its mark on the colonial population, and by winter news was circulating of a witch-hunt in England, which had begun in Essex (half a day's ride from old Springfield) before spilling over into Suffolk. Crusading witchfinders were hiring midwives to search suspects and encouraging witnesses against them. It was a purge that was to make a dark and lasting impression in New England.[105]

2. *Here We Must Be Happy*

In the spring of 1645, as witches were thrown into East Anglian gaols and sects ranted in the streets of faraway London, in Springfield Mary Lewis, a Welsh maidservant, had her hands full. Now in her thirties, she belonged to the household of Henry Smith, William Pynchon's stepson, who as the husband of Pynchon's eldest daughter Anne, was also his son-in-law. Mary's time was taken up with looking after the Smiths' four daughters, aged one, two, four and thirteen, whom she fed and dressed, scolded and entertained.[1] The girls knew all about demons not just from Reverend Moxon's sermons, but also from Old World folktales full of ghosts and hags lurking in forests and glades, mirroring the frontier world that enclosed them. To stray from the homelots, as children often did, was to sense the eeriness of isolation, feelings of foreboding and of being watched. The soundscape, like the landscape, was vast and untameable: a hum of silence pierced by a lapwing's shriek or the tattoo of a woodpecker; the rustle of maize stems like whispers of anticipation.[2] Children heard adults discussing attacks on lonely plantations, and tucked up in bed imagined intruders on the other side of the door or prowling beneath the windowsill: Indians, conflated with demons. It was hard to sort fact from fiction – especially with a nurse like Mary Lewis, who was unusually prone to such fears and fancies.

Mary's day began at sunrise, when she would get ready before rousing the girls. Soon the whole household was in motion. A stream of townsfolk brought produce, delivered messages, ran errands, begged favours and enquired about work. Visitors came from Pynchon's general store, a palisaded warehouse central to Springfield's life. Never had Mary seen a place like it. You could buy tools and utensils, clay pipes and candles, needles and pins and most types of

English cloth. There was dried fruit, sugar, condiments and spices, including cinnamon. The shop also sold purgative pills ('vomits') and other medicines, such as wormseed, ratsbane for killing vermin and gunpowder, which colonists mixed with butter for toothpaste. People also bought goods for trading with Indians: wampum, mouth-harps, tobacco boxes and tin mirrors.[3] Every Springfield household was allowed credit according to its means and made repayments in kind – maize, wheat, turnips, meat and feathers at a shilling a pound – or by labouring in Pynchon's fields, his gristmill or at the store itself. Women did chores such as weeding and plucking to offset their husbands' debts. Boys were employed to string shells into fathoms of wampum, with which Pynchon bought furs. All this he recorded in a narrow, leather-bound ledger, like an English parish register.[4] Debt made everything possible – yet it was a drag on attaining independence, authority, respect, liberty.[5]

For Mary Lewis, the only acceptable route to this liberty was through marriage. Although wifehood ended a single woman's freedom, it promoted her from subordination to a partnership, which, however unequal, offered security in the community.[6] But achieving this state was easier said than done. For, like all resources in New England, Springfield's marriage opportunities were limited: a young man might set up a household – the precondition to marriage, in the Old World and the New – but both sexes found the town had too few single people to offer much choice in making a match. Back in England and Wales, the problem was the reverse: too many unemployed youths, male and female; too little land or work. Young people trekked to towns looking for employment, some ending up in ports, where they boarded ships for the colonies. Yet by the mid-1630s, demand in many New England townships was already outstripping supply, forcing newcomers to search further afield for somewhere to start a new life. Pynchon himself had relocated from Boston to Dorchester to Roxbury, and then onwards to the Connecticut valley. Even in Connecticut, things quickly grew tight. In Springfield no one, not even the son of an established resident, was allowed to stay there unless

Pynchon and his selectmen approved; most new settlers came by invitation because their labour was required.[7] Hired men, who typically were young and single, were not exactly free, but could at least acquire a house and farmland and open an account at the general store – everything that was denied them back across the Atlantic. Almost everything, that is, for in a town of fewer than fifty households there remained the challenge of finding someone suitable to marry.

The challenge was greatest for a woman of Mary Lewis's age. In the four years since she left Wales, most of which she had spent in Springfield, the women she knew who had married were in their early twenties. The previous winter Sarah Chapin, another maid in Henry Smith's household, and recently wed, was paid off near the time her baby was due.[8] Mary wondered anxiously when her own turn would come: spinsters over the age of thirty were mocked as 'thornbacks', prone to 'green sickness', a malady attributed to unsated sexual appetite.[9] And with this longing came loneliness. Henry Smith was a decent man, and his wife Anne well disposed towards Mary. But in moments of solitude, at daybreak and the end of the day, Mary stared into the chasm between her inadequate present and an ideal future, the prospect of bridging it confined to dreams and fantasies. She and Anne Smith had become confidantes, their lives contained by four walls and the dependence of children. Nonetheless, there was one particular detail which Mary, afraid of spoiling her chances of finding a good husband, had not yet told her mistress, nor anyone else in Springfield: she was already married.

Little is known about Mary Lewis's origins. Lewis was probably her married name; her maiden name may have been Reece. She was born in about 1610 in the Welsh Marches, the wild borderlands between England and Wales, a patchwork of traditions bound by folklore and magic and anciently sunk into the landscape.[10] Caves and mountains, ruins and springs, were sites of legends that told of miracles and murders, ghosts and fairies, kings sleeping under hills. Visions of black men and hideous dogs scared travellers, jolting them into mending their ways.[11] Since long before Mary's birth, Wales had been reputed a place of popery and irreligion by puritans like the preacher and pamphleteer John Penry, who demanded godly ministers be sent to the darkest corners of the land.[12] A Welsh MP who took up Penry's cause deplored their country's superstition, idolatry, neglect of services (in Welsh or English) and abuse of water from 'holy' wells. Penry's zeal was ridiculed by mainstream opinion: an English satirist lampooned him for being a Catholic-turned-puritan, and the product of a monstrous birth 'born in that hour when all planets were opposite'. Penry was later hanged for sedition against Elizabeth I: despairing of reform in the English church, he had become a Separatist, linked to the same circle from which a few years later the *Mayflower* pilgrims arose. In her youth Mary Reece or Lewis was a conforming Protestant, obedient to the established religion. Soon, however, she would be drawn into this radical, mystical movement.[13]

For all their supernatural beliefs and confessional strife, the Welsh had little interest in witch-trials. To puritans, though, all magical practices – healing, soothsaying and the like – were acts of witchcraft. Welsh clerical brothers Henry and Robert Holland both wrote treatises on witchcraft, inspired in part by the superstitions polluting their respective parishes in Cambridgeshire and Pembrokeshire. Witchcraft accusations, however, were scarce in Wales, and folk magic only mildly admonished in church courts. In a rare trial of 1607 a poor Pembrokeshire woman, confused by the legal process, incriminated herself by repenting a crime to which she had refused to confess. Frequently, though, the evidence was simply insufficient: the execution of a Welsh witch in 1623 was the first for thirty years and would be the last for a generation.[14] So while Mary grew up aware of witchcraft, she neither saw anybody punished for it nor even heard of such a thing. Her people frequently crossed the River Severn to Bristol, a thriving terminus for the Atlantic trade, but even there the execution of two witches in 1624 was unusual.[15] Witches were paradoxically everywhere and nowhere, which made prosecuting them so urgent and so difficult.

Mary was in her late teens when, around 1627, she married a Catholic man in the Wye valley town of Monmouth. Her husband, probably called David Lewis, publicly conformed to the Church of England, but worshipped in secret. Naturally, he expected his wife to convert, and, abetted by his two Catholic sisters, threatened her when she resisted.[16] Mary was trapped in a divided, doomed household. Divorce was all but impossible, which left only stoical endurance or flight from her home, which by this time – possibly from the time she was married – was somewhere outside Monmouth. But in the late 1630s it was Lewis who departed, leaving Mary alone in the world. They had wasted a childless decade, for which he may have blamed her (even though, considering her later fertility, the problem probably lay with him).[17] Perhaps lovelessness killed intimacy, whether consensual or forced; perhaps she miscarried, or had stillbirths, or had even smothered the issue of this hateful relationship. Nonetheless, Mary searched for her disappeared husband by every means, including, it seems, consulting a cunning man or woman adept at finding stolen property and missing persons. But, clearly, he did not wish to be found.

Mary joined the young independent church of William Wroth at Llanvaches, a hamlet of modest farms and narrow lanes framed by sloping pastures and distant hills. Wroth had been the devoted rector there for over twenty years, orthodox in faith though somewhat Catholic in culture – he liked music and played the fiddle – until, in the late 1620s, his soul was hardened by Calvinism and guided by the memory of John Penry's martyrdom. In 1635 Wroth came to the attention of the bishop of Llandaff, who in turn reported him to Archbishop Laud as a schismatic who 'leads away many simple people'. By 1638 Wroth had been forced out of his living. Prompted by a dream in which he promised to spread the gospel to save himself from a flood, he gave up the fiddle and founded his own church, still in the parish of Llanvaches, assisted by Walter Cradock and another dissenter, Henry Jessey, who came from a London church to help. Their model was the so-called 'New England pattern': truly independent, with a congregation of Saints, ruled by a pastor. In this godly company, Mary prayed, fasted and communed with Christ. Wroth was popular with his parishioners, who had collected money for him when he had lost his living. He told them to spend it on land for the poor, whom he also named as beneficiaries in his will. Mary Lewis was devoted to this venerable man, who some already called 'the Apostle of Wales'. The flame in her heart, snuffed out by the pain of a failed marriage, was relit under Wroth's gentle care and guidance.[18]

Now in his early sixties, Wroth exerted a magnetic charisma as evangelist and prophet: his ministry attracted scores of hearers, to whom he preached in the churchyard, and, though his health was poor, his voice was strong. His sermons told of Christ beckoning believers to the new Jerusalem, meditated on the transience of life and encouraged all to 'think on thy state, before thy life be out of date'. Word spread, drawing followers from Brecknockshire, Glamorganshire, Gloucestershire, Herefordshire, Somerset and Bristol: many were rebellious adolescents questing after truth. A generous host to those who travelled far, and an inclusive preacher who sought others' views on Christ and on God's creation, he would nonetheless strictly examine those wanting to join his communion. Indeed, it was said that Wroth understood every soul, helping people to see the evil in their own hearts. Satan hated Wroth – but Wroth was undaunted. While preaching to a crowd he saw a malevolent apparition approaching. 'There is the devil's servant coming to disturb the service of God,' he announced – and with such confidence that the apparition stumbled and stole away.[19]

Mary was enraptured by Wroth, who perhaps taught her a phrase she would use in America: 'dumb dog'. (Wroth knew it from the writings of John Penry, whose term it was for an ignorant preacher.)[20] In Llanvaches, she was hopeful and happy, secure in a community of friends bound together by the love of Christ. But Wroth was old, and stories of freedom and opportunity in New England gave sharper definition to the shared dreams of his mostly youthful congregation, prompting many to vow to leave Wales when they could. Among them was a man called Alexander Edwards from the town of Usk, eight miles away. Mary may also have been from there; she and Edwards were certainly well acquainted, and perhaps encouraged each other to dream of a new life across the Atlantic.[21]

One day in spring 1640 Mary packed a bundle and walked the ten miles to Chepstow, a bustling port on the Wye estuary. She was alone, though she felt Christ's presence. She crossed the River Wye on the bridge between Welsh Monmouthshire and English Gloucestershire, a dilapidated timber structure that neither jurisdiction could be bothered to maintain. Passing the ruined chapel of St David, she continued her journey south through the Forest of Dean, a place of spectres and standing stones, to the Beachley peninsula, where the Wye flowed into the Severn. She ventured out on the rickety pier, gazing across a mile or so of iron-grey water, and waited for the ferryman to carry her through the strong currents to the village of Aust.[22] From there it was a three-hour walk south, keeping the Severn on her right, until she could see the masts of ships on the Bristol Channel. On reaching the harbour, she enquired about passage to Massachusetts, offering either money – perhaps a gift from Wroth – or her indentured labour upon arrival. She saw a familiar face, then another: her friends from Llanvaches, including Alexander Edwards, leaving for America. Perhaps she had followed them there on impulse, in spite of their discouragements: they were concerned that a married woman should abandon her native land unless she was sure her husband could not be found. She had staked her entire future on this heart-fluttering moment; but they told her to go back. Agreeing to keep looking and also to consult Mr Wroth, Mary slunk off home to Llanvaches.[23]

Back in the hamlet, Mary was received sympathetically. Wroth knew her Catholic husband had mistreated her, felt satisfied she had tried her best to find him and so approved her proposal to start a new life in New England. Probably thinking she should have consulted him in the first place, Mary was given the blessing she needed, from the man she revered like a father. Perhaps he offered her similar advice to that which John Penry gave to his daughters on the eve of his execution in 1593: shun Satan, grow in grace, share Christ's afflictions through the church, live life in holy fear, beat down pride and 'regard not the world nor anything that is therein'.[24] Whatever the case, Wroth knew she would have to hurry. The decade of the Winthrop migration was drawing to a close. Already fewer ships were crossing the Atlantic, and fewer people had a mind to go anyway: with England on the brink of civil war, increasing numbers of puritans felt they were needed at home. Even so, Wroth told her, she should not leave Wales without a household in New England to go to.

Wroth asked William Erbery, a local preacher, to help. In his mid-thirties, Erbery was, like Wroth, a puritan mystic, whose curate was Walter Cradock, co-founder of the church at Llanvaches. Rejecting predestination, he taught that everyone shared in Christ's divinity and had inherited the view of Wales as a spiritual wilderness, but one where 'the Saints of Llanvaches' had lit a beacon: in his view, no puritans were more holy.[25] Like Wroth, Erbery's patrons were the Lewises of Caerphilly – whether Mary's estranged husband was related is unknown – and, after his dismissal by the bishop of Llandaff, he too preached to great crowds. 'My heart cleaves to him in love, more than to any one man in the world,' said one admirer.[26] Erbery wrote on Mary's behalf to Richard Blinman, a young Welsh minister who had relocated to New England. A sympathetic congregationalist – he had witnessed Wroth's will – Blinman had lost his living in Chepstow for failing to conform, after which he had been persuaded by the *Mayflower* pilgrim Edward Winslow to emigrate to New Plymouth with his flock.[27] Introducing Mary as 'a sister', Erbery asked if Blinman could find her a position in a godly household. Blinman did so, arranging for her to settle in Dorchester, where she would enter the employ of William Pynchon.[28] Six weeks after her aborted attempt to leave Wales, and a decade after her new master had made the same crossing, Mary returned to Bristol, and this time there was no one to dissuade her. It was the early summer of 1640.[29]

Mary's high-masted ship stood before her, its sails loose but otherwise ready to depart. A typical vessel bound for New England was repurposed from fishing or haulage of coal or wine. Weighing less than 200 tons, it might carry 120 people, 150 barrels of beef, 40 hogsheads of malt, 40 hogsheads of flour and 100 gallons of oil. There would also be wine, aqua vitae and vinegar, plus basic provisions of bread, pease, biscuit, butter and cheese. Usually, ships were also packed with exported goods: everything from soap to muskets. Sometimes, there were domestic animals: horses, cows, goats and hens.[30] Passengers, many already hired by new masters in America, comprised yeomen, mostly with families; husbandmen; agricultural workers and other servants; and various tradesmen: weavers, tailors, blacksmiths, carpenters and coopers. Everyone waited on deck, surrounded by chests, bundles and barrels, while searchers boarded to inspect licences and administer oaths.[31] Mary was quickly examined, declaring, as all emigrants had to, that she was 'desirous to pass to New England there to inhabit and dwell'.[32] Formalities over, the crew pulled at the rigging, and the ship caught the wind and moved out of harbour. Once the coast had disappeared behind them, all Mary could see was a vast circle of grey-green ocean with her at its centre. Her adventure had begun.

Excitement soon surrendered to boredom. Voyages lasted eight to twelve weeks; five was exceptional, twenty not unheard of. But even on the fastest passage, marking hours and days grew harder and more meaningless. There was little to do except chat, nap and gaze out at this limitless, landless world. Nervous passengers scanned the horizon for pirates and studied one another for signs of smallpox. Many took wormwood for seasickness or tried to exercise on deck. Meals broke the monotony, but offered little variety: salted fish, buttered pease, stale bread, sometimes eggs and goats' milk. 'Bag pudding' with suet and raisins was a treat. Water was usually brackish. The porpoises sailors caught tasted like rancid bacon. Mary's nights were spent in the low-ceilinged hold, which was crammed with baggage, hammocks and canvas drapes for a little privacy. Strangers were pressed together in uncomfortable intimacy and had to endure the pitching, yawing and rolling of the ship; the snoring, bickering and weeping of its passengers; the reek of unwashed bodies, damp blankets and fetid bilges. Storms turned misery to terror. Waves rose twenty feet, and ships were thrown from peak to trough and back again. Some sailors laughed at puritans cringing in prayer; others thought praying bad luck, preferring to sing over the crashing of the ocean.[33]

Like their passengers, sailors were a superstitious lot – even more so, considering the deadly peril they routinely faced on the ocean. Babies' cauls – part of the amniotic sac still attached at birth – were prized as talismans against drowning. Seabirds were regarded as omens, as were the luminous violet apparitions seen in the rigging during thunderstorms – a phenomenon they called St Elmo's Fire, but which crewmen thought was caused by evil spirits. A run of misfortune made passengers suspect witchcraft. Red-hot horseshoes were nailed to masts as protection, and stories were heard of alleged witches thrown overboard – or in one case fatally wounded in the head with a carpenter's axe.[34]

Deckhands often claimed to smell land before it was visible; the appearance of gulls signified that the ordeal was almost over. It was time for Mary Lewis to reappraise her Old World self: after so much nothing, suddenly a pressing something. As the coast grew in size and definition – trees, houses, spires, people – her suspension of reality faded. Pilot boats drew alongside the ship, and harbour cannon boomed salutes across the bay.[35] As she walked unsteadily down the gangplank, it took a while for Mary's head to stop swaying, her legs to stop wobbling. There was a lot to take in, and adjust to, in the New World.

Boston did not detain her as she headed south to Dorchester. Rich in woodland and pasture, cornfields and gardens, its modest streets looked over a bay dotted with fishing boats that joined the Neponset River at its lowest point. The farm once occupied by her new master, William Pynchon, was situated across this river. Mary stayed only a few months in service in Dorchester: Pynchon needed workers for his Springfield plantation, particularly a maidservant for his daughter Anne, who was expecting a baby.[36] Good workers, especially godly ones, were in demand. Alexander Edwards, Mary's friend from Llanvaches, was already in New England. He too had been hired by Pynchon, who by indenture signed men up for eight years, promising bed and board, and at the end of their time a suit and forty shillings, and perhaps some land.[37]

Mary may have arrived in Springfield by river, via the coast in Pynchon's ketch. More likely, she came along the Bay Path, by cart or mule, or even on foot. It was a very different journey to that from Llanvaches to Bristol: 100 miles of rough, forested terrain through the lands of four great nations – the Wampanoags, Narragansetts, Pequots and Mohegans, with Nipmuck villages in between. Perhaps she joined a caravan of others going that way: safety in numbers. There were many lakes, streams and springs, and in parts the trail was boggy or rutted from English horses and livestock driven to Connecticut. The journey took four or five days, depending on the weather. At last the path turned down a wooded hillside and opened out across a log causeway over a swamp. There before Mary was Springfield: the main street, its homesteads facing her; beyond, the river and a band of low, irregular hills.[38]

It was spring or early summer 1641 – a year or so since Mary had left Wales. She immediately saw that Springfield was nothing like Chepstow or Bristol, let alone Boston or Dorchester. It was smaller, rougher, simpler: there were, after all, only forty-five residents.[39] Mary was welcomed by Henry and Anne Smith – Pynchon's stepson and daughter – and shown to her quarters. It was a humble space, and hard work lay ahead, but Mr Wroth's sermons had taught Mary to make Christ her exemplar for a life of humility and service. Mary guessed she was a few years older than her mistress, who was plainly several months into her pregnancy, enough to need help with her two young girls, Anna and another Mary. Mary Lewis did what was asked of her until her mistress began her confinement – a period of antenatal seclusion – and went into labour. Martha Smith was born at 7 a.m. on the last day of July and thrived. By the autumn, however, little Mary, then about two years old, sickened and died.[40]

Children this young were regarded as innocents: the Smiths, who numbered themselves among the elect, would have trusted in their daughter's safe passage to heaven. Yet every soul entered the world in a state of nature: lacking civility, respect for laws and religious understanding. Nurturing infants, therefore, required not only Mary Lewis's love, but also her discipline to save her charges from their base instincts – just as preachers set out to reclaim Indians from savagery. Faith and subservience instilled at home and in sermons were sturdy shields against temptation. Let the devil rage: sons who obeyed fathers defied Satan and frustrated his designs. The Smith girls were also taught to keep evil at bay through prayer, introspection and contemplation. It was never too soon to know and fear God: children as young as four were put through the ordeal of public confession to prove they had been divinely chosen.[41]

Mary got to know her neighbours and, soon, everyone else in Springfield. Alongside the new and the strange, there was plenty that was familiar. People dressed much as they did in Wales and England, albeit without great variety or style. Cloth came in 'sad' shades of russet, green, mauve and brown; much of the fabric in Pynchon's store was 'tawny' or 'liver colour'.[42] Men wore soft high-crowned hats, jackets and breeches of moleskin – heavy brushed cotton – and women full skirts, petticoats and tight bodices with tied-in sleeves over linen smocks or shifts; hair was pinned up under a linen cap or coif. Men and women both wore waistcoats that kept bodies warm but left arms free for work: these came in red or green – a dab of colour in a worker's outfit. Clothing was expensive. A decent man's suit cost over a pound, the price of ten bushels of wheat or six goats. Rips were sewn, holes darned and patched. Men wore woollen stockings and hobnailed boots; but both sexes made do with clogs, the leather uppers hammered into wooden soles. In summer some colonists wore moccasins, good for hunting, and in winter snowshoes, both of Indian design. Men wore rough cloaks, women hooded capes. Children dressed in smaller versions of the garments worn by their parents.[43]

As the months passed, Mary gradually became accustomed to her new life. She first had to get used to the climatic extremes, which, it was said, might upset the balance of the four bodily humours: blood, phlegm, yellow bile and black bile. The almost-tropical torrid summer heat was accompanied by tornadoes that ripped off roofs, uprooted trees and tore ships from anchor; lightning split beams and struck people dead. Hailstones like rocks flattened wheat and maize, smashed shingle roofs and made fist-sized holes in the ground. After seven months of this came the descent into five freezing months that, as one New Englander wrote, made them 'prisoners from the end of November till the beginning of April'.[44] There were forty inches of rain a year (compared to twenty-five in East Anglia), which in November turned to snow. Livestock had to be dug out, beards froze, and Christmas fires roared all winter – so long as the fuel lasted. By the time spring returned, log piles were low, and cows looked like the wild deer of Greenland. Even then, fruit trees sometimes didn't blossom, nor did seeds germinate, until mid-May. Winter at least held down the gastroenteritis that killed so many children in summer; the winter air, sharp and pure, felt healthier than the heat.[45]

The seasons also shaped social life, although there was little time for recreation, especially for servants like Mary. In the cold months, townsfolk gathered in the 'ordinary' or licensed alehouse, drank ale and cider and took tobacco (now grown downriver at Windsor, undercutting Virginian suppliers). Smoking was popular, though some disparaged it as a savage Indian pastime. Drunkenness was punished, as was singing 'filthy corrupting songs', an English practice not tolerated in Massachusetts.[46] Drinking healths was reviled as the sort of thing one might find, so one puritan said, at 'the conventicles and festivals of witches'.[47] The militia always drank on training days, without which busy farmers considered such events a waste of time. Alcohol started fights and made courting couples sin. Intimacy required privacy, so in fine weather young people slipped into the woods and meadows. Grass stains told tales on young women, who wore the 'green gown' – which might be a risk worth taking to secure a husband: better a green gown than to remain a spinster and be mocked as a thornback. All this aside, culture was, in the main, religious culture. Pynchon insisted the Sabbath be kept sacred, likewise days of thanksgiving and humiliation, and prohibited work and profane games such as stoolball, shovelboard and cards – 'the devil's picture book'.[48]

The chief occupation of Sundays was hearing the word of God in George Moxon's sermons, morning and afternoon. (Moxon also gave a more experimental, speculative lecture on Thursday mornings.) Springfield at this point did not yet own a bell – or indeed a meeting house to hang it in – so a drummer summoned Mary and her neighbours to Moxon's house. At twice the width of most homes, it could accommodate everyone, besides Moxon's own growing family: in addition to his two young daughters, Martha and Rebecca, by late summer 1641 his wife Ann was pregnant again. Pynchon had contributed more than half of the £40 to build the house: having persuaded Moxon to come to Springfield, he knew he must keep him there, untempted by a better life in some godly township near Boston. He also gave the minister £55 per annum and generous credit at the general store, including for the purchase of a 73-pound pig. Even so, Moxon was materially ambitious, like the men he preached to, and supplemented his stipend by farming. He hankered after hearths for his hall and parlour, instead of making do with a single, central hearth. But this would mean building brick chimneys at either end of the house – and as yet, in Springfield, there were no bricks to be had.[49]

Sitting in Moxon's unheated parlour, Mary Lewis was soon reassured that Springfield upheld the essentials of faith closest to her heart: prayer, contemplating scripture, keeping the Sabbath. Furthermore, this church was a true congregation, as she defined it. In New England, just as Mary had hoped, a church was a congregation, Moxon's home their place of worship. In the old country, a congregation was the whole parish, whose compulsory presence at services was an act of loyalty to the crown. Puritans, however, deplored that elect Saints had to share pews with those they considered sinners passed over for election. Not everyone in Springfield had yet confessed and been admitted to the covenant, the inner circle of church membership; but that remained the church's objective, and Moxon would help them get there. His sermons were full of simple truths, looping phrases and homespun metaphors, softening

Calvinist theology, and he spoke warmly of courage and optimism. 'We are in a new country', he exhorted, 'and here we must be happy.'[50] New England's ministers debated how best to preach – the consolations of a loving God versus Satan's hellfire – but for now Moxon adhered to the former. God cared for his people like a nursing mother, he said, but could not keep those weak in faith from satanic temptation. 'Love not the world' was a lesson from the book of John that Mary knew well. In Llanvaches it merely confirmed the virtue of the poor; in avaricious Springfield it was a gentle admonition.[51] Moxon exalted the burden of responsibility that he and Pynchon, as minister and magistrate respectively, shouldered for the community, akin to the responsibility of all men for their households. He also spoke of 'an inward spiritual principle', from which true confession must extend – not, that is, just from fear of the devil.[52]

William Pynchon also attended these meetings, as watchful of his people at prayer as he was in every other part of their lives. He had chosen Moxon as a man after his own heart. Though his roots were in East Anglia, Pynchon was more of a West Country puritan in style, which is perhaps why he settled first in Dorchester, which had been founded by puritans from this region of England. His godliness was less extreme, still wedded to the Church of England, a loyalty to which puritans in Boston paid lip service while behaving more like Separatists. Pynchon believed that, the quest for Saints aside, promoting greater religious inclusiveness in a community would promote peace and prosperity, and also valued the distinction between magistracy and ministry that in Boston seemed blurred. He was a Presbyterian, a puritan favouring a national church structure (in contrast to Independency, a more militant spirit) and only a reluctant congregationalist, his reasoning being that Protestants alone in the wilderness had no choice but to form select congregations, like – or so it was believed – the Jews in heathen lands before they reached Canaan.[53]

Pynchon's religious designs were embraced by Moxon, who, like most godly exiles, was simply glad to be in New England. Short and stout, now in his early forties, he was the seventh son of a Yorkshire husbandman, educated at Wakefield Grammar School and Sidney Sussex College, Cambridge, where he emerged as a talented classicist, adept at imitating the Latin poetics of Horace.[54] Moxon was appointed a curate in the Lancashire parish of Prescot, but was reported to the bishop of Chester for omitting key ceremonies. This was an act of resistance typical among puritan ministers, who spurned the prescribed liturgy contained in the Book of Common Prayer, and disparaged sacraments, such as making the sign of the cross at baptisms, wearing the clerical surplice, and bowing to the altar, as crypto-Catholic – even as a kind of witchery. Finding a royal summons pinned to his chapel door in 1637, Moxon had hurried with his wife, in disguise, to Bristol docks, where they caught a ship to New England.[55]

Soon after their arrival in Springfield later that same year, Moxon gathered his church. Congregants pledged 'seriously and very solemnly' to surrender themselves to God through Christ, 'the head of his people in the covenant of grace'.[56] Moxon held that Old England's misery and shame came from straying off this path. From the start, he warned Springfield not to be 'too greedy of comfort' and appealed for love among neighbours. Like Pynchon, Moxon saw Christ as 'a good mediator', or intercessor, between God and man. Universal access to worship was not just Moxon's generous dispensation, but a means for him to teach as yet undiscovered Saints to find grace hidden in their hearts. In this way, Moxon established himself as a gentle shepherd caring for his flock: both a pastor to those who had proved or would soon prove themselves, and a minister to the whole town. For his care, Moxon was admired and respected; but then again, in such an isolated community, who else, apart from Pynchon, could people turn to for guidance? Like Pynchon, then, Moxon exerted an immense spiritual power over the settlers of Springfield.[57]

To worshippers like Mary, aiming 'to walk in all the ways of Christ', as Pynchon put it, the force of this spiritual power was not unwelcome.[58] Every Sunday and Thursday, Mary sat among the upturned faces, gazing at Moxon and soaking up his measured words. Yet still she felt unfulfilled, craving the rapture she had experienced with William Wroth at Llanvaches. There, moreover, she had been a confirmed member of the church; now she would have to prove herself all over again. She knew she was godly; but would others? In the strict religious climes of New England, women were constantly reminded of their innate depravity, more so than at home. Perhaps Mary was like the new arrival in another plantation, who described herself as 'cast in the open field . . . in a sad condition', scorned and full of self-reproach. Or the Essex woman who, having yearned to be in New England, once there felt miserable and estranged from Christ, her heart 'altogether dead and unprofitable'.[59] In Moxon's sermons, Mary heard echoes of Wroth's wilderness spirit, even if all Moxon did was to exhort her to search her conscience for signs of grace. Such grave introspection, though, could – and did – cause melancholy and madness. At Roxbury, where Pynchon himself had founded the church, a woman fell into a blind panic, convinced she was going to hell because her sins proved she was no child of God. Indeed, as the book of John taught: 'he that committeth sin is of the devil; for the devil sinneth from the beginning'.[60]

Public confession had a dark, divisive side: it was, after all, the process by which the drowned were separated from the saved. For many, the preparation for confession was a protracted agony building towards a terrifying climax in the presence of the congregation: one New Englander, 'being fearful and not able to speak in public', fainted at the sound of her own voice. Failure to persuade neighbours already confirmed as Saints, and so admitted to the church, meant not just exile from Christ but a kind of reunion with Satan. Passing this test, on the other hand, came more as relief than triumph, after years of feeling wretchedly lost.[61] It also reminded others, as yet unredeemed, that they were eternally damned until they proved otherwise: addressing his church in 1642, one newly confirmed Connecticut Saint was finally able to look forward to God's judgement, 'punishing the wicked with everlasting perdition from his presence, and joining together the godly with himself in endless glory'. This strained, oppositional

43

way of seeing oneself and the world, poised between flesh and spirit, self-loathing and elation, was part of daily life in Springfield. And there in the midst of it, caught between guilt and righteousness, was Mary Lewis, the seed of her destruction already planted.[62]

This, then, was Mary's life in Springfield, the changeless routines of duty to household and devotion to church, for more than three years. After a sharp autumn, the winter of 1644–5 was mercifully mild – at least until February brought icy blizzards, and snow covered the ground till late March, when spring finally re-greened the land.[63] By now the wartime slump had lifted: trade was brisk, and the town's population had grown to twice what it had been two years earlier. This created demand, stimulated supply and extended the ranks of useful tradesmen with which colonists had been familiar at home. The general store was restocked, and Pynchon could again start moving corn, timber and furs downriver. Indians brought skins from Mohegans in the Hudson River valley, some from animals trapped even further west, in Mohawk territory in New Netherland. This encroachment on their territory antagonized the Dutch, as did the Indian habit of referring to all New Englanders as 'Pynchon's Men', something that also irritated English people in the towns further down the Connecticut valley.[64]

Colonists felt warily ambivalent about native peoples. In Springfield, or Agawam as the Pocumtucks still called it, Indian and English lived side-by-side but not together. From Henry Smith's house where she lived, Mary saw Indians canoeing down the river and going in and out of English homes on business; some came asking for her master. The two peoples mostly understood each other in commerce, but culturally were poles apart. The Pocumtucks of Agawam, at first unaware of the ramifications of the 1636 deed, were now resigned to the transformation of their land: the forest clearings, fenced-off plots, worked-timber structures, orderly rows of homes – suggesting a people who commanded nature rather than sympathized with it. Contrary to English assumption, these Native Americans had long been farmers as well as hunter-gatherers, based in villages on higher ground to the south and west, but more peripatetic than sedentary. They valued seasonal access to natural resources, not exclusive ownership or despoliation, which only confirmed English prejudices about their ignorance and idleness.[65] Pynchon's policy was unwavering: until the day the Indians wished to be governed by the English 'they must be esteemed an independent free people'.[66] He also learned something of native life and language, although it was strange to him and his own way of seeing the world. The Pocumtuck year, for instance, began in early May, and was further complicated by the names given to months: the word for November came from the appearance of frost on a meadow.[67] But Pynchon's gestures, unusual for an Englishman in America, were seated not so much in empathy as in prudent self-interest.

Colonial disdain for Indian ways was heightened by open conflict. Things had been tense in Connecticut due to war between Mohegans and Narragansetts over adjacent former Pequot lands, which had forced the valley's militiamen to pick a side and defend their trading partners, the Mohegans.[68] The Narragansetts, for their part, promised to 'lay the English cattle on heaps as high as their houses and that no Englishman should stir out to piss but he should be killed'.[69] Food shortages had inflamed tensions even with native allies, underscoring for those bonded to Pynchon yet another kind of unmanly dependence: Christians at the mercy of savages and their prices. As a veteran of the corn crisis, and a rationalist in commerce as well as religion, Pynchon accepted this reliance – although his bargains were uneasy, especially with the Narragansetts, whom he considered 'full of subtle postures'.[70] He made Indian agents he sent on business use tally sticks to stop them cheating him. Pynchon's was a widely held view: George Moxon likened a native promise to that of a pig held by the tail.[71] Yet, awkward though it was, trading with Indians was essential to frontier life; Springfield, indeed, had been founded to this end. Fear came only when the English felt like underdogs, which in turn made them aggressive. In the colonial imagination, and in nightmares, this aggression was attributed to the *Indians*, who remained both familiar and unknowable.

In Springfield, distrust between settlers and Indians was just one strain among many. Tensions with the Dutch, and with Windsor, Hartford, Saybrook and other neighbouring English settlements, shaped colonists' beleaguered mentality, much as the topography of the town and its environs shaped their daily lives. Even more immediate were the resentments and recriminations felt towards neighbours with whom they lived cheek by jowl. Distance bred distrust, for sure; but familiarity and proximity nurtured paranoia and spite. When colonists feared and loathed the white person next door, the outbursts of rage were more frequent and intense than usually ensued from similar feelings towards dark-skinned strangers across the river. Few in Springfield's history would prove this more vividly than Mary Lewis.

Settler townships that grew out of migrant congregations suffered disputes, but found some unity in a common heritage, much as the life of English parishes was steadied by custom – a shared cultural ancestry. Springfield's colonists, by contrast, came from all over Britain, including a significant number, like Mary, from Wales. The English mocked the Welsh for their savage manners – but then a man from Middlesex might jeer at a man from Yorkshire, and someone from Norfolk perhaps had little fellow feeling for someone from Cornwall (unless, perhaps, they were both ridiculing a Welshman). Colonial homesickness was firmly attached to place and only loosely to nation.[72] Accordingly, in America traditions and customs collided, dialects and accents jarred; varying rules for land tenure and inheritance led to disagreements. People even dressed differently. Puritans from Dorset had no love for puritans from Chelmsford – but then not all puritans from Chelmsford, like William Pynchon and Thomas Hooker, cared much for each other either. Welsh and West Country folk tended more towards the beliefs and rituals of the old religion than did their reformed compatriots from Essex and Kent.[73]

Rather than evolving haphazardly, like many townships, Springfield was planned, and planned for profit not freedom of conscience. Residents weren't content with a mere 'competency' or 'sufficiency':

they all wanted to do better and have more. A yen for land, common elsewhere in Massachusetts, was rampant in Springfield.[74] Nor was this desire some New World genius; rather, it nurtured England's own growing habit of free enterprise (by contrast, the stable yeoman society aspired to in other plantations was already an anachronism back in the old country). While John Winthrop was dreaming of England's past, William Pynchon was envisioning its future – for himself and for hard-working migrants like Mary Lewis.[75] And as in England and Wales, dynamism meant competition, and that meant friction. Pynchon made more farmland available after 1642, but rather than sating appetites it whetted them. Early in 1645, he commissioned a survey of the long meadow to create new lots for luring new artisans and traders, and to extend the estates of existing tenants, who had been eyeing this land covetously. The selectmen allocated it according to taxable wealth, which, though fair, hardened the divide between the town's prosperous north end and the southern limits, where most new arrivals struggled to get established. The long meadow, the selectmen noted, caused much 'disagreement between the said neighbours'.[76]

Pynchon, who saw industry and competition as virtues not vices, smoothly compatible with Christian morality, was from the outset determined that his town would be no mere trading post, but – in outlook at least – as pious as Hartford, or Roxbury, where he had founded a church. The routine of worship and moral instruction was, as Virginian colonies had found, vital for discipline in a workforce. Pynchon, craving God's favour for his plantation, took seriously the spiritual life of the community: for a man to have rancour in his breast, directed at rivals, was the devil's work. Moralizing rhetoric stressed amity between neighbours largely because so often the glaring reality was asperity.[77]

Back in Wales, Mary Lewis had known strife between neighbours. In England, too, it felt like a curse on every parish, every village and hamlet. Widening gaps between gentry and yeomen on one side and poor tenants and labourers on the other strained social bonds, a strain exacerbated by civil war in the 1640s. The most sensitive fault lines, however, lay between near neighbours of similar status. When *they* were uncivil – abusing boundaries, ignoring requests, forgetting favours – there was much fuming and glowering, scheming, and imagining others scheming. Grudges turned into feuds that simmered away for years in unbreakable stalemate.

In this climate, the idea festered that adversaries, naturally powerless and forbidden to use violence, might resort to magic to get their own way. Poor women who were refused alms on the doorstep, for instance, naturally mumbled harmless imprecations, which then were taken seriously by the refusers, especially if bad luck ensued. Misfortunes attributed to witches – *maleficia* – included ailing children and livestock, spoiled food, milk that wouldn't churn, boats sinking in calm waters, and windmills collapsing on windless days.[78] Witchcraft was the antithesis of communal charity, and suspicions spread insidiously, like a virus. Fear incubated guilt, which was projected and returned as anger – much as colonists in New England imputed their own aggression to Indians, easing their own consciences and justifying drastic counter-measures. A vengeful God could only be humbly appeased; but a vengeful witch could be righteously repelled, and even, using the law, killed.[79]

Like the plague, witchcraft was usually first encountered as news from distant parts, then in reports creeping closer to home. In 1616, back in Old England, eighteen people in the Essex parish of Navestock, twenty miles from the young Pynchon's home, accused a widow and another woman – probably her daughter – of magical murder and entertaining demons. In the same year, not far from Navestock, a glover and his wife were accused of bewitching to death a man, a pig and three horses; meanwhile, a woman was hanged at Chelmsford for using a skull taken from a grave to cast a spell which killed a father and son and consumed a woman's body.[80] William Pynchon may have attended the execution. Ten years later, he certainly would have known the case of Denise Nash, a single woman, accused of laming a youth with witchcraft, because this happened in his own village. The witches in old Springfield's margins had advanced. Already, however, prosecutions were dwindling and convictions harder to achieve, largely because of Charles I's mistrust of the evidence. Denise Nash was arraigned at Chelmsford, but acquitted.[81]

Not every suspicion matured into an accusation, not every accusation led to an indictment, and less than one in four trials ended in conviction. Though wicked, witchcraft was a slippery crime, suspended between fantasy and reality, credulity and scepticism. Most people believed in witches; the thornier question was whether an individual could reasonably be hanged on the testimony of her neighbours.[82] Various factors had to coincide to reach even a fleeting consensus at law: popular pressure, magisterial diligence, judicial receptivity, and a firm belief that witches were threatening life, limb and property.

For the first twenty-five years of New England's existence, there was no appetite for witch-hunting, and in Old England first James I's scepticism, then the anti-Calvinist policies of Charles I and Archbishop Laud, had suppressed it for a generation. But in the mid-1640s fears stirred again: witch-panics flared up in East Anglia, and across the Atlantic in Massachusetts, where so many East Anglians had settled. Near Boston, a minister deplored an 'inundation of abominable filthiness', a wave of sin and dereliction of Christian duty indicating that the devil was thriving among colonists, much as he did among the wantonly godless people of the wilderness.[83] This was the decadent world that Mary Lewis thought she had left behind in Wales but which to her dismay thrived among Christians in their chosen paradise.

Native religion was a backdrop to colonial witch-beliefs in a country as yet unconquered for Christ. Indian culture was spiritualized, sensitive to nature, with unseen forces sensed in everything from bees humming and birdsong to tempests and dreams. But inevitably it was seen through an anxious Christian lens, which polarized goodness and evil. Therefore, like most colonists, Mary supposed that natives were, at least unconsciously, in league with the devil. According to Richard Baxter, an English puritan writer admired by William Pynchon, in New England 'it is a common thing to see spirits appear to men in various shapes day and night', and a minister at Pynchon's old plantation of Dorchester claimed to have witnessed a human sacrifice to Satan, 'with many ugly ceremonies devoted to him'. During the Pequot War, Indians had even been accused of casting spells on the English.[84] Predictably, English and native witchcrafts were linked. In the summer of 1645 John Winthrop's brother-in-law returned to Salem from London, where reports of the East Anglian witches were rife, as was speculation that New England's calamities were divine punishments for tolerating native devil worship.[85]

But mainly the mood that made witchcraft plausible settled in New England because by the mid-1640s its economic and social woes had reached Old World levels. The increased size and complexity of the colony bred competition, and with that the envy and hostility that had long been commonplace in England, and which gave witchcraft its destructive energy. Envy was the emotion of the witch, personified as a cave-dwelling hag, pale and thin, squinting and black-toothed, 'never rejoicing but in others' harms'.[86] It was also the emotion of melancholics, whose 'false conceived want' made them discontented and so 'desire that which they see others to enjoy'. For devout Christians like Mary Lewis, such passions were profoundly spiritual. Neighbourhood squabbles were not just events happening there on the surface: they were all-consuming inner struggles against diabolic wickedness in the heart.[87]

The weeks, and the months, rolled on. By the early summer of 1645 Mary had been in service with Henry and Anne Smith for four years and now had four girls in her care, the eldest aged seven, the youngest nine months: Anna, Martha, Elizabeth and Mary – named after the Mary who had died in 1641, or perhaps after the girls' nursemaid. Day after unvarying day, Mary cherished and raised these children, while hope burned in her heart that before long she would have some of her own. In that blessed subjection lay the true sense of who she was.[88] By this time, newcomers were arriving every week, among them unmarried labourers and artisans who fell under Mary's gaze. For whatever reasons, none was suitable. But then one day a new man appeared, strong, lean and energetic, a vital worker in his prime. He was wearing a lined cap and a distinctive red waistcoat.[89] Mary was captivated: he had for her some dark, mysterious magnetism, a look of inscrutable seriousness. She watched him. He too was silently watchful in return, sucking on his pipe, wreathed in smoke.[90]

3. Temptations of Desire

The scent of woodsmoke was everywhere, so house fires could be hard to detect before it was too late. Families depended on fire for heat and light and cooking, but their homes were made of timber and crammed with combustible material. Urban authorities in Old England prohibited thatching, and parishes kept buckets and fire-hooks to pull down burning roofs. In Springfield, though, the lanes between homelots were only as wide as a cart, and wind easily carried sparks and flames from one property to another. Since 1641 every householder had been required to own a sixteen-rung ladder for roof access, and carrying embers in an uncovered vessel was prohibited. Smoking pipes in public was also banned. But as the town grew, so did the risk of conflagration. Carelessness – discarded tapers, neglected candles, smouldering tobacco – caused accidents, as did lightning strikes, which were more common than back in the motherland. Most fires, however, started in chimneys built of timber and clay, the exposed parts rendered in lime. Poorly clad chimneys, especially at the top, were most vulnerable. In February 1645 residents were ordered to sweep chimneys regularly or pay twelve shillings to have it done for them. Massachusetts Bay Colony had banned wooden chimneys after a spate of fires, but that was not possible here. Boston had bricks; Springfield did not.[1]

Bricks were fireproof, but difficult to manufacture and too heavy to transport in sufficient quantities: a single chimney, with adequate foundations, required several tons. Sometimes bricks that came from England as ballast found their way up the Connecticut River, but it was impractical to transfer them to smaller craft north of Enfield Falls for onward passage to Springfield. And demand out-stripped what little there was: while there were brickworks in eastern Massachusetts, transporting bulky loads along the Bay Path was onerous and costly. Even a man as important as George Moxon would have to wait. So the problem persisted: Springfield needed bricks to prevent fires and upgrade homes, but even securing an irregular supply meant reliance on other towns, whereas Pynchon's overriding aim was independence from Connecticut and, so far as possible, New England as a whole.[2]

There was nothing else for it: Springfield would have to make its own bricks. This solution was consistent with Pynchon's methods to date. Whenever the town needed something the Old World took for granted, be it a barrel or a door or a horseshoe, Pynchon would persuade a tradesman to settle there. He had agents in Old England, and also drew on contacts in Boston or Dorchester or settlements in the valley at Hartford, Wethersfield and Windsor; others he hired came from his old home of Roxbury. Men already in service could be released from their indentures in exchange for a fee or favour offered to their masters.[3] But decent brickmakers were few and far between. Brickmaking was a delicate, almost mysterious art, requiring special skill and years of experience. At last, however, Pynchon found a suitable candidate, perhaps in an established brickyard in Boston or Salem, or one of the newer ones at Dedham or New Haven.[4] Terms were agreed, and soon this artisan was on his way to start a new life in Springfield.

His name was Hugh Parsons. A man of obscure origin, like so many Springfield settlers, he was probably born in the West Country, though, according to some accounts, he came from East Anglia or Wales (or most counties in between). Somehow the mystery fits this enigmatic, taciturn man, with his red waistcoat, and clay pipe clenched between his teeth.[5]

When Hugh Parsons arrived, in mid-1645, Springfield had almost completed its meeting house. It was a milestone of civic progress. Since February every man in the town had been made to give twenty-eight days' labour to finish the work, which sped things up and kept costs below the budget of £80, agreed with the carpenter, Pynchon's near neighbour Thomas Cooper. Hugh probably did his bit under Cooper's direction: daubing the half-timbered walls, fitting windows with small leaded panes or covering the roof in shingles, which were flammable but less so than thatch.[6] Like all new arrivals Hugh was given security of bond – his guarantee of usefulness and right to reside – and was promised a four-acre homestead on the west side of the main street, as well as wetland in the hassock-filled 'muxie meadow' to the east, a six-acre woodlot and planting ground across the river. Hugh also received a share of the long meadow, in line with the agreed allocations that year: a seven-acre plot, four miles south of his house, which was itself a mile south of the town centre.[7]

For Hugh, bricks meant a livelihood, the means to become a householder – the fulfilled destiny of a masculine man. He had a house and land and work: all he needed now was a wife. Hugh and Mary's courtship is lost to us: we can't know when their first glance or word or gesture was exchanged. But both were seeking partnership and love and so drew attention to themselves, each in the other's direction. It may have been the prospect of this new union that encouraged Mary to share her long-held secret. She chose her closest, and perhaps only, confidante in Springfield, her mistress Anne Smith. Finding a moment when they could be alone, Mary confessed that she was married but estranged from her husband, a Catholic who had mistreated and deserted her. It was a risk, but this was an emergency, where Mary's only other emotional outlet was perplexed contemplation and heartfelt prayer. It was an essential rule of the frontier: every public or personal advancement required doubts to be silenced, dangers confronted and faith placed firmly in God. Anne Smith listened with generous patience and promised to consult her father, William Pynchon.

Pynchon's willingness to consider the question was both a favour to his daughter and a kindness to Mary: it also reflected his passion for godly propriety and a desire to act as Solomon in his own Israel. Marriage, provided it was lawful, was to be encouraged because marriages created the households from which strong, stable plantations were built and made the community's lifeblood flow. Pynchon summoned Mary, who naturally kept the appointment, perhaps recalling the critical meeting with William Wroth, her pastor in Llan-vaches, which had propelled her to New England in the first place.

On Monday 2 June 1645, Mary told Pynchon about her miserable situation in Wales and asked whether she might remarry – assuming, she added, God granted her the opportunity. Pynchon considered the matter carefully, then asked if she was currently 'free of all entangle-ments'. Mary replied chastely that she was indeed unattached, and vowed to remain so until she was granted the liberty to find a new husband. She didn't mention Hugh Parsons. Pynchon continued to ponder. For a man to desert his wife was contrary to divine law as laid down in the book of Matthew – and yet for all his boldness, Pynchon was careful never to exceed his authority. Finally, he declined to judge this difficult case, preferring that the deputy governor of Massachu-setts, John Winthrop, should decide. He agreed to write a letter on Mary's behalf, which, instead of sending via a trader or an Indian messenger, he thought Mary should deliver in person. But first he needed to verify her story.[8]

Although some sought to escape troubled pasts in the New World, the past often followed them there. Many emigrants knew someone from home, and memories were long. That which undid fugitive criminals, however, was a boon to those needing an alibi or a testimonial. Alexander Edwards, who had known Mary in Llan-vaches, had since 1642 been a farmer in Springfield, where he had married a young widow, inherited her husband's estate (and their son), received several acres of his own and been accepted as a mem-ber of the church. He was, therefore, respectable and trustworthy.[9] Pynchon sent for him and related Mary's testimony. Edwards said he had known her for about two years when she was a fellow 'hearer' at William Wroth's church, in which time she often com-plained that her husband 'was departed from her and that she could not tell where to find him'. She had made extensive enquiries about him, Edwards recalled, and also 'did use means in inquiring him out', hinting that she visited a soothsayer. Crucially Edwards con-firmed that Mary and her husband had been separated for over seven years, adding that he had often heard her say her husband was 'a rank papist', like his two bullying sisters, and that she lived in constant fear of her life, 'for he did often threaten to do her mischief if she would not be a papist and do as he did'. Mr Wroth and his godly congregation, indeed, had greatly pitied her.[10]

Any colonist could appeal to the Court of Assistants in Boston, by now the upper house of the assembly, regarding matters of moral or legal difficulty. But Pynchon was also able to draw on his personal connection with the deputy governor, whose son, John Winthrop Jr, happened to be visiting Springfield at that time.[11] In his small, untidy hand, Pynchon filled two sheets of paper with Edwards's testimony, together with details of William Erbery's original letter to Richard Blinman seeking work for Mary Lewis in the New World, which had outlined her plight and attested 'that she left the land and so all hopes to find her husband, with counsel and advice of godly ministers'. He said he supposed it was lawful for Mary to remarry, but asked that the deputy governor give his opinion and consult his magistrates, then send her back to Springfield with whatever advice they deemed appropriate, so that she 'may either be fully set at liberty or strictly tied from marriage'. It was crucial, Pynchon stressed, that she not be left dangling in her present state of 'doubtful suspense'. He then folded the letter into a small square, three inches by two, inscribed it 'Testimony about Mary Lewis', and sealed it with red wax and a signet bearing a rose surmounted by a wheel of arrows. Mary was given this precious packet, which she hoped would be her ticket to freedom and fulfilment. Then she set off for Boston, probably down the Connecticut River in Pynchon's pinnace, and possibly in the company of John Winthrop Jr on his way home.[12]

Boston was already like a small European port: a modern city where commerce was brisk, governance decisive, administration efficient and religion precise. God was feared and the devil shamed – for the most part – and disobedience and dissent sharply corrected. The harbour was crowded with wharves and warehouses, the jetties bristling with masts and bustling with stevedores hauling boxes and rolling barrels. Even the wheeling gulls seemed animated by the energy of the place. Leading up from the quay was a broad street of terraced town houses, brick-built with stucco fronts and tiled roofs. Narrow lanes branched left and right. Shopkeepers watched over wares, hawkers shouted, carts and carriages rattled over the cobbles. On the crest of the hill, elegant spires pointed the town's glory to heaven. Beyond lay neat civic squares and parks with abundant trees and flowers. The world that John Winthrop had built from nothing on a bumpy plain a mere twenty years earlier whirred like a giant automaton, the people its cogs and levers. One resident declared Boston a 'wonder of this modern age that a few years should bring forth such great matters by so mean a handful'.[13]

The deputy governor's high-fronted redbrick house was situated near the harbour, on the left side of the main street. Mary delivered Pynchon's letter, which John Winthrop read at once. A serious principle was at stake: the sanctity of marriage and the integrity of the family were the bedrock of order for the colony and needed defending. To this end, bigamists were whipped, stocked, stripped of their assets and sent back across the Atlantic. But adultery was more heinous still, an offence against the edicts that God had handed down to Moses, which were the foundation of the Massachusetts law code. The previous March, Boston had gathered to watch the execution by hanging of an adulterous couple; Winthrop, who was present, noted in his diary that before the woman died she displayed a 'deep apprehension of the foulness of her sin'.[14] Winthrop was a man distinguished by great learning and self-assurance, yet even he hesitated in Mary's case. At length he decided to refer the matter to the magistrates in the House of Deputies, where a committee would debate the matter. Thwarted yet still hopeful, Mary returned to Springfield to wait for this committee to reach a decision.[15]

July 1645 was hot and dry. Field-workers kicked dust from hard, cracked ground and retreated to the shade, quenching thirst with ale. Every day men crossed the river by canoe to check on their maize in the planting grounds and, for all the buckets of water they hauled, were powerless to do anything but watch it shrivel.[16] The prospect of hunger was worsened by unrest. Bulletins came from the Narragansett–Mohegan war, which had broken out the previous year. Sixty miles south, the New England Confederation relieved Mohegans besieged in their fort and threatened to invade the Narragansetts' territory unless they signed a treaty. This they did on 27 August, but the ensuing detente was tense. The English demanded 2,000 fathoms of wampum as reparations and took four Narragansett children hostage as collateral. This caused resentment among the Narragansetts, who didn't feel bound by the truce anyway. Peace was never more than an uneasy pause. Plantations that were distant from the fighting – like Springfield – were more secure but still *felt* vulnerable to attack and nervously imagined their own annihilation.[17] The poor harvest and looming war preyed on Pynchon's mind. Mary Lewis's thoughts, however, were elsewhere. She was preoccupied by one question: when would word arrive from Boston about her situation? Three months of guarded courtship with Hugh Parsons had passed, and she was becoming desperate. Was she by law the single woman she believed herself to be? Might the eligible brickmaker tire of waiting? Again she confided in her mistress Anne Smith, who advised patience. Mary went back to work, prayed earnestly and kept her passions laced tight, like a pair of women's stays.

By mid-September, however, Mary could no longer bear the uncertainty. Again, she went to see William Pynchon. This time she admitted that she had fallen into what she called 'a league of amity' with Hugh Parsons – a phrase Pynchon repeated in a letter of reminder to John Winthrop. Scratching away at his desk, yet choosing his words as carefully as ever, he began by praising God for ending the Narragansett–Mohegan war and the 'disordered hardship' it had brought, then moved on to Mary Lewis's great matter, which had become urgent now that she was 'under temptations of desire of marriage'. Pynchon may also have suspected she was pregnant, which would explain her haste. Referring to his previous letter, in which he had asked the deputy governor to consult his magistrates, he added, with a note of polite urgency, that Mary Lewis hoped soon to be granted permission to marry. The letter was delivered to Winthrop, who replied swiftly. His answer was received in

Springfield early in October, and Pynchon delivered the news to Mary. She was indeed a single woman, free to marry Hugh Parsons. Her prayers were finally being answered.[18]

Marriage preparations were made during autumn storms that battered New England with hurricanes and hailstones the size of musket balls.[19] Reverend Moxon was notified, and a wedding date set for six weeks' time. Hugh and Mary were betrothed. Mary gave notice to Henry and Anne Smith about leaving their service; they, like William Pynchon, gave their blessing. Hugh began acquiring on credit everything they needed to set up home and a week before the wedding agreed a contract with Pynchon to supply him with bricks worth 19s 6d, at a rate of seventeen shillings per thousand. This would help defray the debt to Pynchon for goods purchased and repay him for work that a townsman had done for Hugh, which Pynchon had financed. Somewhat rashly, Hugh also undertook to build a chimney at Pynchon's gristmill by July the following year. The bricks were to be 'well burnt', meaning hard enough to with-stand New England's wind and rain. In a hesitant hand, Hugh signed Pynchon's ledger 'Hugh Parson', as if the pen went dry before he could finish.[20]

On Monday 27 October 1645 George Moxon married Hugh and Mary in the newly finished meeting house.[21] It was a civil contract, as was the custom in New England, but one sanctified before God and witnessed by the town. There was no exchange of rings, which were considered 'a relic of popery' and 'a diabolical circle'. Officiating ministers instead reminded marrying couples of their shared duty to live in imitation of Christ.[22] Moxon had many texts to draw on for his sermon. Ecclesiastes 4:9–10 exalted the mutual sustenance of husband and wife, where one would lift the other if he or she stumbled. But every hope came with a caveat: marriage was also 'a war-faring condition' for which couples needed to wear 'the whole armour of God . . . to stand against the wiles of the devil'.[23] After the ceremony Henry Smith, as town clerk, entered the names of Hugh Parsons and Mary Lewis in his register, and all misgivings (of which, given Mary's past, there must have been some) were for now put aside.[24] William Pynchon missed the occasion, having gone to Hartford to attend another wedding, that of his son John. Yet he noted the Parsons–Lewis union with satisfaction and informed John Winthrop that Mary had been 'newly married to a brickmaker'.[25]

That evening, there was a low-key celebration in Springfield, perhaps with cakes, cider and ale provided by the town, and music played on a fiddle and a drum (though dancing was forbidden by the law of Massachusetts Bay Colony). Before the festivities died down, Hugh and Mary would have headed off down the main street to spend their first night together as husband and wife. They had reached their earthly paradise in America, which they had travelled so far to find.

South of Springfield's town centre, the reassuring sounds and sights faded into the stillness of unmastered countryside. The lower portion of the main street had the same river-facing homelots, barns and young orchards as the rest of the town, but was still more like the forest clearing the whole area had been in 1636, with obstinate tree stumps and encroaching brush, and ahead the empty waterland of the long meadow.[26] The meadow itself was divided east to west by four brooks through which cattle had to be driven.[27] Now that the common land there had been parcelled out, plans to build homelots gathered momentum. Yet residential Springfield's southern boundary remained where the main street met the lower wharf, a remote place damp and misty by day, by night unnervingly dark and quiet. And it was teeming with unhunted wildlife: eagles, vultures and kites gliding overhead; owls and cuckoos calling in the forest; and on the mudflats and riverbank grebes, bitterns, herons and egrets. Grey foxes, bobcats and pine martens were a common sight. The land, stretching into infinite distance, still belonged to nature. This was where Hugh and Mary Parsons set up home, on the extreme edge of a town that itself was situated at the edge of New England.[28]

Their house was the usual two-storey hall-and-parlour affair, roofed in hand-riven oak shingles, with a central front door and casement windows to each side and another in the gable end to allow a little light into the loft. It had a broad chimney at its heart, and was stoutly faced in clapboard and daub of riverine mud. To the rear stood some rudimentary animal pens, a vegetable garden and a small orchard: it was autumn, so the trees were heavy with apples, and further afield there were nuts, blackberries and honey still dripping in the combs. One of Hugh's first jobs was to build a clay-covered clamp or 'scove' kiln, protected from rain by a high-roofed shelter.[29] There was decent clay and sand, though no lime had yet been found in New England, so Hugh may have built another kiln in which to make cement and render from oyster shells. Clay was used as mortar but it tended to dissolve, causing chimneys and walls to collapse, resulting in injury, death and lawsuits.[30]

The hall was Mary's kitchen. The space was dominated by the hearth, with its firedogs, pot-hooks, skillets, trivets and smoothing irons. Vegetables and herbs hung from low rafters. Beneath a trapdoor, a staircase led to the cellar, where Mary kept cured meat and cheese. She made simple meals of maize and pease, oats and barley, turnips and pumpkins: all cooked in a big brass kettle, also used for making cheese and dipping candles. Meat was stewed, and the liquor made into broth. Pork was fried, smoked or preserved in a salt tub; shad were roasted on spits. 'Hard pudding', suet and offal boiled in a linen bag, was a hearty dinner; 'hasty pudding', a mess of maize, flour and milk, more of a staple. Breakfasts were leftovers, together with bread and cheese. Mary budgeted carefully, and luxuries were few. She enlivened meals with pepper, which cost 1s 3d for half a pound – more than half a day's pay; raisins and spices were added to oat porridge to make flummery. Another treat was wheat flour, riddled though hair sieves, for white bread and pastry for apple pies. Housewives learned how to make unleavened cornbread from parched maize, anglicizing the Indian 'nookhik' as 'no cake', though it was blamed for constipation. Other native maize dishes were hominy and succotash (hominy mixed with beans), also pone and samp.[31] Cooking water came from the brook by the main street, kept clean by a town order against washing flax and hemp there.

This water was also used for brewing beer using mashed malt, stale bread and hops gathered from the edges of the swamp; and cider, which 'sang' as it fermented in the cellar in early winter.[32]

Work carried dust into the house – Hugh's boots were caked in clay and sand – as did faggots for the fire and grainsacks; it settled in fine layers along with soot from the hearth. Mary kept surfaces as clean as her tools and time allowed. Chimneys were cleared (and made safe) using long brushes, or dry grass pushed up with poles, or sometimes from the roof by dropping down a flapping chicken. Floors were swept with Indian brooms made from bound lengths of birch or ash, and scrubbed with sand and hard soap. Every now and then, the house might be fumigated with burning herbs and flowers, which banished bugs as well as masking odours. Mary rarely washed her petticoats, but her shifts and aprons needed regular attention, as did Hugh's shirts. Bedlinen came somewhere in between. Laundry meant boiling kettles of brook water and soft soap: it was hot, energetic work. On fine days the backlots of many homesteads were strung with drying sheets, pale flags billowing in the breeze.[33]

The bed that Hugh and Mary shared lay downstairs near the hearth. It had a timber frame with a mattress filled with straw or flax and supported by a sagging mesh of rope. Stuffed bolsters ran along the high headboard, and a blanket, rug and coverlet provided warmth. On cold nights, wealthier families like the Pynchons, Smiths and Moxons took brass warming pans to bed; poorer people made do with hot stones wrapped in cloth, and began to use Hugh's bricks for the same purpose. The house contained little else in the way of furniture: perhaps a table, some stools, a chest and cupboard, most of which Hugh was expected to make himself from sawn timber panels.[34] Coats and bags were hung from nails banged into the posts of the house-frame. Storage space was at a premium. The loft, accessed by a ladder set flush with the clay-clad chimney stack, was, like every other room, crammed with barrels, flour, lumber, skins and tools, also a spinning wheel and loom.[35]

This was the Promised Land where Mary Parsons, doubtless thrilled with her new married name, threw off the chains of a single woman's bondage. The past was dead, supplanted by liberty – a liberty consisting in subjection to her husband's authority: a natural state of submission without which, John Winthrop believed, a woman 'would not think her condition safe and free'.[36] Mary's new role, in addition to myriad domestic duties, was to procreate. This was what she had been waiting for: a task full of purpose and, she imagined, pleasure. It was common knowledge that fertility depended on mixing male and female seed, both of which were released through orgasm. Many long-suffering mothers had cause to doubt this, but the myth was sustained by times of mutual physical satisfaction, the province of newlyweds, which even puritans saw as congruent with God's designs for mankind. Nothing else this indulgent was so blessedly exempt from sin. So for a brief, ecstatic spell, Hugh and Mary faced each other in the hearthglow and its wavering shadows, united by providence or some other force of destiny, cocooned in the silence and blackness of the night.

Within a month of the wedding, Mary's monthly courses stopped, and she told her husband she was expecting a child. It was the next step of Hugh's promotion from Englishman to emigrant, from servant to master and husband, and now to fully realized householder and father. Mary shared the news with her neighbours, hoping perhaps they wouldn't start counting how many days she had been married, and that if they did, by the time her child came they would have forgotten the date of its conception. Then again, people were given to remembering many details about the lives of others, in case they ever came in useful.

By now, Springfield numbered around a hundred souls and was growing steadily. The south end of town, which was where most newcomers set up home, already had a sense of neighbourhood. Many people there were from Wales, which helped Mary feel that she belonged.[37] The Parsonses' neighbour was Jonathan Burt, an unmarried Devon man, who had been in Springfield for a couple of years.[38] Next to Burt, moving up the homelots away from the wharf, lived Benjamin Cooley, a linen weaver and farmer, probably from Hertfordshire. He had moved to the town the previous year with his wife

Sarah, whom he had married in England, and their young daughter Bethia, a name meaning 'daughter of God'.[39] Sarah Cooley's brother George Colton, meanwhile, had recently set up home in the long meadow and was good friends with Benjamin.[40] Their neighbour was Reece Bedortha, a riverman and carter, who had arrived, probably from south-eastern Wales, around the same time as Jonathan Burt. Like Burt, he was single, but courting a young Welsh woman named Blanche Lewis (apparently no relation to Mary). Her gown may have been green, but down here, a mile from the centre, there were fewer people to notice such things.[41]

Griffith Jones, whose homelot was next to Bedortha's, was yet another Welshman. He had come to New England in 1635 and after a spell as one of William Pynchon's fieldhands was now Springfield's tanner.[42] A few weeks earlier his wife had given birth to their first child, but, as Pynchon's stepson Henry Smith recorded, 'it lived not long'.[43] Next in the row came William and Joan Branch, who had relocated from Windsor in 1643; he was a labourer and a barber.[44] Then came John and Pentecost Matthews and their baby Abigail. John was a cooper, brought to Springfield from the town of Rehoboth in 1643. Pynchon needed barrels to ship beaver pelts and pork to the West Indies, but, like all woodworkers, Matthews also made roof shingles by the thousand. He had married Pentecost Bond in Springfield in February 1644, and Abigail had been born in April 1645. Like Griffith Jones's daughter, and so many other children, she didn't live long.[45] In this way, Hugh and Mary dwelt among strangers: strangers who soon became intimately versed in each other's ways and deeds.

South-end dwellers were not cut off from the rest of the town. Springfield's commercial and cultural life brought them into frequent contact with people all along the main street, up as far as the 'end brook', 'three corner meadow' and foot of 'the round hill', which marked the northern boundary. The north end was where the 'better sort' lived: William Pynchon, Henry Smith and George Moxon, as well as Pynchon's servants, whose houses were in the lane down to the upper wharf. Thomas Miller was one such servant, from

Northumberland, brought first to Windsor, then given to Pynchon, who indentured him for eight years. Next to Miller was Simon Beamon, a cobbler in his twenties who worked in Pynchon's store. Opposite them lived John Stebbins, and Francis Pepper, another of Pynchon's labourers, who kept his own heifer.[46] Nearby were Miles and Prudence Morgan, a Welsh couple in their thirties. Miles Morgan came from the town of Llandaff, twenty miles south-west of Llanvaches, and had emigrated in 1636. He reputedly met Prudence Gilbert on the voyage and, once their time in service was up, they married and lived in Plymouth and New Haven before settling in Springfield in 1644. A sawyer who cut boards for Pynchon at a rate of 4s 4d for every hundred feet, Morgan also worked as a butcher: slaughtering pigs (Pynchon paid him 6¾d a piece), gelding bulls, horses and pigs and spaying sows.[47] These folk worked cooperatively side by side, but appearances were deceptive. Below the surface there bubbled grudges, rivalries and jealousies. Pent-up hostility was the fuel of witchcraft accusations in the Old World and the New.

In Old England, many people depended on their local community because they were poor and frequently old. Such impotence strained relationships, but conversely so might a man's economic strength if others relied on him and had to be deferential to get what they wanted. Either way, it was an imbalance of power, and this chafed. New England's rapid growth had increased demand for skilled craftsmen able to hew and square beams, cut mortises and tenons, and assemble frames – which, in turn, meant those men were able to demand more for their work. Massachusetts Bay Colony tried to cap a housewright's wages at two shillings a day but, as Pynchon found during the corn crisis, there were no fair prices in the wilderness. Consequently, wage capping was not strictly enforced, especially in remote places like Springfield.[48] The plain fact was that self-improving townsmen needed bricks, and Hugh Parsons was the man to provide them. Like Pynchon with beaver pelts, Parsons had the monopoly: a commercial disparity resented by customers and competitors alike. Dependence – indentured service, debt at the general store, things borrowed or bought on tick – was necessary to attain a sort of independence; but to preserve peace along the way, the terms had to respect manly honour, and this was where a man like Hugh Parsons fell down.

For his employment as a bricklayer – building walls and chimneys and laying paths – the town set a two-shilling daily rate. Hugh, however, was in a position to unfairly prioritize jobs and accept bribes (though none was ever recorded).[49] Customer satisfaction depended on price, speed of delivery and quality – but all three were unpredictable when it came to bricks. For brickmaking was a laborious, difficult process. It started with digging clay from the riverbank, which in New England was glacial and sticky. This was work for the autumn: after the harvest but before the first frosts, which drew out moisture. The clay would be turned through winter, then in February watered and reworked in a pit by a tethered horse dragging a 'cragg', a spiked beam. If the clay was too stiff, sand would be added. The mixture was put in moulds dusted with sand, allowed to dry, then the 'green' bricks stacked on pallets. Hugh layered the bricks in the scove kiln and lit the fire; when the ensuing smoke went dark, it meant the water had gone. He spent several days adding wood, opening vents and closing shutters to maintain a constant temperature. Some unevenness of firing was inevitable. The stack shifted as it shrank, and some bricks were nearer the fire than others. Those closest were black and warped: known as 'clinker' bricks, they were crushed to make cement. Those furthest were friable 'samel' bricks, so called because they were salmon pink: these were used to line cellars or fill wall cavities. Only those in between were durable enough for exterior walls and chimneys.[50] It was all extremely hard to get right: frustrating for the maker, and disappointing for the client. Hugh's house was at least well sited for transporting the finished bricks to the wharf to be loaded onto boats, from where they were carried downriver to Windsor, and upriver to the north end of Springfield, where they were most needed for the best homes.

Typically the fruits of Hugh's labours disappeared into William Pynchon's account ledger, subtracted from his debt and added to that of other clients. Money rarely changed hands; there was little to be had. Hugh's sense of satisfaction was also muted by everything else he had to do. He felled and sawed trees, dug ditches, hammered in fences, tended, tilled and planted crops. He slaughtered a calf – no need to pay Miles Morgan for this – and gave Pynchon veal worth 3s 6d. Hugh also had to make and mend continually, studding his boots with hobnails and patching them with 'clout leather' from softened sheep's horn. He learned how to sail a birch-wood canoe, which was essential for carrying Pynchon's wheat, peas and furs downriver to the warehouse; and returning with everything from salt, wine and raisins, to leather, linen and felt, to knives, kettles and glass.[51] Hugh also needed this skill to reach his planting ground on the west side, which involved paddling hard against treacherous currents. At Springfield the river was narrow enough to boost its flow yet too wide to be quickly or safely crossed. Few men could swim, and drownings were common. Pynchon once lost a cowhand when a canoe overturned, while two days after Hugh and Mary were married a boat laden with corn was cast away in the torrent, its two-man crew lost.[52]

As in most households Hugh and Mary shared the extra work, drawing on mutual understanding and goodwill. To encourage this, the marital ideal was, according to one puritan writer, a 'continual stream of familiar conversation': honest, amiable chatting throughout the day about everything that needed doing.[53] Mary collected eggs and fruit, weeded the garden and looked after the goats, whose milk they drank and sold.[54] In the autumn she would be expected to help Hugh bring in the maize harvest. Her workload did not abate as her baby quickened inside her, and matrimony began to seem more like service – except with greater responsibility. Hugh, too, felt the weight of expectation. With a child on the way, he would have to make a crib, with a hood against draughts, or borrow one from neighbours enjoying a brief respite between births; but that was only the beginning. Reaching the estate of a householder conferred esteem yet also put manhood on trial, weighed it against custom. He had to balance patriarchal dominance with dependence on his wife – as hard to maintain as the temperature in a kiln. Order was everything.[55] As one New England minister preached that year: 'You husbands, wives, masters, servants: remember if you are not good in your places, you are not good at all.' Falling short of ideals, however, was the more usual outcome.[56]

Marriages were like flawed bricks that exploded during firing, or which looked sturdy but cracked and crumbled under pressure: often, things like a forthcoming harvest or the arrival of a child in a couple's lives. They may not have understood what was happening, what had changed. It may have felt like some malign intervention, unseen and beyond reason or obvious heavenly design. After all, one reliable proof for witchcraft, scholars taught, was 'when married people formerly loving very well, hate one another without any evident cause'. It was easier, perhaps, to imagine a curse inflicted from without than some affliction incubating within. Unhappy marriages were devastating to the reputations of men and women alike because in the sight of God and the community it meant they had failed.[57]

The worries of household life bled into those of the neighbourhood, community and colony beyond – and vice versa. In the autumn of 1645, while Hugh and Mary Parsons were setting up home, townships in the Connecticut valley were buzzing with unsettling rumours of an imminent Dutch assault, supported by native allies.[58] Amid heightened alertness to a common danger, the valley's English settlements were poised to unite against what they believed to be an approaching Indian enemy – but there was no love lost between them either. Pynchon continued to cause frustration and fury by refusing to pay a levy for the fort at Saybrook, believing it to be 'a very great charge and little or no benefit'.[59] And so, fears of the Indian threat persisted. Springfield's men, unable to fight an enemy they couldn't see, contented themselves by making war on the foxes and wolves that crept low among their herds and flocks. Iron hooks baited with offal and grease were strung between trees, which, when swallowed, became embedded in wolves' throats. The selectmen offered a bounty for every wolf caught, paid upon presentation of its severed ears. Dogs that killed sheep were dragged to the woods to be hanged, which seemed like condign punishment for animal felons.[60]

It was one of the earliest and sharpest winters anyone could remember, with icy storms and sickness that spread from the Bay across the colony. Discord between townships and within them was magnified by privation and peril. In December, the authorities at Dorchester, with whom Pynchon kept strong ties, passed emergency legislation to tackle 'the disorders that too often fall out among us' and 'intemperate clashings' in town meetings.[61] Fears of the consequences of disappointing God in this way were borne out by disquieting phenomena. A vast rainbow surrounded by bright lights appeared over Boston. At Ipswich, thirty miles north of there, people gathered to see a calf with three heads, one sunk into the other, causing John Winthrop to write in his journal: 'What these prodigies portended the Lord only knows.' At Springfield, meanwhile, the snow fell steadily, muffling and blurring the edges of life. Soon, the town would be entirely cut off from the outside world: farmers would count days in fodder consumed and remaining; their wives in corn and salt pork. In February 1646, with snow still thick on the ground, Hugh Parsons was forced to buy seven shillings' worth of good hay from Pynchon, a loan repayable in hay of comparable quality that autumn. Should he default, he was warned, the debt would be 8s 9d.[62]

The weather stayed raw into March. Finally, the snow melted, and Hugh and Mary emerged from their first winter together, chilled to the marrow and starved of fresh food, but grateful for their survival. Mary was five months' pregnant, a time when many women started to feel fatigued, as well as worried about carrying their babies to full term. To ward off their fears, they prayed and they drew on magic and other old beliefs. For a hare to cross the path of a pregnant woman was considered bad luck, countered by her friends tearing her clothes.[63] But the coming of warmer weather made everyone feel hopeful. Gardens were cleared of winter deadness, and neighbours lingered to chat, soaking up the weak sun. As the ice broke up and flowed away, traffic on the river increased, and Springfield was reconnected to the world. News of the war in Old England arrived in letters and news books – and the news was good, mostly stories of routed royalists and the surrender of besieged garrisons.[64]

There were also reports from England of the witch-hunt in the eastern counties, which by now had spread from Essex, Suffolk and Norfolk into Huntingdonshire. So far, over 200 suspects had been arrested, male as well as female, many of whom had made extraordinary confessions: sealing diabolic covenants, suckling familiar spirits and bewitching neighbours. These fantastical claims had hardened into convincing reality in the courtroom, especially because they came from the witches' own mouths. One woman admitted that a creature like a large brown mouse had woken her from a dream by nipping her and had demanded a portion of her soul. At first she resisted, but soon accepted two imps as her personal gods: one for killing cattle, the other men. This contributed to widespread consternation in Old England, which had also experienced prodigious rainbows and suns, blood-red rain and thunder like gunfire, as well as monstrous births. A cheap pamphlet juxtaposed a mention of witches executed at Bury St Edmunds with news of a deformed child born in London, both of which were seen as 'signs and wonders from heaven'.[65]

Closer to home in Connecticut, there was also talk of horror crimes in the godly town of New Haven: witchcraft, heresy, blasphemy, bestiality and rape. The governor's wife had been excommunicated for malicious conduct, including falsely accusing her own stepdaughter of being in league with Satan and her servant of bewitching the beer.[66]

Spring was not always benevolent: the rapid change in temperature caused storms and flooding, swamping houses and endangering cattle, followed in April, with cruel irony, by drought. Then came contagion. English and Indian alike were stricken by agues, perhaps marsh fever, with, it was said, 'great prostration of the spirits', 'hot fits' and 'strange stupefaction of the brain'. In Old England a surgeon would let blood, but in New England's warmer climate fevers were treated with cooling drinks – if, that is, they were treated at all. Many died within a week, children the worst affected.[67] Newborn babies, including another daughter born to Mary's former mistress Anne Smith, were anxiously watched for signs of sickness. The pestilence lasted into May, and all a nursing or expectant mother could do was try not to inhale too deeply the air from whatever noxious miasma was believed to be spreading the disease. On the 14th Blanche Lewis, the sweetheart of their neighbour Reece Bedortha, gave birth, after which preparations were hastily made for their marriage. The child perished before it could even be named.[68]

The Bedorthas' fornication was just one of many kinds of misdeed that provoked God right across the Atlantic world. The witches of Huntingdon, it was said, had fallen prey to Satan through their anger, malice, lust, covetousness and idolatry – the same vile sins that afflicted plantations back in the Connecticut valley. Idolatry, it was believed, tended to occur through sheer ignorance; but apostasy – the renunciation of faith – was more of a conscious, deliberate act. The General Court in Boston received a petition from Pynchon's former town of Dorchester warning that 'the prevailing of errors and heresies' was endangering the churches and commonwealth of New England. An influx of subversive books from Old England, it seemed, was promoting untrammelled religious freedom, condemned by one puritan as 'the grand design of the devil, his masterpiece'. Most New England puritans agreed: to tolerate every man interpreting scripture entirely for himself was to be culpably indifferent to the spread of anarchy. William Pynchon was worried it might 'give liberty to Satan to broach such horrid blasphemous opinions as never were the like in any age', and prayed that God would rouse the righteous to confute falsehood.[69]

To some, Pynchon's words were ironic, because he was one of the most irksome freethinkers in New England. The steely entrepreneur was by nature a country churchwarden who believed in Christian inclusion over Calvinist exclusion, and that Christ's obedience to his father, not God's angry sacrifice of his son, had expunged mankind's sin. Since Christ had never assumed the burden of that sin, reasoned

Pynchon, God had no cause to be wrathful. Such wrath belonged entirely to Satan and the executioners he incited, whom Christ forgave so as to keep immaculate his reversal of Adam's disobedience.[70] In this scheme, one that filtered down into George Moxon's preaching, the devil was no mere trickster, but rather a monster defined by perpetual fury and restless intrusion into daily life.[71] For sixteen years Pynchon had been quietly thinking and reading – perhaps, like John Winthrop, ordering books from the Frankfurt book fair.[72] But now, encouraged by dissent in England, he began voicing his opinions on the Atonement – the reconciliation of God and man achieved through Christ's execution. This was a more dangerous activity than by now it would have been in Old England. The Massachusetts law code was uncompromising in its definition of heresy as 'the maintenance of some wicked errors, overthrowing the foundation of Christian religion'. This obstinacy, if combined with a will to seduce others into error, was to be punished with death. The reason for this, the law explained, was that 'a heretic, no less than an idolater, seeketh to thrust the souls of men from the Lord their God'. Heresy, then, was like spiritual murder.[73]

The summer of 1646 was stifling. The earth was parched, and crops withered. A storm around the end of June finally brought rain and relief, but that was not all. In the first week of July, Pynchon wrote to John Winthrop: 'We have a hand of God upon us . . . in that our English corn is much devoured by multitudes of caterpillars: the Lord affect our hearts and humble us kindly in the sight of our sins and provocations.' Eastern Massachusetts was similarly stricken by these pests, which Winthrop said resembled 'a black worm about an inch-and-a-half long'. There, as in Springfield, they consumed wheat, barley, oats, even meadow grass. The immediate cause, people thought, was the 'great thunder shower' in which the caterpillars had fallen to earth, as plantations had been instantly infested. But the deeper cause was heaven's disapproval. Across the colony, churches set aside days for people to pray and fast, until, as suddenly as they had come, the caterpillars disappeared 'to the wonderment of all men'.[74]

Whereas drought and infestation depleted Springfield's food supply, demand increased as its population continued to grow. The town now had forty-two taxable householders, three of whom were women (who, exceptionally, might also be good patriarchs). Every month brought newcomers. Nathaniel Bliss arrived from Hartford with his widowed mother and sister Mary, the woman who later haunted the swamp after dark, and at once hired Hugh to build a chimney. The fee was fifteen shillings, as ever absorbed by Pynchon, who reduced Hugh's debt and raised Bliss's.[75] John Lombard and George Langton, both single men, also arrived in 1646. Lombard, a Somerset herdsman, had migrated from Cape Cod and moved into a homelot immediately south of Hugh and Mary, hard against the wharf lane.[76] Langton, an English carpenter in his thirties, who previously had lived in Wethersfield, set up home a few doors up.[77] Springfield's expansion spurred Pynchon to hire more essential trades. Desiring a second blacksmith, he tasked Miles Morgan and George Colton to find one, which they duly did.[78] This flurry of activity brought strength and prosperity, and with it competition and unrest.

The tensions of that long, hot summer of 1646 were heightened by other fears and disturbances. The valley settlements debated the meaning of congregationalism, reflecting public puritan controversies back across the Atlantic, where such debates were no longer stifled, nor obedience enforced, by king or bishops. Presbyterians wanted a national church structure; Independents, amply represented in Oliver Cromwell's New Model Army, argued for full independence for congregations. Meanwhile Pynchon, keen to preserve Springfield's appeal to migrants, held his ground over the Saybrook levy, protesting that 'no man will dwell here to be brought under such payments'. But even these religious and fiscal disputes paled against the threat of war with the Narragansetts, who were demanding the return of the four children still being held hostage by colonists in Boston. The Agawam Indians, enraged by what they felt to be colonists' provocations, broke into houses in Springfield to steal tools and allegedly also burgled Pynchon's warehouse. English thieves were also at large – one notorious culprit was chained, but still escaped – and there was drunkenness and defamation, fornication and adultery. Springfield, it seemed, was remaking the Old World, warts and all. Pynchon was glad to receive a letter informing him of parliament's final defeat of the royalists; but now he feared war between England and Scotland, who ought to be 'conjoined friends in the common cause of religion', but were increasingly at loggerheads.[79]

Towards the end of July, Mary Parsons lay perspiring in bed, her baby due any day. Hugh worked long hours, racing to finish building the chimney at Pynchon's mill. He was behind schedule. Adding to the pressure was the knowledge that he would soon have to stop to bring in the harvest, his own and that of a neighbour to whom he had pledged his labour. In Hugh's absence, Mary was attended by women chosen from the neighbourhood. These 'godsiblings' assisted the midwife, perhaps soothing Mary with 'groaning beer', brewed longer for strength, and sustained her with caudle, a sweetened drink of milk and eggs. Most of the godsiblings, among them Pentecost Matthews, were young mothers or were pregnant with their first child. They knew the chances and the dangers: several other infants had died that summer, including Pynchon's stillborn granddaughter. Things had not been going well for Pentecost and her husband John. First they lost a healthy cow, a tremendous blow to a poor family, but worse was to follow. On 25 July, their only child, Abigail, just over a year old, died suddenly. For Mary, then, the birthing chamber was an enclosure of grief as well as fear.[80]

In the first week of August, a time when most people were harvesting corn, picking fruit and hunting game, Mary began her labour. What happened during her confinement was as hidden from her husband as it is from posterity: a private time in a sequestered space for the mother, her godsiblings and the midwife. Perhaps Mary was given hedge-nettle plucked from the meadow, or had warm freshly shorn wool pressed upon her belly to relieve the pain. And when the baby finally came, was the midwife careful not to let the umbilical cord touch the floor for fear of causing incontinence, nor cut it too long or short in case it harmed the child's fertility? All we can say is that it was a scene of intense physical and emotional strain, and that on the 7th, a Friday, Hannah Parsons entered the world, her name denoting both piety and the healing power of prayer.[81] In Hannah, like all children, lay hopes for the regeneration of plantation and colony, and a source of joy to her parents. For Hugh and Mary Parsons, though, her birth also marked the beginning of their descent.

4. Sleeveless Errands

Towards the end of 1646 two suns appeared over New England. Boston's elders predicted the end of days, though with more foreboding than joy. Autumn had been blighted by hunger, disease and fear of native conspiracies. Narragansett fury at the detention of their children spread to other indigenous nations. Connecticut Indians came to William Pynchon's house and threatened him, which he regarded as a sign of the times: 'the pillars of the land seem to tremble,' he wrote in a letter. Events in Old England continued to disturb the mood in the New. The last royalist stronghold had fallen (though not yet in Wales) and a parliamentary order to abolish bishops had been published. The witch-hunt was nearly exhausted: the mass trials in Essex, Suffolk and Huntingdon were over. A new book asserted that although the witch was a literal Antichrist – 'for as Christ is a God incarnate, so is a witch (as it were) a devil incarnate' – rampant witch-finding was an abomination.[1] Despite appeals for conciliation after the civil war, a lingering sense of crisis pervaded the Atlantic world. Puritans feared God's silence more than his judgements, but even so omens like the double-sun unsettled people whose waking hours were spent preserving their households and putting food on the table.

In the Parsons household, Mary struggled to perform her domestic duties on top of her new role as a mother. Blanche Bedortha and other neighbours offered help and advice, but the responsibility was hers alone. She breastfed Hannah, soaked her soiled clouts and tried to rest. Mary felt not just wearied by the demands of motherhood, but depressed; yet as ever she put her faith in God. Prayer restored some confidence, as did the thought that even if she failed to measure up as a mother, she wasn't wicked. Wickedness was projected onto the character of the witch – an anti-mother as well an anti-Christ – whose existence was a source of terror but also consolation: there was always a woman worse than oneself. And, as before, Mary had also to serve her husband, who toiled from first light to after sundown and came home famished and exhausted. He had finally finished building the chimney at Pynchon's mill, more than halving his debt; but there were always more obligations and debts, especially for a man with a young family. It was hard to be a model patriarch and householder when feeding a family was so demanding.[2]

God's small mercies were few and fleeting. One of the mildest winters colonists had known was offset by torrential rain that swelled the Connecticut River until its banks burst. Springfield's meadows and cornfields were flooded, as were the river path, landing stages, wharves, burying ground, training field and lower reaches of the homelots. Next came pestilence – shivering colds and burning fevers, 'full of malignity and very dangerous', according to one account.[3] At home with her baby, Mary was somewhat removed from the contagion, but Hugh, like all townsmen, worked in teams and had to move from field to meadow to mill. This was a busy time for all of Pynchon's servants, tasked with sorting through accumulated skins in the warehouse and packing them in barrels for export. Men also returned to the woodlots to help meet demand for planks, shingles, pipe staves and fuel: each family needed at least half an acre of trees every winter. Noting the timber shortage, the selectmen ordered that none be transported out of town. Regulations to prevent wastage and to manage woodland growth were introduced across the colony. William Pynchon worked to make more land available – soon everything east of the river down to the warehouse belonged to the town – but it was never enough.[4]

The demand for chimneys, too, was greater than ever before. In February 1647 Hugh Parsons agreed to supply William Pynchon with 5,000 bricks within three months: some were to be 'weather bricks', others 'well burnt'. He laboured through the worst of the floods and the contagion to meet his obligation.[5] For Pynchon, bricks were another form of currency, useful for increasing the scope and speed of his commercial activity, such as the recouping of his 'Indian purchase' – the money he had spent buying Springfield's land – through a new variable rate imposed on the town's forty-two households.[6] Hugh Parsons now had in his possession 37½ acres and so was charged 10s 4d, which was far less than what Moxon and Smith were charged, but still more than his neighbours Reece Bedortha, John Matthews and Miles Morgan. Even at its lowest rate, this was a tax poorer men could scarcely afford and so increased their indebtedness. Hugh managed to pay his dues early in May, in lengths of wampum. He also bought four dozen 'silk buttons', presumably so Mary could make clothes to sell, and a steel for sharpening blades, which pushed his debt back up to £3 3s.[7]

Pynchon's system impelled men to work ever harder. To make matters worse, Hugh had been made inspector of fences for the long meadow, a routine position that he was obliged to take up for no financial gain.[8] He was gone long hours, far from home. Mary would wait by the window, wondering when he might return. It was warmer now; outside, the rasp of cicadas, livestock stirring in pens and the restless surge of the river. From the side of the house, Mary could see down to the wharf and across the marshes towards the long meadow. One blue-black night, something crept out of the crawling mist. Hovering, dancing lights, like white flames tinged with colour, rose and fell, disappeared and reappeared. She had heard of such things before: the will-o'-the-wisp or 'fool's fire', a false flickering lantern to lead unwary travellers astray. Back in Wales these ghostly apparitions presaged a death.[9]

More new lives entered Springfield's world. As well as his daughters Martha and Rebecca, George Moxon now had three sons, the youngest born on 10 May. Three days later, a year after she lost her newborn child, Blanche Bedortha gave birth to a boy, John, who was to live a little longer. At this time, the Matthewses had a daughter of three months, Sarah; and the Cooleys a four-month-old son. In June came frosts that damaged crops, yet little rain; lamentations and prayers were answered with another biblical plague of caterpillars. Mary watched over Hannah, ten months old, while Hugh hastened to finish Pynchon's brick order.[10]

The summer bore out Springfield's worst fears: epidemics of smallpox and influenza that claimed many lives. Pynchon's old adversary Thomas Hooker died a week after preaching at Windsor on Romans 1:18: 'for the wrath of God is revealed from heaven against all ungodliness'. He had been, intoned the preacher John Eliot, his ally in Old and New England, one of the colony's 'choicest flowers and most precious saints'. Hooker's loss made people at Hartford feel their prayers were ignored in these 'days of our calamity', and they clung to memories of 'pleasant things which we enjoyed in former times'. The fondest memory was of food. After the previous year's bad harvest, grain was scarce, forcing plantations to forbid exports.[11] The devil, it was supposed, rejoiced in such pain and recruited sinners to his cause. News arrived from Hartford, thirty miles downriver, that at the end of May a woman had been hanged as a witch. She came from Windsor and her name was Alice Young. Unable to bear the grief or shame, her husband sold up and left.[12]

Through all this, little Hannah Parsons survived: she was now a year old and in good health. Her mother Mary, though, remained clouded in mind and spirit. Though now living at the opposite end of town, she still sometimes saw her former mistress, Anne Smith, who on 8 August gave birth to her sixth living daughter: still no sign of a son and heir for her husband Henry. That summer Hugh canoed Pynchon's beaver pelts, wheat and pease to the warehouse and returned with a grindstone for the mill, bolts of cloth, a barrel of raisins and a cask of wine. By mid-August he had whittled his debt down to 18s 2d, but at once started spending again: a bushel of corn, five yards of expensive red cloth, a pair of white cotton stockings. By September the debt was back up to £2 19s 6d. This was not crushing – Hugh still ranked in the middle of Springfield's landowners – but he wasn't happy.[13] He compared himself to other men, some of whom seemed to be racing ahead. Thomas Cooper, the carpenter, who left his native Warwickshire aged eighteen, had lived in Springfield for several years. He, too, had spent the summer manning a canoe for Pynchon, though now was buying land while his wife Sarah spent freely at the store, on cloth, linen, pins, paper, powder and shot.

Cooper also co-owned a team of oxen with no less a figure than Mr Moxon.[14]

Hugh wasn't alone in ranking his achievements against others'. They all did it, just as William Pynchon ventured to make Springfield better than Windsor or Wethersfield, a watchfulness in every direction, judgemental as well as jealous. It wasn't just the fruits of labour that came under scrutiny, either: marriages, too, were subject to unspoken rules and appraisals: either conform or feel the glare of disapproval. A household was a mini-commonwealth, a symbol of the state, its management a sacred duty. Negligence was a betrayal of patriarchy, for kings – Charles I, now imprisoned, was accused of failing as father of the nation – and cottagers alike. Erring couples felt abject misery and shame – marital discord being, according to one physician, 'the most lacerating of all grief'. The death of a child was a stab in the heart, but it was a frequent, expected occurrence, and there would be more children. A bad marriage was an earthly eternity of misery, a fate Hugh and Mary struggled to avoid. In September their neighbour John Lombard returned from New Haven with a new wife, Joanna, and they too set about building a good life for themselves, as best they could.[15]

The harvest of 1647 was again meagre after the cold, dry summer, though a farmer who was also a brickmaker and a riverman still had plenty to do. In the wake of harvest bonfires, Hugh and other men collected and boiled the ashes, which the women made into soap – some thought it the hardest day's work of the year.[16] But Mary's ability to help Hugh was limited, what with running the house and watching Hannah, who was now crawling and able to pull herself up precariously onto her feet. Hugh worked every hour, and yet there was never a job done so well that he wasn't impatient to get the next one done. He was forever gauging the scale of other men's estates and debts and dreaded falling behind. His mood blackened. When Mary told him she was expecting another child his feelings were ambivalent: satisfaction that his household was growing, worried about feeding another mouth. Now Mary would be able to do even less to raise their standing, and at a time when he needed her most. Relations between Hugh and Mary cooled, like an early winter after a warm, bright summer. Their neighbours, the Lombards, noticed this with quiet dismay. And yet, bad husbands and wives had a purpose: all neighbourhoods needed a failing household, which made lacklustre marriages look better and provided an object lesson in how not to behave.

The fragility of Mary's happiness was gradually exposed. The loneliness and longing she had felt for a decade, in both Wales and New England, had been alleviated by marriage and motherhood – but only partially. Even if her husband had been considerate and even-tempered, she was inherently prone to anxiety, exacerbated, perhaps, by the puritan equation of satisfaction with sinful pride. Through all her travails, faith had been the thread in the patchwork of her life, but the stitches were starting to come loose. After Hugh finished his daily work, he would return to find Mary sad and listless, fretful and confused, generally 'mopish' – a man's term for a discontented wife's dejection. Her deepening misery went beyond what was considered normal among Springfield's hard-pressed women. It became clear that what she needed was not just the spiritual counsel of Reverend Moxon but a physician. The nearest, however, was at Windsor – and, besides, physicians were expensive.[17]

As far as physical afflictions were concerned, the community had its ways: the Parsonses' neighbours, Thomas and Sarah Cooper, dispensed remedies, and most housewives had their own, such as cobwebs for cuts, powdered sheep's horn for sores and river mud for bee stings. The Coopers also set fractured bones, when farmers were thrown from carts or sawyers fell from trees. Green sickness ('the virgin's disease') was treated with rosemary, infertility with mandrake oil, intestinal worms with wormseed or a diet of salt fish. Draughts and salves were made from herbs like 'gill-go-by-ground', 'freshwater-soldier' and 'Christ's-eye'. Heartmint, burdock and comfrey also had healing properties. Some cures were learned from Indians and absorbed into English medicine, notably for snake bites. More serious illnesses called for more elaborate treatments. Smallpox, which that summer scythed through Springfield, was treated with a drink made from boiled toads, and prevented with a half dose. A medical practitioner at Salem prescribed cow's milk, ants' eggs and the hair of a virgin for birth pains, and for shingles recommended cat's blood and cream applied with moss.[18]

Mental illness was a more subtle affliction; its medicines, however, were not. Spleenwort was considered effective, as was hellebore, a toxic flower used as rat poison but also taken as snuff by 'such as are mad through melancholy'. Neither were doctors the sole source of authority. Body and spirit were understood to be a unified entity, a conception that linked sickness to sin and found cures in abstinence and repentance. John Winthrop speculated that the wife of the governor of Connecticut had lost her 'understanding and reason . . . by occasion of her giving herself wholly to reading and writing'. William Pynchon, who knew something about most things, advised that the 'hot subtle vapour which hath taken possession of her brain' might be removed with medicine and prayer.[19]

In cases like that of Mary Parsons, Pynchon discouraged snorting powders and instead recommended possets with sugar and saffron; lettuce leaves, if they could be had, were also salutary. Making the body sweat released vapours and was 'a good help to the operation of other physic'. By 'physic', Pynchon meant pills – herbal tablets for sale at his store, and of a type common in the Old World – intended to flush away toxins, refreshing Mary's brain and rebalancing her bodily humours. Pynchon's son-in-law William Davis, a druggist in Boston, was almost certainly his supplier. Taking Pynchon's advice, Hugh Parsons started buying these pills for Mary in the winter of 1645 and carried on doing so through 1646: first four, then twelve, then another four. In February 1647 he bought yet another four, and a week later two more. No one in Springfield, apart from George Moxon (for his own, unknown malady), purchased so many pills. They also tried purging Mary, a process usually performed using laxatives or 'vomits'. Hugh bought Mary a vomit, but predictably was against her taking to her bed – an opinion illustrated by the work shoes he bought her at the same time. For the household to thrive, he felt, she needed to stay on her feet and keep going.[20]

That autumn Hugh worked harder to pay for medicine and everything else they needed, including essential nourishment for his wife
and for their second baby, now growing inside her. He strove and he
brooded. His work in the long meadow, inspecting fences and pasturing livestock, meant he often returned late and fell into bed. Mary
would lie awake watching him twist and murmur beside her. The
next day, he was quiet and serious, as if the previous night's dreams
continued to haunt him – dreams that, like all emotional experiences,
the New England man was meant to dominate or risk appearing
diminished, to both himself and others.[21] Like Mary, Hugh could not
banish these thoughts.[22] Melancholy, everyone knew, was the mother
of all terrors of the night, and Hugh was the kind of melancholic soul
whose humours doctors said were flooded with black bile. Such bile
made his body cold and hard, his mind teeming with 'things full of
horror, by reason of a black vapour diversely moving and disturbing
the brain'. Men like him, it was believed, were furious, obsessional,
covetous, mean, 'lovers of solitariness': not inclined, in other words,
to empathize with Mary's condition.[23]

Increasingly, Hugh could not confine these traits to his home. He
had a habit of appearing uninvited at neighbours' houses. This wasn't
odd in itself: cooperation and mutual reliance, borrowing and sharing,
making conversation and sharing news kept the humours of the community in balance. What bothered people was how often he turned up
without explanation or obvious purpose. Such visits were known as
'sleeveless errands' – pointless chores.[24] Hugh's near neighbour William Branch would open the door to find him leaning on the doorframe,
wanting nothing or asking for things that Branch dared not refuse
him. Hugh invited himself in and sat smoking his pipe in terse contemplation. It was hard to know what to say. All the neighbours felt the
same: that he was sizing them up, seeing what they had, feeding a sullen envy that one physician described as 'a sort of grief mixed with
hate'.[25] Everybody made these green-eyed comparisons – but not the
way Hugh did. And when he did speak, he was prickly, self-conscious,
quick to bridle at the least provocation. As a brickmaker in demand,
his disputatious manner was felt all over town, especially when he

quibbled over contractual details or defaulted or reneged on a deal. When his bricks started falling short in quality and well as quantity – he had so little time – he seemed more harassed than ever.

As the autumn of 1647 gave way to winter, spiritual unease stirred along the valley. At Windsor, where witchcraft had so recently been detected, church members renewed their commitment to right-eousness through a creed-covenant in which they vowed to walk together in love, humility, mercy and self-denial, and, pointedly, to 'renounce all other saviours'. The first snowflakes fell a fortnight later, in early November. Men sharpened axes, the iron blades brit-tle with cold, and chopped firewood. The cattle that had grazed all summer on the marshes would soon need hay, so men baled in teams. Women dressed children in layers, stoked hearth fires and busied themselves in the kitchen: salting rough cuts, preserving fruit and pickling vegetables. There was sickness, and it would last until spring. Such adversity fitted into a cosmic whole, with invisible threads linking households to the heavens.[26]

Springfield's trials were part of a wider testing of Massachusetts, itself understood within a context of upheaval across the Protestant world. In England, through the winter of 1647–8, a convergence of constitutional chaos, poor harvests and trade depression had caused strife to gratify Satan. 'The whole commonwealth', it was said, 'is turned into a mutiny.' The fighting of the civil war had ended but had not resolved parliament's differences with the king. A sense of crisis stifled the desire for conciliation. Meanwhile, the spiritual war against the Antichrist continued. On both sides of the Atlantic, puri-tans resisted what were described as 'all the malignant powers, plots and policies of the earth and hell – ever witches, conjurers and infer-nal spirits themselves'. Behind the rhetoric, real forces pinioned souls. Henry Jessey, the preacher in Llanvaches, ministered to a teenaged girl, who, searching in vain for grace, harmed and starved herself, crying in despair: 'The devil fights with me . . . do you not see him?'[27] Mary Parsons was not yet so mentally vexed, so starkly opposed by Satan; but day by day, week by week, it grew harder to face people, harder to pray.[28]

March 1648: the roads were clogged with snow. The town observed a day of penitence and prayer to beg God's forgiveness. Now six months' pregnant, Mary desperately needed to rest. Her husband wanted her to work. He resented what he saw as her idleness, and she felt isolated, oppressed, exiled again – this time from her new life, even from herself. He grew cruel. One night, coming home to find Mary asleep in bed, Hugh ripped off the blankets and doused the fire to make her cold. Another time he scattered a dish of peas on the floor and made her pick them up, which she did, on all fours, burning with shame. Mary stooped and cringed and floundered around him, unable to do right. She confided in Blanche Bedortha and other neighbours, as once she had confided in Anne Smith; but it became more difficult to know who to trust, and at sunset she was all alone.[29]

The snow continued into April, and people were hungry: ongoing skirmishes with Indians added to the hampering of trade by bad weather. As winter finally slackened its grip, Hugh, always eager to earn more, suggested that Mary ask Anne Smith if she could return to her service, as a nursemaid to her youngest daughters, Margaret and Sarah. But Mary did not feel up to it: she was so tired, who would hire her? Hugh took this refusal like treason against his own state, heresy against his religion. If she wouldn't approach the Smiths for work, he would. He marched uptown, knocked on Henry Smith's door and asked to do some ploughing. The two men faced each other: Smith, with his nice house and family, who wanted for nothing – or so Hugh supposed; Hugh, a look of desperation in his eyes, perhaps with a flash of dark menace, who behaved as if he had nothing to lose, daring Smith to refuse him. But Smith did refuse, perhaps because he didn't need a ploughman or because he didn't want a ploughman like Hugh Parsons. Whatever the reason, Hugh came home livid with rage, vowing revenge.[30]

In the early summer of 1648 news spread across New England that hostilities had reignited in the motherland. A royalist uprising in the county of Kent had triggered a second civil war, as well as a spasm of witch-hunting. Mobs were throwing suspects into ponds and mill dams to see if they floated, thereby proving their guilt. This extra-legal test was known as the water ordeal or, more prosaically, as 'swimming'. The rest of the summer, unusually wet in the old country, was in New England unusually hot. A 'great drought' withered the maize, and what was salvaged was mostly stored. Pynchon sent fewer canoes to the warehouse, which meant less food in Boston. Ships returned to London with light loads, causing mariners to mock New England as 'a poor, barren country'. Sickness as ever went hand in hand with dearth. At the end of May, Blanche Bedortha's baby son John died aged a year and a week, although, as was usual in Springfield, she would soon be pregnant again. Before then, she visited the Parsons homestead to assist with the birth of Mary's second child.[31]

Samuel Parsons was born on 8 June, in good health. Mary, however, was exhausted and even more troubled in mind.[32] Hugh, though behind with his brick orders, still craved more income, so decided to take in lodgers. Anthony Dorchester, some thirty years old, had arrived from Windsor with his wife Sarah and three young children. Before Windsor they had lived at Hingham, a township south of Boston so bitterly split by political and religious faction that many fled.[33] Dorchester, a miller by trade, was hired by William Pynchon, who arranged his tenancy with Hugh Parsons before he and Sarah, who was sick with consumption, could be found a permanent home. Around the time of Samuel's birth the family moved in with their meagre possessions – it was as well they were meagre, as there was no spare room in the Parsons home – and a bed made for them. Perhaps Hugh cleared a space in the loft, in the side parlour or at the back of the hall. Like other couples, Hugh and Mary screened off their bed with Indian mats suspended from cords nailed to the beams. Children slept under skins by the fire or in with parents. Upstairs lodgers benefited from heat rising between the floorboards. But through these gaps sound also carried. Nine people now lived in the small house: four adults, and five children, including Hannah Parsons, aged two, John Dorchester, aged four, and the baby Samuel. People cared little for privacy – but there were limits.[34]

Lodgers were meant to live under the householder's authority. In practice many bridled at this and watched their landlords closely, in order that they might bear witness against them should the need arise.[35] So it was with the Dorchesters. Anthony bore no grudge against Mary: despite her own weak state and onerous duties she helped to nurse his wife, whose condition grew steadily worse. It was Hugh that he resented. The two men were of similar age, both driven, and just too close to each other in every way. Anthony was acutely aware that he had neither mill nor homelot, and so was not an independent man; meanwhile, he was forced to witness Hugh, who was, flaunt his privilege as a householder and neglect obligations imposed by that status. Like Mary, he felt the direct heat of Hugh's moods and saw and heard how disrespectfully and cruelly he treated his wife – who, he could tell, was morbidly fretful.

Since childhood, Mary's mind had been filled with images of evil, against which her faith was both sword and shield. But melancholy made her question her resilience to the devil; indeed, it cast doubt on her very salvation. Even in sound puritan minds, virtue teetered on the brink of wretchedness; devotion peered into an abyss of perdition. Witchcraft was anathema; but the lusts that caused it and came of it were close even to the purest heart – uncomfortably close, like an unwelcome lodger. Becoming a witch wasn't necessarily some hellish summons or a path consciously taken; rather, it was an affliction to which delicate souls gradually succumbed, much as infirm bodies might succumb to an ague. Like all sins, witchcraft was seeded inside every person, whether born to damnation or touched by grace. It was a germ to be starved or fed. For the devil was no visible enemy, like a skulking Indian or a predatory wolf: he was a subtle spirit, insinuating himself like a vapour.

News of witches drifted into neighbourhoods as gossip, and there was embellished through repetition. People believed what they heard, less in spite of its outlandishness than because of it.[36] As Mary sat nursing her baby Samuel – surrounded by children now, with Sarah Dorchester lying sick and the men at work – rumours circulated of a witch who had been discovered in Massachusetts Bay. This time, the source of the information was impeccable: William Pynchon himself. He had returned from Boston, where he had been sitting as a magistrate at the General Court, presided over by the governor, John Winthrop, when the case of Margaret Jones came up. The court found her guilty of witchcraft, according to a new legal code, one rooted in English common law and statute, which gave a Mosaic twist to the penalties for serious offences. The English Witchcraft Act of 1604, which had emphasized the pact made between witches and their diabolic imps, was made into an instrument of justice that referred specifically to Leviticus 20:27 and Deuteronomy 18:11.[37] And of course, this most wicked of crimes carried the death penalty, not just because it was an English felony but more particularly in obedience to Exodus 22:18: 'Thou shalt not suffer a witch to live.'

Margaret Jones was hanged on Boston Common on 14 June 1648. A midwife from Charlestown, she was said to have 'such a malignant touch that whomsoever she touched . . . with any affection of displeasure' fell sick. She had quarrelled with neighbours, and when things she bewitched were burned she 'came to the fire and seemed concerned'. Influenced by the recent East Anglian witch-hunt, the court ordered that Jones be watched in case her familiars visited, 'the course which hath been taken in England for discovery of witches . . . the best and surest way'. A body search, another English method, revealed 'an apparent teat in her secret parts as fresh as if it had been newly sucked', and she was seen in daylight with her skirts raised, holding a small child. Margaret denied the charges and refused to yield to her neighbours, who visited to try to make her confess. She admitted a petty theft, but supposed 'there was grace enough in Christ to pardon that'. At her trial she railed against the jury and went to the gallows in the same fury. Margaret's husband Thomas, who was implicated in her crimes, tried to flee to Barbados but was refused passage. Before it even left the Charles River, the ship, loaded with eighty horses, was rocked by a storm for twelve hours. Only when he was arrested did the ship regain an even keel.[38] That same day 'a very great tempest' blasted much of Connecticut, tearing up trees. An apparition of a three-masted ship appeared in New Haven, on deck a spectral figure pointing a sword out to sea.[39]

The arrival of witches in a community was disconcerting, uncanny. Far away until they were near, suddenly they were within the town boundary, across the street, leaning on the windowsill, then knocking on the door, full of secret purpose. And this realization was all the more chilling because, it seemed, perhaps they had been there all along, dripping poison with a smile, plotting mayhem as they waved good morning. How many mothers in Boston shuddered to think that the malignant Margaret Jones had brought their children into the world? Now Springfield worried that it had its own witches in its midst and tensely awaited the first blow, wondering when it would fall and against whom. The answer came all too soon.

That same June of 1648, word spread that Henry and Anne Smith's infant daughters, Margaret aged two, Sarah less than a year, had fallen sick. Neighbours, including the minister Mr Moxon, came to pray earnestly for their recovery. William Pynchon was present, for these were his granddaughters. Their mother Anne, now five months pregnant, was distraught. On the 24th, in a room thick with desperation and the most heartfelt appeals to God, Margaret died. Baby Sarah languished for a few days before she too perished.[40] Henry Smith's heart was clotted with grief and rage, his thoughts spiralling. Would his remaining four daughters also die? Had God taken his youngest girls to punish him for secretly wanting a son? Or was this in fact diabolical revenge for his refusal to employ Hugh Parsons?

The solemn funeral of the Smith girls, witnessed by the whole town, increased the fears of parents for their children. Three weeks later Hugh and Mary's next-door neighbours John and Joanna Lombard welcomed their first child, a son, and prayed fervently for his survival. There were more strange omens. In late July, brown flies the size of a fingertip crawled out of the ground with a loud buzzing. They filled woodlands not just in Springfield but throughout New England, and ate young shoots in orchards, though mercifully they left the maize and wheat alone. Then in August, after the harvest had been brought in, thousands of pigeons descended like a dark cloud; they were shot and netted, destined for spit, pot and pie. At the synod in Boston, a snake appeared on the bench occupied by the elders, taken by John Winthrop as heaven's sign that the devil was vigilant, ready to undermine the godly.[41]

As ever, Satan delighted in puritan suffering. Throughout September 1648 William Pynchon struggled to keep Springfield supplied, although his refusal to pay the river levy worked against this. Saybrook badly needed funds to rebuild the fort after a fire the previous winter; but Pynchon was unmoved.[42] Reports arriving from England, meanwhile, were concerning. Royalist soldiers were on the march again – indeed, they had even passed through old Springfield on their way to the town of Colchester, where, mercifully, they were defeated. Pynchon wrote to John Winthrop in October, eager for more news and pitying Old England more than he pitied the New. 'I look upon that land as in the saddest posture,' he said. 'The Lord in mercy turn the wheel upon the wicked, and them that love the Lord in sincerity shine as the sun in its strength.' Only piety and the punishment of sin could persuade God to restrain the devil from tempting people to damage their souls and their plantations.[43]

Speak of the devil, a proverb taught, and he will be there at your elbow.[44] And Mary's neighbours noticed that she spoke often of the devil and of witches. A bit of gossip was one thing, but too much reflected badly on the person spreading the gossip. English ministers likened the tongue to a witch – dispersing venom into the community.[45] The tragedy of the Smith girls' deaths had further bruised and tangled Mary's thoughts. These were the girls she might have cared for, might have saved. Was she herself to blame? Or someone else? Shut up in her house her mind coiled around the possibilities. There was, however, one woman at the core of her suspicions. Her name was Mercy Marshfield, a middle-aged widow recently arrived in Springfield from Windsor. She had come with her adolescent children Samuel and Sarah – but, Mary thought, she had brought the devil too.[46]

The Marshfield family was known to John Winthrop, who saw in their story a lesson in the vicissitudes of fortune. Mercy had left the Devon city of Exeter for America in 1634 with her husband Thomas. A godly man, Thomas Marshfield had been too poor to emigrate until a wealthy citizen took pity on him after dreaming about his plight and paid Marshfield's passage along with that of his wife and children. The Marshfields settled at Squantum Neck, Dorchester, near William Pynchon's first home; there, Mercy gave birth to a daughter, Priscilla. They moved to Windsor in 1637, where Thomas and Mercy were saintly pillars of the church, as they had been at Dorchester. Yet within a couple of years Priscilla was dead and her father in trouble. According to Winthrop, ever one to blame mishaps on sin, Marshfield 'grew suddenly rich, and then lost his godliness, and his wealth soon after'. His creditors sued after a business venture folded in the early 1640s, forcing him to sell off land. His remaining assets were seized, and he died soon afterwards. Not that this ended the ruthless claims against what was left of his estate. After her eldest daughter was safely married, Mercy, now penniless, moved to Springfield, hoping to escape the shame of the Marshfield name at Windsor.[47]

Opinion at Windsor, and in Hartford, where creditors had been left empty-handed, was that the Marshfields had betrayed their covenant with the town. Witchcraft confessions, notably those in eastern England, held a mirror to such betrayals, reflecting them darkly as covenants with Satan. Mary Parsons's suspicions were born of the rumours from Windsor, where fear of the devil (and those who encouraged him) was intense, inflamed by hardship and hard preaching. The sermons of their minister John Wareham and the lecturer Ephraim Huit often dwelt on Satan's exploitation of pride, ingratitude and hypocrisy.[48] Alice Young, the witch hanged at Hartford the previous summer, came from Windsor. Both towns – Windsor and Hartford – were locked in an existential battle between Christ and Antichrist. Hunger and disease were attributed to sin, Indians and demons were elided as enemies, and survival hinged on the merciful dispensations of grace. And at their beating heart was the message, which the Saints drummed in repeatedly: 'the devil is amongst thee now'.[49]

The discovery of witches was bound to spread along the Connecticut valley. In the winter of 1648, a woman was exposed as a witch in Wethersfield, another township scarred by conflict. Mary Johnson had a poor reputation, having been whipped for theft a couple of years earlier.[50] After her arrest, at which time she was carrying an illegitimate child, she was put in the care of Samuel Stone, a puritan minister and co-founder of Hartford with the Essex emigrant Thomas Hooker. Like Hooker, Stone specialized in 'spiritual cures'. These were exorcisms by any other name: grinding, soul-purging interrogations meant to break Satan's grip upon sinners.[51] Mary Johnson did not disappoint Stone. She confessed that as a discontented servant she had so often cursed in Satan's name that he appeared and helped her with her chores. She liked this, murdered a child, and 'committed uncleanness both with men and with devils', for which now she was sorry. In the first week of December, in a freezing courtroom at Hartford, Mary Johnson was convicted of 'familiarity with the devil' and condemned to death. But rather than being hanged straight away, she was reprieved until after her baby was born.[52]

January 1649 was breathtakingly cold, a return to the adamantine winters of earlier in the decade. Ice crept across New England's rivers. Some people risked walking on them: in Boston, several drowned. Children died from influenza. John and Pentecost Matthews, who had invested such hope in their second daughter Sarah, after losing their first child, passed the days in earnest prayer that she too would not be taken from them and consigned to a grave hacked from the iron-hard earth of the burying ground. Others shared their anxiety. By now, Anne Smith had a three-month-old daughter, named Margaret after the child taken from her by God – or by a witch with God's permission. Three doors up from Hugh and Mary, Blanche Bedortha, who had lost her son John the previous May, was now seven months into her third pregnancy, praying this time that she might bear a viable child: her life, like that of so many other women, was a continual round of exertion and fatigue, hope and fear.[53]

Meanwhile, Widow Marshfield had begun to forge new friendships to replace those she had lost in Windsor, and upon which a poor woman with children depended for survival. She drew close to Blanche, offering help and advice as Blanche's time drew near. And two more babies were born in the south end that month: Eliakim Cooley and Hepzibah Jones. Their names, meaning 'resurrection of God' and 'my delight is in her' respectively, bowed to heaven's authority and begged its protection against evil. Witches were active in the community, and were known to be envious of fertile women, who became victims of their murderous magic. Every mother's worry found substance in the person of the witch.[54]

The Parsons family and their Dorchester tenants had spent all winter cooped up together: Sarah Dorchester in her consumptive state, Mary weary and wan, and the children always underfoot, hungry and bored. Hugh's brickmaking did at least mean he had something to do before the planting season began. He took commissions for chimneys and checked that the freeze had drained moisture from his dug clay. Still he yearned for prosperity and respect. His term as inspector of fences was now up. He had proved himself competent and on 6 February was invited to swear an oath of fidelity to the town – signifying his inclusion rather than doubt about his good faith. Yet every advance in his luck and standing, like a row of faulty weaving on a loom, had some flaw for its own unravelling.[55]

One day Hugh was at the Bedorthas' house, discussing an order of bricks; as was increasingly the case with negotiations involving Hugh, the atmosphere crackled with tension. Blanche, now a month away from her confinement, lost patience listening to her rancorous neighbour going on and made a snide remark. Hugh immediately turned on her. 'Gammer,' he spat, 'you needed not have said anything. I spake not to you, but I shall remember you when you little think on it.' Her husband Reece was aghast that this man should insult his wife – 'gammer' meant an old woman, not a young one like Blanche – and threaten her, in his own home no less; but to save their deal just protested meekly that this 'was no good speech'. Hugh departed, and Reece Bedortha got his six shillings' worth of bricks. Yet the confrontation left the heavily pregnant Blanche ill at ease: Hugh was proving a frightening, unpredictable neighbour. She began to worry about what form his 'remembering' might take.[56]

One evening soon afterwards Blanche was alone in the house after dark, and undressing. Her bed was curtained off from the rest of the hall by a mat slung over a rope, which kept out the hearth light. As she went to hang her shag-cotton waistcoat on a nail, a sinuous and glowing wisp caught her eye, like a marshlight but glimmering on the waistcoat. Afraid, she held up the garment and saw a cold luminescence, like a candle flame, creeping up and down the inside. It left her bewildered and alarmed. She tried to reproduce the effect by holding her waistcoat against the fire, but in vain. She never saw it again.[57]

A month later, early in March, snow still lay in drifts as Blanche's fortnight of confinement began. Mercy Marshfield took charge and stayed all the day, leaving her only at sunset. At the end of the first week of confinement, a Thursday evening, Mercy departed as usual. Blanche, worn out, fell asleep. But after an hour or so she awoke with a start, a pain beneath her left breast and, she supposed, near her heart. Sharper now, it spread to her shoulder and neck. The pain was so intense – like the pricking of knives – that she had to prop herself up on a bolster; yet still it didn't abate. When Widow Marshfield arrived in the morning, she found Blanche in agony. Fearing she was dying, Mercy stayed for the next three days as Blanche's torment grew worse, until midday on the Monday when it eased. By Tuesday Blanche had recovered. But she was convinced that what she called 'this evil' came from the 'threatening speech of Hugh Parsons', leaving her afraid for her unborn baby.[58] On the following Thursday, 15 March, Joseph Bedortha was born, and mother and baby emerged safely from the ordeal.[59] They were lucky. News had arrived from Dorchester of a devil disguised as 'a professed servant of Jesus Christ, in Old England and New': another wicked midwife accused of killing birthing mothers and their babies.[60]

Towards the end of the month, Springfield roused itself from its winter slumber. The brook was cleared of debris, fences mended, canoes resealed with pine pitch. Soon the sheep would need shearing, and the business of washing and drying fleeces would begin. Hugh Parsons set to work mixing clay and cleaning his brick moulds. The seasonal routine was unvaried – but something had changed in the south end of Springfield. Blanche Bedortha's ordeals – the flame on her waistcoat, her painful confinement – had put Hugh firmly on the wrong side of good opinion in the neighbourhood. More people were out and about now, and suspicion spread in the lanes, in the fields, and from door to door. Mercy Marshfield, who thought it possible that witchcraft had caused Blanche's symptoms, and may have wished to deflect doubts about her own good name, had already set her face against Hugh Parsons. Perhaps it was she, or Blanche Bedortha, who told the Bedorthas' next-door neighbour Griffith Jones about what had happened, sharpening his own sense of peril.

One spring Sunday, after the morning sermon, Jones, his wife Sarah and their baby girl Hepzibah visited a neighbour. Sarah Jones accepted an invitation to stay for midday dinner before they returned to the meeting house for the second sermon. For some reason, Griffith left his family and went home to eat. Alone in the house, he fetched some food, resting his plate on Hepzibah's cradle while he looked for a knife. Strangely, he couldn't find one anywhere, and had to use the rusty blade from the shoe-mending basket. He ate, cleared things away, then fed his scraps to the pig. Returning to the table to cut some tobacco, he was startled. Lying next to the rusty blade were three good knives. Frozen by fear, he summoned the courage to look behind him, half expecting to see an intruding Indian. Seeing nobody, he sat down and reached for his pipe. Just then the front door opened. It was Hugh Parsons. 'Where is the man?' he called. 'Are you ready to go to the meeting?' Griffith stammered that he had a mind first to smoke his pipe, perhaps hoping that Hugh would go on without him. But Hugh didn't leave. He came in, sat down at the table and joined Griffith for a smoke. Then the two men went off to the meeting house, as if nothing had happened.[61]

With each small, strange event the atmosphere thickened. Mary Parsons, distanced from her irascible husband and fixated by witches, nonetheless hesitated to point a finger at Mercy Marshfield. Afraid of accusing, and afraid of not accusing, she leaked her obsession in hints. One day in April, Mary was at home with other neighbouring women, chatting by the hearth while carding: teasing wool with brushes. Mercy Marshfield appeared in the doorway and saw what they were doing – jealously, Mary imagined. Later that day, after the women had gone, Mary noticed wool was missing and went to tell Pentecost Matthews, a patient listener (she taught children to read). 'I wonder', Pentecost asked, 'what is become of the half pound of wool'. Mary said she couldn't say, 'except the witch had witched it away'. Pentecost then asked Mary why she was always talking about witches: 'Do you think there is any witch in town?' Mary was certain there was; the wretch had even been to her house. Pentecost asked whom she meant, but couldn't get a straight answer. Mary said she had been at Henry Smith's house when Anne Stebbins, who was also afraid of witches, had said the culprit 'was suspected to be a witch in Windsor'. This identified Widow Marshfield. Mary claimed it was only since Marshfield had arrived that sinister 'strong lights' had been seen in the long meadow. When Pentecost did not respond, Mary grew bolder: Marshfield 'did grudge at other women that had children because her daughter had none'.[62] This daughter was Mercy Dumbleton, still in Windsor, who had been married for over a year without becoming pregnant.[63] Pentecost said no more: there was something unnerving about Mary's obsession.[64] So Mary took her best shot. It was the same time when Marshfield was grudging about this, she informed Pentecost, that 'your child died and your cow died'.[65]

Soon afterwards, Mary also spoke to Pentecost's husband John Matthews, referring to Mercy Marshfield anonymously as 'a widow woman that now lived in Springfield', formerly of Windsor. But now there was something else. Mary claimed that this woman had told her how to identify witches. Mary didn't elaborate, but her meaning was clear: it took one to know one. Matthews knew what Mary was doing and told her firmly 'that he believed no such thing' of this poor widow of Windsor. Losing ground, Mary hit back: 'you need not speak so much for Goody Marshfield' – followed by the killer blow. Marshfield's daughter had finally had a baby, she said, but before then the widow had envied every woman with a child: her jealous rage explained the deaths of his daughter and prized heifer. 'I am persuaded', Mary said, 'they were bewitched.' In Windsor, she added, it was well known that Mercy Marshfield bowed to Satan, who 'for aught I know . . . follows her here'.[66]

By this time news had reached Springfield that John Winthrop, the father of Massachusetts, had died in March 1649. He was, according to his epitaph, 'a man of unbiased justice . . . very humble, courteous, and studious of the general good'.[67] New England's elders regarded the passing of their luminaries as a punishment. Yet Pynchon, pragmatic to his core, now saw an opportunity to expound his dissenting views in the book he had long been contemplating, perhaps having before feared that doing so might provoke controversy with his old friend. (He was probably also moved by the death the previous year of Reverend Henry Smith of Wethersfield, whose sermon three decades earlier had been Pynchon's own epiphany.) Now, Pynchon was ready to pull together thirty years of thinking and reading, not just of the Bible – in both the Geneva and King James translations – but of the works of Calvin and Luther and their followers, and many others besides, even learned Catholics. At the core of Pynchon's contentiously offbeat interests was the doctrine of justification: how the Crucifixion had freed man from the curse of original sin. He had also corresponded with scholars in Old England, notably the anti-Presbyterian Thomas Gataker, with whom he disagreed about the meritorious price – that phrase again – that Christ had paid to redeem mankind.[68]

It may have been one of these correspondents who informed

Pynchon of an even more terrible death. On 30 January 1649 Charles I had been beheaded as a traitor. Pynchon had no love for the English king, whom he found 'corrupt in religion and manners'. Nonetheless, he was of the opinion that wherever they were in the world Englishmen should make laws in the king's name, since it was the law alone that restrained the monarch's absolute powers. 'We are not a free state,' he had reminded Winthrop in 1647, nor should New England aspire to be one, not least because colonists had been protesting in Boston in defence of their 'due and natural rights as freeborn subjects of the English nation', and justifiably urging respect for Magna Carta and England's 'ancient constitution'.[69] It was for trampling on such sacred custom that the autocratic Charles I had been convicted of treason against his people – whose own sovereignty, it transpired, was superior even to his divine right. The king's 'wicked designs' and 'evil practices' – charges made at his trial – painted him as black as any apostate. Some had seen this coming; but Pynchon and others still found the execution deeply shocking. Even parliamentarians, many of whom had hoped for a settlement with the crown, called it heinous regicide, a ghastly emblem of disordered times. Not only was the king dead, but the English monarchy had been entirely abolished. The patriarchy that held the Atlantic world together was a column teetering on its pedestal.

Religious orthodoxy was another creaking pillar of order. Dissent, portending disaster, was resisted by church and state. In February 1647 the English parliament had issued ordinances against heresy and blasphemy, such as questioning the immutable truth of the Holy Trinity. On a day of fasting and prayer the following month, a preacher had told the House of Commons how heresies spread poison, 'destroying by degrees the light of the mind, fascinating and bewitching the spirits of those that swallow them'. Heretics, thundered another, promote conspiracy and murder through 'the devilish spirit of hatred'. The following year a cleric likened heresies to the magic arts, 'diabolical delusions' insinuated into men's minds by Satan himself.[70] Heresy was a disease, like gangrene, for which cutting and burning was the right surgery; or, like rickets in children, swelling the head of the church but enfeebling its body. The execution of heretics was compared favourably to pulling down houses to halt a conflagration.[71]

As life grew stranger, people became more open to strange ideas, and the stain of heresy deepened. And now New England, too, was bewitched by sectaries, 'that rabble of men that went under the names of Independents, whether Anabaptists, Antinomians, Familists, and Seekers'.[72] Whatever crack-brained heterodoxy went unpunished in Old England would not pass in the New: about that, colonial governors were determined. This was the climate in which William Pynchon started writing his book, an act of disobedience to the authorities in Boston that some would feel lured the devil to town, just as witches welcomed the devil into their lives. Meanwhile, George Moxon's sermons grew markedly more forbidding, reflecting Springfield's darkening days and, perhaps too, his disquiet that the maverick Pynchon had begun to put pen to paper. Using vivid metaphors, Moxon spoke of sin and guilt, and of Satan blinding people to wrongdoing and imitating his depraved life. Sin lay dormant in the heart, like a hibernating beast, he said, but once roused it gathered momentum, 'as the horse rusheth into the battle, committing wickedness with greediness'. Moxon asked the congregation at Springfield to imagine the shrieking of those who on earth burned in lust burning for ever in the fiery lake. Spend each day, Moxon advised, in fear and hope: the elect fearing that salvation was at stake, the reprobate hoping they might yet find grace in themselves. Departing from strict Calvinist doctrine, he implied that every person had a choice, and a stark one. 'If you miss heaven,' he warned, 'unavoidably you will drop into hell.'[73]

5.   *I Hear My Child Is Dead*

One night in the spring of 1649, two hours after sundown, Joan Branch was woken up by her husband William in a panic. He had been lying there staring at the darkness when in an instant the room was filled with a great flash of light, from which emerged a small boy 'with a face as red as fire'. The boy approached the bed and reached out, resting his glowing hand beneath Branch's chin. Branch was petrified, speechless. Then, he told his wife, he felt a searing pain down his back – 'something like scalding water' – and heard a voice say: 'It is done. It is done.' Suddenly the room was dark again, and the boy had vanished. The following day William Branch could not stop turning this visitation over in his mind, and wondering what had caused it. Branch was the town barber, who lived next to Griffith Jones – he of the conjured knives – and next but one to the Bedorthas. As such, he was already wary of Hugh's 'sleeveless errands', and his wife Joan had known Mercy Marshfield when she lived in Windsor.[1]

By this time Hugh Parsons had become a repugnant figure in the eyes of the town. People felt his malign influence when he was present and, as Blanche Bedortha and Griffith Jones had found, even when he was not. Hugh even discomfited himself. He, too, had been sleeping badly, tortured by stressful dreams. It was an orthodox belief – admittedly one William Pynchon disputed in his book – that during his Atonement Christ had been forced to visit hell. This was how it felt for Hugh: his soul dragged to some hole, darker than a moonless night, to be racked and goaded. Suffering severe stomach cramps, he cried out, waking Mary, telling her that he felt as if he was being stabbed. She had an idea why.[2]

The devil that Mercy Marshfield had brought with her from Windsor was now in their bed – not that, Mary imagined, her husband was blameless in the matter. Meanwhile, Mary continued to harbour suspicions about Marshfield. She had already sown a seed of doubt in John Matthews's mind regarding his dead child and cow. But such accusations always carried a risk of reversal – as Mary now discovered. Forced to pick a side, John and Pentecost Matthews chose Widow Marshfield, telling her that Goody Parsons had called her a witch. A vulnerable woman, already deep in ignominy, and needing to preserve her fragile reputation, Mercy was quick to complain to William Pynchon. She had been slandered! What would become of her? Pynchon knew there might be witchcraft abroad in Springfield, as in the godly regions of Old England, and also at Boston, Windsor and Wethersfield. But considering the case purely as a magistrate, this seemed to him just a defamation suit, with Mary's word against Mercy's. He set a trial date for the end of the month.[3]

It was May: planting time. The cows had long since calved, and milk rich in butterfat had been heated in cauldrons with rennet from the previous autumn's slaughtering, the whey drained from the curd, and fresh butter worked in. The cheeses, wrapped in muslin, were drying and ageing on shelves: Springfield would eat whatever it could afford not to send downriver to sell.[4] By this time more men had homelots in the long meadow: Alexander Edwards, George Colton, Richard Excell and a few others. These houses were far from the meeting house – something that concerned William Pynchon, who thought that by the time the Sabbath came round, such people were 'more fit to sleep at God's worship than to attend it as they ought to'.[5] But living in the long meadow was handy for pasturing and planting: others with long-meadow plots who lived in the town, like Hugh Parsons, had to ride or walk several miles to get there.

As the weather grew warmer, Hugh chose to make a rough bed outside rather than trek home only to start again at dawn, especially with the long days and short nights. This was not in itself odd behaviour: woodcutting and haymaking took men far from home along primitive paths, through gloomy, resin-scented forests, in which case it made sense to camp at dusk: even hardy woodsmen felt safe only as long as the light lasted. They did not, however, camp alone.

Hugh, though, was different: a melancholic craving solitude, ready to put up with persistent biting insects, and thoughts of wolves, perhaps even Indians, out there in the darkness. Besides, it was a relief from trying to relax in a stuffy, overcrowded house, with Sarah Dorchester sick in body and his wife Mary in her mind. He could lie there and think, staring at a moon of scoured pewter, stars thickening against a sky as deeply black as a beaver pelt. Back home, Mary waited vainly at the window. What might have been rings around Hugh's lantern, shining through a veil of mist, proved to be no more than the bobbing glow of marshlights.[6]

One morning, as his wife's appearance at Pynchon's court approached, Hugh awoke in the meadow with a thirst for fresh milk. The sun was low on the horizon, and the grass grey with dew. He wandered to the house of Alexander Edwards, the Welshman who had vouched for Mary when she sought permission to marry. Edwards himself was out, but his wife Sarah was there. These days few were pleased to see Hugh's face: no good could come of his visits, unless they needed bricks, but even then such liaisons were apt to sour. Hugh reminded Sarah of a debt she owed, which he asked to be settled in milk. Trying to be conciliatory, Sarah said she could spare but a halfpenny's worth. After all, like most families, they had only one cow. Could she not repay him with something else? Hugh insisted on having what was due to him in milk. But she stood her ground, and he went away, aggrieved.[7]

The next time Sarah came to milk her cow, the heifer yielded barely two pints instead of the usual six, and it didn't look right. Yellow milk was rich milk, good for butter, but this was the colour of saffron. There was also a tinge of blood, which may have been caused by pulling too hard, so for the moment Sarah thought no more of it. The cow was otherwise well. But then the milk changed to other colours. Alexander and Sarah showed it to their longmeadow neighbours, George Colton and Richard Excell. Everyone found it peculiar, and Sarah suspected witchcraft: the discolouration was abnormal, it attacked her household by ruining produce, and someone with a motive – resentful envy – had recently called.[8]

Her husband informed William Pynchon that he and his wife believed Hugh Parsons had bewitched their cow. Pynchon suggested that the stoppage of milk was merely 'a sign of some dangerous sickness'; but when the cow remained healthy he was forced to reconsider. In time, he himself would suggest that 'such a sudden change could not come from a natural cause'.[9]

On the morning of Sunday 27 May, townsfolk filed into the meeting house to listen to Reverend Moxon's sermon. They brought with them their suspicions and grudges – thoughts still mostly private, words bitten back, but gradually gaining momentum. In two days' time Pynchon's court would decide whether or not Goodwife Parsons had slandered Widow Marshfield as a witch. Once the congregation was settled, Moxon turned over his hourglass and began. The text of his sermon was Hebrews chapter 11, which told of the Israelites wandering the deserts and mountains looking for a home. The inference was clear: New Englanders were their spiritual heirs in Canaan. Many ministers flattered their congregations this way, but invariably added a caveat: 'For unto whomsoever much is given,' the Bible taught, 'of him shall be much required.'[10] Moxon reminded Springfield that to honour God they must act upon his words. At the afternoon meeting, Moxon repeated a message from an earlier sermon, namely that the elect should live charitably with neighbours so 'that they may get more full assurance of their salvation'. Satan made the elect forget to store up proofs of their grace, like food cellared for winter. Instead, they squandered their time on 'scandalous sins that may exceedingly darken things' in their souls. As the last grains of sand slipped through the hourglass, Moxon's eyes scanned the meeting house, hesitating before his conclusion: 'Take heed of tampering so much with Satan.'[11]

Shortly before her trial, Mary took her sceptical neighbour John Matthews aside for a quiet word. Her subject, as usual, was witchery. This time, however, she didn't repeat the charge against Mercy Marshfield. She had an even more devastating accusation – one that spoke loudly of her confusion and anguish, her growing obsessions about witchcraft and the terror her strange husband instilled in her.

To Matthews's astonishment, Mary accused Hugh himself of being a witch. There was always more going on behind his hard face than came out when he spoke, she said, which was increasingly rarely. Nor did he always attend Mr Moxon's meetings, a disclination that may have been entirely because he was working in the long meadow – or perhaps because Christian worship somehow pained him. So, yes: Hugh was a witch, she was sure of it. But how could she be so certain? asked Matthews. She replied that Satan often came to him in the night to feed from his body, so that he was 'tormented in his bowels and cried out as though he were pricked with pins and daggers'. He was hellishly ensnared, she believed, and now couldn't escape. As the proverb had it, it was easier to raise the devil than to lay him to rest – and the same was true of accusations of heinous crimes in a town like Springfield. By confiding in John Matthews, Mary had lit a fire.[12]

On Tuesday the 29th, the town returned to the meeting house for the court hearing, hiding its excitement behind a mask of solemnity. Pynchon, seated on the dais, would decide whether or not Mary Parsons was a liar – and if not, by implication, whether there was any truth in her opinion of Mercy Marshfield. But first the people had to hear a reading of the laws and liberties of Massachusetts, published the previous year. After a preamble came a list of capital offences, starting with the crime of worshipping anyone or anything but God, followed by this: 'If any man or woman be a witch, that is, hath or consulteth with a familiar spirit, they shall be put to death.'[13] Did Mary Parsons exchange knowing glances with Mercy Marshfield or John Matthews – or her own husband? Surely a shared frisson rippled across the room. For Mercy and now for Hugh, too, Mary's accusations could cost them their lives.

Announcement over, Pynchon's court was declared in session. Owing to its distance from Boston, Springfield had since 1641 enjoyed *de jure* authority to try non-capital crimes and, owing to its small size, needed only to empanel juries of six men rather than the usual twelve. This was, however, the plantation's first slander prosecution: the use of injurious words breached the peace, but strictly speaking it wasn't a crime, so a jury wasn't needed. Pynchon alone would decide the verdict.[14] He feared the devil, but also knew the devil touched more hearts with malice than he incited to commit witchcraft. Yet Pynchon was a scrupulous man, almost pedantically fair. Both sides would have their say in the public forum.

Mercy Marshfield stood humbly at the front of the meeting house. She protested that she was no witch, but rather the victim of Mary Parsons's spite. Pynchon allowed her to call John and Pentecost Matthews as witnesses. Mary, they said, had suggested that Widow Marshfield had brought the devil from Windsor and had bewitched their daughter and cow. As the weight of evidence accumulated, the hearing spilled into Wednesday. Mary, for her part, hotly denied defamation but had no one to back her, no witnesses to call; her low spirits and gabbling about witches had left her isolated. Marshfield, on the other hand, had not only friends and family but also an expanding network of townsfolk, who – thanks to Hugh's misconduct – harboured a low opinion of the Parsons household. Pynchon found it easier to believe that an inconstant woman with a rebarbative husband might make a rash accusation than to believe Marshfield guilty of witchcraft, that most devilishly difficult of crimes to detect. And besides, the prosecution witnesses had sworn on oath, whereas Mary as the defendant was not required to do so, to avoid incriminating herself. Drawing proceedings to a close, Pynchon sentenced Mary to be 'well whipped': twenty lashes that coming Friday, 1 June. The sentence would be commuted, should Mary prefer, to a fine of £3, payable to Widow Marshfield in silver or twenty-four bushels of corn come harvest time. She chose the fine.[15]

Hugh was infuriated. He worked so hard for so little, and now Mary's addled head was wasting the fruit of his labours. To add to his sense of unfair persecution, he had been fined ten shillings at the same session for smoking his pipe in the street: a prohibited fire risk. Hugh hit back by charging a witness against him with smoking in his back yard – a futile lashing-out that only further depleted the dregs of Hugh's honour.[16] There was shame enough in being the unreliable brickmaker and defective patriarch, unable to bring his wife to heel. But he was also the unwelcome visitor, the obtuse neighbour, the magician of knives and milk and creeping flames. And the black looks he now received from Springfield's townsfolk only deepened his discontent. He was a walking fit of rage, the kind of man who, as one preacher put it, was 'angry with his enemies and angry with his friends; angry for little things, angry for nothing; angry at his world, angry at his meat; angry in health, angry in sickness'. Anger could be virtuous; it righted wrongs. Christ had shown anger to the Pharisees and Sadducees, to traders in the Temple. But unjustified anger was a feminine thing, which Satan nurtured into malice, revenge and civil war.[17] By yielding to his passion, it was said, a man unmanned himself, opening his heart to the evils he feared most. Exactly this, people concluded, had happened to Hugh. It was anger that eroded the relationships with his wife and community, from which no man could be parted and still prosper.[18]

Mary was not by nature so easily enraged. Yet she too felt wronged by Pynchon's judgement and began muttering that the Matthewses had perjured themselves. Her comments only brought further opprobrium from her neighbours. But even these neighbours needed the bricks that only Hugh could supply. So when John Matthews decided that he wanted two chimneys built in his house, he had no choice but to engage Hugh's services. Hugh gave him a price and took a down payment of £1 14s 6d. Matthews should have known better.[19]

Between May and August 1649 the drought that had beset New England for five years threatened the entire harvest. 'An innumerable company of caterpillars' returned to eat whatever greenery remained, including the leaves from the trees, until it looked like winter. There were quirks: the creatures ate the pea shoots but left the peas.[20] It didn't seem natural – but then, as people knew, the lines between natural and supernatural were blurred. Springfielders felt they were part of a cosmic scheme of angels and demons, but none pretended to understand its mysteries: they prayed, but were also prepared for prayers to go unanswered. A poor harvest would mean dependence on Indians, requiring negotiations in which Pynchon was at least well practised. That summer, he was excused attendance at the General Court in Boston in order to concentrate his efforts closer to home. Connecticut's General Court, meanwhile, urged him to settle his ongoing dispute with Saybrook 'in a way of love and peace, and according to truth'. But Pynchon focused instead on Springfield's problems, from within and without: the darts fired from heaven that turned their food to dust, and the vitriol welling up in the hearts of his people.[21]

Colonists across New England contemplated their own sins and misdemeanours while censuring others, a desire for unity and uniformity mixing with righteous anger, nervous guilt and rank hypocrisy. George Moxon's sermons and lectures continued to spell out the force of heaven's mercy, the virtue of charity and the relief from spiritual worry delivered by grace. At the same time, like a stern physician, he also scrutinized Springfield's infirmities, diagnosing divine retribution and prescribing repentance: 'pray in secret, search your own soul, humble your heart, meditate, spend time between God and your own soul, wrestle with corruption'. There were absences from the meeting house that summer, Hugh Parsons included, which were duly noted. In June, Moxon reproached those who made feeble excuses for non-attendance, such as the inclement weather, or having no hat or shoes. And he condemned idleness more generally: 'the sluggard will not plough and therefore he shall beg in harvest time and have nothing'. The irony was that many stayed away because they had so much to do to save the harvest; but worship was vital and brooked no compromises.[22]

A cloud of suspicion hung over Springfield. Widow Marshfield had been exonerated in court, but such accusations left a stain upon both accuser and accused, especially when the accuser herself belonged to a household of dubious reputation. It was perhaps with this blemish in mind that on Sunday 8 July Reverend Moxon preached about the value of truth and swearing oaths to settle disputes. A fortnight later he commanded his loyal hearers in the meeting house, Mary Parsons among them, to resist the devil by learning to distinguish his voice from God's. The danger, thought the minister, had never been greater. On the morning of 5 August, Moxon likened faithful Springfield to a ship anchored by hope but rocked by storms. 'A man may be a godly man', he reasoned, 'and yet be strangely exercised with tossings and tumblings, both outward and inward.' The pure in heart would face many troubles and be tempted; yet they must cleave to the Lord.[23]

Attentive minds may have detected a hidden message in the sermon. Was Moxon thinking of any particular godly man, who for all his tossings and tumblings, troubles and temptations, should still be thought pure? If so, it wasn't Hugh Parsons: it was the town's founding father, William Pynchon. Moxon didn't disagree with Pynchon's theological ideas, but broadcasting them in a book, he felt, was to dissent from the Massachusetts regime to which Springfield, however remote, was still answerable. Publication would have consequences for the town.

Pynchon, though, was animated by events further afield. Across the Atlantic, Old England was in a state of upheaval in the wake of the king's execution. This included a fresh wave of witch-hunting, most severely in north-east England and across the border in Scotland, but also in Worcestershire, Gloucestershire, Hertfordshire, Essex, Kent and other counties besides, where men and women alike were accused.[24]

He was also inspired by a new book recently arrived in America. Richard Baxter's *Aphorismes of Justification* criticized the fervour of the New Model Army, in which Baxter had served as a chaplain, urging Christians simply to worship and obey God. Perhaps grace was universal after all, and Christ's righteousness belonged to everyone with faith in their hearts. Like Baxter, Pynchon saw more love than wrath in God, love that should unite Christians in inclusive congregations. Relying on public confession to sort the drowned from the saved, surmised Baxter, amounted to 'taking a very few that can talk more than the rest, and making them the church'.[25] That summer, Pynchon sailed down to Windsor to hear John Wareham give a sermon denouncing Baxter, who Wareham felt held with the popish idea of justification by good works. Pynchon stood up in Windsor's meeting house to disagree with Wareham, whom he thought 'transported with passionate zeal'.[26] Awareness of Pynchon's dissent was not, therefore, confined to Springfield: it seems he was prepared to defend his beliefs about the true nature of the Holy Trinity wherever and whenever he chose. But he could not escape the consequences. And like others, Wareham was affronted by Pynchon's rebuttal. He continued to argue, as did orthodox preachers at Hartford and elsewhere, that only those confirmed as Saints could live within the covenant. If they abandoned that principle, Wareham concluded, God's heart would harden and hell would gape for them all.[27]

From this time onwards, Moxon conducted a kind of dialogue with Pynchon, openly yet codedly in the meeting house. On the Sunday after he had spoken about the tossings and tumblings of the godly man, 12 August, Moxon preached about Christ's sacrifice and again earnestly enjoined the townsfolk of Springfield – including Mary Parsons, who continued to attend meetings even if her husband did not – to make hope their anchor and hold tight amid Satan's storms. That much was familiar and easily digested. But the afternoon sermon that same day concerned Melchizedek, an obscure figure from the book of Genesis, whose significance perhaps only Pynchon – and Mary and her fellow Llanvaches hearer, Alexander Edwards – would have understood. The previous year Pynchon had written about Melchizedek in a tract about the difference between Presbyterians, like himself, and Independents, like the politically driven soldiers of the New Model Army away in revolutionary Old England.[28]

A week later the congregation was surprised to see not Moxon in the pulpit but Pynchon himself. With the minister away on business, here was Pynchon's chance to reply publicly. His text was Matthew 5:1–12, the start of Christ's Sermon on the Mount – which had inspired John Winthrop's lecture to the fleet in which Pynchon had sailed to America. Pynchon used the same tone as Winthrop twenty years earlier. Blessed are the poor in spirit, for theirs is the kingdom of heaven, he said; blessed are the meek, for they shall inherit the earth; blessed are the peacemakers, for they shall be called the children of God. The blessed yearned for righteousness as the body yearns food, he said, adding that 'the appetite of hunger and thirst hath a strange violent passion – it will make men break through stone walls'. From there Pynchon ventured into his own theology, speaking of the blessing conferred on mankind by God's free grace, a gift given by Christ the mediator. This was a different interpretation of the Trinity, and of the road to salvation, than the one Springfield was used to, and a dangerous one. It fundamentally changed the identity of God and Christ, and their relationship to each other and to mankind – a departure from Calvinist orthodoxy that Boston's godly elite would have found blatantly heretical. Citing the book of Romans, Pynchon opined that Christ had not merely washed away sin: 'we shall be saved from wrath by him'.[29] For this was a sermon about earthly conduct as well as salvation, about love and obedience, just as Christ's Atonement consisted in his loving obedience to God. Whatever wrath existed between men in Springfield, Pynchon taught, it came from the machinations of Satan. This was bittersweet comfort to ordinary listeners like Mary Parsons, for it meant the devil raged all around. There were now several households in the town who had reason to believe it, knowing how the devil cramped their lives, invaded their thoughts and dreams and turned wicked souls against them. The devil tempted them to feel hatred and resentment, just as he had done to Christ at Calvary.[30]

The people of Springfield didn't need to grasp the finer points of Pynchon's theology to be unsettled to hear him voice heretical opinions. Heresy and witchcraft were different sins; but they shared a diabolic source and were believed to exert a malign force that divided nations, neighbourhoods, even households – and as the Bible warned, 'if a house be divided against itself, that house cannot stand'.[31] Since the early years of the Reformation, orthodox clerics had feared the devil slipping into the pulpit, from where he could corrupt impressionable souls.[32] Pynchon spoke the truth, Moxon believed, yet inevitably the unlawfulness of his words served to undermine his authority as a magistrate and leader in the eyes of the people. Patriarchy was Springfield's basic principle of government, and upon the integrity of that principle everything depended. Now it was at risk. Furthermore, this was the year of patriarchal failure, writ large in the disgrace of an English king beheaded for treason. Springfield's faltering confidence in Pynchon, together with the sordid end of Charles I, in turn inflamed hostile feelings towards the town's most hopeless patriarch, Hugh Parsons.[33]

When people were most agitated, and their families, churches, communities and polities off-kilter, then witchcraft, which often seemed ethereal or dubious, became most plausible and real. This is how it felt across New England, in Springfield's public discourse and in the life of individuals like Hugh Parsons's neighbour William Branch: his nocturnal encounter with the fiery boy had left him feeling so sick in heart and mind he thought he might die. One day later that summer, as he passed Parsons's front door on his way to the long meadow, he suffered another uncanny affliction. As he told his wife, he 'was taken with a strange stiffness . . . as if two stakes had been bound to my thighs', so only with great difficulty was he able to drag himself forwards down the main street. This malady lasted two days, accompanied by the sensation of burning in the soles of his feet. All this, he vehemently suspected, was caused by the witchcraft of Hugh Parsons.[34]

That September brought what a minister called 'a general visitation' of smallpox, which killed many people in New England. As ever, fear was greatest in the most overcrowded households, and in those with infants and young children. Anthony Dorchester, his wife Sarah and their three young children were still living with Hugh and Mary and their children: Hannah, now three, and Samuel, just a year old. And Sarah Dorchester was dying. A few weeks earlier her husband had bought medicine he could ill afford to treat her consumption: five pills and a vomit, followed by another five pills and a poultice. All to no avail. Mary helped to nurse the sick woman, but she was exhausted herself and vexed by bleak,

perplexing thoughts. Hugh showed no sympathy and resented
Mary wasting time on what did not increase household prosperity,
like comforting Sarah Dorchester and sharing precious food. The
fine owed to Widow Marshfield, to be paid in corn and already over-
due, was bad enough. Hugh had to feed his family. A cow worth £7
was slaughtered – probably one of Pynchon's – and Hugh and
Anthony each bought quarter shares. With the other two men, they
also agreed to draw lots for the various cuts, the best of which they
would sell while keeping the tougher bits and offal for themselves.
Hugh wanted the root of the tongue, which could be made to last
all winter. And when Anthony won it Hugh didn't hide his irritation,
even though he knew Anthony wanted it to provide nourishment
for his wife, whose condition grew graver by the day. It especially
rankled that the tongue was then stored in Hugh's own salt tub.[35]

The pent-up discontent erupted in a series of disturbing events.
One afternoon, when Hugh was craving more paid work, he sent
Mary to Jonathan Taylor's house to offer Taylor his labour. Mary
thought this odd: normally Hugh would have run such an errand
himself. Still, she set off along the river path behind the homelots,
and by the time she returned it was already twilight, the curved line
of the hills standing out against a pale sky. Then she saw something:
a flicker of dark movement, just off the path; then the looming
shape of a great marsh dog. Terrified, she hurried onwards, glan-
cing over her shoulder until, relieved, she reached the safety of her
front door. The dog did not follow and melted back into the
shadows.[36]

In the following hours and days, Mary didn't tell her husband what
had happened, having already decided that this had been no natural
creature, and furthermore that he was to blame for it – almost as if his
pitch-black passion had conjured a stalking apparition. By now, she
no longer shared much with Hugh, preferring to confide in the few
female companions who had not yet turned against her, and who
may have pitied her, she being plainly ill and stuck with that man.
What Mary called her 'private talk', however, seemed less private
when Hugh revealed that he knew everything she said. Her friends

could be trusted – couldn't they? To Mary's mind, there was only one explanation: supernatural eavesdropping.[37]

Nowadays almost everything Hugh did seemed portentous, every motive questionable. Sometimes he disappeared for twenty-four hours, and if he returned late – which he did, on occasion, after midnight – shortly before he walked through the door she heard a loud rumbling around the house, an unearthly phenomenon that happened only when he was absent yet nearby. It couldn't have been caused by the weather, for there was no wind in the chimney or creaking beams: it was unnatural, as if Hugh had imbalanced the very humours of her home. Mary's fear of her husband was manifested not only in uncanny episodes such as this, but also in more mundane yet furious confrontations, at home and in public. She criticized him to his face, accusing him of things he seemed silently to accept, or at least did not deny. Once, perhaps, he would have retaliated, but this was the broken frame of government into which husband and wife had settled. Neighbours, on the other hand, continued to take offence at this epitome of mercurial chaos in their midst. Men grumbled to each other. It wasn't just unseemly for a woman to scold her husband. It confused the order of nature, as did Hugh's unmanly failure to throw off the saddle she had tied to his back and instead rein her in.[38]

The suspicion was mutual. The more that Mary became convinced of her husband's witchery, the more Hugh himself began to wonder about his wife. Would somebody with nothing to hide be so keen to accuse others? But, as Mercy Marshfield's case had shown, accusations were nothing without proof. It was widely known that in England suspects were searched for a secret raw spot where imps fed, thereby proving familiarity with the devil. The idea stewed in Hugh's mind until he could contain it no longer. He demanded to examine his wife's body, but received the brush-off he feared: Mary was shocked and refused, calling it 'an immodest thing'. Perhaps she had such marks – women who had given birth often did – and feared them being used against her as evidence. He didn't force her, and no more was said; yet the conversation lingered in Mary's mind.

As she had told John Matthews, she was already convinced that Hugh's stomach pains were caused by his infernal master, who tortured him while he slept. Once when he cried out Mary had been horrified to think it was because 'the devil came to him in the night on the bed and sucked him'.[39]

Watched over by a hillside forest turning russet and gold, the townsfolk headed to the meeting house. As if speaking only to Hugh and Mary Parsons, Moxon instructed every person to turn away from sin and keep their thoughts pure.[40] If Mary heard a warning in these words she did not heed it. One night soon afterwards, when she was sure Hugh was asleep, she peeled back the bed sheets, waited in case he stirred, then lifted up his linen shift. From either fire glow or candle, there was enough light for her to see his naked body. She began to search, half expecting to find an unnatural wart or teat, but there was nothing. She didn't, however, examine 'his secret parts' – the genitals, where the devil's marks were usually located. This was too difficult, or degrading, or both. Her thoughts may have turned back to the belief, promoted by ministers, that the covenant with Satan, like that with Christ, was purely spiritual, the idea of nursing demons a disgusting distraction. Moxon's recent sermon had also cautioned against yielding to violent passions. 'A man cannot always quench a fire when he pleases,' he had warned. It was best, therefore, never to start one. But in Mary's case it was too late: that fire was already burning brightly.[41]

It was around this time, when the maize was ripe, that little Samuel Parsons fell sick. Caring for her baby boy, three-year-old Hannah, and Sarah Dorchester took up more of Mary's time than Hugh could stand when there was so much to be done. One day, George Colton, one of the long-meadow farmers, called at the house looking for Hugh. He wasn't at home, but Mary was by the fire as usual, her ailing baby in her lap. When Colton asked what was wrong, she showed him the boy's naked body. He noticed Samuel's shrivelled genitals, and that Mary's distress was dulled by fatigue. She did not disguise her belief that Hugh was the cause of her misery: 'Though my child be ill and I have so much to do with it', she said, 'yet my husband keeps ado at me to help him about his corn.' Colton was sympathetic: he had two young sons, and his wife Deborah was about to give birth again. 'Your husband had more need to get *you* some help', he told her stiffly, 'than to keep ado at you to help *him*.'[42]

Soon afterwards Mary and Hugh were woken in the night by Samuel's cries. They hurried to the cradle, lit a candle and turned back the covers. They watched as trembling in the child's toes crept up his body until it reached his throat, when he began struggling for breath. In a panic they held him up to clear his airway, then Hugh ran to the Cooleys' house, two doors up. He banged on the door, begging for help. Sarah Cooley hurried from her bed and saw that Hugh was crying hot, desperate tears.[43] She ran back with him, accompanied by Blanche Bedortha, also disturbed by the commotion; two other women were not far behind. Together they laid hands on Samuel, and soon he was breathing again. Their experience of raising children had saved his life, but this didn't mean they thought his condition was natural. Sarah Cooley had heard that victims of witchcraft often felt a lump rising in their chests before they choked to death.[44] They examined the baby's body thoroughly and, like George Colton, noticed that his 'secrets' were diseased. What they all knew but didn't say was that for a witch to attack a person's genitals was in effect an attack on the regeneration, and so the future, of the plantation. Only a weak, malicious person would even contemplate such a thing.[45]

On the last Sunday in September, Hugh and Mary were getting ready for the church meeting. Anthony Dorchester was going too, but alone: Sarah could no longer walk, nor could she even get up unaided. Before he went, Anthony decided to put some broth on to simmer, something hot and nourishing to give Sarah when he returned. He went to the salt tub, took out the root of the cow's tongue and washed it. Mary watched him work, then she and Hugh left with their children: Hannah holding her mother's hand, Hugh carrying baby Samuel, still poorly. Anthony put the meat in a kettle of water and hung it over the fire. Then he smartened himself and, leaving his three children with their bedridden mother, hurried to the meeting house.[46]

By now, Hugh and Mary were halfway there. He seemed in a good mood and, his wife later recalled, 'was very pleasing to her, more than usually he had been a great while'; perhaps both were feeling kinder to each other after so nearly losing Samuel. There they were, walking to the meeting as a family. Even so, something wasn't right. She knew he still resented having lost that bit of tongue and guessed that when he returned to a savoury aroma in his house his anger – 'a cruel tempest of the mind' – would erupt. They reached the house of Thomas Merrick, now Springfield's constable, near the meeting house, when abruptly Hugh laid the baby on the ground and walked away. Why, Mary had no idea; nor did she know where he was going. She picked up little Samuel and continued to the meeting house without him.[47] Taking her seat, she tried to focus on Mr Moxon's sermon, which drew on the book of Job. The topic was the wages of sin. Workers of iniquity – the deceitful, the proud, the unchaste – should expect eternal death, Moxon declaimed, but first they would be scourged in life. He cited example after example: the annihilation of decadent Sodom and Gomorrah; the flood survived by Noah's family alone; Judas made to hang himself; Herod consumed by worms; the children who mocked Elijah's baldness mauled by a bear. 'If ye be about to sin,' concluded Moxon, 'think with yourself it will bring destruction.'[48]

After the sermon, Anthony Dorchester arrived home before Mary. He lifted the bubbling pot off the fire and stirred it. The chunk of tongue had gone. He was astonished and angry. When Mary came back – still without Hugh – he told her what had happened. She was at a loss to explain it. His wife had been there all the time, and their children were too small to take it out. For what it was worth, Mary helped Anthony look around the house, including in the salt tub, in case somehow he had forgotten to put it in the pot. But Anthony insisted that he had put it in the kettle, whereupon she remembered seeing him wash off the salt. She also admitted she had 'feared her husband might convey it away'. She told Anthony about Hugh's bizarre flit en route to the meeting house, adding that she saw him again briefly at the end of the meeting but that was all. In the afternoon they returned to hear Mr Moxon's second sermon, which contained a reminder that rang in their ears. 'Though you can hide your wickedness from man', he said, 'yet you cannot from God: he knows it and takes notice of it; there is no juggling with God.' Once again, the prescience of his counsel struck home. 'Juggling' meant conjuring tricks: making things disappear.[49] Afterwards, the town was soon buzzing with what was described as 'talk about the strange going away of this root of the tongue'.[50]

Hugh did not come home. After his fleeting appearance in the meeting house, Mary didn't see him again till the following day. She spent the night nursing Samuel, whose condition deteriorated so rapidly that she and the Dorchesters feared the worst. Her husband, meanwhile, lay out in the long meadow beneath the cold stars; at first light, he rose and continued working. Some time between the hours of eight and nine, he was toiling near the great oak, a prominent landmark, when he saw his next-door neighbour Jonathan Burt striding purposefully towards him. As Burt drew closer, his grim expression announced the bad news even before he spoke. Samuel had died. Hugh said little in reply and to Burt's amazement showed no emotion. Sauntering off across the meadow, he disappeared into George Colton's house.[51]

Colton was at home with his wife Deborah, who was nursing their newly arrived baby girl Mary, and their sons Isaac, nearly three, and the eighteen-month-old Ephraim. They were surprised to see Hugh Parsons so early in the morning. Knowing how sick his son was, George thought to himself that Hugh should have been at home with his wife, supporting her like a good husband. Yet by now he had Hugh's measure. Even so, George and Deborah found his offhand manner disconcerting. 'I hear my child is dead,' he remarked. 'But I will cut a pipe of tobacco first before I go home.' He took out his knife, pared a few bits off a lump of tobacco, packed his pipe and lit it with a taper. They all stared at him. Hugh stood there smoking a while, as if lost in thought, then took his leave. Like Jonathan Burt, the Coltons were appalled by his lack of sorrow, his calmness even.[52]

Hugh trudged back over the fields, past the lower wharf, until he reached the homelots. He found Mary sitting with Samuel's corpse, Anthony Dorchester and Blanche Bedortha beside her. Again he said little and seemed unbothered, quite unlike his frantic state when Samuel had been ill. After a while, he got up and returned to work in the meadow, leaving everybody dumbstruck by his indifference. It went beyond insensitivity: it was downright suspicious.[53] Mary was convinced she knew what her husband was thinking: Samuel's death would free her up to help him. And Anthony Dorchester guessed what *she* was thinking, too.[54]

Reverend Moxon was informed and the gravedigger instructed: Samuel would be buried that same day. Later Hugh came home and called at the houses of his neighbours, inviting them to his son's funeral. Wrapped in a linen shroud, the tiny body of Samuel Parsons was carried the length of the main street, followed by his parents and mourners. No bell tolled: the town could not yet afford one. At the graveside Moxon followed the puritan custom of quiet meditation: there was neither prayer nor sermon. The bundle that was once a life was lowered into the hole and earth shovelled in. Samuel's grave would have its simple memorial. A slab of Welsh slate, as some New Englanders chose, would have been a slice of home for Mary. But these were expensive imports. Her son would have wood, which would blacken and rot; or sandstone, quickly weathered away by storms and frosts.[55]

The people who had gathered at the burial ground wondered grimly who would be next. Samuel's funeral was on the Monday, the first day of October 1649. On the Thursday, Rowland Stebbins's wife Sarah died. Her body was laid out, the limbs washed and arranged, tied into a winding sheet, and the dismal ritual of interment repeated. During that month of fevers and influenza, rumours of demons and witches invaded conversation by day and thoughts by night. With this in mind, on 4 November, Moxon contemplated Matthew 15:22, where a woman of Canaan cried out to Jesus: 'Have mercy on me, O Lord . . . my daughter is grievously vexed with a devil.' Moxon warned that even the children of godly parents might be possessed by demons, however strong their trust in the power of heaven, as Satan would for ever be an instrument of retribution for correcting the sinful.[56]

Soon, death called again at the Parsons homestead. Sarah Dorchester died on 8 November and was buried the following day. As usual, George Moxon consoled her bereaved husband Anthony and back home fretted about his own family, especially his children: the two daughters he had brought to Springfield, plus the three sons born there, the youngest aged just two. There had been sickness in his own household: late that summer he had bought no fewer than thirty-three medicinal pills, for some unknown malady.[57] And naturally, as he was a pillar of the community, the trauma of fatal disease inflicted on the daughters of Henry and Anne Smith – William Pynchon's granddaughters – in June the previous year remained vivid in his memory. How they had prayed for their deliverance; how they had wept when these prayers were not answered. Who could say if God would ever be merciful again.

George Moxon was not universally liked. He was close to Pynchon, whom everyone feared; he directed everyone's thoughts and actions; he had prospered, and had arguably the best house in Springfield. But he no longer seemed entirely committed to Springfield's salvation: his thoughts were conflicted; there had been controversy about his salary of £55, which he wanted raising to £70; and he speculated openly about leaving the town – not for another colony but for Old England, where, now that a puritan government had replaced the monarchy, he imagined he might live in peace. But it was already November, too late in the year to sail. As the pasture grew thin, Moxon, like other men, took his cattle across the river to graze. There, they ate the corn stems, which, like all incursions and impositions among Springfield's townsfolk, caused 'disorders' between farmers.[58]

The source of spiritual disorders lay, some supposed, with William Pynchon and his heretical views, and perhaps also with George

Moxon, who did nothing to restrain him. On Sunday the 18th, Henry Smith followed his stepfather William Pynchon's example and delivered his own lay sermon, in keeping with the tenebrous mood settling over the town. Taking as his text Psalm 85:8 ('I will hear what God the Lord will speak . . . to his Saints; but let them not turn again to folly'), Smith reminded people that they must suffer heaven's afflictions as they waited for their prayers to be answered. Rather than repeat Pynchon's emphasis on love and free grace, he stressed instead the cosmic repercussions of communal discord: godly chastisement. Let every member of the town, he inveighed, examine his or her heart to find the source of divine displeasure. 'What is the cause that God seems to shake us?' he wondered. 'See whether we are not guilty of some rebellion, of some unworthy walking.' More than ever, they must confront and atone for a litany of sins. Was Smith hinting at witchcraft, heresy even? It was common knowledge that, as Samuel 15:23 instructed, 'rebellion is as the sin of witchcraft'.[59]

This tone of reproach, to the town in general and its leaders in particular, was maintained in the afternoon, when Samuel Wright, the church deacon, ascended the pulpit. Invoking Ezra 8:21, he spoke of danger, the need for fasting and prayer, and a duty to find a righteous path to God – a path from which colonists had strayed, like travellers lost in the dark, misled by the false lights of the will-o'-the-wisp. None could deny, he said, that God had planted New England with his choicest vines. And yet what was its yield? 'Wild grapes of pride, unbelief, murmuration, discontent', regretted Wright, already causing God to pull up his plants and break down the hedges between garden and wilderness. 'For our own parts', he continued ominously, 'you know what trouble befalls us.' Candles had been snuffed out, leaving people fumbling in the gloom – which brought Wright to the electrifying, devastating nub of his sermon. 'How many of great learning suffer their souls to be drawn away – and draw multitudes after them,' he added, pointedly. He can only have meant that the devil was luring Pynchon, and perhaps Moxon too, into grievous religious error and, through their pronouncements, infecting the spirits of all Springfield. That much was clear to all who heard him.[60]

As winter set in, cloaks were lined with wolfskins, boots and clogs packed with straw. Powdery snow first picked out the detail of the landscape, and the timbered lines of the town, then, thickening, obscured them. It grew deep underfoot. Men mended fences, dragging sleighs effortfully behind them. Livestock were brought in from the frozen marshes and meadows, and began consuming the hay stacked in barns, built bigger than in Old England for the longer winters. Families furthest from the meeting house – which was as cold in winter as it was stuffy in summer – stayed away; those who came brought flat stones or grass hassocks to keep their feet off the cold ground. As the bustle of trade died down, people withdrew indoors to spin and weave wool and flax. Fires blazed, and blankets were nailed over windows. Families drew on food stocks laid down in autumn: smoked fish and pork, oats and parched corn, hard cheese and preserves.[61] Hugh Parsons had no work – it was difficult to make and lay bricks in winter – and less income, since Anthony Dorchester had moved out after his wife died.[62] Hugh went to Henry Smith's house to beg for some dried pease and other things but was turned away. He came home enraged, for a second time swearing vengeance against Smith. Nor was Hugh the only one tangled in neighbourly disputes. On 2 December he was summoned to court as a witness in a dispute between townsmen over a land sale: Springfield's frontiers of unrest and alliance were intricate and shifting. Faced with these ongoing quarrels, Reverend Moxon had earlier that day exalted the virtues of charity and piety, noting that 'an evil heart of unbelief' caused men to desert God, rendering them unable to quench Satan's flaming arrows.[63]

By unbelief Moxon meant not atheism but disobedience to God and dishonour to Christ, who was both saviour and exemplar, whose gentle life of patience and kindness was to be emulated. From this perspective, Hugh Parsons indeed had an evil heart: envious and vindictive. He still nursed a grudge against the Matthewses for testifying against his wife; Blanche Bedortha for sniping at him over a brick deal; Henry Smith for denying him work and food; and other folk besides. And he still owed Mercy Marshfield the damages she had been awarded for defamation by his wife. From that moment, her family had rallied round her, namely her adult son Samuel and sixteen-year-old daughter Sarah, who had strengthened her own position in the town that October by marrying Thomas Miller, Pynchon's servant from Northumberland, released early from his eight-year indenture. The Millers set up home in the more affluent north end, near the upper wharf not far from where Pynchon himself lived. Sarah bought fabric and buttons on credit to make coats to order, for Reece Bedortha and others.[64] Thomas Miller had no time for Hugh Parsons or his idle threats. Nor had his new mother-in-law softened her heart towards Hugh's wife, who had defamed her as a witch.

With her relatives (and probably Pynchon) behind her, Mercy Marshfield was now in a position to insist that Hugh settled his – or, rather, Mary's – debt to her. One day in the icy depths of winter Hugh Parsons arrived at the widow's door, a reluctant penitent, laden with maize: twenty-four bushels to be exact. She kept him on her front step in a biting wind, while he pleaded to be spared a third of what he owed, citing a rumour that she might be so willing. Mercy replied she would do no such thing, because his wife had been putting it about that her witnesses had sworn a false oath. Hugh, already tense, flew into a rage, swearing that if she refused to lower the fine his corn would never truly be hers. Echoing Moxon in the meeting house, and some half-recalled scripture, he predicted: 'it shall be but as wild fire in your house and as a moth in your clothes'. The words felt like a curse. Hugh threw down his maize at her feet and stormed off home through the snow.[65]

The thought nagged away at Mercy Marshfield that Hugh Parsons might now be about to bewitch her family. She realized that, rather than drawing a line under her dispute with the Parsons household, Mary's conviction for slander had both made an enemy of the feared Hugh, and moved Mercy's supporters, some of whom had their own grievances, to carry the affair from whispered huddles loudly into public discourse. John Matthews, defamed by Mary for bearing false witness, and no longer wanting the chimneys he had ordered from Hugh in the summer, cancelled his contract and asked for his deposit back.[66] But as the lines of accusation stretched and twisted, Mary and Mercy did have one thing in common: they both believed Hugh Parsons to be devilish. Mary had confronted Hugh about his coldness over Samuel's death; she had also revealed to Sarah Cooley's husband Benjamin that her suspicions had compelled her, like some witchfinder or midwife, to search his body while he slept. Even though she had not found anything, she could not stop thinking about Hugh's lack of feeling, and even worse, how Samuel's death had seemed not to surprise him. Steadily, her thoughts led to a single, terrible conclusion. Soon everyone in the town would know what was increasingly clear to Mary: that her husband had murdered their own son with witchcraft.[67]

6. Strange Dreams

The Parsons bed was a battleground. Where once they had drawn close in love and trust, now it forced unwelcome intimacy on Hugh and Mary, who lay within touching distance, listening to each other breathe. The winter nights of 1649–50 were long and restless. Mary's mind churned with bitter memories of her son. Did she dream of him, as mothers often did of their dead children? Samuel's spirit may have visited her – or perhaps it was just a cruel demonic impersonation.[1] Demons came to Hugh; she was sure about that. He was often doubled up with stomach ache, or held just beneath the surface of sleep, shifting and moaning, recriminations bubbling up. And now that witchcraft had infected the town, even waking hours were like nightmares. The worst of it was that there was no easy way to act against witches, or escape them. It didn't matter how detested Hugh and Mary had become: there they were, following the same routines, persistently present – not predators to be trapped or Indians to be shot at, or even homicidal colonists who could be dragged into court. They were ordinary neighbours, difficult to shun in a social world of mutual dependence.

Neighbours were at once scared of Hugh and offended by him. He couldn't curb his wife's tongue and he himself spat imprecations; his minatory stares were the look not of a strong man but an impotent one leaning on a diabolic crutch. Witchcraft was a weapon of the weak; and the weaker vessel, the Bible taught, was the woman. Hugh's speech was intemperate, waspish; his silence, above all when his wife berated him, a measure of his emasculation.[2] Mary traduced her husband's reputation in other ways. Whereas once she had guarded her secrets, now she shared her suspicions that he was a witch with all and sundry – as many as forty people, she later claimed. And these people told others, spreading tales in

Springfield's tight-knit world like smallpox on a packed ship.[3] Hugh was powerless to halt the contagion; nor did he do anything to improve his own standing. In his commercial dealings, his word was far from his bond. Early in February 1650, a month of raging snow-storms, he was sued by John Matthews to recover the down payment from his cancelled contract. The jury, which included Henry Smith, Benjamin Cooley and Thomas Stebbins, voted in Matthews's favour. William Pynchon ordered Hugh to return the £1 14s 6d, and pay a shilling's damages and 10s costs. Hugh, still fuming about his debt to Mercy Marshfield, was incensed. Every circumstance conspired to sap his money and time.[4]

If, as Mary supposed, Hugh had killed their child to make her work longer hours, it was a scheme defeated when she became pregnant for a third time. Also expecting a child was Sarah Miller, daughter of the Parsonses' enemy Mercy Marshfield, just seventeen years old. What-ever satisfaction Marshfield felt about the long-awaited arrival of grandchildren was vitiated by worry: Hugh Parsons's cursing of her on her own doorstep was hard to forget. Of nervous disposition, Sarah was also afraid and, as the spring of 1650 arrived, began to suffer seizures, her body racked with spasms – 'strange fits', the family called them. Sarah screamed that Hugh Parsons was tormenting her and addressed him directly as 'sirrah' and 'thou witch'.[5] She was literally not herself, her body not her own, the thin membrane between her interior world and the supernatural world punctured.[6]

George Moxon prayed for Sarah Miller. Spring had reawakened his thoughts of leaving Springfield, but Pynchon persuaded him to stay. Moxon knew his spiritual guidance was needed in the town. Sin invited demons into communities, households and individual souls – the 'unworthy walking' that Henry Smith had spoken of. By this time, some townsfolk had come to believe that Pynchon's theological opinions were one such invitation, as hinted at in Deacon Wright's sermon. Moxon, however, reserved judgement and remained loyal to his patron. More than that, he abetted him. When Pynchon finished his book, Moxon sent the manuscript to a kinsman in London, a printer specializing in puritan pamphlets, to be published.[7] As they waited for copies to be sent back over the Atlantic, disease spread across New England, its symptoms fever and 'gripings in the bowels, with violent vomiting and purging', which often proved fatal, especially in children. These were what one clergyman termed 'awakening dispensations . . . to cause us to consider and examine whether we have not provoked the Lord with some general and unwonted sins'.[8] How should people appease God? In June, Mary Johnson, the Wethersfield witch convicted eighteen months previously, was finally hanged at Hartford. She died penitently, it was said, 'in a frame extremely to the satisfaction of them that were spectators of it'.[9]

From summer into autumn 1650 the fortunes of Hugh Parsons and William Pynchon declined together, though in a gradual, piecemeal fashion. For a while yet, each continued to work with others in the town and perform his civic duties. Pynchon was at the apex of his power and profit in the fur trade, a thorn driven ever deeper into the side of Dutch traders. Some consignments he sent downriver contained as many as 200 pelts weighing 300 pounds – a staggering amount by usual standards.[10] In commerce – meeting Indian traders at the wharf, revising his balance sheets – and in his studies – reading whatever he could lay his hands on, comparing biblical translations – Pynchon seemed to be girded by grace and guided by God. Hugh meanwhile took his turn as a warder, responsible for patrolling the main street with his neighbour John Lombard. One Sunday in July, he and Lombard spotted Pynchon's servant Samuel Terry leaning against the meeting house masturbating while Mr Moxon was inside preaching – a defiant, albeit unusual, insult to authority. They reported Terry to his master Pynchon, who chose to keep the matter private; instead, he took a stick and gave the youth six sharp blows on his bare back. No one would need to know – especially the linen weaver Benjamin Cooley, set to take Terry on as an apprentice in October (for the sum of £9). Perhaps Pynchon wanted to be rid of the boy – or was simply reducing his obligations in anticipation of what would happen once his incendiary book arrived in Massachusetts.[11]

He did not have long to wait. In London copies had already left the print shop. Early in June, *The Meritorious Price of Our Redemption* by William Pynchon went on sale in Cornhill, near the Royal Exchange. In these revolutionary times, titles covering everything from foreign news to animal husbandry, from cookery to cosmology, were on offer. Not everyone welcomed this variety, especially when the subject was religion and the author an amateur enthusiast. 'What more uncharitable and un-Christian-like scribbling was ever produced', protested one critic, 'than the pens of these men have in frequent editions manifested.'[12] George Walker, a member of the Westminster Assembly of Divines that had been convened to reform the Church of England, suggested the devil might impersonate authors to 'belch out desperate lies and forgeries' for the giddy multitude, whom Walker likened to clouds blown by the 'winds of every new and strange doctrine'.[13] Nor did he hesitate to link these lies to heresy, blasphemy, sorcery and witchcraft.[14] Meanwhile, the *Mayflower* pilgrim Edward Winslow, in London to promote the interests of New England, kept his eyes peeled and his ear to the ground for anything that challenged the colony's authority. It was probably he who noticed *The Meritorious Price of Our Redemption* and saw at a glance that it was heretical. 'Christ did not suffer for us those unutterable torments of God's wrath', read the title page, 'to redeem our souls from them.' Instead, Christ saved mankind from the curse on Adam by performing perfect 'mediatorial obedience' to his father, who then welcomed him in heaven.[15]

Pynchon devoted 158 pages to this idea: that the Atonement came from Christ acquiescing to God, rather than enraging him by absorbing the sins of the world. The book was lucid but full of ponderous exegesis, pulling together arguments from theologians, translators, historians and classical authorities. Pynchon the autodidact employed homespun metaphors, like George Moxon in his sermons. Love for his own son John helped Pynchon to imagine God's feelings for Christ. He was intent on separating literal truths, such as God's perfection, from mere allegories and rejected a Catholic construction of hell that included purgatory. He also thought Catholics and Lutheran Protestants alike were wrong about the

Eucharist, 'for they place the meritorious price of their redemption in the gross substance of Christ's flesh and blood', whereas the 'miracle' was entirely symbolic and in no way spiritual or mystical.[16] *The Meritorious Price of Our Redemption* was bracingly rational – modern – and intensely heretical. There is no record of who in London (apart from Winslow) read the book or what their reaction was. But this mattered less than the fact that copies were already on their way to an ocean-bound vessel and would soon be in New England.

For the moment, back in Springfield, no one was aware of the book's publication. Besides, there were other things to worry about. It was harvest time, and Mary Parsons was heavily pregnant. With his wife unable to work in the fields, Hugh relied on others – and they relied on him, despite misgivings about his secret means and intentions. Everyone had to pull together if they were to get through the cold months ahead. But many felt reluctant to help Hugh Parsons, or did so warily and grudgingly. He managed to get his grain to the gristmill but struggled to bring the flour home: it wasn't far from his house, but the sacks were heavy. He asked Pynchon's servant Simon Beamon, who was at the mill on horseback, to lend a hand. Beamon refused, which irked Hugh. Beamon trotted back up the main street on his 'gentle quiet horse', his own flour slung over the saddle. He had travelled only a short distance when he fell off, and the sack thudded on top of him. Coming to his senses, he checked his horse: it was calm, and hadn't spooked or shied. Beamon reloaded the sack, remounted, shortened the reins and set off. But he had only gone thirty feet when he tumbled again, even though, as before, he had been sitting tight and the horse was perfectly composed. Then it happened a third time 'and yet the horse stood quietly in his place'. There was nothing Beamon could do except keep trying, even though by now he was bruised and rattled. Finally he made it safely home. It wouldn't be the last time he came to grief after crossing Hugh Parsons.[17]

Hugh's presence, as immovable in their landscape as the river or the forest, was hardest to bear for Hugh's nearest neighbours. John Lombard, Hugh's warding companion, lived with his wife and baby son in the next-door house, on the corner of the main street and the track that led down to the wharf: the southern tip of the town before the long meadow. His wife Joanna was, like her neighbour Mary, heavily pregnant, her baby due in October. Like everyone else, they were preparing for winter. To stop the frost creeping into the render on their house and widening the cracks, Lombard borrowed a trowel from George Langton and set to work daubing the walls with mud or dung mixed with ground shells. After he'd been working for a while, a pair of Indians arrived to discuss some matter, at which point Lombard set down the trowel on the sill of the door. Their business finished, the Indians left, and he returned to his work, only to find the trowel gone. His natural assumption was that the Indians had stolen it. The next day he borrowed Hugh Parsons's trowel and carried on daubing until he spotted the same Indians from the day before. Lombard called; they didn't seem to hear him. But Hugh had heard and came to ask what business his neighbour had with them. 'They have stole my trowel,' replied Lombard. At this Hugh simply pointed to the ground and said: 'Here it is.' And there it was, Langton's trowel, on the sill just where Lombard had left it. This incident unnerved John and Joanna Lombard: it was inconceivable that Hugh could have slipped the trowel back without either of them seeing. It might have been a joke, but to them Hugh was meddling in the business of daily life – a man who couldn't get his own house in order interfering with the homes of others.[18]

In Boston, another Springfielder, William Pynchon, was causing a different kind of stir. Copies of his book arrived there early in October, just as magistrates were assembling for the General Court. *The Meritorious Price of Our Redemption* was discussed as a matter of urgency, the fear not only of its influence in New England but that the puritan government in London might think that Massachusetts Bay endorsed it. It was especially galling that Pynchon had styled himself 'Gentleman, in New England' on the title page. The magistrates were aghast at what they saw as a manifesto of treachery adding 'to the heap of many errors and heresies already too much abounding' in Old England. A letter to the English parliament, professing 'their orthodox faith against all destructive paradoxes and dangerous innovations', was duly rushed to the harbour, where a transatlantic ship was waiting to depart.[19] Condemning *The Meritorious Price* became an article of faith in New England. Even Pynchon's old friend John Eliot judged it to be 'a book full of error and weakness, and some heresies'. Such language echoed the censure of Antinomians in Boston in the mid-1630s and expressed worry that any public departure from Calvinist orthodoxy might cause Old England to impose a governor upon them, as had been proposed in a petition of 1646 that everyone knew Pynchon had defended.[20]

On 16 October 1650 the General Court issued a declaration against Pynchon's book, which for questioning orthodox views of the Holy Trinity and Christ's redemptive power was 'false, erroneous and heretical'. Its author was summoned to the next court on its first day in session, and informed that a retraction must be issued, and furthermore printed in England. John Norton, the minister at Ipswich, Massachusetts, was also commissioned to write a book-length refutation on behalf of the colony. A university-educated scholar, Norton preached a very different interpretation of Christ as mediator between heaven and earth and had already had a sermon published as an antidote to 'these giddy times, wherein poor souls seem to be bewitched and led captive with the enticing words of men's doctrines'. Now he was tasked with sweeping away Pynchon's dead, tangled arguments, much as the Indians opened forest trails with brush fires, leaving only the healthy trees. This analogy was to be taken literally. The court ordered that a copy of *The Meritorious Price* be handed to the city hangman. Four days later, on the Sabbath after the lecture, a crowd assembled in the market place to watch the hangman put Pynchon's words on a bonfire. Meanwhile, John Norton went through his copy line by line, identifying in it three major 'damnable heresies'.[21]

By the 23rd news had arrived in Rhode Island, a colony known as 'a receptacle of many varieties of opinion'. The puritan freethinker Roger Williams, whose own book had been burned in London in

1644, wrote to Boston asking to read *The Meritorious Price*, predicting archly that Pynchon's case would now reveal 'what liberty conscience hath in this land'.[22] When news of the burning of Pynchon's book reached England, Sir Henry Vane Jr, the governor of Massachusetts during the furore of the 1630s, was similarly indignant. A champion of toleration, Vane had spoken out in defence of the radicals John Biddle and John Fry, who had been inspired by a tract entitled *England's New Chains Discovered*, published in March. Its author John Lilburne, a Leveller who believed sovereignty lay with the people, argued that putting Cromwell's army in charge of the country simply replaced one tyranny with another: unsurprisingly, it proved inflammatory. Vane thought that men like Biddle and Fry, Lilburne and Pynchon, had a right to speak their minds; he had also helped Roger Williams secure a charter for Rhode Island, granting the colony both a corporate existence and, uniquely, freedom of religion.[23] Vane believed in a 'happy union' between Christians, prizing their simple core beliefs – faith, honesty, charity, forbearance – over the complex ones that divided them.[24] To Vane, heresies were just ideas that evolved into articles of faith – as one churchman put it: 'every age hath its proper verities, which the former age was ignorant of'.[25] Even so, the war between censorship and freedom of speech would be a long one.

It wasn't necessary to read *The Meritorious Price* to be outraged by it, or, on the other side of the debate, outraged by its prohibition. For the latter camp, it symbolized dissent's challenge to despotism, William Pynchon being only the latest figurehead for these contentions. Freethinkers noted that the Bible was full of so-called 'heretics' like Pynchon: 'did they not call our Saviour deceiver, conjurer, blasphemer?' asked one. Luther and Calvin had been heretics, too. How could heretics possibly be 'soul killers', scoffed Roger Williams – and, besides, which mortal was pure and wise enough to judge them? Men should be allowed to speak freely, he averred, and be whatever they wanted: 'a heretic, a Balaam, a spiritual witch . . . breathing out blasphemies against Christ'.[26] Back in Springfield, word had spread that a book by their leader, containing opinions he had expressed orally, was in circulation, and with this news a sense that no good could come of it. If Boston's godly leaders condemned it, why should God himself not do so? Through such disobedience was paradise reclaimed by the wilderness, the rose strangled by the briar. Pynchon's heterodoxies were a threat to the town, which was still struggling to hold on, and waylaid by spiritual trials of its own.

On 26 October Mary Parsons was delivered of a son, Joshua, a hopeful name for a new Israelite in this American Canaan.[27] But the strain on Mary's body and mind, and on her marriage, was greater than ever. The most trivial domestic matters, relating to housework or cooking or caring for children, led to misunderstanding and rancour with her husband. Daily routines that created bonds of mutual respect in other households were for Mary and Hugh tight channels in which they faced off and collided. Lost in recrimination and quick to anger, they saw only the worst in one another, and their arguing became louder and more frequent. They were no longer in love, nor were they in control of their lives, among neighbours who demanded such control. The fears and failings of the husband were personified in the wife and vice versa, turning in a perpetual vicious circle. Neither spouse could bear the other, and neither was going to fall without bringing the other down with them.

Hugh's disputes had not abated throughout the year. He had harsh words for his neighbour Benjamin Cooley, who was working sedulously to extend his property. He quarrelled with James Bridgman over a tree and continued to blame John Matthews for the judgement in the Marshfield case.[28] He was reserved, tetchy, cavilling, then irate. It was practically a matter of habit, whenever anyone crossed him, to threaten that he would be even with them.[29] Feeling out of charity with everyone, Hugh now rarely attended public meetings, including Moxon's sermons – both the consequence and confirmation of his spleen.

Although Hugh was no more acquisitive than his neighbours, they saw in him something abnormally grasping – a toxic concentration, perhaps, of their own sinful desires. Colonists were perforce steadfast and stubborn, but few were so compulsively possessive.

The puritan adventure in New England had from the start demanded industry and profit – but how much was too much? Nobody knew, and in practice, in the normal dealings of the day, few especially cared, least of all in Springfield. Even so, beneath this desire lay troubled feelings that were hard to allay and easier to dump, unconsciously, on the town's moody brickmaker. Hostility towards Hugh may even have symbolized the frustrations felt by townsfolk towards their untouchable overlord Pynchon, or their doubts about his authority: they attacked the symbolic anti-patriarch because the arch patriarch was himself being unmanned by the taint of heresy.[30]

Indians had taught English farmers to predict bad winters by the thickness of maize husks. So perhaps they foresaw how dire that of 1650–51 would be. Everything was petrified in ice, and thick snow shut off all routes. Clear night skies brought sharp frosts by morning. Cattle shifted and stamped in stalls; hogs steamed in their sties. Horses, always the last animals to be sheltered, waded through drifts until exhausted or lamed by hoof rot or mud fever; the heifer kept by Pynchon's household servant, Francis Pepper, sickened.[31] Fields and gardens were veiled in mist, and dung piles eerily smoked and flickered with red fire as pockets of bad air combusted. Winds howled through the homelots like vengeful furies, searching for cracks and gaps around shuttered homes. The people confined inside piled mats and blankets on beds, and lay still as corpses to trap warmth after the embers had died.

It was on such a bleak night that a crashing sound outside Jonathan Taylor's window pulled him from his warm huddle and out of the door. He looked around his backlot and into the lane, where he noticed his neighbour John Matthews's buckets had fallen down. What had caused it, it was too dark to say: the wind perhaps, or a scavenging wolf. As Taylor went back inside, he sensed someone on the other side of the door, seizing the handle just as he let go. The door creaked open. There was Hugh Parsons, a looming silhouette against the moonlight. He entered and asked Taylor to sit down. Hugh proceeded to tell him that Samuel Terry, the disgraced apprentice Benjamin Cooley bought from Pynchon, had been beating his – Hugh's – calf, and that if his master wouldn't discipline him, he would. It was an odd message to deliver at night, and it was all he said before he left. A day or so afterwards Sarah Cooley sent Terry on an errand. He did not return. She went out looking for him. Encountering Taylor, she asked him to help her search the outhouses and haymows, 'hooping and hallowing'. Taylor asked Goodwife Cooley if Hugh Parsons had indeed reprimanded the boy. She didn't know, but her suspicions were aroused. When finally Samuel Terry came home, he accused Parsons of having thrown him head first into 'a great cellar', then falling upon him.[32]

Other tales of violence circulated in Springfield. William Pynchon had given two Scots prisoners of war, who had arrived in town in the summer, to Henry Smith to work his farmland.[33] They brought with them stories of war and persecution. In the previous twelve months, 300 witches had been burned in the Scottish Lowlands. Away on mainland Europe, even worse horrors had occurred: mass executions for witchcraft, dividing opinion between sceptics of the evidence and those who insisted that diabolists abounded. Such stories fed the tense atmosphere in New England. At the port of Marblehead a woman was seen out sailing in the form of a cat, having already been blamed for blighting the fruit harvest. At Dorchester, four children had to be fostered after their mother was executed for covenanting with Satan and their father, ruined by the shame of it, fled to Rhode Island.[34] Everywhere adversity and despair bred such paranoia – and particularly in the isolated, vulnerable Connecticut valley. In January 1651, acutely aware of the threat presented by Dutchmen, Indians and wolves, Springfield's selectmen voted that the town should invest more of its precious capital in gunpowder, musket balls and match cord, and that cattle owners should pay bounties to the wolf-slayers. What Springfield needed most was strong leadership – which, in previous years, it had had. But now that leadership was wobbling, with a magistrate who invited accusations of heresy and a minister itching to leave. Though Pynchon raised Moxon's salary to a handsome £70 per annum, persuading him to stay, rumours then began circulating that Pynchon himself wanted to return to Old England.[35]

At this time, every few days the gravedigger was out chipping away at the frozen burying ground. John and Pentecost Matthews's only child, Sarah, perished before her fourth birthday; her grieving parents could not forget that Mary Parsons had blamed the death of her sister Abigail, back in the summer of 1646, on Mercy Marshfield's witchcraft. And it was not long before Mary's three-month-old baby, Joshua, lay sick in his cradle.[36]

Mary had already lost one child – a loss she ascribed to her husband's witchcraft. Now, as she fretted over her sick infant, her maternal pain was like a blade pressed against her heart. What was she to think? These days, her husband's sleep was more disrupted than ever, and he gabbled deliriously. Mary would lean over him, holding her ear close to his mouth, trying to make out what he was saying. If he awoke with a start, she asked what he'd been struggling to say; but he was confused, replying only that he had 'strange dreams'.[37]

Hugh's troubled nights continued to colour his turbulent days. That February, the smouldering feud with Pynchon's servant Simon Beamon flared up.[38] Hugh had not forgotten Beamon's refusal to carry his flour; Beamon had not forgotten tumbling from his horse afterwards. Beamon was working in the general store when Hugh, who had been threshing for Pynchon, came on an errand – 'in his master's name', or so he claimed. What he wanted was a small piece of whiteleather to replace the hinge or 'cap' that joined the swingle of his flail to its wooden handle. Beamon said he didn't have time to serve him. Hugh suspected the real reason Beamon refused to help was his evident dislike of him: after all, as an employee in the store and the town cobbler, he had access to leather whenever he wanted. But Beamon apologized, explaining that he was just off to the woods to fetch lumber and that the horses were already harnessed to the cart. He promised to help another time. Hugh snapped that Beamon would have done better to serve him there and then and stomped out. Evidently this was another of his sinister threats – the sort a failing, frustrated man might carry out with magic.[39]

Storming home, Hugh found Jonathan Taylor, who had come by on an errand. He was talking to Mary, who braced herself for the latest furious complaint – though she was increasingly outspoken against her husband, in the presence of others as well as in private. Hugh related what had happened at the store, insisting that Simon Beamon should have made time for him: 'He shall get nothing by it,' he ranted, 'I will be even with him.' Taylor said nothing, but Mary tried to reason with him: 'Husband, why do you threaten the fellow so? It is like he was busy.' Hugh sneered that Beamon would have responded differently if Benjamin Cooley 'or any one else that he liked' had asked him for leather. Never mind, though, he said: 'I'll remember him.' They were dangerous words indeed: to threaten William Pynchon's servant was, by extension, to threaten Pynchon himself.[40]

Later that day Beamon was returning along a well-worn route from the forest, sawn timber slung beneath his cart, when the horses bolted, as if startled, and galloped away. Beamon pulled hard on the thill-horse, which steadied the shafts of the cart, but was himself hurled forwards, out of the cart, landing heavily on the ground. As he fell, he just managed to kick the horse so that it veered off with the cart, or else he would have gone under the wheels. Instead, one rim just clipped the hem of his jacket before the cart crashed to a halt against a stump. Beamon cast a glance among the silent, towering trees, but could see nothing that might have spooked the horses. Then he lay back panting on the forest floor, shaken, viscerally afraid.[41]

In those first weeks of 1651 stories of more witches in England and its colonies bored deeper into Springfield's consciousness. They may have heard of the scare in the islands of Bermuda, where religious schism and reforming zeal had spurred puritan colonists to hunt witches, using the same diagnostic methods employed back across the Atlantic.[42] Reports also arrived from nearer to home. A carpenter named John Carrington and his wife Joan, from witch-fearing Wethersfield, were tried for having 'entertained familiarity with Satan, the great enemy of God and mankind', to perform 'works above the course of nature'. Both were hanged.[43] Hugh Parsons, who seems to have known Carrington, returned from a neighbour's house where the Carringtons were the topic of conversation and told his wife the news. Mary was piously indignant, saying: 'I hope that God will find out all such wicked persons and purge New England of all witches 'ere it be long.' Hugh gave her 'a naughty look' – that is, glowered in silent fury. After the trouble his wife had caused by accusing Mercy Marshfield, he had vowed she should meddle no more. But she wondered whether there was something else in his baleful expression: a guilty suspicion, perhaps, that the devil was in him, too. Later he flew into a rage and, grabbing a block of wood from the hearth, raised it as if to throw it at Mary. She flinched and cowered, but he let his arm drop and cast the wood into the fire.[44]

New England men were forbidden to strike their wives. Such brutality was considered not only a violation of their sacred union and a breach of the peace but also a dereliction of patriarchal responsibility. The man who sought respect through physical coercion rather than by consent had failed as a husband and a householder.[45] Words and gestures also broke the natural reciprocal chain of authority in a marriage. For a generation or more, men had feared women swapping places with men, flipping nature on its head.[46] 'Since the days of Adam women were never so masculine,' thought one satirist. If men didn't take a stand, they might as well make 'the wild Irish' and 'the naked Indian' their masters.[47] The obvious disdain that Mary Parsons felt for her husband was matched by the disdain he showed to her. Moreover, Hugh's disrespect was also apparent in his dealings with his social superiors: William Pynchon, at least indirectly through Pynchon's servant Simon Beamon; Henry Smith, whom he had threatened and whose daughters some believed he had bewitched to death in the summer of 1648; and George Moxon, first by absenting himself from services, and then reneging on a deal.

This deal, predictably, concerned bricks. Moxon had been doing well for himself: to persuade him not to leave Springfield, Pynchon had not only increased his salary but extended him £7 16s 4d credit so he could add chimneys to his house. Moxon also had the walls of the meeting house, which was freezing in winter, lined with timber and a comfortable seat made for himself. He struck a deal with Hugh Parsons for a consignment of bricks; but the deadline for their delivery came and went. When Moxon queried this, there was an altercation. Later Hugh, still seething, swore to Mary, in the way she had come to expect, that 'if Mr Moxon do force me to make bricks according to the bargain, I will be even with him.' Soon afterwards, John Matthews came to Hugh's yard to collect some soft samel bricks, used for infill, and asked if he intended to honour his contract to the minister. 'He will stay with us now', observed Matthews, 'and then I believe he will have up his chimneys.' Hugh said nothing, so Matthews persisted: would the work go ahead? 'Not that I know of,' mumbled the brick-maker. Matthews said he expected Reverend Moxon would hold him to their arrangement – to which Hugh responded, robustly and to no one's surprise, 'If he do, I will be even with him.'[48]

Within a few days of the row came news of more illness. George Moxon's young daughters Martha and Rebecca had sickened, writh-ing and squalling in their beds. Only too aware of what happened to Henry Smith's daughters after Smith crossed Hugh Parsons, Moxon nervously blamed the brickmaker's 'ill purpose'.[49] The minister's household prayed with earnest concentration for their recovery, but God's test – or was it a penalty for Moxon's love of luxury? – would not be that simple. Martha and Rebecca's twitches became tremors, which grew in violent intensity into lurching, shuddering convul-sions, like those exhibited by Sarah Miller. As an ordained minister, Moxon took it upon himself to confront the demons in his daugh-ters' bodies, willing the powers of heaven to evict them. If the devil really did interfere in temporal affairs, here was the proof before their eyes.[50]

Visitors came to Moxon's house, prompted by concern, morbid curiosity and a desire to be part of this involving drama. Standing in the girls' bedchamber, spectators' emotions were purged through such a close encounter with Satan: they could feel the heat of his power and yet stand back and escape his clutches.[51] Samuel

Marshfield judged the girls' fits to be even more severe than those of his own sister, Sarah Miller, although her convulsions and hallucinations had also worsened since the girls had fallen ill.[52] Some neighbours were convinced that Martha and Rebecca were possessed by demons, but Moxon and his wife leaned towards a diagnosis of witchcraft, which stressed the innocence of the victims and banished suspicion they had brought the affliction upon themselves through faint devotion.[53] By the time Simon Beamon saw the girls struggling *in extremis*, a consensus had already formed that they were bewitched. If some illegal counter-magic was deployed as an attempted cure, as it almost certainly was (if not by Moxon, then by someone else), it went unrecorded. All that mattered in the end was that the girls recovered – which they did, to universal relief and rejoicing.[54]

But in the last fortnight of February 1651, Springfield's spiritual crisis became uncontrollable, like a canoe dragged by rapids to the falls. By the time the Moxon girls regained their senses, the contagion had spread to the meeting house, where, as one puritan put it later, townsfolk were 'supposed to be under an evil hand' – meaning either possessed or bewitched. Things came to a head on Sunday the 16th, during the break between George Moxon's sermons. Mary Parsons was sitting with neighbours in the alehouse owned by Robert and Mary Ashley. She seemed unfocused, gazing into nowhere. She began rambling that the death of Anne Smith's daughters 'lay very sad upon her'. When Goodwife Ashley asked why, Mary answered: 'because my husband would have had me to have nursed her children'. Mary Parsons examined their worried faces and asked who would 'think me a fit nurse for them'? Goodwife Ashley broke the ensuing silence: why did Hugh want her to be the Smiths' nurse? 'For lucre and gain', replied Mary, 'one may well know his reason.' With a heavy sigh, she said: 'Little doth anyone think how the death of those children lies upon me.' Then she murmured something to imply that she blamed her husband for the deaths, adding: 'It is better for others to bring him out than for me – but I can speak a great deal of him, if others bring him out.'[55]

Then Pynchon's servant Francis Pepper joined the group, fresh from tending to his ailing heifer. Mary looked up and in an agitated voice told him straight away that the cow was cursed. How did she know this? Pepper asked. My husband, she replied: my husband bewitched it. 'And now', she continued, slapping her thigh, 'he hath bewitched me, and he knows now what I say and he now terrifies me.' This conversation, she knew, was not private: Hugh could always use his witchery to listen in, even when he was nowhere nearby. But somehow, now, this only encouraged her to pour out all the troubles in her heart. Hugh bullied her about work, Mary said, just as her previous husband had bullied her over her faith. He had threatened her with a lump of firewood, and his desires had drawn wickedness into their lives. Did it not seem odd, Mary asked her small audience, now rapt with fear and fascination, that he 'cannot abide that anything should be spoken against witches'?[56]

At this point, Mary appeared to slip into a trance: she was glazed and unresponsive. What the company in the alehouse didn't know was that an infernal voice was booming inside her, a voice that only Mary could hear. Satan told her he had entered Hugh's body not carnally, but through an invisible surge. In a quavering whisper, Mary admitted to the devil that she, too, might have become a witch before now had she not been so afraid. 'I will not come in any apparition', Satan reassured her in his manly, masterful way, 'but only come into thy body like a wind and trouble thee a little while and presently go forth again.' She would be spared the usual diabolic consummation described by witches: the hot breath, damp skin and icy semen. Nor would her blood, pricked by the devil's claw, be used to sign his ledger – an account book, like Pynchon's. At this moment, slumped in the Ashleys' alehouse, Mary consented in her heart to Satan and was transported. Leaving her body in the room, her soul was whisked away to a witches' meeting in John Stebbins's homelot. It was dark there, but in the firelight she could make out her husband, and two other witches: the constable's wife, Sarah Merrick, and Bess Sewell, the wife of another townsman. There was revelry and gleeful shape shifting from human to animal forms, but the witches, angry with Mary for revealing so much, made her walk barefoot over the stony ground to gather sticks for the fire. Ever the wayward servant and disappointing wife, even in this fantasy world of escape from the mundane, she was being punished by her cruel husband and judgemental female neighbours.[57]

The spell was broken by the clang of the meeting-house bell. The company escorted Mary from the alehouse and across the way to the meeting. Still dazed, for the moment she said nothing of what had just happened. As he began his sermon, George Moxon found it hard to settle the people and hold their attention. Then there was movement, followed by gasps. The wife of Joseph Parsons, confusingly another Mary, who had roamed the dark meadow in a trance, had collapsed and was flailing around on the floor. Two men struggled to hold her down. Then other women began dropping around her. All had convulsions – like the Moxon girls – and were carried one by one from the meeting house, limbs stiff and shaking, lips foaming, eyes rolled back. In this way, Satan mocked George Moxon in his place of worship.[58] As for the victims, hauled off to their beds by friends and relations, they were like lunatics in whose bodies, it was said, demons bathed in black bile.[59] When they spoke, the words of such wretches tended to be blasphemous and obscene. Others jabbered about storms and tornadoes lashing their souls; mice and other vermin scurrying inside them; tides rolling up and down their bodies; and hallucinations and voices, softly inciting transgression.[60]

Mortal fear seeped like marsh mist into every home. On the Tuesday after the hysterical scene in the meeting house, 18 February 1651, Hugh was working in the long meadow until after sunset. It was cold, but he was used to it. Mary sat up at home, her mind besieged, while Hannah, now four, and the ailing baby Joshua slept. Flames cast shadows round the room, which was quiet except for the wind in the eaves and the sputter of resin in the hearth. In a heartbeat a deafening rumble 'as if forty horses had been there' filled the entire house. This ended abruptly, leaving Mary shaking in terror. A moment later, Hugh strolled through the door. She eyed him accusingly, but he didn't respond to her gaze, just climbed into bed. Late into the night, still shocked by the loud noise, Mary lay awake while her husband turned fitfully in his sleep. In the morning, when Mary asked what had ailed him, he was surprisingly candid: he had dreamed he was fighting with the devil, he said, 'and the devil had almost overcome him, but at last he got the victory'. It was perplexing and distressing. If all souls were feminine, as ministers taught, then Hugh was trapped in his own abusive spiritual marriage: a partnership with Satan that he could resist but not evade. It was the dread opposite of the puritan ideal: the heart's loving, sustaining union with Christ.[61]

Hugh spent the day labouring with his neighbour John Lombard. No one felt comfortable doing anything with Hugh any more – but still, he was not easily avoided. They looked up as George Langton passed. Langton, a carpenter, had married two years previously and now had an infant daughter. Like all townsmen, he had to manage his resources to provide for his dependants. So when Hugh asked Langton to sell him some hay, he had to say no. Inevitably, Hugh felt insulted and aggrieved – a grievance he took home and was still nursing the following day, Thursday, when he turned up at work.[62] Lombard tried to placate him, explaining that Langton simply had no hay to spare. Why else would he deny a neighbour? But to Hugh, this only meant that Lombard had taken Langton's side against him. Whatever paranoia the town felt towards Hugh was more than matched in Hugh's own roiling mind.[63]

The afternoon of Friday 21st, and Hannah Langton was making a bag pudding, a hearty dinner served now and then on colonial tables. A muslin bag was stuffed with offal and oats or pounded maize, tied tightly, and set to simmer. When ready it was slipped from its cloth sheath, as fat as a marrow, glistening, magnificent. This was Hannah's second attempt at the dish. When she had tried ten days earlier, it had failed – and in a way that shamed a wife expected to put food on her husband's table. Now she nervously lifted the steaming bundle from the kettle and laid it on the table.

Exactly as before, the pudding slid out easily – but was neatly split end to end, 'as smooth as any knife could cut it', she thought. This could not be her fault, and she was relieved her husband didn't blame her either. George Langton knew Hugh Parsons was angry about the hay: that very morning he had been railing to John Lombard – for the third day running – and once again Lombard had failed to pacify him. When a neighbour put his head round the door, Hannah showed him the pudding. As they considered it, the three minds converged on witchcraft. The neighbour suggested putting a slice in the fire: a spell to summon a witch. This was against the law – ministers taught that counter-magic was itself witchcraft – but they knew it might work, and besides what else could they do? In these fraught times, ends justified means, even if that meant turning Satan's power against himself.[64]

As the scrap of pudding sizzled in the grate, Bess Sewell called at the Langtons' house. She had been going round frantically trying to quash the aspersions that, by now, Mary had cast against her and Sarah Merrick. Might Goodwife Sewell be the witch, the Langtons wondered? Bess's timing was unfortunate. But she was absolved: the company had set their sights elsewhere: clearly they sought confirmation rather than revelation. Back on the side of the righteous, Bess joined them as they waited for the spell to work. An hour or so passed, heavy with expectation. It was fully dark now. At last Hannah Langton thought she heard 'someone mutter and mumble at the door'. Bess was nearest, so lifted the latch.

Who is it? asked Goody Langton.

Hugh Parsons, Bess whispered.

George Langton remained quiet, just out of sight. There, framed in the dark doorway, lurking on the threshold, the border between the hostile night and the glow of a warm hall, stood the menacing figure of Hugh. Is George at home? he asked. Hannah had the presence of mind to lie that he was not. Hugh turned and left, without saying what he had wanted or leaving a message. They might have guessed what the visit concerned, but Hugh's terseness made it seem yet another sleeveless errand. The Langtons and their neighbours present agreed that it was peculiar that Goodman Parsons should come calling without an explicit purpose – as if drawn there against his will by their counter-magic, pained by the effluvium of witchcraft transferred from his body to the pudding.[65]

In the morning, George and Hannah Langton went to William Pynchon to complain. Like most people who initiated proceedings against witches, their fear and anger had tipped them over from suspicion to accusation. If Hugh had indeed spoiled their pudding, they would have justice – but in the short term they wanted only to remove a threat to their household, in particular their young child. Pynchon, preoccupied with accusations of heresy against him over his book, did his proper duty as a magistrate. He listened to the Langtons, taking careful note of their concerns. It was not long before other townsfolk came knocking. Hearing that the Langtons had set things in motion, Mercy Marshfield was the next to stand in Pynchon's parlour, appearing not so much for herself, it seemed, as on behalf of Blanche Bedortha, who was suspected to have been tormented by Hugh during childbirth.[66]

The next day was Sunday 23rd, which the Langtons decided was a good time to attempt another pudding. If it worked, Hannah would please George with a perfect dinner; if it failed, they would have more proof of Hugh Parsons's magical malevolence. This time, when the pudding was opened, it divided into three long, even slices, a phenomenon they made sure their neighbour Roger Pritchard witnessed before returning to the magistrate. Pynchon was receptive but kept his own counsel, weighing these private passions against the wider public mood. The town was full of gossip, an atmosphere of fluttering anticipation almost like hope. Frail fantasy was hardening into the hard fact of Hugh Parsons's witchcraft.[67]

On Tuesday 25 February Hugh Parsons went with several men to the woodlots: felling and sawing lumber was not a job easily or safely done alone. Also present was Thomas Burnham, a visitor in Springfield, the carpenter Thomas Cooper and Thomas Miller, who believed Hugh had bewitched his wife. At midday, the men put down their axes and saws and opened their packets of food.

They were, Miller thought, 'merry together', until Hugh climbed up to an overhead bough to eat his lunch. Someone asked why he had gone up there. 'To see what we have,' scoffed Miller, meaning Parsons was so envious he even had to know what everyone's wives had given them. The light mood was clouded. Miller had not finished. What's all this about puddings, he demanded to know, referring to the Langtons' uncanny cooking. Cooper fidgeted, worried such provocation would end badly.[68] The men glanced at Hugh, reading his features. But he was impassive and just sat on his perch, looking down on them, chewing.[69] Break over, the men went back to work. Miller picked up his saw, and nothing else was said. But a quarter of an hour later he cried out. The others turned to see that his blade had slipped, the teeth embedded in his leg, blood pouring. They laid him down and made a bandage from a strip of cloth. Then they carried him down the hillside into town. It was not a serious wound: the likely cause, however – Hugh's witchcraft – was terrifying.[70]

That same day Pynchon received a visit from Hugh Parsons's former lodger Anthony Dorchester. He had recently returned from Hartford, where he had married again, to a widow named Martha Kicherell, and had brought her and her children to live in Springfield with his own children. By this time Dorchester, who was slowly getting on in the world, had bought property: the homelot of Griffith Jones, who had moved out, situated between Jonathan Taylor and Reece Bedortha; a parcel of wet meadow land east of the brook; and planting ground across the Agawam and Connecticut Rivers, which Hugh had recently been forced to sell. Dorchester told Pynchon about the disappearance of the beef tongue as his first wife lay dying, swearing: 'I have ever since believed that no hand of man did take it away: but that it was taken away by witchcraft', adding that Mary Parsons 'did much wonder' at it too. Pynchon's notes were growing into a file of complaints against Hugh Parsons. Later that day Griffith Jones pitched in to say that when he used to live near Hugh and Mary his knives had vanished and reappeared, which, he confessed, had 'made me blush', meaning hot with alarm.[71]

In the evening, Hugh sat quietly in the company of his neighbours: they could hardly stop him being among them.[72] Those present included the visitor, Thomas Burnham, and Benjamin Munn, a labourer who had moved from Hartford to Springfield a couple of years earlier and married a widow named Abigail Ball, who was herself there, listening in. Burnham turned to look at Hugh. 'Here is strange doings in town', he said, 'about cutting of puddings and whetting of saws in the night.' It was a question disguised as a statement, and for a second they thought Hugh would ignore it. But they sensed his agitation. After a beat, Hugh replied: 'I never heard of these things before.' Burnham pretended to be taken aback. 'That is strange,' he said. 'And I being but a stranger in town do hear of it in all places wherever I come.' Hugh cast his eyes to the floor. At length the conversation resumed, whereupon Hugh joined in again, talking 'as pleasantly as anybody else', thought Burnham, although 'to the matter of the pudding he would say nothing'. Unable to let things lie, Burnham kept returning to the subject of the puddings, and the rumour that Hugh had sharpened his saw on the Sabbath night. Still, Hugh held his tongue. Benjamin Munn, a devout man, wished that all who worked on the Lord's Day be shamed, to which Burnham said it was up to them to do something about it. Munn and the others refocused on Hugh, agreeing that they'd never heard anything like these weird tales before, and pointedly asking him if *he* had. Hugh remained silent.[73]

Time was running out for Hugh, as surely as sand in the hourglass near the end of a sermon. It was Wednesday 26 February, five days since a split pudding had triggered a witch-hunt, and Springfield's 'strange dreams' had become 'strange doings'. For now, Mary Parsons held on to her secret that she had given herself to the devil and attended his meeting, even though she had now pointed the finger at Sarah Merrick and Bess Sewell. But she was nonetheless vehemently suspected of some wrongdoing – a woman obsessed with witches, married to a man whom she herself suspected of witchcraft, including that he had bewitched the Smith girls to death. This much was common knowledge in Springfield.

Under pressure to redraw the town's moral boundaries – boundaries he himself had breached – William Pynchon issued a warrant for the arrest of Mary Parsons. The town constable Thomas Merrick, whose own wife was now tainted by suspicion, escorted Mary to Pynchon's house for questioning. It was then that Hugh, hearing the news, went looking for Merrick but instead found Jonathan Taylor labouring in Merrick's barn. This encounter led to the awkward joke about witches, over beer in Sarah Merrick's cellar, and that same evening ended with the petrifying intrusion of demonic snakes into Taylor's house, slithering across the floor, menacing his family. Taylor was the demons' chosen victim: bitten, traumatized and cursed by a voice that said 'death' – the unmistakable voice of Hugh Parsons.[74]

Once Pynchon had finished interrogating Mary and returned her to the custody of the constable, Merrick arranged for her to be detained, probably in the hall of his own house, and instructed the up-and-coming townsmen Anthony Dorchester and Benjamin Cooley to watch her closely for any unusual activity. It would be a long, unsettling night.[75]

7.   That Dumb Dog

Witches confessed to meeting the devil, accepting his offers, even to copulating with him. But the devil couldn't be everywhere, so he relied on an army of imps. These came in many shapes – insects, rodents, reptiles, dogs, even children – and were thought to seal the deal with Satan's human acolytes by feeding at teats on their bodies. The experience was partly maternal, partly sexual, usually uncomfortable and often painful. In exchange for blood, these imps, sometimes known as familiar spirits, made the witch feel powerful whenever she sent them after her enemies.[1] Some familiars even entered the witch's body: the ultimate intimacy and mastery. The imp's real purpose, however, was to remind the witch of her contract, and to stop her thinking about the consequences of her actions: stretching a rope or burning for eternity. Most common in England, the idea of witch familiars was exported to America.[2]

Even so, such imps could be a weak point in the devil's scheme. To prove a case against a witch, the trick was to catch her familiars in the act – as watchers had done with striking success in the East Anglian witchfinding campaign a few years earlier, when beetles, toads and rabbits had entered the rooms where suspects were held. If the imps never came, it might mean Satan had deserted the witch, as he invariably did: after all, the devil promised much but rarely delivered. Legends told of greedy witches who by night were given piles of gleaming gold, yet in the cold light of day found nothing but withered leaves.[3]

Godly ministers, for whom the witch's covenant was the spiritual opposite of union with Christ, rejected the idea of such parasitic imps as a gross superstition – a thought that may have stopped Mary Parsons properly searching her husband's body. But hopes were nonetheless pinned on watching suspects and the discovery of devil marks as inducements to confession. Exposure of a witch would force Satan to give up his side of the bargain, casting the witch back on the mercies of heaven and its earthly agents. Only then would the soul's bondage be broken, leaving the edifying sight of a penitent sinner dissolved in tears. The witch would still have to die, of course – but obediently, to be redeemed by Christ, in whose own obedience to God the Father William Pynchon saw the essence of salvation. If Reverend George Moxon had an opinion of imps it was not recorded. Pynchon, however, was content to allow the case against Mary Parsons to proceed using the methods of the English witchfinders, as already used against Margaret Jones in Boston in 1648. After the episode at the Ashleys' alehouse Mary may have been close to testifying against her husband, or even to confessing that she was a witch herself – but Pynchon knew she was melancholic, possibly delusional. He would need proof to pursue a pre-trial investigation. So too would the authorities in Boston, where according to law serious crimes like witchcraft were indicted and tried.

No creature came scuttling on the night of Mary's detention, nor did her minders Benjamin Cooley and Anthony Dorchester, blinking through the half-light, perceive her to be distracted by anything except fatigue. The devil was neither beneath her clothes nor in her head. Instead, Mary stared into the eyes of these men she knew well: the land-hungry neighbour, whose wife had helped her nurse her dying son; and her ambitious ex-lodger, whose dying wife she in turn had nursed. When at last she spoke, it was not about herself but about Hugh, the malevolent man she really *had* contracted with, who had let her down like her first husband in Wales, and whose soft words of courtship had turned to ash, darkness and despair. Hugh kept faith with no one and like the devil broke his pledges and tore up contracts.

Mary started talking to her watchers. She opened with something only too familiar: her husband swore to be even with everyone who crossed him. Honour had to be defended against slurs and insults – but there were limits, which Hugh habitually exceeded by demanding vengeance rather than redress. Yet there was more spilling out of Mary now: nothing less than an indictment of her husband's hot blood and lethal malice against his enemies, apparently including his own wife and son. Mary said she feared he had bewitched Samuel to death to free her up for the maize harvest. However busy or tired she was, he always expected her to help, and was annoyed that 'her time was taken up about her child'. He was jealously ambitious: 'eager after the world', as she put it – beyond what was conscionable or even possible. One lesson from the East Anglian witch-hunt had been that the devil made witches of those 'who with greediness gape after worldly wealth, or fear poverty'. And so it proved on the other side of the Atlantic, in Springfield, concentrated in the person of Hugh Parsons.[4]

Yet, for all Hugh's envious striving, nothing he did had actually advanced his ambitions – at least, not to his own satisfaction. He couldn't overcome the inadequacy of his existence, the essential misery of it, in order to magnify his public self – the self aspired to by every man in Springfield. Mary alleged that everything he produced, principally bricks, was substandard, and his customers never prospered with what they bought from him. His indifference to this was unneighbourly, as was his settled aversion to public meetings, religious or civil. He had become so reluctant that he or Mary should visit the meeting house that she had threatened to complain to William Pynchon; otherwise, she thought, 'he would not let her go once in the year'. She also told Cooley and Dorchester about the haunting noises, Hugh's disturbed sleep and how he had brawled with the devil, who 'had almost overcome him' until, manfully, he got the upper hand.[5]

The following day, Mary Parsons, dull with exhaustion, was brought before William Pynchon, who then took statements from several neighbours. Standing in the magistrate's parlour, John Matthews described how Mary had spoken to him about witches just before her slander trial, revealing that her husband was a witch. Then Mary Ashley recounted the story of Mary's lament in the alehouse: how she grieved for the Smith girls and thought Hugh was to blame for their deaths. If Pynchon was pained by the mention of his granddaughters he didn't show it. Once Goody Ashley had sat down, he turned back to Mary Parsons. What grounds did she have, he wondered, for supposing that her husband had bewitched the children? She answered: 'My husband would often say that he would be even with Mr Smith', demanding satisfaction when, having been denied something, he felt disrespected. Pynchon made a note, making sure he had heard correctly. Yes, Mary repeated, her husband did often say: 'I would be even with him', meaning Pynchon's stepson, Henry Smith.[6]

Pynchon shifted in his chair and shook the cramp from the hand grasping the pen, as he scratched line after line of testimony. Some who had already given statements would return; many others had yet to speak. Sarah Edwards retold the story that Pynchon had heard from her husband Alexander nearly two years earlier, about how, following Hugh Parsons's demand that a debt be repaid, their milk had turned 'as yellow as saffron'. George Colton stood up to verify this. The day's most engaging witnesses were Benjamin Cooley and Anthony Dorchester, Mary's guards during her night in custody. Cooley repeated Mary's story of how she had searched her sleeping husband to see where he fed his imps. Dorchester followed with his own recollections of being the Parsonses' tenant: how Hugh threatened people, disappeared for days on end, seemed to know Mary's 'private talk' and made the house rumble. He confirmed what Cooley had said about Mary suspecting her husband to be a witch. Then the two watchers related the previous night's conversation with Mary. It was a story which, when told in Pynchon's presence, became a watershed in Hugh's fortunes.[7]

Hugh Parsons was arrested later that day in the north end of town.[8] There was relief among all who saw Merrick the constable escort his prisoner through the streets – until, as the pair passed the house of John and Anne Stebbins, something happened. Anne Stebbins was a delicate soul, often unwell – she had, perhaps, never recovered from the death of her son, buried in April 1650, before he was two years old – and her husband bought medicine on credit, including a pint of sack – fortified wine – to make posset. Anne certainly had witches on her mind: it was she who had gossiped to Mary about Widow Marshfield at Henry Smith's house. Now she was at her gate when Hugh was led past, and, crying out, 'Ah witch! Ah witch!' she collapsed, her husband hurrying to her side. Merrick, who happened to be John Stebbins's brother-in-law, kept going until he reached his own home, where he chained Hugh up by the fire. There, Hugh stayed until morning. Meanwhile, across town, Anne Stebbins's seizures continued, each preceded by an apparition only she could see. Transfixed by something she felt was hiding in the chimney, she peered up and exclaimed: 'Oh dear . . . there hangs Hugh Parsons!' She stumbled backwards, wailing that he would fall on her. Then she passed out, her body jerking and shaking.[9]

Anne was not the only one terrorized by apparitions that day. In the south end of town, the two-year-old Joseph Bedortha, who had picked up on his mother's fear of Hugh, clambered onto his father's lap, crying: 'I'm afraid of the dog!'[10] Reece and Blanche looked round the room: no dog. Where had it gone? In his distress, Joseph managed to reply: under the bed. They paused for a second, then looked: there was nothing there. Whose dog is it? Reece asked gently. John Lombard's, Joseph stammered; then, when his father told him Lombard had no dog, the child said it belonged to Goodman Parsons. Hugh didn't have a dog either – and yet the boy remained terrified. He stood there shaking, pointing a finger at the creature invisible to everyone except himself. The spectral dog, the Bedorthas decided, could be a figment of childish imagination, or it 'might be some evil thing from Hugh Parsons'.[11]

Chained up at Merrick's house, Hugh was fed and watered by Sarah Merrick, no longer so light-hearted as when she had served him beer in her cellar. He dreaded the next day to come, when he was to be brought before William Pynchon and informed of the charges against him. This would not be a trial, which could only happen in Boston, simply a pre-trial hearing. But Hugh knew enough about the law to realize that what was said in Springfield's meeting house might one day soon echo in a courtroom on the other side of the colony.

Saturday 1 March 1651. Townsfolk – the Langtons, the Bedorthas, Simon Beamon, Anthony Dorchester, George Colton, Griffith Jones and others – assembled in Springfield's meeting house. At the front sat William Pynchon and, beside him, his ally George Moxon, who was present both to temper and bolster proceedings – for he too had a beef with Hugh Parsons. Henry Smith was also there in his double capacity as town clerk and as the father of children thought to have been bewitched to death. As for Pynchon, if the stain of heresy had harmed his position as the town's leader, his authority as a magistrate was, for now, intact. Truth and justice, consonant with God's will, were his objectives. Pynchon was, however, less ardent than some other magistrates in Massachusetts Bay Colony, who, though guided by English law, bore down on suspects like inquisitors in Spain, France and the Holy Roman Empire. Pynchon followed the advice of his well-thumbed copy of Dalton's *Countrey Justice*, the magistrate's handbook: *nullus tenetur seipsum prodere* – no man's guilt should be extracted by torture, but proved by testimony freely given by witnesses.[12]

Thomas Merrick brought in his prisoner, and Pynchon called the room to order. Hugh looked into the faces of his neighbours, their expressions furtive and defiant by turns. No more whispered asides or huddled confidences: now, anything there was to say would be said openly. Hugh noticed that his wife wasn't there: Pynchon planned to repeat the proceedings at a later hearing with Mary present, to check consistency in the stories and increase the pressure on husband and wife to confess.[13] Reece and Blanche Bedortha were summoned first. Standing side by side, they told of how, two years earlier at their house, Hugh had threatened Blanche for making a snide comment about him. The accused, standing at the front of the room beside the seated Pynchon, Moxon and Smith, said nothing. Inviting Hugh to consider the 'evil events that did follow not long after this threatening', Pynchon asked Blanche to describe her ordeal. She emphasized her overwhelming fear and the severity of the pain she had suffered. 'Suddenly afterwards', she recalled, 'my thoughts were that this evil might have come upon me from the said threatening speech of Hugh Parsons.'[14]

The Bedorthas sat down. Next came the sufferings of George Moxon. Pynchon asked Hugh whether he thought there might be witchery in the sickness of Moxon's children. Careful not to trip himself up, Hugh replied: 'I question not but there is witchcraft in it – but I wish the saddle may be set upon the right horse.' It was a barbed answer. 'Who is the right horse?' asked Pynchon. Were there other suspects whose names they had not yet heard? Hugh retreated, saying only that he was innocent, 'neither do I suspect any other'. But Pynchon kept going. Did Hugh suspect his own wife as a witch? Hugh shook his head wearily, saying: 'No, I do not know that I ever had any such thought of her.' Hugh's denial risked putting him in a double-bind: if Mary wasn't to blame, then perhaps he knew who was. Was it one of the women she had accused: Bess Sewell or Sarah Merrick? Or, more likely, was it Hugh himself? George Moxon, pained by the memory of his daughters' suffering, believed it was.[15]

Pynchon decided to wait before calling Moxon. Instead, he asked the Langtons to repeat the now familiar story of their culinary failure. Perhaps because her husband was afraid to admit it, Hannah Langton alone told of their counter-magical spell, the slice of bag pudding fizzing in the fire that lured Hugh Parsons to their door, a visit unexplained then or since. She was careful enough not to specify who had performed the spell – or if she did, Pynchon failed to record it. (Either way, everyone in the meeting house knew such magic was superstitious and illegal; but it was hard to condemn if it had trapped a witch.) By now Pynchon, for one, was persuaded, and made a note: Hugh had come to the Langtons' house not on any errand of his own, but because 'the spirit that bewitched the pudding brought him thither'.[16] The townsfolk, bunched up on the meeting-house benches, watched avidly: after hearing so many stories of witches, cruelly at large then held to account, both in Old England and increasingly in the New, they were now living through their own drama of diabolism, unfolding around them in real time. Work could wait: this was where they needed to be.

Now Pynchon asked Hugh why he had gone to the Langtons' house. Hugh shuffled his feet and changed the subject. So Pynchon asked a second time, upon which, again, he spoke evasively, 'not to the question'. His patience wearing thin, Pynchon asked once more, this time pressing him for a direct answer. Looking up, Hugh admitted that he had wanted hay – this, despite John Lombard advising him to let the matter lie – but hadn't asked, because Langton hadn't been at home (though he had, of course, been hiding). In that case, Pynchon demanded to know, had he approached George Langton about the hay since then? Hugh shrugged: he hadn't even seen Langton. At this point, there were shouts from the onlookers: Reece Bedortha and Simon Beamon insisted they had seen Hugh with Langton the following day. An interjection by George Langton that Hugh hadn't mentioned hay only made him look more of a liar. Pynchon let the matter rest – for now. There was a lot more to get through.[17]

Next Pynchon called on Sarah Edwards to go through her deposition, made two days earlier, regarding her spoiled milk. Then he asked Hugh to reply. Hugh cast his mind back to the summer of 1649. He was sure he hadn't slept in the long meadow then, only in spring: March, or at the latest early April, when he had been there putting up fences. He admitted asking Sarah Edwards for some milk, but doubted a skinny heifer like hers ever gave as much as three quarts, as she claimed. Discoloured milk was not perhaps the most compelling evidence of Hugh's witchcraft. But his sleeping out alone, away from his family, struck people as unusual, sinister even. Learned opinion would have agreed. To remove oneself from the community was voluntary exile from the binding covenant that kept it together. King James I himself, the author of a treatise on witches fifty years earlier, had alerted his subjects to the witch's 'natural melancholic humour', signs of which included 'desire of solitude'.[18]

So far, five of the charges that Pynchon had prepared from the preliminary testimonies had been levelled at Hugh Parsons. There were three more to go. Griffith Jones confirmed his statement about the knife mystery, to which Hugh replied that he was ignorant of any such thing and that, with God as his witness, he could clear his conscience. Why did he say 'conscience' when 'name' would have been more appropriate? Was his conscience not already clear? If Pynchon noticed this slip, he didn't press Hugh on it but clearly thought something was awry. He put it to Hugh that, as with the pudding spell, 'such a strange thing, falling out just at his coming in, did minister just occasion of suspicion of witchcraft'. Hugh was legalistically defiant. Jones was the only witness to this event, he smartly pointed out, and one witness was insufficient.[19] The towns-folk looked at each other: Hugh had a point.[20]

The seventh charge came from Goodwife Ashley's testimony, which Pynchon summarized for Hugh. 'Your wife', he began, meaning Mary Parsons, 'saith that one reason why she doth suspect you to be a witch is because you cannot abide that anything should be spoken against witches.' Pynchon then reminded Hugh of the time when, according to his wife, they had discussed John and Joan Carrington, the witches hanged at Hartford, and he had lost his temper with Mary for hoping God would purge New England of such devilish malefactors. Had he not then, in his ire, raised a block of wood as if to strike her? And did he deny, Pynchon asked, that 'this expression of your anger was because she wished the ruin of all witches'? At first Hugh said he couldn't recall threatening her; then, pressed by Pynchon, he admitted he had done once, but had no memory of when or why. After a pause, he added that he might have said such things 'because in his anger he is impatient and doth speak what he should not'.[21]

The final charge concerned Hugh and Mary's dead son, Samuel. George Colton from the long meadow related how Hugh had called at his house after receiving the news of the boy's death, and that he and his wife 'did much wonder for the lightness of his carriage because he showed no affection of sorrow'. It wasn't natural, and no one present in the meeting house thought it was. Anthony Dorchester picked up the story from the time Hugh arrived home, when he had 'carried himself as at other times', apparently unaffected by grief. Blanche Bedortha confirmed this to be true. Pynchon waited for Hugh to speak.[22]

There was silence. Hugh took a deep breath. Then he spoke, his words cutting through the air of tension that had built up in the meeting house. He was, he said, 'very full of sorrow' for the death of his son – 'in private though not in public'. Of course, like any father, he had been 'much troubled' to lose a child, but in the overwhelming shock of the moment had felt so stunned that he simply told the Coltons what had happened – without, he now acknowledged, showing appropriate emotion, the display of feeling everyone expected of him.[23] Time and the room froze in that moment, as if there were nothing else to say. With the sun hanging low in the sky, Pynchon adjourned the hearing until the following Monday. Hugh was taken back to Merrick's, where he was re-shackled and fed by Merrick's wife. It was still cold: he was at least lucky Springfield had no gaol, which at this time of year would have been like an icy tomb. He lay in front of the fire. He felt ill with stomach pains, but also dog-tired. He slept.

Sunday passed uneventfully. But that night, Hugh went over and over the destructive words of his neighbours, who were like woodsmen hacking at the stump of his reputation. The swelling and pricking in his guts worsened. Towards dawn on Monday, Thomas and Sarah Merrick were woken up by cries of agony. Lighting a candle, Merrick saw his prisoner writhing by the hearth, clutching his stomach. 'Goodman,' Hugh pleaded, 'come and lance my belly, for I am in lamentable pain.' Horrified, Merrick refused. Hugh begged him, upon which Merrick offered to unchain him so that he could at least move his bowels in the back yard. But Hugh shook his head, protesting: 'I have no need that way.' An intolerable pressure was building up in his insides, like an overboiled pudding fit to burst.[24]

The next morning, Monday 3 March, Thomas Merrick took Hugh back to the meeting house and told Pynchon about the stomach pains, which by now had eased a little. Had his imps come to remind him of his loyalty to the devil? Sarah Merrick came along too, to back her husband up and stifle Mary's rumours that she was one of the witches.[25] At the end of the conversation, Pynchon ordered – or at least approved – the witchfinders' experiment of searching Hugh's body, possibly his wife's too.[26]

While all this had been happening, Mary had been under house arrest with her daughter and baby boy. Then on the Tuesday Joshua died suddenly. Everyone at once assumed that his mother had murdered him. Nor did she deny it, overwhelmed, perhaps, by an inrushing surge of alarm and remorse the second her hands had done their deadly work. Her tacit admission precluded any further investigation of how the boy had died. The body wrapped in a cloth was removed for burial, and a note made by Henry Smith in the town register: 'Joshua Parsons, the son of Hugh Parsons, was killed by Mary Parsons, his wife.'[27] In this way, another Springfield tragedy was recorded, prosaically, without a glimmer of the emotion – the anguish and turmoil – that consumed Joshua's disturbed mother and heartbroken father.

Hannah Parsons, Hugh and Mary's firstborn, was now four years and seven months old. How she fared, what she knew, or even where she was it's hard to say, perhaps because at the time she was barely noticed. Was she still at home, or taken in by a kind neighbour? Elsewhere, fostering was the custom when parents disappeared from a child's life. It was a Christian duty. If anyone was truly cursed in Springfield, and deserving of pity, it was Hannah. Her father was in chains; her mother, mentally ill, lost in a maelstrom of paranoid agitation. Everyone was calling her father a witch and saying he murdered her brother Samuel. Now, too, her baby brother was dead: allegedly killed by her mother, who herself was also accused of witchcraft. Hannah might have been old enough to say her prayers and take in everything around her; but it was asking a lot of her to join these painful pieces into a story that made sense or that gave her the security of the holy, hardworking households in which other children were raised.

William Pynchon didn't mention Hannah, at least not in a way that caused him to put pen to paper. Events were overtaking Spring-field, and the light of the divine purpose that had guided it out of the wilderness had dimmed. In this, as in so many ways, Pynchon *was* Springfield: its fatherly creator and its spiritual embodiment. Nowadays, though, the man of action who had made everything happen, more often at the age of sixty let things happen to him. He had no choice in the matter. Now that he had spoken through his book, and this book had been burned, his destiny was in God's hands. He feared that worse was to come. In the meantime, all he could do was to continue discharging his duties as magistrate. The week after Joshua Parsons died, the demanding work of gathering evidence against his parents paused. Then, on Wednesday 12 March, the hearings resumed, though without Hugh and Mary Parsons. First to speak were the Marshfields. Samuel Marshfield informed Pynchon that Goodman Parsons had cursed his mother, in the winter after she won her damages against his wife. Then, Marshfield continued, in the spring his sister Sarah 'was taken with strange fits', which intensified when the Moxon girls were similarly afflicted.[28]

The following day, it was the turn of William Branch, who feared Hugh intensely and believed he had bewitched him. Branch, a settler in the long meadow, thought back to when he used to live on the main street, a few doors up from the witches. He had often heard Hugh Parsons venting his spleen, and his harsh refrain about getting even with people. Branch recalled how Hugh cursed others, including John Matthews over a 'bargain of bricks'. Branch told of the apparitions he had seen – the lights and the fiery boy – and how they ruined his life. 'I have been ill ever since,' he told Pynchon, adding that he 'thought Hugh Parsons to be naught'. Branch couldn't get away from him either, even down in the meadow, where, he claimed, Hugh had made 'so many sleeveless errands to my house for several things, and yet I could not tell how to deny him what he desired'. Then there was the stiffness in his legs as he passed Hugh's house, which he had long supposed was 'some work of witchcraft from him'.[29]

Meanwhile, away from the meeting house, Thomas Cooper the

carpenter was tasked with keeping watch on Mary – not that they feared she would escape, rather that Pynchon still hoped her imps might come to her, inducing her to confess.[30] By now, perhaps, Mary was absorbed by the secret fantasy of being a witch, by the knowledge, as yet undisclosed, that Satan had sublimated her soul, allowing her to frolic on Stebbins's lot without leaving the alehouse. The guilt of witchcraft, even of murder, may have slipped into the thrill of notoriety – a desperate, reckless thrill considering the prospect of damnation lying just beyond. For having become a witch surely precluded any possibility – the possibility that gave her life meaning – that she was a Saint, predestined for salvation and an eternity of paradise.[31]

Cooper was sceptical about witchcraft, but could plainly see Mary's anxiety: a stew of contrition and rage. After all, this was a woman who, moved by whatever wicked desperation, had killed her own child. She spoke freely with him, admitting that she felt 'hampered' by everything she'd said against her husband – and was sorry for it, but his silence had left her no choice. 'If that dumb dog would but have spoken it would have been better with me,' she said. Why didn't he confess instead of just standing there, muttering like a fool? What kind of a man was he? The lament became a rant, until Cooper sensed that she no longer regretted anything. No: she was eager for the next hearing, when she would have it out with Hugh. 'If I might but speak with him before Mr Pynchon face to face,' Mary railed, 'I would make that dumb dog to speak!' A dumb dog: the term for an ignorant preacher, which Mary had heard William Wroth use at Llanvaches, now resurfacing from her past. If Hugh was the ignorant preacher, she would play the confessing Saint, seeking spiritual reconciliation with her neighbours and her own guilty self, even if her earthly life was over. New England magistrates had been known to treat penitential murderers with sympathy, reserving the ultimate judgement for God.[32]

Like George Colton, Cooper blenched to hear Mary dishonour her husband. She was a confessed murderer: that was horrific enough. But heinous crimes were believed to originate in the unnatural rebellions of disordered households as well as in disordered minds. Mary's slurs against Hugh, thought Cooper, had to be challenged. 'Methinks, if he were a witch there would some apparent sign or mark of it,' he told Mary, 'for they say witches have teats upon some part or other of their body.' And yet, he continued, Hugh had been examined and no such mark found. To this Mary replied: 'It is not always so.' For a heartbeat, she retreated: how would she know any-way? – 'I have no skill in witchery.' But perhaps, she then thought to herself, Hugh experienced the devil much as she had done that time in the alehouse. 'The devil may come into his body only like a wind and so go forth again,' she explained, 'for so the devil told me that night.' Then she recounted, for the first time in full, what had hap-pened to her in the alehouse. Satan came to her, she said, and eased her fear of becoming a witch: 'And so', she said, 'I consented.' Cooper listened to this fresh revelation in horror. Mary went on to describe cavorting in the darkness with Hugh, Goodwife Sewell and Goodwife Merrick, their faces lit by the campfire. 'We were sometimes like cats and sometimes in our own shape,' she said, and made merry – although the other witches had ticked her off for speaking indiscreetly. Cooper was shocked, hardly able to speak – but he did, at least, have a new piece of the story to share with William Pynchon.[33]

On Monday 17 March John Lombard turned up at Pynchon's house, wanting to make a statement. He began by telling Pynchon how his missing trowel had reappeared in Hugh Parsons's presence, saying, 'I verily think it came thither by witchcraft.' Then he said he'd overheard Hugh and Mary say that 'the corn which they paid to the Widow Marshfield for the slander would do her no good', and that Hugh was discontented about being refused hay by George Langton. As Lombard gave his statement, a few doors up from Pyn-chon's house Sarah Miller was having more fits. The butcher Miles Morgan, his wife Prudence and Griffith Jones held her as she shook and struck and kicked. 'Get thee gone, Hugh Parsons, get thee gone,' she bawled. 'If thou wilt not go, I will go to Mr Pynchon and he shall have thee away!'[34]

The next day, Tuesday the 18th, the townsfolk poured back into the meeting house. Hugh Parsons was brought in for a second examination, this time in the presence of his wife, who, having already confessed to murder and witchcraft, was now just a prosecution witness against her husband. She was not, perhaps, the most reliable witness; but who else in the town knew Hugh Parsons better? Not everything hinged on Mary, however. By now most households contained someone who had turned against him: at least thirty-five townsfolk had already testified or were about to, some for the second or third time: after a fortnight of speculation, Pynchon had to verify the accusations. The Bedorthas repeated their evidence, as instructed, but again Hugh was silent. Mercy Marshfield recalled the 'lamentable torment' of Blanche's labour, how she had screamed as if 'pricked with knives'. Marshfield had seen many women suffer with babies twisted in the womb, twins, stillbirths and monsters – but never anything like this, and she had feared Blanche would die. The Bedorthas also told of the spectral dog their son saw crouched beneath a stool or the baby's cradle, which, said Goody Bedortha, had to be some present evil from Hugh Parsons. Her husband stressed the boy's utter terror, saying, 'He will often speak of it and point at it with such earnestness that he hath often made me afraid.'[35]

Nothing new was learned, but Pynchon was set on doing things the English magistrate's way, collecting evidence by an informal, intuitive, even rather haphazard, process of enquiry – not, as in most European states, according to prescribed rules, and using the thumbscrew and the rack. Proving felony in Old and New England largely depended on witnesses testifying on oath, and the trust placed in such oaths, which is why Pynchon had upheld the Marshfields' action for slander against Mary Parsons. Yet sworn testimony would not perhaps be enough for the Boston court, where a crime like witchcraft was concerned. For, unlike other heinous crimes, witchcraft bore what one authority called 'no reality of fact': it rarely left significant physical evidence, and its perpetrators were never caught in flagrante.[36]

Therefore, Hugh Parsons would most likely have to betray himself, through confession or some accidental admission. Hugh, though, was a man of few words – quick with curses and threats, but tight-lipped when required to explain his actions. Pynchon had been brought up to know that words offended more often than silence: the man who restrained his tongue also restrained his emotions and preserved order. On the other hand, silence might also come from stupidity. As one Jacobean writer put it, 'You see clowns or dull persons not able to speak in a wide company.'[37] Hugh, though, was far from stupid: he was sharp-witted and kept his own counsel. Yet this silence, by pushing him even further from his neighbours, came across as incriminating. Dalton's *Countrey Justice* taught Pynchon that witches were so 'hardened and sealed up against all touch' that even under interrogation they might say nothing, and that he should watch for 'blushing, looking downwards, silence'.[38]

Considering his prisoner with a shrewd eye, Pynchon scribbled a note: 'Hugh Parsons, having heard all these testimonies alleged, stood still at this second examination as at the first and made no answer.' Then he leafed through his papers to the testimony given by Mary against her husband. 'Your wife saith that she suspects you may be the cause of all the evil that is befallen to Mr Moxon's children,' said Pynchon. Had Hugh not, after all, been annoyed by the minister's insistence that he supply chimney bricks according to their contract? Mary says, Pynchon continued, that 'you vowed to be even with him or he shall get nothing by it'. The meeting house was silent, expectant. At last Hugh gave his answer, gently contradicting his wife. 'I said not that I would be even with him,' he said of his response to Moxon, 'but this I said: if he would hold me to my bargain, I could pussle him' – meaning outwit him. John Matthews cut in to say that he too had heard Hugh threaten Moxon, to which Hugh made no comment.[39] Now Pynchon brought in Moxon himself, who testified that it was just after the row that his daughter Martha started having fits. However, Moxon admitted, details of who said what to whom were not sharp in his mind. He remembered Hugh refusing to honour their deal but was unsure he had actually cursed him. Even so, Moxon was certain about 'the ill purpose of his former threatening'.[40]

Ticking off the charges on his sheet, Pynchon questioned Hugh again about Sarah Edwards's allegation that he had slept in the long meadow. Realizing that Sarah's husband would swear to the truth of this, Hugh admitted 'that he lay a night there in planting time about the end of May'. Clearly his memory, like Moxon's, was not infallible. William Pynchon followed this with his own account of Alexander Edwards informing him about the queer-looking milk. 'He was persuaded the cow was bewitched by Hugh Parsons,' Pynchon recalled, 'but I did not believe him at that time. I rather conceived that the cow was falling into some dangerous sickness.' However, when the cow remained healthy, Pynchon had changed his mind: 'Such a sudden change could not come from a natural cause,' he concluded, and he had told Hugh Parsons as much at the time.[41]

After hearing about Griffith Jones's knives, all of which Hugh again denied, Pynchon returned to the substantive business of Hugh's anger. Had he not, he asked again, threatened his wife with a piece of wood? Not on the occasion she claimed, came the reply. But surely it could have been then, insisted Pynchon: hadn't he recently told her that if he ever got into trouble it would be because of her, even that she had the power to hang him? She may well say that, remarked Hugh, given 'she is the worst enemy I have – considering the relation that is between us'. When anyone spoke evil of him, Hugh went on, Mary was only too ready to join in. And, Pynchon persisted, was he not angry because she wished ruin upon all New England's witches? On this point, Hugh kept his characteristic silence.[42]

Now Pynchon asked Mary's opinion of her husband. She hesitated. The crowd leaned in. Mary cleared her throat. 'I have often entreated him to confess whether he were a witch or no,' she replied earnestly. 'I told him that if he would acknowledge it I would beg the prayers of God's people on my knees.' Then she primly echoed Pynchon's heresy about the meritorious price of redemption. 'We are not our own,' she said, 'we are bought with a price.' This was God's bargain for freeing people from Satan and expunging their sins.[43]

Pynchon turned to Hugh Parsons. Was this true? he asked. Did your wife ask you to confess to witchcraft? Hugh and Mary were now both standing, like characters in a tragedy, alone on the stage before a riveted audience. Hugh said he had no memory of any such entreaty. Mary at once rounded on him: 'Did not I speak to you of it upon the death of my child? Did not I tell you then that I had jealousies that you had bewitched your own child to death?' Her furious words hung in the air; there was no answer. Sustaining the momentum of his interrogation, Pynchon quickly asked Anthony Dorchester if he had been aware of Mary's suspicions when he lodged with them. He replied she had never told him directly – but he knew her mind. Mary then said it was not just Samuel that Hugh had bewitched. When Joshua was sick, she told Hugh that she suspected he had bewitched him too. Nor had she made a secret of her feelings but had broadcast them throughout the town.[44]

For the rows of townsfolk immersed in the drama, this was the strangest thing they had ever seen in Springfield. A confessed witch accusing her husband of the same crime: it was unheard of. Turning the screw yet further, Pynchon put it to Hugh that 'he might well be suspected to have bewitched his former child to death, because he expressed no kind of sorrow at the death of it'. By this point, Hugh knew perfectly well that the mismanagement of his emotions was the crux of the charge. Everything else was circumstantial, lacking in corroboration – but his apparent absence of love and grief looked like murderous intent in a man already suspected as a witch. Whatever his inward feelings, to the wider community, it was the visible manifestation of feelings towards the little victim – his own flesh and blood – that counted. Hugh explained solemnly that he had been 'loath to express any sorrow before his wife, because of the weak condition that she was in'. Struggling to contain himself, he had fled the piteous scene where his child lay dead, returning to the fields to weep alone. In turmoil, his first thought had been that family and neighbours would think him unmanly for crying – not acting like a man should. He had thought his devastation was implicit: it had literally gone without saying.[45]

At this juncture, with crashing obtuseness, Moxon interjected: if Hugh and his wife had already shared their distress when Samuel lay sick, why 'should he forbear to express the affection of sorrow before her'? Why did he think his tears would grieve her more? Hugh retorted that Mary might well wonder why he tried to hide his true feelings, yet a desire to protect her 'was the true reason of it'. Pynchon asked why, if he had been so worried, he didn't show more respect for his family, but instead 'went into the long meadow and lay there all night when his child lay at the point of death.' Hugh didn't reply.[46]

Pynchon's quartermaster George Colton was as mystified as his employer. He had seen Samuel Parsons's shrivelled genitals, knew how Hugh nagged Mary, demanding more and more of her, and shared Thomas Cooper's concern that she said 'very harsh things against him before his face . . . as are not ordinary for persons to speak one of another'. More alarmingly still, Hugh had said nothing to contradict his own acerbic wife, whereas, Colton supposed, 'if he had been innocent he would have blamed her for her speeches'. Pynchon looked at Hugh: Well? With a shrug of resignation, he said he was used to the abuse: 'he had such speeches from her daily and therefore he made the less of it'. Hugh also denied needing her help with the harvest, and had 'set her not about business' except to bring in the maize that he stacked by the door. On the contrary, worried she would exhaust herself, he had 'bid her do less'.[47]

Could Anthony Dorchester, the Parsonses' former tenant, attest to this generosity of spirit? Dorchester replied that he never known Hugh tell Mary not to work – except when she nursed his sick wife, 'which work did not bring any profit to him'. What about Hugh's claim that he stoppered his emotions to spare Mary in her frailty? Dorchester scoffed at the idea: 'He never feared either to grieve or displease his wife.' Pynchon turned to Hugh: Did you do anything to comfort your wife over the death of her child? He didn't answer, so Mary spoke for him: 'No, he did nothing to comfort me, but still when he came home he kept ado at me to throw in the corn.' This was no way to treat a wife: that much was clear to the assembly.

And in fact, Mary added, Hugh had made things worse. 'When I saw my husband in this frame of mind,' she said, 'it added more grief to my sorrow.' Dorchester nodded: this was all true. Asked by Pynchon about Hugh's reaction to Samuel's death, Colton said, 'He showed no natural sorrow' – which Jonathan Burt, who had brought Hugh the news, verified.[48]

Colton spoke confidently about Springfield's emotional expectations and refused to believe Hugh could have been so composed had he been genuinely upset. Now Hugh, who spoke so rarely, was suddenly eager to be heard. He implored Benjamin Cooley to testify to his anguish when he had invited him to Samuel's burial, at which time Hugh could barely 'speak to him for weeping'. All eyes fell upon Cooley. Had someone seen Hugh cry after all? This mattered, not least because witches, with their imbalanced humours and hot, parched bodies, were thought to be incapable of shedding tears.[49] Cooley didn't remember him appearing to be sad, only that he had been casually smoking his pipe. Exasperated, Hugh swore to Pynchon that he had cared deeply about Samuel. He begged Sarah Cooley to tell everyone about the first time Samuel had been ill, when he had run 'barefoot and barelegged, and with tears' to her house. Goodwife Cooley simply replied that they had suspected Samuel was bewitched because of the choking lump in his throat. Other signs confirmed that the child's sickness was unnatural. Mary Ashley and Sarah Leonard testified that what they called the baby's 'secrets' had rotted away.[50]

The day continued in this vein: witnesses rehearsing suspicions on which Hugh was asked to comment in his wife's presence. Goodwife Ashley recounted Mary's unusual episode in the alehouse. Cooley and Dorchester described Hugh fighting the devil in his dreams.[51] Francis Pepper said Mary told him her husband had bewitched his cow. When John Lombard spoke about his trowel, Hugh just 'stood dumb and answered no more'. He admitted wanting Anthony Dorchester's meat, but had no idea – any more than an unborn child, he said – what had happened to it. When someone suggested that Mary might be the thief, Pynchon said he considered her presence in the meeting house at the time to be a reasonable alibi. This left the small matter of Hugh abandoning his family in the street. Where had he gone, Pynchon asked, and why hadn't he returned until the end of the meeting? Hugh looked blank. He didn't recall going anywhere, except perhaps to Merrick's for a smoke; and, besides, who could say he only came back at the end? He might have been there all along, standing unseen in the doorway. None could gainsay that.[52]

Then came the moment when Pynchon asked Mary Parsons to sum up why she believed her husband was a witch. Her response electrified the meeting house. First, she maintained, Hugh always knew what she had been talking about – including with Anne Smith, Pynchon's daughter, whose discretion was beyond question. Secondly, Hugh's return home after long absence was heralded by strange noises, while he was often 'in a distempered frame' and abused her. Pynchon asked if she had ever known Hugh 'do anything beyond the power of nature' – the charge on which the Carringtons had been convicted at Hartford. She told the story of the marsh dog she saw at twilight, and her suspicion that 'it was done by witchcraft from my husband'. The misfortunes of Hugh's enemies, she said, made for even more compelling proof. She glanced over at Thomas Miller, whose leg was still bandaged from the accident in the woods. 'I am sorry . . . for that poor man,' she said, noting that his injury had occurred just two days after he argued with her husband about a land sale. Hugh was impassive, including when Miller himself limped before the assembly and said his piece.[53]

That long Tuesday in the meeting house ended with stories of bodily torment. Miller told of his wife Sarah's rigid-limbed seizures, backed by others who attested how she had screamed at a vision of Hugh Parsons.[54] John Stebbins described his wife's fit after seeing Hugh Parsons up their chimney, which his father – who, like William Pynchon, had been born in Essex in the 1590s at the height of the witch-trials there – swore was true.[55] Stebbins's co-tenant, William Brooks, saw Goodwife Stebbins collapse as the constable led Hugh Parsons past her gate. Merrick corroborated this story, then, with his wife Sarah, told the room how Hugh had asked for his swollen stomach to be pierced to release the pressure. Hugh seemed puzzled by the suggestion, remembering only that 'he had a pain in his belly'.[56]

Pynchon wrapped up the hearing, and the meeting house emptied. But the pre-trial proceedings were not quite over. Four days later, on Saturday 22 March, Jonathan Taylor, victim of the snake demon, went to see William Pynchon. With him were Mercy Marshfield, John Lombard and the constable Thomas Merrick, whom Pynchon promptly dispatched to fetch the prisoners in order that they could hear what was being said against them. Taylor was especially keen to see Hugh Parsons punished: indeed, this was the latest in a string of visits he had made to Pynchon's house. Merrick returned with Hugh and Mary. Eyeing them warily, Taylor said that on the day of Mary's arrest Hugh told him in Merrick's barn that 'he had often been afraid that his wife was a witch' and wished she would let him search her body. Pynchon recorded this and turned to Widow Marshfield, who took the opportunity once again to say that Hugh had given her 'threatening speeches that he uttered with much anger'. The following spring, Marshfield continued, her daughter had been struck down with 'fits of witchcraft', which Lombard confirmed. There was a pause: so far, neither prisoner had said anything. Then Hugh frowned at Mercy Marshfield: 'when did I give such threatening words?' he asked. Pynchon answered for her: it was when he had brought the corn as compensation for his wife's slander. Unable to remember, Hugh said that if he had remonstrated with Marshfield it was only because he believed his wife had been falsely accused.[57]

And you, Goodwife Parsons, asked Pynchon, what do you say to this? Through a welter of thoughts and memories, muddled by exhaustion, Mary recalled that winter day. Hugh had come home in a sulphurous mood about Widow Marshfield's intransigence. But of course the truth was that she *had* slandered Mercy Marshfield – and ironically so, considering that now she herself had confessed to dealing with Satan, with her husband beside her similarly accused.[58]

As the light faded, the Sabbath began. William Pynchon gathered his papers and scraped back his chair. He would hear no more testimony until next week. He instructed Jonathan Taylor to watch over Mary until daybreak: perhaps, after all, her imps would come to feed – as the executed Margaret Jones's had in Boston – or would threaten her to stop her talking.[59] Not that this mattered much now: Pynchon had everything in his file he imagined the General Court would need. And so it was to Boston that the proceedings would now move. The enormity of Hugh and Mary's crimes had finally outgrown the fretful, furious town of Springfield.

8.   *Converse with the Devil*

Sunrise on 24 March: the last day of the calendrical year, a border-land between pale winter and spring's revival. Mary sat in the cart beside her husband, their hands tied, ready to be transported to Boston for trial. Dust was already settling in their deserted house, the hearth cold and greasy; rodents were bolder now, undisturbed by their hosts. The bed where Hugh had writhed in pain now lay empty, as did the crib where Samuel withered and died. Mary had worked so hard to turn the place into a home – stitching and sweeping, making and mending, hauling water, feeding her children, washing, drying and smoothing linen. Then the evenings Hugh returned home from the fields, stretching aching limbs by the fire, draining the beer she poured for him, while she sat there gazing into his silence, trying to divine his mood. Lightly she told him the small things of the day, yearning for his interest, hoping she might draw kindness from him. Also hanging in the past now, not long gone but as dead as legends, were the days when he raged – raising Cain and, she thought, the devil as well. In those four walls she had stared at her thoughts until they took shape as monsters and devils, and she expressed a wish to see the ruin of all witches. And with that desire, through her smothering melancholy, and under the weight of Hugh's fury, she became a witch herself. A few had seen appari-tions, others demons that entered people's bodies and shook them. But Hugh and Mary knew ghosts: the spirits of remorse that now circled them continually.

Hugh and Mary waited in blank, awful silence: bound together in their fate, estranged from each other and the world. Doubtless Han-nah was elsewhere. Now an orphan in all but name, her innocence was enlarged by her parents' sins. Urged forward, the horses broke into a walk, and the cart clattered slowly down the main street towards the causeway over the hassocky marsh, the start of a spine-jolting hundred-mile trek along the Bay Path to Boston.

William Pynchon had informed Hugh and Mary that they were to face trial by the magistrates of the colony, the charges against them too grave for Pynchon to adjudicate himself. Besides, Pynchon realized, his authority in the community, perhaps beyond, had been dented by the heresy charges against him – charges that he too would soon have to answer in Boston. Now, Springfield went about its business more calmly, as if a boil had been pricked and drained of poisonous corruption. No misgivings were apparent on the part of the townsfolk, no twinge of hypocritical regret, just neighbours with a keen eye on the property that Hugh and Mary had vacated: Jonathan Burt, long interested in the Parsons homelot and garden; the constable Thomas Merrick hankering after other lands that might be available if the property were broken up. The only unease that lingered among the townsfolk was the thought that life would not fully return to normal until the outcasts had been hanged.

To Springfielders, the effects of Hugh and Mary's witchcraft remained all too visibly present. They manifested in the behaviour of Mary Parsons's namesake, the frantic wandering wife of Joseph Parsons. The paroxysms into which she and others had fallen in the meeting house were as severe as ever. Her husband called her 'a distracted woman', who ran around madly, then 'would fall down like one dead'; regaining consciousness, she raved uncontrollably, striking herself and others. By now Joseph had taken to imprisoning his wife in the cellar at night, whereupon she would hurl her bedding at the locked hatch, screaming in her Devon accent that 'the cellar was full of spirits'. But it wasn't just at night when the spirits came. One time, she was washing clothes in the brook when they appeared, like a row of rag dolls silently watching her. Her terror triggered a fit. She came to her senses prostrate in the meadow, with no idea how she got there: an experience that happened with increasing frequency. On another occasion, she shrieked that 'the witches would kill them' unless they hid. Her marriage was as fraught as in the other Parsons household. John Matthews had overheard Joseph accusing his wife of being 'led by an evil spirit', to which she snarled that if that were so, he was to blame for locking her up with demons. She was in a frenzy.[1]

Sarah Miller likewise had more fits, saw more apparitions. On 27 March, three days after Hugh and Mary were taken to Boston, she was at Prudence Morgan's house, opposite hers on the lane to the upper wharf. Her body began to jerk and shake; then, recovering a little, she stared out towards Thomas Cooper's farmstead. 'Look you,' she said, pointing, 'there is a man at Goodman Cooper's barn.' Prudence couldn't see anyone. 'You might see him if you would,' chided Sarah. 'But now he is gone.' After a brief seizure, she again saw the sinister figure. Sarah's brother Samuel arrived and assured her there was no one on Cooper's land, but she would not be swayed. Prudence asked her to describe him. 'It is one in a red waistcoat and a lined cap,' came the reply. 'It is like Hugh Parsons.' He was beckoning with a curling finger, she said, and 'would have me come to him'. He did dress exactly like that, Prudence acknowledged. But, as they all knew, Hugh was in Boston, probably already in gaol.[2]

Shortly afterwards, Prudence Morgan visited William Pynchon to discuss Sarah's disconcerting behaviour. With her went the Bedorthas, who even now hadn't finished saying their piece. Blanche again told of the time when she butted into her husband's conversation with Hugh, Reece insisting that he was 'much offended' but was used to Hugh speaking that way. Pynchon had heard all this before but diligently noted it down – as if he understood that the seismic upheaval of Hugh and Mary's crimes must have its aftershocks.[3]

Spring came early. The April days were mild and fresh, work quickened, and traffic returned to the river, soon teeming with shad and salmon. William Pynchon began streamlining his affairs, selling what he could and ceding various responsibilities. He continued to record scraps of testimony about the Parsonses, such as Thomas Cooper's recollection of watching Mary, when she claimed to have attended a witches' sabbath on John Stebbins's lot.[4] These additional testimonies would in due course be sent to Boston to be added to the file that had gone with the prisoners. For Pynchon, the Parsons affair was now in the hands of God and the courts – though, like his own travails, yet to be concluded. Not only must he, in effect, serve as a court prosecutor on behalf of his witnesses but he still had to atone for his own sins by publicly repudiating his book. Gossip in Springfield about witchcraft and heresy in the town implied some vague yet unmistakable diabolic link between the two. In Boston, the connection was never made explicit, but the swift severity of Pynchon's censure was a sign of how concerned the authorities were about Satan's gains in western New England.[5] And in Springfield itself the danger had not yet passed.

It was the Sabbath, Sunday 6 April 1651, and Jonathan Taylor had two things on his mind. He sat in the meeting house reflecting on the dreadful events of five weeks earlier, preparing a detailed account of the conversation he had had with Hugh in Merrick's barn, which he was to give to Pynchon the next day. His second preoccupation was his wife, at home in the throes of labour, attended by female neighbours and watched by her namesake daughter, now eighteen months old. At last, word came from the birthing chamber that the Taylors had been blessed with another daughter, and all was well.[6]

On Monday morning Jonathan arrived in William Pynchon's parlour, where the magistrate sat waiting, pen in hand, a ream of paper on his table. He asked Taylor to begin. It was, Taylor recalled, 27 February, at a time when Mary was under arrest but her husband was still at liberty. Hugh had asked who accused him, to which Taylor had replied: 'I cannot tell.' Parsons had then demanded, testily: 'Why do you say so? You can tell, I know you can tell. Was it ever known that a man should be accused and not know his accusers? Tell me who they are!' Taylor was reluctant, but Hugh kept on at him, swearing to keep his secret. Writing this down, Pynchon asked Taylor what he had said next to Hugh. Taylor remembered his words being: 'I wonder why you are so earnest with me to tell you. You will know soon enough. I will not tell you anything, but . . . I believe your wife will be your biggest accuser.' It was then that the two men had seen Mary being escorted by the constable. 'It is like I shall be examined now,' was all Hugh had said.[7]

Taylor went on to relate how, that evening, he had been in Sarah Merrick's cellar. The peg in the beer barrel was stiff, so he knocked it with a piece of wood but still couldn't twist it out. Goody Merrick laughed, saying, 'I will fetch it out with my little finger', which she did, just as Hugh appeared. Taylor asked his host, now a suspect, if she were a witch – even though he didn't really think she was. The rest of Taylor's statement concerned the venomous snake demon, which had appeared in the night with a bite that 'pricked like a needle' and the voice of the equally venomous Hugh Parsons. Taylor was anxious that, had she seen it, his pregnant wife's life might have been endangered. As it was, Taylor had suffered, 'as if one limb had been rent from another', and had suffered 'griping pains' ever since. Pynchon also heard new evidence relating to events on the night Taylor had watched Mary. All this convinced him that Taylor could be a key witness at the trial in Boston.[8]

Jonathan Taylor went home to his family, relieved to unburden himself of these dark stories and glad to oil the wheels of justice. But perhaps he was also unsettled about having fired a salvo of evidence at his nemesis, whose wickedness would remain as long as he drew breath. And so it transpired. A fortnight later, the Taylors' baby Anna, little more than a week old, sickened in a way they could not conceive to be natural. Jonathan and Mary agonized and prayed. It did no good. Anna died and was buried on the Sabbath, 20 April. Her distraught parents were convinced that Hugh Parsons, perhaps in league with his wife, had sent some vengeful magic soaring through the Massachusetts air.[9]

The trial was still some weeks off, but now Taylor was determined to see Hugh Parsons hang. Pynchon invited him to come to Boston with the other witnesses to give evidence. Not everyone had accepted. They would be away for several days, and it was hard for men to abandon their work, and women their children, even if the court reimbursed them.[10] But Taylor did. Others who felt compelled to go included Mercy Marshfield, whose vendetta against

Hugh and Mary burned in her heart, for her own sake and that of her daughter, son-in-law and friend Blanche Bedortha. They had all suffered. Mercy's son Samuel would keep her company and was resolved to testify himself. Hannah Langton also agreed to go, as did Simon Beamon, to support his master. Henry Smith would remain in Springfield as acting magistrate, though not yet with the authority that Pynchon would request for him in Boston. George Moxon also stayed behind, even though one of the charges against Mary or Hugh would surely be the bewitching of his daughters. Pynchon assured his loyal friend that he would look after his interests. At the end of April, the party made preparations to leave.[11]

A rite of spring, traditionally marked with processions and dancing, May Day festivities had been suppressed in Old and New England as 'a heathenish vanity, generally abused to superstition and wickedness'.[12] The devil had a stake in pagan idolatry – and besides, there were no holidays in the Bible. Better to use the time fighting Satan than flattering him. There was certainly no question of a celebration for Springfield's small, solemn band of witnesses when they arrived in Boston that week, although beneath their commitment to Christian duty lay an ebullition of vengeance. The early May skies were bright and clear, as William Pynchon and his party settled in lodgings near the courthouse. The prospect of testifying was nerve-racking, but Pynchon briefed them carefully as to what would be expected. His own thoughts flitted between the case against Hugh and Mary Parsons and the charge of heresy hanging over his head. He knew the timing was more than coincidence. To appear as both prosecutor and defendant in the same week was humiliating: a stratagem, no doubt, by the authorities to expose the impossibility of his own future in America.

Together the General Court and the Court of Assistants made up a two-tier trial and appeal tribunal for the Massachusetts Bay Colony: like a governing body with the powers of English courts combined.[13] The General Court had a mainly legislative function but heard appeals when the magistrates – the Assistants, that is – failed to agree or disagreed with juries.[14] Presumably because Mary Parsons had already confessed, her case went straight to the General Court, the spring session of which would commence at 8 a.m. on Thursday 8 May.

Early that morning, Pynchon guided Jonathan Taylor, Mercy Marshfield and the others through the already busy streets into the square between Treamont Street and Cornhill. Boston awed them as a metropolis of confidence and grandeur – and of varied sounds and smells and colours – compared to the more roughly hewn environment of Springfield. Nervous now, they passed the hulking prison where Hugh and Mary Parsons awaited their fate.

The courtroom was an intimidating place, with whitewashed walls and dark wood fixtures, equal parts majesty and misery. Facing the platform where witnesses appeared was the jury bench occupied by twelve freeholders of the city. Spectators crammed into the creaking gallery, alive with excitement at the prospect of the sensational hearing ahead. The clerk ordered 'all rise'; the noise subsided. Three judges, sombre in black gowns and caps, entered the chamber and sat on their dais, the table before them stacked with papers and books. The chief justice was John Endecott, a West Countryman, who had succeeded John Winthrop as governor. Compared to Old England, New England relied less heavily on jurors, who, after all, lacked the magistrate's special warrant from God to discover truth. Instead, more like inquisitors, they would inquire earnestly into the facts of character, relationship and event, and find guilt in the recesses of a defendant's heart. The pressure to confess could be too much, all resistance broken by the promise of compassion for unburdened sinners. New England held dear its rituals of contrition: tear-soaked dramas, where the servant's renewed obedience banished the master's wrath, and grace could be seen, not merely felt.[15]

Gawpers hoping to see a witch paraded before their eyes were disappointed. The bench received word from the gaol that Mary Parsons had fallen sick – too sick to appear, in fact. This, the judges grudgingly accepted, with the proviso that she must be tried soon:

afraid she would die if they waited too long, Endecott granted a day's grace.[16]

The Mary Parsons witchcraft case dovetailed with the other business at hand: the matter of William Pynchon's heresy. Later that same day, the bench invited Pynchon to a meeting with the minister John Norton, who had been commissioned to refute the egregious arguments of his book *The Meritorious Price of Our Redemption*. John Cotton, a venerable cleric from Boston in Lincolnshire, would also attend. Cotton had written the Massachusetts law code, which held that heretics deserved to die, like idolaters and witches, because they sought 'to thrust the souls of men from the Lord their God'. Norton and Cotton proposed that a minister of Pynchon's choosing also join them. The agenda would be the composition of a short, precise retraction of Pynchon's book, which they urged Pynchon to make, in order to clear his name. The possible consequences of his refusal to comply were not spelled out, but included banishment, imprisonment or worse. When they met that evening, the conclave was relieved to hear that Pynchon accepted the orthodox position – at least to outward appearances.[17]

The next morning the court session resumed, but again Endecott was told that Mary Parsons was unfit for trial. Reluctantly, the judges postponed until the 13th, four days' time. The Springfield witnesses, keyed up for justice, would have to wait, occupying themselves in Boston as best they could – although some felt compelled to return home. One of those who remained was Jonathan Taylor, who would see the matter to its end. It was Friday now; the case was scheduled for Tuesday. Pynchon had to stay in order to present Taylor to the court and finish his own statement of retraction, which the court was expecting, signed and sealed, on the 13th. He braced himself to be put on the stand, in the same shameful spot as the witch who he himself had sent to the court, and on the same day.[18]

Boston gaol was a sullen stone fortress with dripping walls three feet thick and doors of iron-studded oak that echoed like thunder when slammed. Contemporaries compared it to a grave for the living, the valley of the shadow of death and the suburbs of hell. It reeked of human waste and despair. The cells were partitioned by heavy planks, vertically arranged, the tiny unglazed windows latticed with iron bars.[19] Around seven in the morning on Tuesday 13 May, the keeper unlocked the room where Mary Parsons had been held for the past seven weeks. Her health, already poor, had deteriorated. She lay on a bed of dank, flattened straw, rarely changed. In the corner was an unspeakable wooden bucket. What physical affliction had joined her mental illness is unclear – perhaps typhus, caused by overcrowding and dirt and lice, and known as 'gaol fever'. This morning she was still unfit for trial, but the court couldn't wait any longer. The gaoler led Mary out of the prison, into the square and across the way. They entered the sessions building, then into its main chamber.

From the languor of the dungeon to the clamour of the courtroom; from faeces and sweat to the scent of beeswax and herbs to ward off infection; from wailing to chatter; and shadowy gloom to the high-ceilinged brightness of plain white walls. Cowed by the austere splendour of the chamber, Mary squinted at the boxed-in seating, bobbing with heads in hats and wigs, and above, on the dais, the judges, all heavy robes and flint-like faces. They were men of godly conviction, yet also cool rationality: they saw hard facts (or their absence) beneath the froth of emotion – the sort of emotion that had dominated proceedings in Springfield.

Mary's cloudy eyes surveyed the room. She saw William Pynchon and Henry Smith, Pynchon clutching copies of the depositions, his renunciation of heresy in his pocket. Mary Parsons shuffled to the low-railed bar, where the gaoler removed her chains so that, according to custom, she could be tried as a free woman. She was dishevelled, stooped; her time in prison seemed to have added years to her. The clerk asked her to look upon the jury, to see if there was any man she objected to. She shook her head. Then he read out the first of two indictments against her: one for witchcraft, the other for murdering her son.[20] By the name of Mary Parsons, began the clerk, she was charged in the name of the commonwealth that without the fear of God before her eyes she had allowed herself to be seduced by the devil. She now stood arraigned for covenanting with a familiar spirit, and at the end of February last, in Springfield, using 'diverse devilish practices by witchcraft to the hurt of the persons of Martha and Rebecca Moxon, against the word of God and all the laws of this jurisdiction'.[21]

A hush settled over the court, all eyes on the bewildered figure supporting herself on the bar as the clerk solicited her plea. The Springfield contingent hoped Mary would repeat her confession of witchcraft, thus sparing them as witnesses and allowing the judges to proceed directly to sentencing. But she didn't: she pleaded not guilty. As shocked chatter broke out around the courtroom, Mary feebly held up her right hand and, as convention dictated, murmured her willingness to be tried by God and her fellow countrymen. After all, she had never confessed to hurting George Moxon's daughters, for which she blamed her husband. Furthermore, although she persisted in her accusation of Hugh, Bess Sewell and Sarah Merrick, she denied being a witch herself, despite admitting back in Springfield that she had allowed the devil to enter her body. Now, through his star witness Jonathan Taylor, Pynchon had the hard task of convincing Boston's level-headed judges and jurors that Mary was guilty. No witch had been executed in Massachusetts Bay Colony since Margaret Jones, three years earlier, at which time Pynchon himself had been one of the judges.[22]

Then the court proceeded to hear the testimony of thirty townsfolk – stories all too familiar in Springfield, but told for the first time in sceptical Boston. Of these thirty witnesses, however, only seven were present, the words of the rest submitted in writing only, albeit authenticated by Pynchon. Accusations that had felt incontrovertibly true in back Springfield, reinforced by so much passionate testimony, seemed more dubious in this city, where truth was weighed according to legal measures.[23]

Hannah Langton spoke first. The bench listened intently and patiently, waiting for evidential substance to emerge from a hotchpotch of trivia and inference. The strength of Hannah's story consisted mainly in the result of burning a piece of a bewitched pudding – but this could hardly be admitted in the General Court when counter-magic was itself illegal, even if Pynchon was persuaded of the spell's efficacy.[24] Next came Jonathan Taylor, whose story, heard previously only by Pynchon, was more compelling. He began by saying that two nights before Mary Parsons was brought to Boston, he had watched over her. She revealed that she had two things to tell him: firstly that she forgave him any wrong he had done her, and secondly that the snakes he had seen were 'three witches', one of whom was her husband. She hadn't named the other two, but clearly meant Goody Sewell and Goody Merrick. She had supposed that Taylor wouldn't believe her; perhaps no one would. 'I am counted but as a dreamer,' she said, 'but when this dreamer is hanged, then remember what I said to you: this town will not be clear yet.' That voice you heard, Mary continued: if you had believed its malediction – 'death' – you would have died. 'But seeing you spake to it and resisted it, it had not power to kill you.' Taylor had no idea, she assured him, how badly her husband wished him harm.[25]

This was powerful testimony from a man who had suffered so grievously, and who swore to have heard these words from Mary Parsons's own lips. Regardless of whether she herself was a reliable witness, Taylor's allegations bore the ring of truth. Furthermore, although on this occasion she had not confessed to being a witch, the authority behind Mary's knowledge had to come from some unholy alliance with her husband, who, in the eyes of the Springfield witnesses, if not yet the Boston court, definitely *was* a witch.

But, for all its homespun power, Taylor's evidence was flawed. The everyday detail of such testimony was what made it so convincing – but only in the sense that it proved witnesses to be sincere in their beliefs, not that it confirmed their beliefs to be true. Scepticism about what constituted reliable proof usually prevailed, as in Old England, where three-quarters of indictments against witches failed. Even if the judges were moved by Taylor's story, they detected little probative strength in it. Where, for example, was the second witness required in cases of felony? This was the same objection Hugh Parsons had put to William Pynchon during his interrogation – and might explain why the court secretary, Edward Rawson, noted that Taylor was 'ill sworn'.²⁶ And was Mary's confession that night to be trusted? None from Springfield could have declared on oath that she was sound in mind. Did Taylor's sincerity extend from anything other than fury and grief? Could the snakes have been a dream, or a hallucination – even one conjured by Satan? Might the death of his baby daughter not simply have been God recalling a soul to heaven? Such doubts were legion, and no judge or juror wanted innocent blood on his hands. When William Pynchon was growing up in Essex, in the last years of Elizabeth I's reign, a witch had been hanged at nearly every session of the assizes. But these days the heinousness of the crime could no longer be allowed to triumph over reasonable doubt, in Old or New England.²⁷

There was another problem with the case against Mary Parsons. Having conferred with the other judges, John Endecott announced with scholarly detachment that the real issue was that too few Springfield witnesses had come to testify in person. In English common law, the delivery of evidence affected its credibility: words scrawled on a page flattened out the truth, whereas words spoken to an audience with passion and a pointing finger might lead a court to what was called 'clear discovery'. But even then there needed to be *enough* testimony, from multiple witnesses, to be even half-sure, and, besides, this was witchcraft: that most difficult of crimes to prove, in any circumstance.²⁸

The trial, it seemed, was almost at an end. Mary remained at the bar, her body looking like it might crumple, her face a wan mask of such fatigue and despair she was almost indifferent to what was happening. Governor Endecott asked the jurors to retire to consider their verdict touching the first indictment, relating to the bewitch-ing of Rebecca and Martha Moxon. The spectators stayed seated, leaning across one another and turning round to discuss the case so far, until the jury returned, and Endecott called for quiet. The jurors had not kept the court waiting long: the decision was simple for these reasonable burghers. The foreman rose and cleared his throat, against an expectant hush. For all the suspicion that hung around

Mary Parsons, the foreman announced they had given her the benefit of the doubt, judging the evidence 'not sufficient to prove her a witch'. After the years of pain, fear and recrimination in Springfield, Endecott ordered that Mary be acquitted.[29]

There was fresh uproar in the courtroom. Mary remained expressionless, her hands resting limply on the bar. Pynchon and his witnesses looked at each other in dismay: what they knew to be true back in Springfield in Boston had been publicly declared untrue. What would happen now? Endecott again called for quiet: again the noise tailed off.

The clerk moved to the second indictment, which charged Mary with having in or near her own house 'wilfully and most wickedly', and at the devil's instigation, murdered her infant, Joshua Parsons. Once more the court waited tensely for her answer. She remained silent. Endecott pressed her for an answer. Perhaps her mind was blank – or perhaps she thought about Joshua, lifeless in her arms, and her sudden horror and confusion. Then, with the expectation of the room bearing down on her, at last she summoned the strength to speak. Guilty, she said. I'm guilty. Mary Parsons had confessed: there would be no trial.[30]

Infanticide was rebellion against nature: even snakes and wolves, it was said, cared for their young. Endecott knew well the cases of Anne Hett and Dorothy Talby, recorded by his predecessor John Winthrop. Hett, a cooper's wife, fearing that her sins were unpardonable, 'in a sad melancholic distemper near to frenzy' threw her child into a creek. Hett was spared execution; Talby was less fortunate. She had been a church member at Salem, who through 'melancholy or spiritual delusions' tried to kill her husband and children. Talby was whipped, but remained 'possessed with Satan' and was hanged in 1638.[31] Mary Parsons, the judges could see, displayed the same melancholic distemper as both these unfortunate women – perhaps caused by a culpable weakness that allowed Satan into her humours, where he could 'chop and change our imaginations'.[32] Within the precincts of her delusion, Mary understood her crime and believed the devil had done his bit. How else to make sense of it all? Bringing Satan into her life had made her murder her child, like the wretch who confessed that the fiend lay at her heart, so 'ravenous and greedy . . . that she cannot feed him fast enough'.[33]

The sins that had grown too great for Springfield now outgrew the world: Mary was fit only for a heavenly tribunal. John Endecott passed sentence accordingly. 'You shall be carried from this place to the place from whence you came', he declared, 'and from thence to the place of execution, and there hang till you be dead.' By now Mary was swaying, barely able to stand, which moved Endecott to grant her a reprieve until 29 May. Boston now had two weeks in which to look forward to the incomparable spectacle of a hanging.[34]

For godly magistrates and clergy, confession more than execution was the desired outcome of felony proceedings: confession removed recrimination and allowed God's mercy to flood in. But the people of Boston – its traders and artisans, sailors and stevedores – felt otherwise. Punishment, to them, was an exciting event; a confession, less so. They enjoyed seeing a felon like Mary drawn in a cart up Boston Hill, where to the beat of a drum she would be dragged down, then pushed up the gallows ladder. There, facing the crowd, a rope around her neck, her face covered with a sack, the preacher's words muffled by blood pumping in her ears, this confessed killer would be pushed off. The onlookers would watch in queasy horror as she choked, jerking around, all control of her bladder and bowels gone. But no one could ever be sure how things would play out. If Mary was penitent, it would be a moving sight; but resistance was also enthralling. Dorothy Talby had shown no repentance, and pulling the cloth from her face had refused spiritual comfort from the ministers. Swinging by her neck, twice she grabbed at the ladder as if to save herself, but then died like the rest.[35]

After Mary Parsons was carried back to the prison, William Pynchon was called to the bar, where he presented his written retraction to the court. In it, he bowed to the authority of the colony and to John Norton's wisdom. He admitted a degree of error and was glad to have a chance to justify himself to Cotton and Norton, to whom he explained his ideas 'to take off the worst construction', or interpretation, of their meaning. He accepted that Christ's death was not merely an act of obedience to a loving father, but God's 'due punishment of our sins by way of satisfaction to divine justice for man's redemption'. The court accepted Pynchon's recantation 'in a hopeful way . . . as a fruit of his ingenuity and a pledge of more full satisfaction': meaning that they would expect to receive a fuller, less equivocal statement of renunciation from him later in the year. Pynchon was then allowed to return to Springfield the following week 'respecting the present troubles of his family' – troubles that perhaps related to his daughter Anne being eight months pregnant, or which, perhaps, he had fabricated in order to escape the stifling atmosphere of Boston.[36]

Before Pynchon was dismissed, John Endecott ordered him to return on Tuesday 14 October to respond; and Norton presented him with a draft copy of his own book, which Pynchon accepted graciously. Ostensibly to allow him to read Norton's thesis properly, Pynchon requested that his stepson Henry Smith, Springfield's deputy magistrate, be invested with full powers to govern. The court granted this request. The real reason for asking for a break from his duties, however, was to give Pynchon enough time to prepare for his departure from New England and his return to the old country after more than twenty years – an outcome which the court may have been implicitly seeking.[37]

William Pynchon would never return to the General Court, nor would Mary Parsons go to the gallows. On a day that passed unrecorded, some time between the 13th and 29th of May, she died alone and uncomforted in prison, on a scatter of filthy straw. Mary was in her late thirties, perhaps forty. She hadn't seen her five-year-old daughter, Hannah, since she left Springfield two months earlier – nor, in that time, had she seen anyone she knew, apart from the few witnesses in the courtroom. The only mercy, though it can hardly have been a consolation, was that she had been spared the ordeal of a sordid, brutal public hanging. What happened to her body we can only guess. She may have been buried within the prison grounds or in some far corner of the burying ground in nearby Treamont

Street. There, she would have been tipped unceremoniously into a pit – her final resting place unmarked, unvisited, unremembered.[38]

This was the wretched end of Mary Parsons's arduous journey from the Welsh Marches to the American wilderness; through two abusive marriages, the loss of two babies and a twisted thicket of delusion, resentment and remorse. At the hour of her death, perhaps she saw heaven, or the figure of Mr Wroth, the good shepherd of Llanvaches, pointing that way. He had been the one truly decent man in her life, who faced down approaching demons, spread charity to all and rejoiced in the light of Christ's love.

By the time William Pynchon arrived home, Henry Smith had already assumed the role of magistrate, as his stepfather had instructed, and with Pynchon's return now had an official mandate. Townsfolk continued to come to Smith with testimony against Hugh Parsons: the stones of the rumour mill refused to stop grinding. There was little that was new – bucking horses, vanishing trowels, festering milk – but in Henry Smith witnesses had a new magistrate to listen to their complaints. Besides, Hugh Parsons had yet to be tried, and given that the evidence of witchcraft against his wife had failed to impress the punctilious judges and jurors of Boston, it seemed worthwhile to add as much paper to the file as possible.[39] News of Mary Parsons's death circulated quickly around the town, though who can say with what reaction? Perhaps feelings were mixed: relief that she was gone; dissatisfaction that she had cheated the hangman; pity for a miserable, sick, downtrodden woman.

Meanwhile in Boston the General Court ordered that John Norton be awarded £20 for his work in demolishing Pynchon's treatise. This item of business was followed by an order that a day of public prayer and humiliation be observed on 18 June, 'taking into consideration how far Satan prevails amongst us in respect of witchcrafts, as also by drawing away some from the truth to the profession and practice of strange opinions'.[40]

By mid-June 1651, Hugh Parsons had been in Boston gaol for nearly three months. The days spent awaiting trial were long and unvaried.

The gaoler came by at intervals with stale bread, filthy gruel and rank water. It was scarcely enough to preserve life, but then there was little physical activity on which to expend energy. Some prisoners were employed making saltpetre – the main ingredient of gunpowder – in a clapboard hut out in the prison yard, but the most heinous offenders, such as murderers and witches, were usually kept shackled 'close', meaning in chains. Prisoners were beaten with pitch-dipped ropes as a punishment, or for no reason at all.[41] The gnawing boredom and torpor were almost unbearable. Hugh Parsons had once been a hard worker from dawn till dusk. But his muscles had atrophied, and his mind, once fixed on whatever task was in hand, floated off. It is likely he was informed of Mary's death, and he must have wondered about his daughter Hannah, wherever she was. He had lost everything: his home, his farmland, three children and his wife. Perhaps he regretted leaving England to start over in America. It had done him no good at all.

Around this time Henry Smith arrived in Boston in his capacity as a magistrate, in order to prosecute Hugh. This spared his stepfather William Pynchon, still under a cloud of heresy, the prolonged humiliation of having to go back there, while also allowing him to concentrate on ordering his affairs at home. With Smith went George Colton, Jonathan Taylor and Simon Beamon, barely a tenth of the witnesses who ideally would have appeared for the prosecution. But no more were willing or able to come. On Tuesday 17 June, Smith entered the General Court holding copies of Pynchon's depositions and the new ones he himself had heard, and took a seat for the trial that all Springfield had anticipated for many months.[42]

Hugh Parsons was brought into the courtroom, carrying with him the stench of the gaol. He stood at the bar, his hair and beard unkempt, his clothes greasy and worn. Striving to show dignity, he listened to the indictment against him: that he had no fear of God and had consorted with the devil. He took a deep breath and pleaded not guilty, thereby initiating the trial. Then John Endecott asked the clerk to summon the first witness, Simon Beamon, who was duly sworn in. Beamon repeated the story of how he had offended Parsons by not immediately fetching leather for his flail, and the subsequent accident with his cart. 'I thought there was some mischief in it from Hugh Parsons,' he told the court, 'for my horse had often gone that road, and never did the like before, nor ever since.' Next up, Jonathan Taylor confirmed how after this incident Parsons had sworn to be even with Beamon, adding the story about Parsons wanting the portion of cow tongue given to his then lodger Anthony Dorchester, even though Dorchester had needed it to nourish his dying wife.[43]

Dorchester himself had not made the journey to Boston, for his stepson had died a few days earlier. For the prosecution, this was unfortunate, since his insight into the Parsons household was unique.[44] A heavy burden of proof now rested on the written submissions presented by Henry Smith. In a neat hand, the clerk Edward Rawson made marginal notes against the handful of testimonies repeated by witnesses in open court.[45] The most compelling account came from George Colton, who described Hugh's affectless reaction to his son's death.[46] But too soon the stories recounted in person, which in Springfield had seemed vivid and endless, were over. Smith's reading of the rest sounded dispassionate.

It was time for the jurymen to consider their verdict: again, they withdrew, then filed back into an expectant courtroom. Their foreman stood. Addressing the judges, he explained that, although the testimonies had impressed them with a 'deep suspicion of witchcraft', they judged this to be 'no sufficient evidence'. Even if more witnesses were to have appeared in person, their stories would have lacked corroboration – again, the point of law that Parsons had raised with Pynchon. For instance, the foreman elucidated, although Taylor's testimony suggested supernatural mischief, he was 'but one witness'. He added that the jurors had been much taken with John Matthews's evidence as well – but, unfortunately, Matthews hadn't been present to give it in person. The judges considered this statement and declared the proceedings finely poised between acquittal and the impossibility of reaching a guilty verdict. John

Endecott suspended the hearing, pending the opinion of the Court of Assistants.[47]

The following day, Wednesday the 18th, Massachusetts performed its prescribed public act of contrition – a day of prayer and fasting – to propitiate God and restore righteousness. Copies of the order had been sent throughout the colony, all the way to Springfield, where it was obvious to William Pynchon not only what 'witchcrafts' were being referred to, but also that 'the profession and practice of strange opinions' referred to him personally. All of which hardened Pynchon's resolve to leave America. That summer he received sympathetic letters, mostly from Old England, where it was well known that Boston's elders had burned his book. Pynchon's supporters, among them Sir Henry Vane, the former Massachusetts governor, were shocked and rushed to defend freedom of conscience and speech.[48]

Pynchon had not in fact changed his views: in court, he had yielded only slightly, and even then disingenuously, to John Norton's objections. By now, he had had a chance to read Norton's book, which was unsparing in its exposure of Pynchon's lack of erudition, his false inferences, inconsistencies and rhetorical blind alleys. Christ *had* felt the wrath of God, Norton insisted: only through wrath could he atone for the sins imputed to him. Norton also observed that by relocating God's wrath, and so responsibility for the Crucifixion, to the devil, Pynchon credited the devil with more power than any Christian could stomach. To regard Satan or man as anything other than God's hapless instruments was heretical.[49]

But, while John Endecott and the General Court of Massachusetts may have forced William Pynchon out, it wasn't much of a victory. Many within the colony and without believed the authorities had demonstrated not the strength of the status quo, but rather its inherent weakness. By silencing Pynchon, and others before him, they were asserting an orthodoxy – a monopoly of faith – that could never prevail.[50] In New England, the desire for a more liberal, relaxed policy regarding doctrine and admission to church membership was growing: church attendance in many townships was already waning, and fines for non-attendance were in decline. Newcomers to the Connecti-cut valley arrived without written dispensations from former churches or recommendations of admission to a new one. Such things had become an irrelevance. Behind this drift from orthodoxy lay some-thing more than indifference: a current of thinking rooted in an English rationalist tradition of which William Pynchon was both heir and exponent. His heresy was not spiritually intense. Rather, it was a rational argument for toleration and universal enjoyment of the truth of salvation. This was revolutionary in both ways: it harked back to the simplicity of the early church, and it anticipated change. It also depended on common sense and engagement with scripture, while eschewing the mysticism of both reactionary Catholics and puritan rebels.[51]

John Cotton and three other elders in Boston received a letter from Old England, bearing several signatures, one of which was probably Sir Henry Vane's. It asked them to intercede with the Gen-eral Court, considering that Pynchon was 'a gentleman pious and well deserving'. If the letter was intended to pour oil on troubled waters, it had the opposite effect. The elders showed the letter to the magistrates, who replied in writing that any man who sup-ported Pynchon could not have read his book properly; had they done, they would have spotted 'fundamental errors in it, meet to be duly witnessed against'. Cotton and his brethren prayed that Christ would help them 'stand in the gap against the inundation of all the errors and heresies of this present age'. Pynchon's book, it was unsubtly implied, was part of that inundation. In New England, he was out in the religious cold.[52]

By the beginning of autumn 1651, Pynchon had transferred most of his property to his son John: his homelot and house; fifty-four acres of arable upland and wet meadow between the river and the main street; and other land besides. John Pynchon took the book of possessions, which listed all this, crossed out his father's name at the top and at the bottom of the page and wrote: 'This land abovesaid now appertains to John Pynchon.' The gristmill, its house, a seventeen-acre plot at the mouth of the Mill River and another at the mouth of the Agawam was shared between John Pynchon and his brothers-in-law, Henry Smith and Elizur Holyoke. To Spring-field, Pynchon bequeathed a tract of land he had bought from an Indian a decade earlier.[53] Practical concerns aside, it was also an emotional time – a time for reflection, perhaps some regret, as well as for resolution. The Pynchons had spent their final summer together in Springfield, along with kinsfolk and friends, the Smiths, the Holyokes and the Moxons. Henry Smith, who was about to return to Boston without his stepfather, now had a son – the boy he had been waiting for, after the birth of nine daughters. Pynchon would be leaving his new grandson and all other family behind when he sailed for the old country.[54]

It was the second time Pynchon had made that leap. Twenty years earlier at Southampton, however, he had been venturing into the unknown; now he had spent a third of his life in America and was returning to Old England, albeit a politically different country from the one he had left behind. In the first week of October, he briefed his stepson Henry Smith, wished God's favour upon him and said farewell as Smith started out on the Bay Path to Boston, where he would continue to pursue the case against Hugh Parsons on behalf of the town. Pynchon, remaining in Springfield a while longer, would keep the mark of a heretic, branded upon him by the General Court – but he would not hang or burn, or be thrown into the prison where Hugh Parsons was still waiting for the authorities to put together a viable case against him. Such were the privileges of rank. Pynchon was a gentleman and an adventurer, who, prior to his disgrace, had done New England sterling service; Parsons was neither.

Now, though, it was too late in the year to sail: the wintry North Atlantic seas were treacherous. Pynchon would lie low in Spring-field in the months to come, sheltering from whatever counterblast came back at Boston, and then would depart the following spring, as soon as the weather permitted. Heresy and witchcraft, mean-while, would continue to overshadow New England. In the township of Lynn, the Holyokes, kin to Pynchon's son-in-law Elizur in

Springfield, heard their preacher liken heretics to sorcerers who 'out of pretence of conscience bewitch souls to death by their enchanting doctrines'.[55]

The General Court reconvened on 14 October, and John Endecott and his judges were surprised to see Henry Smith show up without William Pynchon. Rather than condemn Pynchon, however, the court was willing to be patient with him, in order that he may yet 'renounce the errors and heresies published in his book' – as described in John Norton's critique, soon to be published in London. Endecott sent Smith back to Springfield with two messages for his stepfather: return to Boston in May 1652 to recant fully, on pain of a fine of £100; and, at the same time, present 'the most material witnesses' against Hugh Parsons. Parsons, whose trial was now on the Court of Assistants' calendar for that same month, remained indicted but not yet convicted. He would now have to stay in prison, untried, for the next seven months. Smith promised to deliver the messages and asked to be excused from further appearances at the General Court for that session. The magistrates acceded to this request, he 'having a long journey to travail and urgent occasions to return home'.[56]

The winter of 1651–2 was astonishingly cold. Hugh had to endure it or give up and die, like so many other prisoners in grim, frigid gaols across the Atlantic world. He prayed to hold out at least until the prosecution against him resumed, when he knew he had a chance. Spring brought warmth and hope, and the spread of typhus and dysentery: whenever such diseases entered gaols, almost everyone died. Early on the morning of 12 May 1652, by which time, in total, he had been detained for over a year, Hugh was led out blinking into the sunshine and brought before the Court of Assistants. A pitiful figure in soiled rags, Hugh scanned the courtroom. He noticed that William Pynchon was not there, only the vengeful Henry Smith. He also recognized a few former neighbours, including Samuel Marshfield, who was there to tell the court about the curse on his family and the beckoning apparition seen by his sister.[57]

The judge gestured to the grand jury, whose foreman stood to confirm there was still a legal case to answer, and with that Hugh Parsons was again put on trial for his life. The clerk read out the indictment, accusing Hugh of 'familiar and wicked converse with the devil' and harming people with 'devilish practices and witch-craft'. As in the General Court, the Assistants worked on defendants' 'natural conscience', to expose the truth but also to reclaim their souls, humiliating them into seeing their own depravity: a similar procedure to that which colonists endured to be admitted to a con-gregation. In court as in church, resistance frustrated God's aims, compounding his wrath. Many defendants, confronted by the evi-dence against them, lacked the strength to carry on denying the charges.[58]

The trial jury then heard the testimony, mostly still in the form of written depositions presented by Henry Smith, and most of which had been recorded by the absent Pynchon. Springfield's stories about Hugh Parsons focused squarely on *maleficium* – causing harm with witchcraft – whereas by law a witch was a woman or man who 'hath or consulteth with a familiar spirit'. There was, however, no shred of proof that Hugh had ever consulted a familiar or had any truck with Satan. He may have been stalked by demons that disturbed his sleep; but he had never knelt before them, as witches did. The depositions heard, the jurors retired to confer over this delicate matter. When they returned, the foreman, whose name was Edward Hutchinson, stood and faced the bench. The court-room hubbub died away.

Hugh's heart thumped hard and fast; he felt dizzy, and his head and body ached. Now, after so much agonized waiting, he would know his fate. The jurors for the commonwealth of Massachusetts, Hutchinson declared, were unanimous. Provided the General Court accepted scribal versions of Mary Parsons's confession, the accusa-tions of alleged victims and other depositions as 'authentic testimonies according to law', without corroboration by witnesses before the court, then they were content to find Hugh Parsons guilty of witchcraft.[59] Stunned, Hugh was carried back to gaol, awaiting approval of the verdict. Boston's citizens prepared for the hanging they had so greatly anticipated, and which Mary's untimely death had denied them.

A fortnight later, Hugh Parsons appeared before the General Court. He must have expected he was soon to die, painfully and in shame. But there was a new development. John Endecott's judges, dissatisfied by written testimonies not repeated live in court, took issue with the verdict passed in the Court of Assistants. What was more, the chief witness against Hugh – his wife – was dead.[60] Even though suspicion against Parsons was strong, such suspicion was deemed to be irrelevant without proof of a diabolic covenant. 'On perusal of the evidences brought in against him', the bench of the General Court concluded, 'they do judge that he is not legally guilty of witchcraft, and so not to die by our law'. As in so many other witchcraft trials, the written word constituted flimsy proof for this obscure, elusive crime. Neither judge nor juror had voiced scepticism of witchcraft, nor even any doubt about the defendant's culpability: all that mattered was a formal failure to demonstrate guilt. And so, on 1 June 1652, after fifteen torturous months in captivity, Hugh Parsons was released from the clutches of justice and, pending payment of gaol fees, discharged. Here, at last, was Hugh's deliverance.[61]

9. New Witchland

Since the first execution in New England, in 1647, news of witches had crackled through the land like a brush fire. Fear spread even into native communities: in autumn 1650 the Mohegan sachem Uncas asked colonists to help him find the witches attacking his people, so 'that he might be righted therein'.[1] Inevitably, then, word of the Parsons affair reached Indian and English ears alike: it was sensational. By holding Hugh Parsons and William Pynchon to account in the same week, moreover, and demanding public penance for witchcraft *and* heresy, the authorities in Boston blurred a line between the two offences, made one seem the begetter of the other. Not that this was hard: both pricked a primal fear. Living in the wilderness made settlers peculiarly anxious about being dragged down in nature's hierarchy. And witchcraft and heresy were unnatural – sins against God and man – like sodomy and buggery, for which trials were more frequent in America than in England, and had a special didactic use. A man hanged for sex crimes at New Haven was held up as 'a monster in human shape', which also perfectly defined the witch.[2] Rituals of retribution reset boundaries; but they couldn't hold back the tide of heterodoxy, especially with the arrival of Quakers and Baptists by the mid-1650s, stirring fears that were measurable in fresh panic about witchcraft and sexual deviance.[3]

The persecution of dissenters as heretics raised questions of tyranny versus liberty throughout the seventeenth-century Atlantic world. Where did right and good reside in a society? Was religious toleration the bedrock of justice or the seedbed of corruption? Freethinkers from Massachusetts Bay, who had relocated to Rhode Island and other less oppressive plantations, thought they knew the answers. And they, too, made their own connection between heresy and witchcraft, namely, that both 'crimes' were, to all practical ends, non-existent. In the aftermath of the Springfield episode, and witch-trials elsewhere, these dissidents damned the fanatics who 'putteth people to death for witches'. Puritan zealots, they said, censured alleged heretics and witches without first searching their own hearts to see if the monstrosity that so frightened them actually lay there. Perhaps Satan made *real* monsters of the righteous by deceiving them into fighting imaginary ones.[4]

Reports of New England's witches continued to arrive on the shores of the old country. A garbled tale reached Bulstrode White-locke, Keeper of the Great Seal at Westminster, in a letter from Boston. Whitelocke learned of three unidentified witches: two women and a man. The man claimed to have nursed a chicken-like familiar at his 'paps', which he showed to his interrogators. Along with the women, he also confessed to signing the devil's ledger. The English, who teased New Englanders for their pious hypocrisy, enjoyed hearing about such lapses. For Old England, too, still had witches in the 1650s, a sign of ongoing political and religious fac-tiousness. Smaller panics had followed the witch-hunt of 1645–7, including a purge in Newcastle-upon-Tyne, where no fewer than thirty women were identified as witches. A labourer's wife near old Springfield, accused of feeding a butterfly imp, was committed for trial in spring 1651 – just as, 3,000 miles away, William Pynchon had been building a case against Hugh Parsons. Home and away, cau-tion tempered credulity. A grand jury at Chelmsford rejected the testimony about the Essex woman's imp, and she was discharged.[5]

In July 1651 John Eliot, formerly of Essex, now 'Apostle to the Indi-ans' in New England, sent a letter to London, probably to the colony's agent there, Edward Winslow. Eliot, who had known Pynchon for many years, had an eye for Satan's progress in America's contested spiritual territories. Lately, he said, they had felt the 'sad frowns of the Lord upon us, chiefly in regard of fascinations and witchcraft'. It was inevitable, however, that as God communed with his children 'in visible and explicit covenant', so witches would appear. Springfield had exposed four, and he supposed that the woman who had murdered her child – 'doubtless a witch' – had been executed: Mary Parsons, though he didn't name her. More witches, Eliot continued, had been found elsewhere: one from Dorchester was condemned; others were suspected at Ipswich. But Springfield, he stated confidently, was surely the hub of the plot. His letter was printed in a pamphlet, which reminded readers that the devil built his chapel hard against the churches of the righteous.[6] As one New England puritan put it, the colony was so plagued with melancholy and witchery because the devil was sure to be most malicious 'where he is hated and hateth most'. For all the doubts it threw up, witchcraft remained a serious issue. Like colonization itself, it was a matter of life and death.[7]

In intellectual life, far from being some feeble superstition, witchcraft was still the hard-edged, durable tool for thinking about contrariety in society, religion, politics and law it had always been. In April 1651, as proceedings opened against Hugh and Mary Parsons, in London the philosopher Thomas Hobbes published *Leviathan*, a meditation on strong, centralized rule. For fifteen years Springfield had been in miniature the kind of state Hobbes admired, especially as it was sited among 'the savage people in many places of America', whose 'anarchy' helped to idealize its desirable opposite: 'sovereignty'. Pynchon had asserted supreme control over land and trade, using an unwritten constitution of paternalism and deference with tenants, employees and debtors. And he had tried, as Hobbes advised, to unite public and private interests, stabilizing his society with work. But greed risked a 'perpetual war of every man against his neighbour'. Disputes arose from what Hobbes called 'the natural passions of men when there is no visible power to keep them in awe' – and in Springfield that visible power had been diminished by Pynchon's heresy and his avowed belief in witchcraft.[8]

In fact, Hobbes shared Pynchon's opinion, feeling that 'though he could not rationally believe in witches, yet he could not be fully satisfied to believe there were none'. Why else would they freely confess? Witches may not in reality cause anyone harm, but deserved to die anyway 'for the false belief they have that they can do such mischief, joined with their purpose to do it'.[9] Thus witchcraft became a thought-crime, an offence involving a *mens rea* – the intention to harm – without an *actus reus*, actually *causing* harm. Once this idea became established in the courts, so the indictable felony of witchcraft was doomed. All that was left were the spite and rage that neighbours imputed to witches – and in this regard, New Englanders were little different from their English cousins. John Eliot's suggestion that witches clustered round the righteous was merely a defiant spin on an emerging, uncomfortable truth: puritans were selfish and venal after all. Like everyone else.

In the early 1650s the puritan writer Edward Johnson was preparing a history of New England. In it, he mentioned the Springfield witches, who, he believed, had 'bewitched not a few persons, among whom two of the reverend elder's children'.[10] The legacy would endure. In 1682 the royal hydrographer John Seller published his *Description of New England*, in which he described Springfield as 'infamous by reason of the witches therein'.[11] But Springfield was not alone in this infamy, nor did its crisis signal the end of witch-hunting in the Connecticut valley, whose townships were continually plagued by enmity. In the 1650s Windsor, Wethersfield and Hartford were all plunged into 'schism . . . and horrible prejudices', which divided them into factions, then tore them apart. The issues were perennially land, authority and religion.[12] Tensions with Indians were inflamed by the same rumours in circulation a decade earlier: their conspiracy with the Dutch 'to cut off the English'. Boston, concerned for Springfield's welfare, warned of imminent attack. By 1654 these rumours had been disproved, but the fear of attack persisted – a fear that encompassed not only foreign and native enemies but any perceived adversary in the wilderness, natural or supernatural.[13]

Panic about witches, and the urge to be rid of them, came in waves.[14] Mary Parsons was not the last Springfield woman accused of witchcraft; she wasn't even the last witch called Mary Parsons. For Mary Bliss Parsons, the disturbed wife of Joseph Parsons, was destined to be suspect as well as victim. In the 1650s Mary and Joseph moved twenty miles upriver to the new town of Northampton, where they fell out with their neighbours, including James Bridgman, another former Springfield enemy of Hugh Parsons. A girl fell sick, a pig died in a swamp and a cow was bitten on the tongue by a rattlesnake. Bridgman's son, in agony with a dislocated knee, said he saw Mary Bliss Parsons sitting on a shelf beside a black mouse. The boy's mother heard a bang on the door, which, she said, 'made me think there is wickedness in the place'. The accusations divided Northampton. In summer 1656, backed by two Springfield men – William Pynchon's son John and his former servant Simon Beamon – Mary won a slander case.[15] Implying that she was the victim of a witch rather than a witch herself, Beamon said Mary's fits were just like those George Moxon's daughters had suffered five years earlier.[16]

There were other dark ripples. John Pynchon's wife, Amy, incapacited by illness, lived for a year in New London with John Winthrop Jr, who as well as being a colonial governor was also a physician. In 1654 Amy's druggist brother-in-law William Davis recommended red coral, a charm against witches, to protect her and her baby son. But no red coral was available. The child's death that summer was 'a most sad and heavy stroke' to his father, who, unlike Hugh Parsons, knew how to show grief. Amy, meanwhile, was treated with powdered sea pearls, conserve of roses and oil from the groin sacs of beavers.[17] Her symptoms resembled those exhibited by the bewitched, particularly the infant Samuel Parsons, with a lump in her stomach rising up her throat, causing 'listlessness all over her body'. Witchcraft was not specifically cited as a cause – though it would be when Amy died, forty years later.[18] The year 1654 also saw a feud in Windsor against Lydia Gilbert, a relative of Mary Bliss Parsons, end with her conviction as a witch. Yet, by now, doubts were creeping in. Not only was Gilbert destined to be the last convicted witch from Windsor but opinion elsewhere was divided. At an execution in New Haven in 1654, a woman peeping under the skirts of a neighbour hanging from the gallows remarked:

'if these be the marks of a witch, then she was one herself' – and so were half the women of the town.[19]

Nevertheless, witchcraft endured for decades, along ninety miles of valley from Hadley in the north down to the fort at Saybrook. In 1659 Saybrook asked Hartford for help in investigating 'suspicions about witchery' against a married couple, which led to a trial that divided jurors. In 1662 Anne Cole at Hartford admitted entertaining a demon that skipped like a fawn to seduce her, and to meeting with other witches, including her husband, who was hanged beside her. The devil had promised Cole a party for Christmas, not a feast celebrated in New England. In 1668 Katherine Harrison, the widow of Wethersfield's town crier, was charged with various *maleficia*, as well as conjuring a spectre of herself and commanding a swarm of bees. Twice she split a jury before being found guilty, but even then the General Court overturned the conviction, though Harrison was made to leave Wethersfield for 'her own safety and the contentment of the people'. She fled to Westchester, New York, to the loud objections of its inhabitants. In 1670 John Pynchon dismissed complaints against a Hadley youth accused of witchcraft and instead had him whipped for 'wretched lying'.[20]

Northampton hadn't moved on either. Twenty acrimonious years after the first accusations against her, in 1675 Mary Bliss Parsons was tried for murdering a woman and her daughter, which she denied. John Pynchon referred the case to the Boston Court of Assistants, where the 'six sober and discreet women' who had searched her body testified, as did the Stebbins family, on whose homelot in Springfield witches had once frolicked. The jury acquitted her.[21] In 1679 John Stebbins died in a sawmill accident blamed on witches. The towns-women were brought before the corpse, which bled when a suspect touched it. John Pynchon referred the case to Boston, where no more came of it.[22] Other prosecutions followed. In 1683 Pynchon tried James Fuller of Springfield, who was acquitted. That winter Mary Webster of Hadley was indicted for covenanting with an imp like a black wildcat of the woods. Like Fuller, she was acquitted and returned to Hadley, where youths dragged her from her house, strung her up, then buried her in snow, an ordeal she barely survived. In 1691 Pynchon also presided at what would be the last witch-trial for Hampshire County, that of Mary Randall, another Springfield resident, a case that was quietly dropped.[23]

Measured by convictions alone, witchcraft was waning, but accusations continued to do irreparable harm to the lives of vulnerable people, mostly women. And stories of witches resounded in the community. In 1677, after Simon Beamon died at Springfield, a Hadley man slandered Beamon's widow Alice as a witch, adding that her adolescent son looked like one, too. It seemed as if Alice Beamon's blood was cursed: she came from Windsor, where her namesake mother – Alice Young – had been the first witch hanged in New England.[24] These tales echoed into the next century. In 1702 Pelatiah Glover Jr, merchant of Springfield, prosecuted Betty Negro, an African slave, for saying that his mother-in-law was a witch who had murdered John Pynchon's wife Amy. The alleged witch was Mary Bliss Parsons, and Glover's wife Hannah was her daughter – 'half a witch', according to Betty Negro.[25]

Evidently its purge of witches in 1651 had not reset Springfield on the path of righteousness – at least as far as local lore was concerned. 'I am counted but as a dreamer,' Mary Lewis Parsons had told Jonathan Taylor that night he watched her, 'but when this dreamer is hanged, then remember what I said to you: this town will not be clear yet.' She was proved right: neither her death nor the ruin of her husband solved anything at all.[26]

The persistence of witchcraft accusations in Springfield was linked to the rapacity of its economy. John Pynchon, who led the town for the rest of the century, was a ruthless capitalist who extended the fur trade with trading posts at Westfield, Hadley and Northampton. Pynchon expanded his estates, buying land from poorer neighbours like Thomas Cooper and William Branch in the 1650s, and other territory from the Indians, including by 1666 all the meadow west of the river. In 1672 he snapped up another plot from 'the old woman, the mother of Wuttawwaluncksun' for some beaver skins, two coats and sixty fathoms of wampum. In the same year he built a gristmill at a new plantation named Suffield, using two slaves. He had already established a sawmill on the Mill River and was exporting timber, meat, wool and corn to the West Indies, exports that gradually replaced his involvement in the fur trade. Investing in a ship at Boston, Pynchon imported molasses, rum, sugar and tobacco. In 1697 he built a blast furnace so Springfield could smelt its own iron. No one stood in his way.[27]

Springfield's grumbling hive sent forth swarms: new towns, prominently Northampton, which was granted township status in 1653. The following year a boundary dispute between Northampton and Springfield over the Nonotuck plantation was settled to define both places precisely.[28] Woronoco, once part of Springfield, was incorporated in 1658 and became Westfield. For years to come, Westfield men would complain that their Springfield neighbours trespassed to cut timber and make tar.[29] In 1670 Springfield men petitioned the General Court to found Suffield between Springfield and Westfield, among them the sometime pursuers of Hugh Parsons: Benjamin Cooley, Samuel Marshfield, Anthony Dorchester and Miles Morgan. The boundaries of this new township caused no end of arguments.[30]

What became of the people who had tried to hang Hugh Parsons? While he was still on remand, in 1651, more land was released in the long meadow, for which George Colton, Alexander Edwards, Anthony Dorchester, Thomas Miller, William Branch and Thomas Merrick were waiting.[31] Other acquisitive former witnesses against Hugh included Benjamin Cooley and George Langton.[32] All these men went on to live better than they had back when they were fussing about bewitched trowels and puddings. They ate more meat and bought magnifying glasses, paper, ink, starch and soap.[33] Prosperity shone from their houses. After Hugh Parsons's departure, Springfield bought bricks from Francis Hacklington of Northampton: John Pynchon ordered 50,000 to extend his father's house, a project that also required 156 loads of stone and fifty-six trees. The home of Hugh Parsons's next-door neighbour Jonathan Burt was similarly fortified, and in 1665 the Ely Tavern was built from stone, a change in style that provided security as tension with Indians grew.

In 1668 Springfield finally got its prison, as once it had waited for a meeting house.[34]

By then the ministry was occupied by Pelatiah Glover Sr, father of the merchant, whose family hailed from Prescot in Lancashire, where George Moxon had been a curate, and whose namesake son had married the daughter of Mary Bliss Parsons.[35] After Moxon left, Springfield initially struggled to attract a preacher, and upon arrival Glover found it in a 'forlorn and despairing condition', the spirits of the people depressed.[36] Glover was to spend thirty miserable years in the town, mired in contention, unable to reach dispersed congregants, who resented paying rates for a distant meeting house.[37] Most vexing were the doubts cast on his ownership of his property. He rightly claimed it had been assigned to him and his heirs for ever – a hasty concession made by a church desperate for a minister – but in 1681 this was challenged. 'I have suffered bitterly with them', moaned Glover, 'and for them.'[38]

Disputes multiplied, over everything from breaches of contract and broken fences to straying livestock and dangerous dogs. The brickmaker Francis Hacklington proved as difficult to work with as Hugh Parsons had been and was replaced as a supplier by a Springfield man, Samuel Ball, who built chimneys for Reverend Glover and others.[39] The witnesses against Hugh and Mary fought among themselves. Jonathan Burt accused John Matthews of having 'scandalously reviled him' and Thomas Merrick of calling him a 'lying man'. As a selectman and juror Burt kept the peace, but as a farmer he disturbed it throughout his long life.[40] Thomas Merrick, who had been the constable in 1651, performed other public duties, but to the end of his days he, too, was embroiled in lawsuits.[41] Hugh and Mary's turbulent spirit also lived on in others' marital problems, notably the 'sad bickering and strife' between Obediah Miller and his wife Joan. She beat and scratched him, called him 'fool', 'toad' and 'vermin' and said she didn't love him, had never loved him and would never love him.[42]

The fortunes of other participants in the witch-trials of 1651–2 varied. The Parsonses' former tenant Anthony Dorchester rented part of the Pynchons' gristmill and then all of it, but also invested in land and cattle, and ran a ferry below the Agawam River. He exported wheat to Barbados and died one of Springfield's richest men.[43] Benjamin Cooley, who started out as a linen weaver, amassed an estate worth over a thousand pounds. Reece Bedortha expanded his holdings along the Mill River and west of the Connecticut and bought a tannery from John Pynchon. He drowned in 1683, with his son, daughter-in-law and granddaughter, when their canoe capsized. His wife Blanche died around the same time.[44] A descendant praised Reece as 'devout, liberal, industrious, modest . . . one whom his neighbours could trust'. Hugh Parsons, by contrast, was 'a worthless fellow'. George Colton, to whom Hugh had resorted when his son died, became a wealthy farmer and distinguished lieutenant of militia.[45] No action, it seems, was ever taken against the other suspects: Bess Sewell and Sarah Merrick. Even so, the witch-crisis took its toll on them. Soon afterwards, Bess left Springfield with her husband and baby daughter to settle in Wickford, Rhode Island, a tolerant community overlooking Narragansett Bay. Around the same time, Sarah died, partly due perhaps to the stress of accusation, after which her quarrelsome husband Thomas remarried.[46]

Jonathan Taylor, the seer of snake demons, fared less well. His wife Mary gave birth another five times, and the family grew poorer. Taylor never cleared his debts, lost his house, and was forced to move to Suffield. When Jonathan and Mary died weeks apart in 1682, their estate was valued at £47, but repayment of his creditors left only £7.[47] The cooper John Matthews drank, abused the minister and lost John Pynchon's patronage when he fell behind at work. Pynchon reclaimed his debt, as he always did when productivity fell, forcing Matthews to remortgage. His wife Pentecost made ends meet by teaching Pynchon's son, but after she died Matthews was left with their only child, who was made a ward because of his father's incompetence. Matthews died in 1684, with debts five times the size of his estate.[48] Pynchon also ruined Samuel Marshfield, who lost his estate over a debt of £54. Marshfield's mother Mercy had died soon after the Parsons affair, aged around fifty and in poor health.[49] Many more neither excelled nor failed, but never left Pynchon's grip. Everyone did better than Hugh Parsons, though, who lost everything except his daughter and his life.

After his release from prison in June 1652, Hugh Parsons stayed in Boston with his daughter Hannah, now nearly six years old. Springfield had nothing for them any more. During Hugh and Hannah's first summer in Boston, the city was troubled by an epidemic, probably of smallpox, that lasted into winter. On 10 November, disease-ridden Boston observed a fast day to appease God for, once again, the double blight of witchcraft and heresy. All Hugh and Hannah could do was avoid people with symptoms, and hope and pray.[50]

How Hugh fed Hannah is unclear: perhaps he laboured at the docks or in the city's brickyard. He had no money. In April the previous year – just three weeks after he was sent to Boston for trial – John Pynchon had appropriated his estate: the homelot, six acres of woodlot, eight acres across the two rivers and another seven acres. Henry Smith and the selectmen agreed that some of 'the broken up land of Hugh Parsons' would be sold to Thomas Merrick for £12 'in merchantable corn'. The following month Merrick was replaced as constable by Elizur Holyoke, having done well out of the job. That summer John Pynchon disposed of Hugh Parsons's property and settled his debts; by November, some lands had passed to Merrick, but most to Jonathan Burt. By then Burt was living in Hugh and Mary's old house, where neighbours visited, among them Henry and Anne Smith's daughter Hannah, whose young sisters were suspected to have been bewitched by the former occupants.[51] Perhaps Hugh and Mary's possessions remained with the house; they were not listed. Apart from his goats and pigs and hens, there would have been a flail, a plough chain, a musket, brick-making apparatus, a salt-tub, a table and – the scene of so much marital conflict – a bed, with its frame, bolster and blankets. All the things they had worked for and lost.[52]

In autumn 1652 Hugh received a letter from John Pynchon saying Hugh had been owed 13s 6d, but that after the clearance of his debts – in Hartford as well as Springfield – only five shillings remained. Pynchon also made Hugh cover the rent and upkeep of his appropriated farmland from the time he was in prison. Adding the value of Hugh's possessions left a miserable balance of £1 5s 8½d, which Pynchon equated to six-and-a-half bushels of wheat, plus another two-and-a-half reaped from Hugh's own land. Pynchon wrote again, offering to send the nine bushels to Boston if Hugh met the transportation costs. Parsons replied that he would accept six if Pynchon sent them straight away free of charge. Pynchon agreed, and in May 1654, eighteen months after his first letter, shipped the wheat to his brother-in-law, the druggist William Davis, from whose shop it could be collected. John Pynchon put a line through Hugh's account, with a note: 'all reckonings are evened'.[53]

When Hugh and Hannah finally left Boston, they went either to Watertown or to Portsmouth, Rhode Island.[54] The latter is much more likely, which, the records suggest, would mean they arrived in 1658, when Hannah was twelve. Portsmouth was a township of happily co-existing opinions, as was Rhode Island more generally. (It was later reported in Old England that Rhode Island's leaders 'allow liberty of conscience and worship to all who live civilly', tolerating every denomination, faction or sect, even Quakers – everyone, in fact, who 'the Massachusetts would not suffer to live among them'.) As a refuge for the persecuted, Portsmouth was reputed to be 'generally hated by the other colonies'. In 1654 John Wightman, whose father had been the last English heretic executed, back in 1612, settled in Newport with his younger son and was reunited with an elder son already living contentedly at Providence. It was that kind of place: a haven where neither books nor people were burned.[55]

The unstinting devotion to work that had been Hugh Parsons's undoing in Springfield allowed him to rebuild his life in Portsmouth and, more than that, to prosper.[56] He acquired land adjoining the estate of John Wood, one of John Winthrop's sea captains, married Wood's widow Elizabeth and raised her daughters as his own, although their husbands later sued him over a legacy. So Hannah Parsons, long an orphan of sorts, had parents and siblings again – and, after her childhood trauma, something approximating to stability. Only now and then did her father cross his neighbours. He served as a juror, a deputy in the assembly and a mounted trooper – the model of a respectable freeman of New England.[57] If rumours of Hugh's past followed him there, they don't seem to have caused him any trouble. There was nobody to persecute witches in Portsmouth; indeed, there were no witches at all. At the age of twenty-four, Hannah Parsons married one Henry Matteson, had seven children and led a long and contented life. So, too, it seems did Hugh. He died on 18 June 1685, leaving Hannah four ewes and, perhaps due to the lawsuit over the legacy, the rest of his estate to his stepdaughters.[58]

The ship carrying William and Frances Pynchon back to Old England arrived in Southampton in spring 1652.[59] As their coach passed through the countryside, through Hampshire and Surrey towards London, things looked much as they had done twenty years earlier. The roads were as rutted as ever, the rolling fields as green, the people where they stopped for refreshment just as coarse. Yet manners and fashions had changed, to the extent that, as a ballad joked, the real New England was not across the Atlantic, but was simply the old one reborn. Government had been radically transformed. When the Pynchons had left for America, England was a monarchy. Now it was a commonwealth and free state: a puritan republic in all but name. Monarchy had been abolished; so too had the Privy Council, House of Lords and established church. Parliamentary power was underwritten by the army, and a council of state wielded an executive fiat. Many challenges lay ahead. Scotland had been defeated the previous summer, but fighting continued in Ireland, and war with the Dutch was imminent. Trade faltered, which led to unemployment, made worse by the steady drift of demobilized soldiers looking for work.

The Pynchons lodged in Hackney, a London suburb north-east of the city walls, with kinsfolk of the Massachusetts Holyoke family.[60] The summer was hot, and drought threatened the harvest. News spread of a witch-trial in Kent involving six women, one of whom, it was reported in the capital, 'fell into an ecstasy before the bench, and swelled into a monstrous and vast bigness'. The political theorist Sir Robert Filmer questioned the evidence, as did parliament, which issued reprieves that came too late: all six women were executed.[61] Meanwhile, parliament tried to restrain religious sects, chiefly Baptists, Quakers and Ranters, whose activity, one commentator said, was 'more dangerous to us than our civil wars'. The state's weapon of choice was a new law, which attacked heresy by criminalizing blasphemy. A pamphlet went on sale about a Ranter woman whose heresy had mutated into atheism: 'there was no God, no heaven, no hell', she said, before giving birth to 'the most ugliest ill-shaped monster that ever eyes beheld'. In this way, horror crimes were manipulated as parables to expose the wickedness of free-thinking, free speech and disobedience.[62]

But an unrestrained outpouring of print in the 1640s and 1650s also meant that there were now two very public sides to this debate. It was in this new context that Pynchon's case resonated. On a visit to England Roger Williams, the founder of Providence, Rhode Island, published a book disputing that heresy was a crime. Williams wondered whether Satan had deluded John Endecott and his fellow Boston magistrates: 'as in witchcraft, a stronger and super-natural power lays hold upon the powers of nature', he wrote, enfeebling the wisest of God's creatures.[63] Meanwhile Williams's English ally Sir Henry Vane sent Endecott another letter, deploring Pynchon's persecution. Soon afterwards Vane published a tract repeating Williams's arguments. Civil magistrates had no right to try matters of conscience, Vane stated, and a desire to punish heresy was more corrupt than heresy itself. 'The subtlety of the Serpent', wrote Vane, 'is such that he ever endeavours to turn our eyes outward towards others, so that we may not see what is in our own hearts.'[64]

By the autumn of 1652 Endecott had read Vane's letter – and doubtless his and Williams's publications, as had Pynchon's antag-onist John Norton. On 7 October, thirty miles north of Boston, the people of Ipswich gathered for Norton's Thursday lecture. In

Ipswich, too, heresy and witchcraft grew like weeds: the town was cursed by 'intolerable excess', and a man suspected of 'having familiarity with the devil' had recently been censured. Norton rebuked those who confused their own scriptural interpretations with the mind of God. 'The penmen of corrupt books', he railed, 'must hold up their hands as highly guilty of the evil of the times.'[65] A fortnight later, the council wrote to Vane saying that Pynchon might have kept his views to himself, as he had done for thirty years when he 'lived amongst us with honour, much respect and love'. The elders expressed grief at the encouragement Pynchon had received, adding that they had done only what they had to 'in conscience to God's command'.[66]

On 11 December that year Thomas Clendon, a member of the Westminster Assembly of Divines, preached that Christ had *not* suffered God's wrath and willingly mediated between heaven and earth. This was Pynchon's view, too. Blind adherence to tradition, Clendon continued, was tyranny, enslaving men's judgement – 'witness the late proceedings of the General Court in New England', he said, 'against that ancient, pious and prudent gentleman, Mr Pynchon'.[67] The same month, perhaps buoyed by this support, William Pynchon published another book in which he exalted the power of love: of God to man, and between neighbours.[68] The same spirit infused a new edition of *The Discoverie of Witchcraft*, a treatise by the Elizabethan sceptic Reginald Scot, which argued that confessed witches were in fact harmless melancholics in need of food and medicine.[69] James I had reputedly burned Scot's book – but now thinkers were more receptive to its message. 'A Christian moderation must be had in passing uncharitable terms upon the persons of witches and wizards,' noted one cleric. 'Let us behold in them a spectacle of man's misery . . . and be moved with compassion.'[70]

The year 1653 brought war with Holland and political upheaval. Parliament was dissolved, and during another dry summer, a new, smaller parliament met. By December hopes of stability through representative government were dead, and England became a fully fledged republic, with Oliver Cromwell as Lord Protector. There were more witchcraft trials, though Cromwell showed no interest in them, nor were they successful. Of five women arraigned that year at the south-eastern assizes, two were discharged, two acquitted, and the fifth, who confessed, reprieved.[71] Yet, as if to fan the flames of paranoia, Norton's book was published in England, warning of false teachers and urging readers to 'discern Satan though transformed into an angel of light'. The book contained a letter by John Cotton and others refuting Pynchon's thesis. The frame for ordering truth, though, was shifting.[72]

Pynchon kept himself busy, rebuffing Norton and his other critics, while corresponding with his son John in Springfield. He also shared letters with his grandson John Holyoke, whom he had taught that Christ epitomized God's love and to resist 'devils that ingest evil thoughts into us'. In December 1653, using liquidated American assets, Pynchon bought a Buckinghamshire estate from a London merchant. Set beside the Thames in three acres of land, Wyardisbury House at Wraysbury had outbuildings, a dovecot, a garden and an orchard.[73] Across the river lay Runnymede, where King John had agreed Magna Carta, a long-distant event that in recent times had inspired English common lawyers and colonists in America to protest they were freeborn subjects, not slaves to monarchs and magistrates.[74] A long-time exponent of liberty, as in the antithesis of tyranny, Pynchon had never fully endorsed unfettered religious toleration. Now he was more sympathetic – and he himself embodied what he preached, having become one of New England's great dissenters.

George Moxon returned to the old country soon after Pynchon. Although he never defended his friend's views, it was plain where his sympathies lay. Hugh Parsons's acquittal, mixed with unease about Pynchon's crisis, perhaps left Moxon feeling discontented. Besides, he had been thinking of leaving for some time. In September 1652 Springfield's selectmen began transferring title to Moxon's estate to Springfield's ministry, to remain in perpetuity. He didn't wait for the selectmen to calculate the proceeds, which they promised to send later on.[75] Moxon paid off most of his debts and bought hinges for a sea chest. An anonymous valedictory poem praised his toil, courage and fortitude, even 'when errors crowd close to thyself and friends' and 'wicked men and devils' were raging. By November the Moxon family had arrived back in England. In promoting trust in God's love and Christ's sacrifice, Moxon had laid a path to spiritual healing and salvation for his wilderness community. Now he would have to start over again, in the country of his birth.[76]

Pynchon's stepson Henry Smith also returned permanently to England in autumn 1652, leaving his wife Anne to follow behind him. The son that the couple had waited so long for had died in June, a week before his first birthday. The Smiths, though, retained their Springfield estate, with Anne granted power of attorney. John Pynchon took over as chief magistrate. In autumn 1654 Anne Smith departed for England with her children, having ceded to her brother John her interest in the mill and most of the other property.[77] They arrived in London in mid-December; Anne's father, William Pynchon, was there to meet them. They were all sick. Pynchon hurried them to Wraysbury, forgoing a meeting with Richard Baxter, the puritan preacher he so admired. Pynchon had recently attended a sermon of Baxter's at St Paul's Cross, which exhorted the crowd to fight Satan, who cynically befriended Saints and witches alike. 'All wicked men', Baxter had inveighed, 'do entertain him in a more full and constant familiarity with their souls than these witches do with their bodies.'[78]

Having failed to see Baxter, Pynchon instead sent him letters and books, including his 440-page reply to John Norton's demolition of *The Meritorious Price of Our Redemption*. Dedicated to the Lord Chief Justice of Common Pleas, this riposte appealed to the moral law of nature, yet came with an apology. Given the gravity of the subject, Pynchon wished it had been written by an abler theologian than himself, for, he said, 'I am no bred scholar'. At least, he hoped, it might 'vindicate the truth of my former book from the odium of heresy'.[79]

Like Baxter, Sir Henry Vane argued for a pan-Protestant bulwark against the forces of Antichrist.[80] The answer was not, Vane felt, the puritan authoritarianism that many Englishmen found unpalatable about New England. In the summer of 1655, however, England itself got just that. Cromwell appointed eleven 'major-generals' to run local government, the most draconian of whom advocated executing heretics, blasphemers and witches, all 'under the same enumeration'.[81] The experiment lasted until 1657, when their powers were rescinded. In this year, William Pynchon had his portrait painted, which, according to one nineteenth-century writer, was 'the impersonation of quiet dignity and patriarchal grace'.[82]

By this time, George Moxon had re-established himself as a congregational minister, helped by Walter Cradock, formerly of the Llanvaches church.[83] As in Springfield, Moxon was an inclusive congregationalist, and shared a pulpit with a Presbyterian preacher at Newbold Astbury in Cheshire. With the Restoration of Charles II in 1660, the Church of England was also restored, the orthodox liturgy reinstituted and non-conforming preachers banished. Moxon was duly ejected and spent his remaining years as a preacher in Congleton, the last fifteen as a licensed teacher after the king granted toleration to dissenters. In 1674, still aligned with Pynchon's unorthodoxy, Moxon was censured for his views 'concerning the satisfaction of Christ'. He would go down fighting. Partly disabled by strokes, for the second time in his life his congregation built him a place of worship, a more modest affair than the one in Springfield, but still somewhere to conduct prayer in his own way. Moxon died in September 1687, his funeral the first service to be held in the new meeting house.[84]

By this time, Mary Parsons's former congregation in Wales had long since dispersed. At the start of the civil war, the 'Saints of Llanvaches' fled to parliamentarian Bristol, where William Wroth's disciple William Erbery, who had helped Mary get to America, also sheltered his people. When the city fell to the royalists, they continued their exodus to London.[85] After serving as a chaplain in the New Model Army, Erbery toured the country promoting independent churches, like those in Wales and New England, as 'a pure democracy', unlike the 'aristocracy' of Presbyterianism. This led to his being accused as a Ranter, followed by censure for heresy and blasphemy in March 1653.[86] When he died the following year his wife and daughter became campaigning Quakers, a legacy that William Penn, the founder of Pennsylvania, hailed as seminal for the movement.[87]

William Pynchon never wrote about witchcraft, despite (or perhaps because of) his experiences in Springfield. Buckinghamshire, his new home, had witches – but not many.[88] Instead this grand old man spent his final years, like the previous decade, writing inflammatory theology and annotating his repetitive books, ever his own most attentive reader.[89] Throughout the 1650s he remained a target for the campaigning enemies of heresy, who likened his apparent renunciation of the Holy Trinity to a witch compacting with Satan and even accused him of trying to revive paganism in the worship of English people.[90]

Pynchon's wife Frances died at Wraysbury in October 1657, a few days before their daughter Mary Holyoke in Springfield. Pynchon spent winter alone, drawing little comfort from his closest relatives, Henry and Anne Smith, whose mental health had suffered since their return to England. 'I am the more solitary', Pynchon lamented, 'as my son Smith is of a reserved melancholy and my daughter Anne is crazy.'[91] Pynchon sent out more of his books, unsolicited, signed and dedicated. Copies of his treatise on the observation of the Sabbath were received by clerics from the rector of a tiny Yorkshire parish to the Dean of Rochester. His yearning to be taken seriously as a theologian was never satisfied.[92]

There were more omens and prodigies of the sort Pynchon had known all his life: an indication that the times remained out of joint. In the spring of 1662 from the West Country town of Hereford came reports of an earthquake that toppled the steeple, giant hailstones that killed cattle and a celestial apparition that boomed, 'Woe, woe to the land!'[93] That year, Pynchon finished writing his final meditation on the Atonement and fired one last fusillade against John Norton. Norton, meanwhile, had continued to denounce 'heresy turbulent', the worst type in that it incurably infected others.

Pynchon, he thought, had been a particularly powerful vector of the disease, in Springfield and beyond.[94]

New England had beaten Pynchon, but its authority was waning. Charles II excoriated those who harboured his father's murderers, who had fled there. In 1662 John Norton joined a delegation to the king in Whitehall, pleading, unsuccessfully, for his merciful favour towards the colony; Norton returned to Boston consumed by melancholy and died soon afterwards. This was the same summer when Sir Henry Vane was beheaded as a traitor, his promotion of civil and religious liberties having offended Charles II, who judged him 'too dangerous . . . to let live'. Vane died just as puritans were starting to lose their grip. Within a year, New England's great witch fear had subsided: in the space of seventeen years, since 1647, seventy-nine people had been accused, thirty-three tried and fifteen hanged.[95]

William Pynchon died at Wraysbury on 29 October 1662. His estate was shared among relatives in Old and New England, two worlds that had bridged and sundered his life.[96] His son John, the main beneficiary, learned he had inherited Wyardisbury House the following spring, in a letter from his stepbrother Henry Smith. Offering the consolation that after a lifetime of trials their father had found perfection in heaven, Smith also informed John that as executor he must untangle the complications of probate. Accordingly in November, 'not knowing how the Lord may deal with me', John Pynchon prepared for his journey back to England by making a will of his own, dividing everything between his wife and three children; and bequeathing some small 'tokens of love' for his brothers-in-law and Pelatiah Glover, the minister of Springfield, as well as £3 to relieve the town's 'honest poor'.[97]

Over a decade later, on 5 October 1675, John Pynchon was riding home to Springfield when he saw smoke rising above the town. In June, war had broken out across New England, a rebellion led by Chief Metacom of the Wampanoags against English domination of Indian lands; Pynchon had been away fighting at Hadley, twenty miles to the north. He moved quickly onward, dreading what he would find. Relations with the local Indians had been tense for a while. Although some were held to be good neighbours, 'generally clothed in English apparel and their hair cut after the manner of the English', others, principally the Mohawks, stole corn and killed cattle. The militia patrolled, lookouts were posted, and houses garrisoned, including the old Parsons homestead. But as John reached the town his father had founded, he saw this hadn't been enough. Springfield lay in ruins: houses pillaged, dead and injured all around, including key witnesses from the Parsons witch-hunt all those years ago. Caught in the open, Thomas Cooper and Thomas Miller never made it back to the redoubt. Pentecost Matthews was slain in her own home, others running to the meeting house. Pelatiah Glover's grand home, built for George Moxon, was destroyed along with its library, heaped up into a bonfire. The town that for so long had been fit to tear itself apart, ever vigilant for witchery and other evils, had been destroyed, apocalyptically, by an enemy from outside its boundaries.[98]

The cause of this calamity seemed plain enough: the Indian attackers were 'devilish enemies of religion'. But, as ever, the devil was no more than an instrument of heavenly vengeance. As John Pynchon wrote to his son in London: 'the sore contending of God with us for our sins, unthankfulness for former mercies, and unfruitfulness under our precious enjoyments, hath evidently demonstrated that he is very angry with this country'. Pynchon specifically blamed Springfield's toleration of 'vile enormities . . . which as a flood do threaten to overwhelm us'.[99] Survival depended on heeding dire warnings from heaven – and yet this town, like all New England, was set on a path of industry and trade, moving ever further from the righteousness cherished by the first generation of migrants. Even though the old idea of waning morality in New England, or 'declension', has long been exposed as a myth – puritans had always embraced commerce – rampant capitalism threatened the godly community, as idealized by John Winthrop back in 1630, when he imagined his 'city on a hill' in America.[100] So when Springfield was rebuilt and repopulated, rising like a phoenix from its ashes, there too flourished sin: the pride, greed, self-love ensuing from worldly desire for possessions. 'Land hath been the idol of New England,' declaimed a minister. 'Christians have forsaken churches and ordinances, all for land.'[101]

Richard Blinman, who had introduced Mary Parsons to William Pynchon, had returned to the Welsh town of Chepstow just before the Restoration. In August 1677 he wrote to Increase Mather, an eminent puritan divine in Boston, complaining 'that so little reformation hath been wrought by the awful dispensations of God to New England'. But Wales and England were in crisis, too: a wet summer had wiped out the harvest, a judgement provoked, so Blinham supposed, by sin and licentious stage plays. 'The scarlet whore makes nations drunk with the cup of her fornications,' he blazed, 'the Lord hasten her ruin.'[102] This was the hellfire of an elderly puritan; yet behind his fears for the colony lay real danger: the declining authority of the Saints, which was to find its accelerant and apotheosis in the tragedy of Salem.

Images of assault by Indians and demons had shaped nightmares at Springfield prior to the Parsons trials. But Metacom's War of 1675–8, of which the Springfield attack was part, fused these colonial enemies into a single 'other'. Metacom himself was demonized, then killed and dismembered.[103] In the 1680s Increase Mather and his son Cotton (who kept Metacom's jawbone as a totemic souvenir) wrote books linking colonists' irreligion to native superstition.[104] As New England's peril increased, so too did the incidence of witchcraft: an English visitor in 1686 was shocked to find a 'great many witches in this country'.[105] As ever, paranoia fed on political uncertainty. The Glorious Revolution of 1688–9, which erupted (with only a small lag) in New England as well as in the Old, cast doubts on the legitimacy of law and government and reignited hostilities with Indian allies of the French, with whom, back in Europe, Old England was now at war. The following year, New England was stricken by smallpox. Spirits sagged, tempers flared, social bonds snapped.

Early in 1692, long after the peak of European witchcraft trials, a witch-hunt blew up at Salem. Sir William Phips, the royal governor of Massachusetts, arrived to find the region 'miserably harassed by a most horrible possession of devils, and many persons in a strange ferment of dissatisfaction'. When the Salem judges ignored doubts about the evidence, Phips was forced to intervene. 'The devil took upon him the shape of innocent persons,' he said, 'some of the accused being of unblameable life.'[106]

The Salem witch-hunt, in which twenty people died, ensued from family feuds, religious politics, legal confusion and sheer terror.[107] As at Springfield, anger was projected by people unable to reconcile Christian obligation with thrusting ambition. Even at the time, Salem was blamed on 'sinful and unruly passions, such as envy, malice, or hatred of our neighbours'.[108] Puritan leadership in New England collapsed mainly from the franchise shifting from church membership to land ownership. But the civil injustice of Salem eclipsed the menace of religious dissent. The original godly 'errand in the wilderness' had been tarnished, the spirit of charity abraded by commercial endeavour. And wherever self-interest took away from altruism, causing resentment, anxiety and a sense of guilt, witchcraft was apt to flourish, to the detriment of decency and order. In 1694 Joshua Scottow, a merchant, wrote that 'the horrid shriekings and screamings of obsessed, possessed and bewitched persons' had turned the virtuous New English into detestable Old Devils. The colony might be renamed 'New Witchland', Scottow mocked. Prior to Salem, nowhere deserved the name more than Springfield.[109]

By the time of John Pynchon's death in 1703, Springfield's fortunes, over a quarter of a century after its sacking in Metacom's War, had revived. Not only did Pynchon leave a fortune to strengthen his dynasty, but the town's population had grown to 800 and was set to double within a generation. Property prices soared: by 1707 Hugh Parsons's homestead was worth the tidy sum of £80.[110] Shortly before Pynchon's death, the town was granted an eastward plantation for seventy families. Springfielders west of the Connecticut River, uninhabited in William Pynchon's day, reclaimed the ministry land bought from George Moxon, and demanded that townsmen on the east side contribute to the cost of building their own meeting house.

Residents in the long meadow echoed this independent-spirited petition and sought to establish a township up the hill away from the flood plain. Springfield demurred, protesting that the exemption of southerners from taxation would cause 'intolerable difficulties'. But the agitators prevailed, and Longmeadow was born.[111]

As puritan authority ebbed, New England's preachers still dangled the torments of hell before their congregations. In an execution sermon of 1698, for a Springfield woman convicted of smothering her baby, a minister promised murderers an eternity with idolaters and witches in the fiery lake.[112] Even a century later Springfield's preachers were still warning of the 'diabolical distempers of pride, malice and envy' and 'evil spirits acting invisibly on the passions and imaginations of mankind'.[113] Yet eighteenth-century congregations took such words figuratively, assuming they noticed them at all. The Connecticut valley was more politically stable, its towns economically varied and better governed. Controversies were brief: clashing neighbours calmed by litigation.[114] Keeping the peace was an end in itself rather than a means to appease God. The summary justice of magistrates, and their love for confession, gave way to the judgement of juries. By allowing for diversity, the law nurtured the confidence to prosper, while governors felt less threatened by dissent.[115]

Among other changes was a shift in sensibilities about the seen and unseen worlds. In civil discourse, and prominently in the courts, confidence in sensory evidence of the supernatural diminished. William Pynchon was a harbinger of that change. He wasn't a heretic; but he was a freethinker, who, like the philosopher John Locke, exchanged medieval scholasticism for secular empiricism. Pynchon may have been gullible about witches, but his belief that divinity resided in everyone was truly humanist.[116] And after the horrors of Salem, it was this humanism rather than his alleged superstition that endured. Early in the eighteenth century a minister named John Hale debunked the proofs of witchcraft, including everything believed at Springfield in 1651. Apparitions were phantasms, demons beasts, afflictions natural, witch marks meaningless, and suspects summoned by counter-magic mere coincidences. These things only seemed real because of people's fear, credulity and malice. Evil constructions had been put on innocent actions, averred Hale, causing neighbours to 'look upon other actions with a squint eye', and 'through the multiplying glass of their own jealousies, make a molehill seem a mountain'. This was how the despised were discredited and ostracized.[117]

After Salem no more witches were hanged in New England, and no more heretics banished. New anxieties, more material than religious, replaced the old.[118] The idea of diabolism, however, did not disappear overnight. Not only would European witch-trials continue to happen for decades to come – the last English conviction was in 1712 – but even in states where the evidence for witchcraft became inadmissible at law, the existence of witches could not be disproved. Defenders of the kingdom of heaven resisted scepticism owing to its atheistical implications, but also argued that the melancholy that weakened witches' minds did not affect the sane majority who for so long had believed their crimes to be real.[119] In the end, the city of devils – 'pandaemonium', the capital of hell – was not demolished: it could only be starved of attention by people with fewer uses for magic than their parents and grandparents. After 1800 the demonic foes of Christian civilization were not chased away: witchcraft faded into irrelevance, and its adherents sank back into the ether. Before then, however, many more lives would be destroyed by fearful men and women, for whom the ruin of all witches, so earnestly desired by Mary Parsons, was not yet complete.[120]

Epilogue: An End to All Affection

Springfield, 3 May 2015, a humid Sunday around noon. I was pacing down the south end of Main Street away from the centre, the route taken by Jonathan Taylor 364 years earlier as he hurried home to his wife. The road is six feet higher today: Taylor's ghostly head would have been gliding beneath my feet. The place was deserted. The odd low-slung car growled past, drivers slowing to check me out. I looked like a lost tourist – not that Springfield is much of a tourist town. In my hands were a street-plan of the twenty-first-century city and a map of the place Jonathan Taylor would have known, a spectral outline of its modern incarnation.

Passing pawnshops, laundromats and mini-marts, mostly shut, I stopped at Loring Street. On the corner with Main the redbrick façade of a Pentecostal church abutted Dillon's Liquors, with its pink shop-front and 'Checks Cashed' neon sign. On this spot, Taylor had stopped that night in February 1651, ready for his bed, unaware of the great terror he was about to face. I kept going, not wanting to loiter and keen to find where Hugh and Mary Parsons had lived – a moment I'd been imagining since my arrival two days earlier.

I came by train from Boston, where I'd been researching in archives and libraries. Once these closed for the day, I went walking: up the hill on Boston Common, envisioning execution crowds; along Court Street, formerly Prison Lane, where Mary Parsons died; and down State Street, which when Mary came to see John Winthrop was shorter, the harbour further inland. The site of Winthrop's house is marked with a plaque on the old Stock Exchange. It felt good to get the lie of the land. And present-day Boston is prosperous, populous, reassuring. I was about to learn how neglected and left behind Springfield felt in comparison. Even the terrain, viewed from my train window, signalled a change in mood from built-up modernity to a more timeless, haunting landscape: far-off undulating hills, scrubland, lanky pines and birches and glimpses of creeks and marshes clumped with tough grass. This, then, was the lonely wilderness that had both threatened Pynchon's colonists and driven them to tame it.

I emerged from Springfield's desolate railway station as the sun was setting and hurried through an underpass to my hotel. I slept badly and left early. The Springfield History Library and Archives was a few boarded-up blocks away. In the basement search room I met Maggie, the archivist. She was concerned that I hadn't hired a car: walking in some parts of the city, she said, wasn't a great idea. She ringed three restaurants on a map, all near my hotel and safe to visit in daylight. I took a seat at one of the library's formica-topped tables, and Maggie wheeled over a trolley stacked with parchment scrolls and paper files. Some had been brought from England in 1630, others written locally, but all had moved barely a mile in nearly four centuries. As I began reading something caught my eye. Outside the security-grilled window a man was looking up and down, fumbling with a roll of banknotes. Maggie had told me I might see drug deals. It was distracting, unnerving. But for now, at least, the reading room was an air-conditioned sanctuary from the world outside.

As I ploughed through the documents, Maggie told me how Springfield had once been a boomtown alive with businesses, societies, schools and churches. It was the birthplace of basketball, vulcanized rubber and the Merriam-Webster dictionary – 'the City of Firsts'. During the Revolutionary War, George Washington had seen advantage in Springfield's location, much as William Pynchon had. The US Armory was built there in 1777, manufacturing weapons through the American Civil War and beyond. In 1852 the town of Springfield was formally mandated as a city and within a generation had become supremely self-assured. Its paper factories supplied the nation. Dickens visited on the steamboat *Massachusetts*.

The Pynchons lost pre-eminence but went on to serve as doctors, clergymen and lawyers, and so contributed to making Springfield a model of municipal grandeur.[1]

There were echoes of a supernatural past. In 1814 a consumptive's remains were exhumed and burned as a cure for afflicted relatives. The ghost of a murdered man rendered a property on the Mill River, near the old Parsons house, unsaleable. There was a witch in Longmeadow, whom a doctor saw raise a wind to blow away chaff at threshing time. A clergyman at an inn claimed witches visited his room to invite him to a nocturnal feast. Citizens were also prone to hysterical gossip, as when a spate of fires was blamed on a sinister arsonist.[2] Yet these were faint relics in an era of burgeoning progress, albeit one set to end in agonized decline. Springfield's golden age lasted a while longer into the twentieth century. Rolls-Royce manufactured there in the 1920s, when Theodor Geisel, the son of a successful Springfield brewer, was growing up. Geisel became Dr Seuss, the children's writer, who remains the city's most famous son – something I had learned that morning when I stumbled into his memorial sculpture park, trying to lose a man wanting money for 'medicine'.

The Geisel brewery was ruined by Prohibition, and many other businesses went bust in the Depression. In the mid-1930s catastrophic floods consumed large areas of the north and south ends, which never fully recovered. In these years, William Pynchon's last direct descendant in Springfield died.[3] After the war, economic decline steepened, civic pride waned. By the 1960s investment had dried up, and jobs were scarce, a demise accelerated by the closing of the Armory during the Vietnam War. By the 1990s the city had gained a reputation for urban decay, drug crime and political corruption.

Today, Maggie told me, immigrants were ghettoized, and many young people, mostly Hispanic, slipped into a marginal existence. Some not only failed to graduate from high school but didn't even expect to live that long. The situation had deteriorated after 9/11, when the security budgets of Washington DC and New York were flooded with federal money, which pushed metropolitan drug gangs further afield into smaller cities like Springfield. The semi-derelict buildings I passed were scheduled for demolition to make way for a super casino, which Maggie feared would only create dead-end jobs while feeding the addictions of the poor. Images I'd seen online gave the impression of a confident city clustered with shiny office blocks and green spaces. This wasn't quite how it felt on the ground.

Evenings were spent reading in a Cajun restaurant – one of Maggie's tips. My books included an archival miscellany edited by Henry M. Burt, a descendant of Hugh Parsons's neighbour Jonathan Burt; and Stephen Innes's *Labor in a New Land*, which contrasts the Springfield known to Hugh Parsons with the dreamy pastoral community that, for many, still characterizes New England's townships. Innes nailed Parsons as 'a virtual parody of Springfield's self-image: acquisitiveness becoming greed, individualism becoming vengefulness, deviance becoming diabolical'.[4] It felt strange rereading these books in Springfield itself, a reminder that beneath the built environment – beneath where I was sitting eating Chef Wayne's jambalaya – lay a silent early iteration of the town.

Some months earlier I'd waded through William Pynchon's works, and a few academic studies of the theology that inspired them. Pynchon's writing, turgid and obtuse even in its own time, had no lasting impact. His own volumes passed down the generations as curious heirlooms.[5] Today just nine copies of *The Meritorious Price of Our Redemption* survive. I came across one in the Springfield archive, which had belonged to Increase Mather, then his son Cotton, infamous from the Salem trials. The Mathers hated Pynchon's heresy, much as they hated witches. Against a passage where Pynchon asserts that Christ could not have visited hell, Cotton Mather has penned the cutting remark: 'as some blind Protestants affirm'.[6]

As Pynchon's writings faded, so did his social world. Generations of entrepreneurial Springfielders fanned out to build their own communities; others moved down the Connecticut valley as far as Saybrook. Reece Bedortha's descendants were prominent in Windsor until their mill was demolished in 1963, thereby ending a life where people were sustained by their own land and the power of rushing water. But for many, the shift was almost imperceptible. Photographs in the Bedortha archive depict a historical bridge between the seventeenth and twentieth centuries, one marked more by continuity than change. The captions read: 'landscape, path through the woods'; 'plowed field with fence and houses/cabins in distance'; 'woman in bonnet, standing outside'; 'man watering a horse'; 'people in canoes on a river'. The last word in all these descriptions is 'undated'. 'Timeless' would do just as well.[7]

Springfield's early buildings have gone, too. At the junction of State and Main, the mind's eye conjures colonists crossing the causeway. You can sit in the German pub on the footprint of William Pynchon's house and imagine the constable arriving with Mary Parsons. But there's little to look at. Three churches have replaced George Moxon's meeting house; the present one, now defunct, was built in 1819. The Dwight House, the last colonial homestead, was moved to Deerfield in 1950. The burial ground has been lost to roads and rail tracks; its 'sacred dust' was taken to a new cemetery in 1841. John Pynchon's brick fortress was pulled down in 1831; the Bliss residence, built in the south end around 1645, sixty years later.[8] The most evocative survival is the river. All but obscured by the raised highway of Interstate 91, the best you can do is to survey its length from the Memorial Bridge, and visualize puritan farmers canoeing to their planting grounds on the west side. Over the bridge and five miles south in Agawam, you can also gaze across the river to a place between a ploughed field and a nature reserve where Hugh Parsons's seven-acre long meadow plot used to be.

There are some historical markers in Springfield: a plaque for Pynchon's 'old fort' (the German pub), one for the site of the 1645 meeting house, and another for a tavern, almost certainly the location of Robert Ashley's alehouse, from where Mary Parsons's soul was spirited away to the witches' sabbath. Springfield also has a couple of statues: *The Puritan*, commissioned in 1881 by Chester W. Chapin, a railroad magnate and descendant of Henry Chapin, one of William Pynchon's field workers. The following year the J. P. Morgan banking family erected in Court Square a bronze of their first American forebear Miles Morgan, another labourer bonded to Pynchon, who died in 1699 owning fourteen shillings' worth of swamp. Having never learned to write his name, Morgan's signature had been an arrow, rather like that of an Indian.[9]

No statue commemorates William Pynchon, though a few streets and buildings bear his name. When the Connecticut Valley History Museum relocated to its present site, the house it had occupied was renamed the William Pynchon Memorial Building. Since 1915 distinguished residents have received the Order of William Pynchon, a bronze medal depicting Pynchon as he appears in his portrait of 1657, which today hangs in a museum in Salem. Other reminders are scattered across the city. The Massachusetts State Office Building is decorated with a mural from 1937 entitled 'Mr Pynchon and the Settling of Springfield', where Pynchon looks more debonair cavalier than drab puritan. A black-clad witch flees on a broomstick, a fantasy of witchcraft concealing the deadly festering of suspicion, and how in the marriage of Hugh and Mary Parsons, as a nineteenth-century writer put it, 'altercations arose, and were continued until an entire estrangement and hatred put an end to all affection'.[10]

I had intended to hire a bike to scope out the original town from the riverside, but the cycle paths were overgrown and clogged with rubbish. I caught the bus to Northampton, now a smart bohemian retreat, where the Forbes Library preserves William Pynchon's remarkable account book. Apart from that, I travelled on foot – which is how I ended up at the wrong end of Main Street, feeling conspicuous and dripping from the midday heat.

I was drawing closer to the ghosts that obsessed me most, to the scene of crimes no less real for having passed from sight and largely from memory. The spirits I'd summoned so far had been indifferent, inert. But the thought of visiting the site of Hugh and Mary's home made me feel uneasy. On a wall next to a discount supermarket, a colourful mural asked: 'What Makes a Man?' This was also the question asked of Hugh Parsons as he struggled to meet local expectations – a question that, in the end, he failed to answer to anyone's satisfaction.

I stopped outside a power-tool store at the top of Elmwood Street where the Parsons homestead once stood. The air was thick, the silence oppressive – as it had been in the seventeenth century. Elmwood was a short road with a car-hire firm and a parking lot. But there was a small house. With its clapboards and pitched roof, it might have been the Parsons house, though there was no age to it. That it was uninhabited, with climbing vegetation and a hole where the upstairs window had been, bristled the hair on my neck. After all, this was where Hugh tore off Mary's bedclothes, where she searched him as he slept, where their children were conceived and died. Passion swelled and was spent, tragically, and for Mary fatally. There, once, stood the little house, beside a great river at the edge of a forest, where, as in so many folktales, demons closed in and desire ended in death.

All around these streets, the dead and forgotten – mostly travellers born three thousand miles away, and four hundred years ago – once dreamed and schemed, full of sound and fury. They were real and vital, as yet undimmed by posterity, and lived and loved with every imaginable kind of human feeling until at last they returned to dust. Even as I felt moved by their memory, standing where they had once stood, I could sense Hugh and Mary edging from the shadows, insisting that I couldn't possibly know who they were. As W. G. Sebald once said of history's grand illusions and confident assurances: 'We, the survivors, see everything from above, see everything at once. And still we do not know how it was.'[11]

That wasn't quite the end. I returned to Springfield in July 2018 to tie up loose ends of research and have another look round. An article I'd published had made Springfield sound like a ghost town, prompting a journalist, Jim Kinney, to respond in print that apart from the $800 million MGM mega-casino, $2.7 billion had been invested in other projects. He said he'd never felt threatened in downtown Springfield. Local residents weighed in on my side, inviting Kinney to join them there at night. Others regretted the decline of a great city, some pointing to the incredible feat of its foundation. But I conceded that perhaps I'd been spooked because I was a stranger. In Boston, I'd heard that Springfield was on the up.

A warm breeze was drawing clouds across the sky. My cab took me to an Airbnb apartment, an imposing mock-Tudor house on Maple Street, along the hillside parallel to Main. The code for the key safe didn't work, and when I phoned the contact number no one answered. The wind was up now, thunder rumbling. A couple of passers-by stopped to stare. Finally, a caretaker let me into the flat, which had a stale tang but was clean. The bedroom window looked out over what had been the woodlot of Jonathan Taylor, where he had once worked, haunted by the memory of the slithering demons sent by Hugh Parsons.

The storm clouds didn't break until dusk, as I was returning from a pizzeria on Main Street. The streets were empty. A few fat drops fell. I arrived back at the apartment, a downpour behind me. On TV the weather map was covered in temperature warnings, some in the low hundreds. Sitting by the humming air-con unit, I read the 1973 novel *Gravity's Rainbow*, about the deceptively perfect arc of destiny and history. The author, Thomas Pynchon, casts his direct ancestor as William Slothrop, 'a peculiar bird' who returns miserably from America to England after his heretical book is burned in Boston.[12] I also flicked through *The Bay-Path*, a novel from 1857 about tension between the feminine Hugh Parsons and his wife Mary, 'lonely in her thoughts, and passionate under restraint', who behaved more like a man.[13]

I was woken up at 5 a.m. by hammering rain and the distant blare of trains. From my window, I surveyed the city, lightning forking against a sky of washed-out lilac and charcoal. By the time I went out the rain had stopped, but it was still muggy. The streets were as I remembered them from three years previously: weeds between the cracks, glass in the gutters, timber houses peeling paint. Heading south, I found myself on Pine Street, which was in a better state. As the way curved down I reached the line of the Mill River, once vital to Springfield's settlers. It could hear it thundering through the sewers, frantic to reach the Connecticut River. Over a fence in the car park of a funeral parlour, I found a short stretch of furious, frothing water – an exhilarating relic from the world of Hugh and Mary Parsons.

At the junction with Main Street stood a boulder set with a plaque commemorating the deaths of Thomas Cooper and Thomas Miller, who near that place on 5 October 1675 became the first casualties of the attack in Metacom's War, which remains, proportionally, America's bloodiest yet least remembered conflict. I continued along Main, through the traditionally Italian south end, past a statue of Christopher Columbus, as far as Elmwood Street. I was back at the site of the Parsons homestead, arriving from the opposite direction. But the abandoned clapboard house had gone. It felt appropriate that a phantom house should have vanished from the landscape, and also encouraging that someone was building there.

Gradually, I began to get a more positive impression. Downtown, I noticed new saplings and kerbstones. Construction sites were busy, and the boarded-up premises had been cleared or renovated. The pace seemed brisker, the mood buoyant. Perhaps Springfield was shaking off its post-industrial gloom. I visited the Hampden County Courthouse, where friendly staff brought the deeds I wanted. Afterwards I crossed the square to City Hall and wandered its corridors of marble and varnished oak until I found the Clerk's office. I waited, watching people ask for forms, apply for licences and pay parking fines.

The Clerk appeared and shook my hand. He seemed busy but spared the time to sit me down in a windowless room full of collapsing cardboard boxes. Apologizing that City Hall had no archivist, he dashed out and returned with a tower of bound manuscripts. There I stayed for three hours, photographing town records until my phone died. Every detail of Springfield's infancy had been recorded, from regulations about felling timber and subletting houses, to a note that proved the constable, Thomas Merrick, had benefited from Hugh Parsons's downfall.

Every now and then the Clerk swept through the room, paying me no attention, even though from all the sprawling clutter I was virtually in his way. But then I found something so remarkable I called him over. It was William Pynchon's foundational agreement for the town of Springfield, dated 14 May 1636. The City Clerk from 1846 had annotated it: 'Preserve this record – it is the beginning of this town.' The present Clerk stood still, startled, the document resting in his hands. I suggested he might put it on public display, to show people where Springfield had come from. Smiling now, he promised he would.[14]

Perhaps displaying Pynchon's faded charter will lead to some broader, deeper understanding about the city that Hugh and Mary Parsons helped to build, and about their private lives: their dreams, distress and the emotional gravity of ruin. They currently have no memorial in Springfield – the sort of sober monument found in other places, like Salem, where convicted witches suffered – nor have their names been cleared.[15] That Springfield has so far neglected to remember Hugh and Mary has been blamed on the reluctance of historians to write a definitive account. Hopefully this book is somewhere to begin.[16]

Acknowledgements

I am indebted to my editor, Tom Penn, and his assistant, Eva Hodgkin, both of whom read drafts of this book with extraordinary patience, dedication and insight. There is hardly a paragraph that has not been improved by their astute comments. Their colleagues at Penguin have also been a pleasure to work with, especially the copy-editor David Watson, editorial manager Ruth Pietroni, production manager Imogen Scott, designer Samantha Johnson and proofreaders Stephen Ryan and Louisa Watson. Jeff Edwards drew the beautiful maps. I'd also like to thank Natasha Fairweather, my agent at Rogers, Coleridge & White, and Peter Robinson, Natasha's predecessor, who first believed in this project. Peter transformed the initial proposal, as did Kate Summerscale, Rebecca Watson and James Brown. James also contributed research and helped me get to the point of what I was trying to say.

I'm also grateful to the staff of The National Archives, British Library, Cambridge University Library, Bodleian Library, Royal Society, Dr Williams's Library, National Library of Wales and various county record offices. Much of the research was done in the US. I would especially like to thank Tal Nadan in the Manuscripts and Archives Division of the New York Public Library for granting access to William Pynchon's deposition book; Kim Reynolds and Jay Moschella at the Boston Public Library; Jane Kelly in the Harvard Law School Library; various assistants at the Massachusetts Historical Society; John Harrington at the Massachusetts State Archives in Dorchester, who supplied original documents instead of fiddly microfilms; and most of all Maggie Humberston of the Springfield Library and Archives for her knowledge and generosity. At the Hampden County Registry of Deeds, Donna Brown produced the 'Record Book of Deeds', and just across Court Square Springfield's City Clerk,

Acknowledgements

Anthony Wilson, was courteously obliging. In Northampton, hard-pressed staff made time to find boxes of seventeenth-century wills, and Julie Bartlett-Nelson and Elise Bernier-Feeley of the Forbes Library allowed me to spend an afternoon with Pynchon's account book.

Financial support from the University of East Anglia, the British Academy and the Leverhulme Trust was invaluable. Ideas were tried out at seminars and conferences in London, Norwich, Manchester, Dublin, Berlin and Melbourne. Sally Gardner and Kate Summerscale commented on drafts and greatly encouraged me. Over the years, I've also benefited from the kind words of Kerry Apps, Cathie Carmichael, Sarah Dunant, Mike Farrar, Spenser Frearson, Philippa Gregory, Chris Jones, David Kynaston, Hilary Mantel, Chris Marsh, Geoffrey Munn, Rosamond Roughton, Jess Sharkey, Edmund Slater, Graeme Small and Anna Whitelock. And from academic friends in my field: Tad Baker, Owen Davies, John Demos, Marion Gibson, Richard Godbeer, Steve Hindle, Ronald Hutton, Laura Kounine, Brian Levack, Charlotte-Rose Millar, Alison Rowlands, Jim Sharpe, Mark Stoyle, John Walter, Andy Wood, Blair Worden and Charles Zika. Special thanks go to Stuart Clark and Lyndal Roper for writing so many letters of reference. Roger Thompson, an eminent historian of colonial America, gave me his library, or as much of it as I could fit in the car. My debt to Keith Wrightson rolls over between books. He taught me to be both imaginative and empirical, and to show empathy while preserving the essential otherness of the past.

Finally I'm grateful to my family, without whose support none of what I do would be worthwhile or viable. I couldn't have wished for more from my parents, Audrey and Eddie Gaskill, and my inlaws, Roger and Rosina Peirse. This leaves only my wife Sheena Peirse, a tirelessly patient, cheerful and loving companion, and our children Kate, Tom and Lily, compared to whom the writing of books seems an unremarkable achievement.

Sources and Methods

In 1828 George Bliss, whose ancestors came to Springfield in the 1640s, mentioned Hugh and Mary Parsons in a speech, but declined to elaborate, as 'there is nothing on our records on the subject'. This wasn't quite true, but the principal source certainly lay elsewhere. Today William Pynchon's unique book of testimonies is preserved in the New York Public Library. Written mostly in William Pynchon's crabbed hand, it measures 15 cm by 19 cm, and contains fifty-two grubby, water-stained pages. With only a little exaggeration, the antiquarian Samuel Gardner Drake wrote: 'The proceedings and strange evidence given in the case of Hugh Parsons are probably the most extraordinary of any upon record.'[1]

The material has never before been fully exploited. Drake published a transcription, which David D. Hall modernized. Yet neither tackles the puzzles of dating and ordering, complicated further by Drake, who believed the depositions had been misbound in the eighteenth century; more likely, they were a chaotic copy made for the trial. Marion Gibson, whose insight this is, writes optimistically about this maddening document's potential: 'We can make what we like of the texts supplied.'[2] Clearly there are limits, but I've filled gaps imaginatively and made plausible inferences.[3] I've been sparing with qualifications such as 'probably' and 'doubtless', while avoiding outright invention. This book is a historical reconstruction, not a novel. Yet it aspires to that most difficult of historical undertakings: suspending hindsight to reveal 'the embeddedness of events in a flow of experience'.[4]

I have drawn on many sources: court records, sermons, pamphlets, proclamations, letters, diaries, deeds and wills. Springfield's church records, alas, do not predate 1735.[5] I'm indebted to David M. Powers's transcription of Moxon's sermon notes, and to the late

Stephen Innes for doing so much groundwork. My aim was to scavenge 'a landscape cluttered with the detritus of past living' to see what the reassembled pieces said about what people once saw and felt.[6] This is micro-history, which by drilling deep unearths evidence of human consciousness, both familiar and extraordinary.[7] Past lives are dots in a big picture, yet they were lived largely in ignorance of historical forces such as advancing individualism, modernity or secularization. Poor, fretful people thought only of survival, and perhaps escape.[8]

According to Katharine Hodgkin, the study of witchcraft is 'a place where history asks questions about itself'. It involves language, representation and narrative truth – like history itself. Witchcraft is (and always was) perplexing, opening up endless possibilities of meaning. 'Notions of rationality, certain knowledge, history and fiction', Hodgkin writes, 'are all called into question, to remind us of their own provisionality, their temporal and cultural boundedness'. We are denied certainty – but no more than baffled contemporaries were.[9]

My book is not a straightforward retelling, uncluttered by analysis, nor is it 'oppressively instructive', as a critic said of *The Crucible*, Arthur Miller's play about Salem. The aim was not to belittle the characters in the story by suggesting that we now know better.[10] Instead, it treats witchcraft as *witchcraft*: a category unstable in 1650 and ever since at risk of being explained away as fraud, hysteria or delusion. Objective 'reality' must sometimes be played down to point up the subjective quality of experience.[11] Only by taking the strange on its own terms can we understand ourselves in time. This is the purpose of history, which my doctoral supervisor was taught then passed on to me. It remains the name of the game.[12]

Notes

Abbreviations

AAS
American Antiquarian Society, Worcester, Massachusetts

AHR
American Historical Review

AWNE
Samuel Drake, *Annals of Witchcraft in New England* (Boston, 1869)

BL
British Library, London

Bodl.
Bodleian Library, Oxford

BPL
Boston Public Library

CJWM
Joseph H. Smith (ed.), *Colonial Justice in Western Massachusetts (1639–1702)* (Cambridge, MA, 1961)

CSL
Connecticut Archives, 1629–1820, Connecticut State Library, Hartford, Connecticut

CUL
Cambridge University Library

DH
David M. Powers, *Damnable Heresy: William Pynchon, the Indians, and the First Book Banned (and Burned) in Boston* (Eugene, OR, 2015)

Dow
George Francis Dow, *Every Day Life in the Massachusetts Bay Colony* (New York, 1988)

Notes

DWL
Dr Williams's Library, London

ESMC
Early Springfield Manuscripts Collection, Series 4–7 (in HLAS)

FCHS
Henry M. Burt, *The First Century of the History of Springfield: The Official Records from 1636 to 1736*, 2 vols. (Springfield, MA, 1898–9), vol. 1

GACW
David M. Powers, *Good and Comfortable Words: The Coded Sermon Notes of John Pynchon and the Frontier Preaching Ministry of George Moxon* (Eugene, OR, 2017)

GHNE
William Hubbard, *A General History of New England* (Boston, 1848)

Green
Mason A. Green, *Springfield, 1636–1886: History of Town and City* (Springfield, MA, 1888)

Hampden County
Clifton Johnson, *Hampden County, 1636–1936*, vol. I (New York, 1936)

Hawke
David Freeman Hawke, *Everyday Life in Early America* (New York, 1989)

HCRP
Hampshire County Registry of Probate, Northampton, Massachusetts

HLAS
History Library & Archives, Springfield, Massachusetts

HLSL
Harvard Law School Library, Harvard University

Hosmer
James Kendall Hosmer, *Winthrop's Journal . . . 1630–1649*, 2 vols. (New York, 1908)

HRBD
'Record Book of Deeds . . . for the County of Hampshire', Volume A–B, 1673–1704, Hampden County Registry of Deeds, Springfield, Massachusetts

JJW
Richard S. Dunn and Laetitia Yeandle (eds.), *The Journal of John Winthrop, 1630–1649* (Cambridge, MA, 1996)

LNL

Stephen Innes, *Labor in a New Land: Economy and Society in Seventeenth-Century Springfield* (Princeton, NJ, 1983)

LWP

Worthington Chauncey Ford (ed.), 'Letters of William Pynchon', *Proceedings of the Massachusetts Historical Society*, 48 (1914–16), pp. 35–56

MC

Massachusetts Collection ('Felt Collection'), Massachusetts State Archives, Boston

MHS

Massachusetts Historical Society, Boston

MS1649

'Notes of the Rev. Mr Moxon's Sermons [1649], by the Hon. John Pynchon of Springfield', Simon Gratz Collection (0250A), Historical Society of Pennsylvania, Philadelphia

NEHGR

New England Historical and Genealogical Register

NEHGS

New England Historic Genealogical Society

NEQ

New England Quarterly

NLW

National Library of Wales, Aberystwyth

ODNB

Oxford Dictionary of National Biography

PP

Carl Bridenbaugh and Juliette Tomlinson (eds.), *The Pynchon Papers*, 2 vols. (Boston, 1982–5)

Pynchons of Springfield

Frances Armytage and Juliette Tomlinson, *The Pynchons of Springfield: Founders and Colonizers, 1636–1702* (Springfield, MA, 1969)

Records of Possessions

History Library & Archives, Springfield, Massachusetts, Springfield Municipal Records, Land Divisions: Records of Possessions, 1647–1709 (Book 16)

Notes

RLCR
Report of the Record Commissioners of the City of Boston, vol. 6: *Roxbury Land and Church Records* (Boston, 1881)

RO
Record Office

Savage
James Savage et al. (eds), *A Genealogical Dictionary of the First Settlers of New England*, 4 vols. (Boston, 1860–62)

Shurtleff
Nathaniel B. Shurtleff (ed.), *Records of the Governor and Company of the Massachusetts Bay in New England*, 5 vols. (Boston, 1853–4)

Sylvester
Nathaniel Bartlett Sylvester, *History of the Connecticut Valley in Massachusetts*, 2 vols. (Philadelphia, 1879), vol. 1

Thistlethwaite
Frank Thistlethwaite, *Dorset Pilgrims: The Story of West Country Pilgrims Who Went to New England in the 17th Century* (London, 1989)

TNA
The National Archives, Kew, UK

TRSR
Town Records, Volumes 1 & 2: Selectmen's Records, 1644–82, City Clerk's Office, City Hall, Springfield, Massachusetts

Ulrich
Laurel Thatcher Ulrich, *Good Wives: Image and Reality in the Lives of Women in Northern New England, 1650–1750* (New York, 1982)

VRS
Clifford L. Stott (ed.), *Vital Records of Springfield*, 4 vols. (Boston, 1944–5), vol. 1

WMQ
William and Mary Quarterly

WP
The Winthrop Papers, 1557–1654, ed. MHS, 6 vols. (Boston, 1929–92)

WPAB
William Pynchon's Account Book, 1645–50, Judd Papers, HKBC/P993, Forbes Library, Northampton, Massachusetts

WPDB
William Pynchon's Deposition Book, 1650–51, New York Public Library, Mss Col. 1900 ('Testimony against Hugh Parsons, charged with witchcraft')

Wright, *Early Springfield*
Harry A. Wright, *Early Springfield and Longmeadow, Massachusetts, with Special Reference to Benjamin Cooley, Pioneer* (Rutland, VT, 1940)

Wright, *Genesis*
Harry A. Wright, *The Genesis of Springfield: The Development of the Town* (Springfield, MA, 1936)

Wyllys
Samuel Wyllys Papers, 1663–1728, Brown University Library, Providence, Rhode Island

1. A Voice That Said 'Death'

1 For Jonathan Taylor's deposition: WPDB, ff. 24v–25r (7 April 1651). The Taylors probably arrived late 1648: *DH*, p. 100; *FCHS*, p. 43; *CJWM*, p. 217. Parish registers have several possibilities for Jonathan's birth, from Cornwall to Kent; the latter is most likely.

2 WPDB, f. 7r (William Branch, 13 March 1651).

3 The best general works on Pynchon are: David M. Powers, *Damnable Heresy: William Pynchon, the Indians, and the First Book Banned (and Burned) in Boston* (Eugene, OR, 2015); Robert Anderson, 'William Pynchon', *ODNB*; Ruth A. McIntyre, *William Pynchon: Merchant and Colonizer* (Springfield, MA, 1961).

4 Stephen Innes's *Labor in a New Land* (*LNL*) sees Pynchon almost exclusively as a secular entrepreneur. For the puritan scholar: Philip F. Gura, *A Glimpse of Sion's Glory: Puritan Radicalism in New England, 1620–1660* (Middletown, CT, 1984), ch. 11; Michael P. Winship, 'Contesting control of orthodoxy among the godly: William Pynchon reexamined', *WMQ*, 54 (1997), pp. 795–822. He was 'acute, restive, and singularly self-assertive . . . a person of broad and aggressive thought who loved both money and adventure': *Hampden County*, pp. 18–19.

5 The 'William Pinchon' who matriculated at Hart Hall, Oxford, in 1596 was probably a cousin: Donald Lines Jacobus and Edgar Francis Waterman, *Hale, House and Related Families, Mainly of the Connecticut River Valley* (Hartford, CT, 1952), pp. 723–4; Joseph Foster (ed.), *Alumni Oxonienses: The Members of the University of Oxford, 1500–1714*, 4 vols. (Oxford, 1891), iii, p. 1165; TNA, PROB 11/119/541 (William Pynchon, 1612).

6 E.g. Pynchon's letter of 1647: MHS, Ms. N-760 (i).

7 *LNL*, pp. 6–8; *DH*, p. 45; Green, pp. 50–51.

8 Henry Morris, *History of the First Church in Springfield* (Springfield, MA, 1875), p. 7; Harry Andrew Wright, *Meeting Houses of the First Church of Christ, Springfield, Massachusetts* (Springfield, MA, 1945), p. 10; *DH*, pp. 89–90. Pynchon bought the bell for £5 in January 1651, but expected to be reimbursed: TRSR, p. 102; *FCHS*, pp. 143, 183.

9 Peter Gregg Slater, *Children in the New England Mind: In Death and in Life* (Hampden, CT, 1977), pp. 35–6. On parental grief: Michael MacDonald, *Mystical Bedlam: Madness, Anxiety, and Healing in Seventeenth-Century England* (Cambridge, 1981), pp. 80–84.

10 *FCHS*, pp. 11, 19, 46, 144.

11 *LNL*, pp. 14, 45–8; TRSR, p. 10; Ezra Hoyt Byington, *The Puritan in England and New England* (Boston, 1896), p. 213 n.3.

12 *FCHS*, p. 144; *DH*, p. 89; Green, p. 43; Morris, *First Church*, p. 7; Wright, *Meeting Houses*, p. 4; *WPAB*, p. 208.

13 Howard Millar Chapin, *Life of Deacon Samuel Chapin, of Springfield* (Providence, RI, 1908), ch. 4; *FCHS*, pp. 54–7; Green, pp. 17–19.

14 Mark Goldie, 'The unacknowledged republic: officeholding in early modern England', in Tim Harris (ed.), *The Politics of the Excluded, c. 1500–1850* (Basingstoke, 2001), pp. 153–94. On continuity: T. H. Breen, 'Persistent localism: English social change and the shaping of New England institutions', *WMQ*, 32 (1975), pp. 3–28; David Grayson Allen, *In English Ways: The Movement of Societies and the Transferal of English Local Law and Custom to Massachusetts Bay in the Seventeenth Century* (Chapel Hill, NC, 1981), pp. 115–18; Phillip H. Round, *By Nature and by Custom Cursed: Transatlantic Civil Discourse and New England Cultural Production, 1620–1660* (Hanover, NH, 1999), ch. 2; Stephen Foster, *The Long Argument: English Puritanism and the Shaping of New England Culture, 1570–1700* (Chapel Hill, NC, 1991).

15 Robert Emmet Wall Jr, *Massachusetts Bay: The Crucial Decade, 1640–1650* (New Haven, CT, 1972), pp. 5–7, 17–19.

16 *GACW*, p. 15; *CJWM*, p. 203; *JJW*, pp. 280 n.94, 282–3; William Lambarde, *Eirenarcha, or Of the Office of the Justices of the Peace*, 4th edn (London, 1599), p. 10; Bernard Bailyn, *The New England Merchants in the Seventeenth Century* (Cambridge, MA, 1955), pp. 54–5.

17 *LNL*, p. 149. Springfield practised 'collective individualism': M. M. Knappen, *Tudor Puritanism: A Chapter in the History of Idealism* (Chicago, 1939), p. 348.

18 *LNL*, pp. 112–13, 307–12, 461; *Hampden County*, p. 381; *Pynchons of Springfield*, p. 32.

19 Royal Society, London, RBO/2i/19, p. 81; *Hampden County*, pp. 246, 265; *LNL*, pp. 113–17; Thistlethwaite, pp. 86–7; Hawke, p. 37.

20 William Pynchon, *Holy Time: or, The True Limits of the Lords Day* (London, 1654), sig. U3r; Gura, *Glimpse of Sion's Glory*, p. 378 n.45.

21 Ulrich, pp. 22–3, 51–2; Hawke, pp. 34, 38, 159–60; *LNL*, pp. 117–21, 300–302; Thistlethwaite, p. 85; *Hampden County*, p. 76; Mary Beth Norton, *Founding Mothers and Fathers: Gendered Power and the Forming of American Society* (New York, 1996), ch. 5.

22 Carl Bridenbaugh, 'Yankee use and abuse of the forest in the building of New England, 1620–1660', *Proceedings of the MHS*, 89 (1977), pp. 5–7; Abbott Lowell Cummings, *The Framed Houses of Massachusetts Bay, 1625–1725* (Cambridge, MA, 1979), pp. 23–5, 29–30; Wright, *Early Springfield*, p. 20; *LNL*, p. 436; WPAB, p. 218; Wright, *Genesis*, pp. 21–2; John Demos, *Circles and Lines: The Shape of Life in Early America* (Cambridge, MA, 2004), pp. 2–4, 5–6. On buying glass in Springfield in 1653: HLAS, ESMC, ESM-05-01-01, p. 95.

23 Dow, pp. 96–7; *Hampden County*, p. 76; Thomas Franklin Waters, *Ipswich in the Massachusetts Bay Colony*, 2 vols. (Ipswich, MA, 1905–7), i, p. 26.

24 Ulrich, pp. 94–5.

25 Robert Blair St George, 'Witchcraft, bodily affliction, and domestic space in seventeenth-century New England', in Janet Moore Lindman and Michele Lise Tarter (eds.), *A Center of Wonders: The Body in Early America* (Ithaca, NY, 2001), pp. 14–15, 18–19.

26 William Ames, *Conscience* (n.p., 1639), pp. 50, 93.

27 Increase Mather, *An Essay for the Recording of Illustrious Providences* (Boston, 1684), pp. 178–9; Ann Marie Plane, *Dreams and the Invisible World in Colonial New England: Indians, Colonists and the Seventeenth Century* (Philadelphia, 2014), chs. 3–4; Katharine Hodgkin, 'Dreaming meanings: some early modern dream thoughts', in Katharine Hodgkin, Michelle O'Callaghan and S. J. Wiseman (eds.), *Reading the Early Modern Dream: The Terrors of the Night* (London, 2008), pp. 109–24.

28 George Selement and Bruce C. Woolley (eds.), *Thomas Shepard's Confessions* (Boston, 1981), p. 86; Darren Oldridge, *The Devil in Early Modern England* (Stroud, 2000), chs. 2–4; Nathan Johnstone, *The Devil and Demonism in Early Modern England* (Cambridge, 2006), chs. 4–5.

29 Ulrich, p. 159; Deborah Willis, *Malevolent Nurture: Witch-Hunting and Maternal Power in Early Modern England* (Ithaca, NY, 1995), p. 14.

30 David Thomas Konig, *Law and Society in Puritan Massachusetts: Essex County, 1629–1692* (Chapel Hill, NC, 1979), pp. 177–82.

31 *Hampden County*, pp. 79–80; Mather, *Illustrious Providences*, pp. 155, 266–70; Deodat Lawson, *Christ's Fidelity the Only Shield Against Satan's Malignity* (Boston, 1693), pp. 64–5; Ulrich, p. 52; Richard Weisman, *Witchcraft, Magic, and Religion in 17th-Century Massachusetts* (Amherst, MA, 1984), pp. 60–61.

32 David D. Hall, *Worlds of Wonder, Days of Judgment: Popular Religious Belief in Early New England* (New York, 1989), ch. 2.

33 Thomas Hutchinson, *The History of the Colony and Province of Massachusetts-Bay*, 3 vols., ed. Lawrence Shaw Mayo (Cambridge, MA, 1936), i, pp. 399–400; *GHNE*, pp. 26–9, 34–5; Cotton Mather, *Magnalia Christi Americana*, 2 vols. (New York, 1967), ii, pp. 425–6. Archbishop George Abbot thought New England's natives 'marvellously addicted to witchcraft and adoration of devils': *A Briefe Description of the Whole World* (London, 1656), p. 294.

34 On this problem: John Rylands Library, Manchester, English MS 524, f. 9; George Gifford, *A Dialogue Concerning Witches and Witchcraftes* (London, 1593), sigs. B3v, I4r–K3r.

35 Richard Bernard, *A Guide to Grand-Jury Men . . . in Cases of Witchcraft* (London, 1629); Richard S. Ross III, *Before Salem: Witch Hunting in the Connecticut River Valley, 1647–1663* (Jefferson, NC, 2017), pp. 19–21. On Pynchon's law books: *LNL*, p. 13; *CJWM*, p. 31; *DH*, p. 78; *WP*, v, p. 135; MHS, Ms. N-760 (iii), p. 22; HCRP, Wills (John Pynchon, 1703).

36 William Perkins, *A Discourse of the Damned Art of Witchcraft* (Cambridge, 1608), pp. 200–205, 210, 213–14, 218–19; see also Gifford, *Dialogue*, sigs. H3r–H4v. Pynchon may not have owned these texts, but John Winthrop did: MHS, Winthrop Library; New York Society Library, no. 78.

37 *An Abstract of the Lawes of New England* (1641), in Peter Force (ed.), *Tracts and Other Papers Relating to . . . North America*, 4 vols. (New York, 1947), iii, no. 9, p. 12. On problems of proof: Edgar J. McManus, *Law and Liberty in Early New England: Criminal Justice and Due Process, 1620–1692* (Amherst, MA, 1993), ch. 3; Richard Godbeer, *The Devil's Dominion: Magic and Religion in Early New England* (Cambridge, 1992), ch. 5. See also Sanford J. Fox, *Science and Justice: The Massachusetts Witchcraft Trials* (Baltimore, 1968), ch. 4.

38 The dating is conjectural. It does not predate 1647 as Mary Bliss married Joseph Parsons in November 1646 at Hartford. William Branch, who consulted Pynchon, was living in the town in March 1649 and moved to the long meadow in late 1649 or early 1650: WPDB, f. 7r.

39 Sylvester, p. 21.

40 *JJW*, p. 153; Hosmer, ii, pp. 155–6.

41 Henry M. Burt et al., *Cornet Joseph Parsons: One of the Founders of Springfield and Northampton, Massachusetts* (Garden City, NY, 1898), pp. 11–12; *FCHS*, p. 40; *VRS*, pp. 12, 20, 60; Willard S. Allen, 'Longmeadow (Mass.) families', *NEHGR*, 31 (1877), p. 320. There is no record of Widow Bliss or her sons in relation to land in Springfield in 1647, but Nathaniel Bliss's son was born there on 7 November 1647, suggesting arrival around that time.

42 HLSL, Small Manuscript Collection (Special Collections), Testimony taken on behalf of Sarah the wife of James Bridgeman of Northampton, 11 August 1656), f. 2.

43 William Perkins, *A Direction for the Government of the Tongue* (Edinburgh, 1593), pp. 3–5; Peter Elmer, *Witchcraft, Witch-Hunting, and Politics in Early Modern England* (Oxford, 2016), p. 104.

44 Anderson, 'Pynchon'.

45 TNA, C 142 321/130 (7 Oct. 1611). J. C. Pynchon, *Record of the Pynchon Family in England and America* (Springfield, MA, 1885), pp. 3–5; Henry F. Waters, *Genealogical Gleanings in England*, 2 vols. (Boston, 1907), ii, pp. 846, 854–5, 866–7; McIntyre, *Pynchon*, pp. 5–6; *DH*, pp. 9, 16–17, 19. See also Essex RO, D/DGe P 2/1; D/DGe P3; D/DGe M100; T/G 209.

46 Peter H. Wilson, *Europe's Tragedy: A New History of the Thirty Years War* (London, 2009), chs. 22–3; Roger Thompson, *Mobility and Migration: East Anglian Founders of New England, 1629–1640* (Boston, 1994), pp. 20–23.

47 Brian P. Levack, 'Possession, witchcraft, and the law in Jacobean England', *Washington and Lee Law Review*, 52 (1996), pp. 1613–40; G. L. Kittredge, 'King James I and *The Devil is an Ass*', *Modern Philology*, 9 (1911), pp. 195–209. On the politics of exorcism: Michael MacDonald (ed.), *Witchcraft and Hysteria in Elizabethan London* (London, 1991).

48 Barbara Rosen (ed.), *Witchcraft in England, 1558–1618* (Amherst, MA, 1991), p. 376.

49 Helen I. Paynter, *A Short History of All Saints' Church, Springfield, Essex*, 3rd edn (n.p., 1949), pp. 5–6, 13–14, 22; Essex RO, T/G 209/1, p. 1; D/ABW 32/302; Q/SR 227/13 (Epiphany, 1620); Q/SR 247/48A (Epiphany, 1625).

50 Frank Hugh Foster, *A Genetic History of the New England Theology* (Chicago, 1907), pp. 16–20; John H. Lockwood et al. (eds.), *Western Massachusetts: A History, 1636–1925*, 4 vols. (New York, 1926), i, pp. 101–10; H. John McLachlan, *Socinianism in Seventeenth-Century England* (Oxford, 1951), pp. 1–4, 12–15, 234–9. See also Gura, *Glimpse of Sion's Glory*, pp. 311–12. In a tract of 1624, Anthony Wotton said 'Christ's obedience is the meritorious cause of justification': ibid., p. 378 n.48.

51 William Pynchon, *The Meritorious Price of Our Redemption* (London, 1650), p. 15. In 1655 Pynchon said of his first book, published in 1650, that he had 'a resolution when I went from England [in 1630] to publish something on that subject when I should get time': DWL, Baxter Letters, 3.186–7 (1655), f. 186f.

52 Pynchon, *Meritorious Price*, sig. A4v; *Alumni Cantabrigienses, Pt. 1, Volume 4* (Cambridge, 1927), p. 99; Henry R. Stiles, *The History of Ancient Wethersfield, Connecticut*, 2 vols. (New York, 1904), ii, p. 628.

53 Winship, 'Contesting control', pp. 795–7; Hugh Broughton, *A Revelation of the Holy Apocalyps[e]* (Middelburg, 1610), sig. B2r, p. 48; idem, *Declaration of General Corruption, of Religion, Scripture, and All Learninge* (London, 1604), p. 24; Charles W. A. Prior, *Defining the Jacobean Church: The Politics of Religious Controversy, 1603–1625* (Cambridge, 2005), pp. 49–50 n.108.

54 Sargent Bush Jr, 'Thomas Hooker', *ODNB*; David D. Hall, *The Puritans: A Transatlantic History* (Princeton, NJ, 2019), p. 162. On Hooker's exorcism: John Hart, *Trodden Down Strength* (London, 1647), pp. 119–29, 159–60.

55 E[dward] W[inslow], *Good Newes from New England* (London, 1624), p. 64; Thompson, *Mobility and Migration*, pp. 39–44; TNA, CO 5/902, pp. 33–6.

56 *WP*, ii, pp. 151–2; Samuel Eliot Morison, *Builders of the Bay Colony* (Cambridge, MA, 1930), pp. 68–70; 'Pincheon papers', *Collections of the MHS*, 8 (1819), p. 228; Francis J. Bremer, 'The heritage of John Winthrop: religion along the Stour valley, 1548–1630', *NEQ*, 70 (1997), pp. 536–8, 544–7.

57 Essex RO, D/ABW 50/45; *DH*, p. 20; Charles Edward Banks, *The Winthrop Fleet of 1630* (Boston, 1930), p. 3.

58 Possibly the *Jewell*; definitely not the *Arbella*: Samuel E. Morison, 'William Pynchon: the founder of Springfield', *Proceedings of the MHS*, 64 (1931), p. 72; Gura, *Glimpse of Sion's Glory*, p. 305. On 23 April, Pynchon sailed across to join Winthrop for dinner: *WP*, ii, p. 294.

59 Abram C. Van Engen, *City on a Hill: A History of American Exceptionalism* (New Haven, CT, 2020), ch. 3; Thomas Dudley et al., *Massachusetts, or The First Planters of New-England* (Boston, 1696), pp. 1–5, quotations at pp. 2, 5.

60 Dudley et al., *Massachusetts*, pp. 12–18; Thistlethwaite, pp. 78–9; *WP*, ii, pp. 266, 312; Morison, *Builders of the Bay Colony*, p. 79.

61 John Cotton, *Gods Promise to His Plantation* (London, 1630), pp. 14–16. The phrase comes from Isaiah 61:3.

62 Francis J. Bremer, *John Winthrop: America's Forgotten Founding Father* (Oxford, 2003), p. 193; *DH*, p. 23; Dudley et al., *Massachusetts*, pp. 16, 20–21; *GHNE*, p. 136; Thistlethwaite, pp. 80–82; Hosmer, i, pp. 69–70.

63 BL, Egerton MS 784 (April 1630); Robert C. Anderson, *The Great Migration Begins: Immigrants to New England, 1620–1633*, 3 vols. (Boston, 1995), iii, pp. 1691–2; *RLCR*, p. 73.

64 Walter Eliot Thwing, *History of the First Church in Roxbury, Massachusetts, 1630–1904* (Boston, 1908), pp. v, x–xi; Theodore Dwight Bozeman, *To Live Ancient Lives: The Primitivist Dimension in Puritanism* (Chapel Hill, NC, 1988), pp. 284–5.

65 BL, Sloane MS 922, ff. 90–93v, quotations at ff. 91, 93v.

66 John Noble and John F. Cronin (eds.), *Records of the Court of Assistants of the Colony of Massachusetts Bay, 1630–1692*, 3 vols. (Boston, 1901–28), ii, pp. 1, 4, 26, 173–5; 'Pincheon papers', pp. 234–5.

67 John Josselyn, *An Account of Two Voyages to New-England* (London, 1674), p. 254.

68 *WP*, iii, pp. 86, 116, 169, 255; Roger Williams, *A Key into the Language of America* (London, 1643), p. 105; Nick Bunker, *Making Haste from Babylon: The Mayflower Pilgrims and Their World* (London, 2010), ch. 12; Lockwood (ed.), *Western*

Massachusetts, i, pp. 89–91; *LNL*, pp. 5–6; *Pynchons of Springfield*, pp. 11–12; McIntyre, *Pynchon*, pp. 9–13.

69 *Dorchester Town Records, 1632–87*, 3rd edn (Boston, 1896), p. 7.

70 Lambeth Palace Library, London, MS 841, Pt. 7, ff. 4v–5r; 'Pratt's apology', *Collections of the MHS*, 7 (1826), pp. 126–7; Sylvester, pp. 14–15. See also Beinecke Library, Yale University, OSB MSS File 16794, ff. 1v–2r.

71 *GHNE*, p. 305; Thistlethwaite, p. 108; Mather, *Magnalia*, i, pp. 80–81.

72 Thomas Weld, *A Short Story of the Rise, Reign and Ruin of the Antinomians, Familists, and Libertines* (London, 1644), sigs. B3v–B4r; 'Pincheon papers', p. 236; Emil Oberholzer Jr, *Delinquent Saints: Disciplinary Action in the Early Congregational Churches of Massachusetts* (New York, 1956), pp. 85–6; Stephen Foster, 'New England and the challenge of heresy, 1630 to 1660: the puritan crisis in transatlantic perspective', *WMQ*, 38 (1981), pp. 624–60.

73 *FCHS*, p. 13; Hawke, p. 14; Daniel Howard, *A New History of Old Windsor, Connecticut* (Windsor Locks, CT, 1935), pp. 9–12.

74 Simeon E. Baldwin, 'The secession of Springfield from Connecticut', *Publications of the Colonial Society of Massachusetts*, 12 (1908), pp. 57–8; Sylvester, p. 29; *PP*, ii, p. 23.

75 Harry A. Wright, *Indian Deeds of Hampden County* (Springfield, MA, 1905), pp. 13–14; Sylvester, pp. 15, 21; *DH*, p. 37; Howard, *Old Windsor*, p. 14.

76 *WP*, iii, pp. 238, 254–5; Thwing, *First Church in Roxbury*, p. 45.

77 Byington, *The Puritan*, p. 131; Wright, *Genesis*, pp. 8–10; Stiles, *Ancient Wethersfield*, i, p. 182; Pynchon, *Meritorious Price*, sig. A4v.

78 Sylvester, pp. 31–2; Wright, *Early Springfield*, pp. 1–6, 12; *NEHGR*, 13 (1859), pp. 295–7; *Pynchons of Springfield*, p. 15; Wright, *Genesis*, pp. 11–14.

79 Sir Edward Hoby: BL, Add. MS 38,823, f. 6v.

80 Wright, *Early Springfield*, pp. 5–6; *GACW*, p. 14; Moses King (ed.), *King's Handbook of Springfield, Massachusetts* (Springfield, MA, 1884), p. 10; Sylvester, p. 19.

81 Wright, *Genesis*, p. 11; Wright, *Indian Deeds*, pp. 11–14.

82 *WP*, iii, p. 314; McIntyre, *Pynchon*, pp. 13–15, 29–30; *Pynchons of Springfield*, pp. 22, 27. Colonists who sold gunpowder to Indians were fined: *TRSR*, p. 23.

83 *GHNE*, p. 308; Mather, *Magnalia*, i, p. 81 (quotations).

84 *LNL*, pp. 8–9; *Records of the First Church at Dorchester in New England, 1636–1734* (Boston, 1891), p. 3; Green, p. 74; Savage, iii, p. 251; 'Pincheon papers', p. 235; Maude Pinney Kuhns, *The 'Mary and John': A Story of the Founding of Dorchester, Massachusetts* (Rutland, VT, 1971), p. 3; Howard, *Old Windsor*, p. 14.

85 Baldwin, 'Secession of Springfield', pp. 63–4; *DH*, ch. 5; Sylvester, pp. 37–8.

86 Sylvester, p. 32; Thistlethwaite, p. 108; MHS, Ms. N-760 (iii), p. 18.

87 Mark Valeri, *Heavenly Merchandize: How Religion Shaped Commerce in Puritan America* (Princeton, NJ, 2010), pp. 46–7; William E. Nelson, *The Common Law*

in *Colonial America*, vol. 1: *The Chesapeake and New England, 1607–1660* (Oxford, 2008), pp. 57–8.

88 'Letter of William Pynchon, 1638', *Proceedings of the MHS*, 58 (1924–5), p. 387; *WP*, iv, p. 10; Richard S. Dunn, James Savage and Laetitia Yeandle (eds.), *The Journal of John Winthrop, 1630–1649* (Cambridge, MA, 1996), p. 256.

89 Green, ch. 2; Michael W. Vella, Lance Schachterle and Louis Mackey (eds.), *The Meritorious Price of Our Redemption by William Pynchon* (New York, 1992), pp. xix, xix, xxiii–xxiv. The corn crisis gave Pynchon's book 'a secular subtextual dimension': ibid., p. xix. See also: Valeri, *Heavenly Merchandize*, pp. 47–8; Morison, 'Pynchon', pp. 86–7.

90 MHS, Ms. N-760 (iii), pp. 3–4, 13, 15–17; Green, p. 29; Hall, *Puritans*, p. 153.

91 *JJW*, pp. 151–2; Gura, *Glimpse of Sion's Glory*, p. 307; Hosmer, i, pp. 290–91; Baldwin, 'Secession of Springfield', pp. 72–4.

92 Edward Johnson, *A History of New-England* (London, 1654), p. 131; BPL, Ms. Am. 1506/2/13; Ms. N-791, p. 6; Nathaniel Morton, *New-Englands Memoriall* (Cambridge, MA, 1669), pp. 111–12; Hosmer, i, pp. 278–9.

93 Lancashire RO, DDKE/HMC/166 ('pretty plantations'); Hooker quoted in Ross, *Before Salem*, pp. 68–9; Josselyn, *Two Voyages*, pp. 260–61.

94 LWP, pp. 37–8, 47–8; J. Hammond Trumbull and Charles J. Hoadley (eds.), *The Public Records of the Colony of Connecticut*, 15 vols. (Hartford, CT, 1850–90), i, pp. 11–20.

95 *WP*, iv, pp. 98–9; *JJW*, pp. 152–3.

96 MHS, Ms. N-760 (ii); Hutchinson, *History*, i, pp. 131–2 ; 'Letter of William Pynchon', p. 388; Baldwin, 'Secession of Springfield', p. 65; Eric Jay Dolin, *Fur, Fortune and Empire: The Epic History of the Fur Trade in America* (New York, 2010), pp. 71–2, 82.

97 Johnson, *History*, p. 170; Edward E. Hale (ed.), *Note-Book Kept by Thomas Lechford* (Cambridge, MA, 1885), p. 85.

98 Douglas H. Shepard, 'The Wolcott shorthand notebook transcribed', unpublished PhD thesis, University of Iowa (1957), p. 210; GACW, pp. 2, 25, 36; TRSR, p. 25; Green, pp. 55–7; LWP, pp. 48–9, 49–51; *WP*, iv, p. 254.

99 BL, Egerton MS 2646, ff. 182r–182v.

100 Josselyn, *Two Voyages*, p. 261; *JJW*, pp. 211–12, 238–9; Peter N. Carroll, *Puritanism and the Wilderness: The Intellectual Significance of the New England Frontier, 1629–1700* (New York, 1969), pp. 92–3; GHNE, p. 264; *JJW*, pp. 151–2, 273; *WP*, iii, pp. 285–6; iv, pp. 495–6; Dow, ch. 12. In 1640 Henry Smith told John Winthrop Jr 'money is not to be gotten with us for any goods we have': *WP*, iv, p. 296. See also ibid., pp. 330–31.

101 William Hooke, *New Englands Teares, for Old Englands Feares* (London, 1641), p. 7.

102 CSL, Colonial New England Records, Hartford CT, Col. 52, 1643–70, p. 1. See also MHS, Ms. N-1182, Carton 1: SH 113L S, Folder 1 (John Endecott, 26 July 1643).

103 Hosmer, ii, pp. 91–2; BL, Egerton MS 2648, f. IV; *DH*, pp. 70–71; *FCHS*, pp. 19–20.

104 BL, Stowe MS 184, f. 125; Susan Hardman Moore, *Pilgrims: New World Settlers and the Call of Home* (New Haven, CT, 2007), pp. 64–72; *GHNE*, pp. 375–80.

105 On the impact of the East Anglian witch-hunt in New England: Francis J. Bremer, *First Founders: American Puritans and Puritanism in an Atlantic World* (Durham, NH, 2012), p. 258; Ross, *Before Salem*, pp. 22–4, 31–2, 35–6; Malcolm Gaskill, *Witch-finders: A Seventeenth-Century English Tragedy* (London, 2005), p. 272.

2. *Here We Must Be Happy*

1 Anna (b. *c*.1632), Martha (b. 1641), Mary (b. 1643), Elizabeth (b. 1644): *DH*, p. 75.

2 Peter Charles Hoffer, *Sensory Worlds in Early America* (Baltimore, 2003), pp. 43–4, 75–6.

3 WPAB, *passim*. See also the transcription of one man's account, 1652–69: Burt et al., *Cornet Joseph Parsons*, pp. 18–42. On toothpaste: David Hackett Fischer, *Albion's Seed: Four British Folkways in America* (Oxford, 1989), p. 144.

4 WPAB, *passim*. On wampum: WPAB, pp. 245, 252–3; *LNL*, pp. 454–8; *PP*, ii, p. 77n. Between 1634 and 1664 New Englanders swapped 7 million beads for furs worth £5–10m: Alan Taylor, *American Colonies: The Settling of North America* (London, 2002), p. 194.

5 Susan Dwyer Amussen, '"The part of a Christian man": the cultural politics of manhood in early modern England', in Susan D. Amussen and Mark A. Kishlansky (eds.), *Political Culture and Cultural Politics in Early Modern England* (Manchester, 1995), pp. 214–17, 227.

6 Ulrich, ch. 2 calls wives 'deputy husbands'.

7 Josiah H. Benton, *Warning Out in New England, 1656–1817* (Boston, 1911), pp. 27–8.

8 *LNL*, p. 401; *VRS*, p. 10.

9 Alice Morse Earle, *Customs and Fashions in Old New England* (New York, 1893), pp. 38–9; Fischer, *Albion's Seed*, p. 77; Alexandra Shepard, 'Gender, the body and sexuality', in Keith Wrightson (ed.), *A Social History of England, 1500–1750* (Cambridge, 2017), pp. 335, 339.

10 Mary Lewis's origins are obscure. David M. Powers suggests Bristol or south-eastern Wales: *DH*, p. 41 n.10. There are many MLs in the parish registers for Monmouthshire but no candidates for the Springfield ML: the earliest was born in 1629, so was too young. An ML (aged thirty-two) sailed with her husband from Ipswich in April 1634, but she was too old and Ipswich unlikely: P. William

Filby (ed.), *Passenger and Immigration Lists Index*, 3 vols. (Detroit, 1981), ii, p. 1215. There are baptism records for two women, one in St Ishmael, Carmarthenshire, 1 April 1612 (https://search.findmypast.co.uk/record?id=gbprs%2fb%2f8 55889934%2f1); the other in Panteg, Monmouthshire, 27 September 1612 (https://search.findmypast.co.uk/record?id=gbprs%2fb%2f914040465%2f1). If either is Mary Lewis of Springfield, her marriage age would have been sixteen or fifteen – young, but not unheard of.

11 T. Gwynn Jones, *Welsh Folklore and Folk-Custom* (London, 1930), chs. 3–8; Edmund Jones, *A Relation of Apparitions of Spirits, in the County of Monmouth, and the Principality of Wales* (Newport, 1813), pp. 42–8.

12 John Penry, *A Treatise Containing the Aequity of an Humble Supplication*, in David Williams (ed.), *Three Treatises Concerning Wales* (Cardiff, 1960), pp. 1–46; Thomas Richards, *A History of the Puritan Movement in Wales* (London, 1920), ch. 1.

13 J. E. Neale, *Elizabeth I and Her Parliaments, 1584–1601* (London, 1957), p. 153; Thomas Nashe, *An Almond for a Parrat* (London, 1589), p. 13; John Waddington, *John Penry, the Pilgrim Martyr, 1559–1593* (London, 1854), chs. 8–10.

14 Richard Suggett, *Welsh Witches: Narratives of Witchcraft and Magic from 16th- and 17th-Century Wales* (n.p., 2018), pp. 14–15, 17, 25, 51–3; Henry Holland, *A Treatise Against Witchcraft* (Cambridge, 1590), sig. A2v; NLW, Cwrtmawr MS. 114B, ff. 243–65; Stuart Clark and P. T. J. Morgan, 'Religion and magic in Elizabethan Wales: Robert Holland's *Dialogue on Witchcraft*', *Journal of Ecclesiastical History*, 27 (1976), pp. 31–46.

15 C. L'Estrange Ewen, *Witchcraft and Demonianism* (London, 1933), p. 435.

16 *DH*, p. 98. If, as seems probable, Lewis was Mary's married name, there are six plausible marriages of Marys to men with the surname Lewis; most likely (given the Monmouthshire connection) is the Mary Reece who married David Lewis in Monmouth, 30 July 1627, the only fit in all South Wales: https://search.findmypast.co.uk/record?id=gbprs%2fm%2f913136307%2f1. However, if Lewis was her maiden name, several marriages fit: in 1615 to Griffith Hughes in Kerry, Montgomeryshire (http://search.findmypast.co.uk/record?id=gbprs%2fm%2f 448039967%2f2); in 1615 to Richard ap Evan in Wenvoe, Glamorganshire (http:// search.findmypast.co.uk/record?id=gbprs%2fm%2f16011598%2f3); in 1630 to Owen ap Evan in Llanidloes, Montgomeryshire (http://search.findmypast. co.uk/record?id=gbprs%2fm%2f448027033%2f2); in 1632 to David [unknown] in Llanfair Caereinion (http://search.findmypast.co.uk/record?id=gbprs%2fm% 2f448005900%2f3); and in 1633 to Thomas David in Kerry, Montgomeryshire (http://search.findmypast.co.uk/record?id=gbprs%2fm%2f448040101%2f2).

17 MC, vol. 3, pp. 2–2v. According to Alexander Edwards, in his testimony to William Pynchon on 2 June 1645, 'it is a full seven years since her husband left her': ibid., p. 2.

18 Stephen K. Roberts, 'William Wroth', *ODNB*; Hall, *Puritans*, pp. 283–4; NLW, MS 13072B, 'An epitaph upon old dotard Wroth', f. 155r; J. D. Griffith Davies, 'Protestant nonconformity in Monmouthshire before 1715', *Monmouthshire Review*, 1 (1933), pp. 359–64; Edward Whiston, *The Life and Death of Mr Henry Jessey* (London, 1671), p. 9; Benjamin Brook, *The Lives of the Puritans*, 2 vols. (London, 1813), ii, p. 469; NLW, LL 1641/40.

19 NLW, File A76, 'Carolls English & Welsh' (unfol.); NLW, MS 128C, Thomas Charles, *c.* 1800, ff. 78b–80b.

20 Leo F. Solt, *Church and State in Early Modern England, 1509–1640* (Oxford, 1990), p. 116; Waddington, *Penry*, pp. 30–32, 100, 191.

21 See https://familysearch.org/photos/artifacts/17484543. Edwards was certainly Welsh, probably lived in the Monmouthshire town of Usk and may have come from the adjacent village of Llanbadoc (not, as this genealogical website states, Llangadog, which is in Carmarthenshire: https://www.geni.com/people/Alexander-Edwards/6000000008300659021).

22 Ivor Waters, *Chepstow Road Bridges*, 2nd edn (Chepstow 1980); H. G. Nicholls, *The Forest of Dean: An Historical and Descriptive Account* (London, 1858), chs. 1–2. Daniel Defoe describes the Aust ferry, unfavourably, in *A Tour Through the Whole Island of Great Britain*, 4 vols. (London, 1761), ii, pp. 310–11.

23 MC, vol. 3, p. 2; Savage, ii, pp. 102–3.

24 Waddington, *Penry*, pp. 136–45, quotation at p. 138.

25 McLachlan, *Socinianism*, pp. 227, 232–3; *The Testimony of William Erbery* (London, 1658), pp. 42, 152–3, 156, 162; William Erbery, *Apocrypha* (London, 1652), pp. 8–9.

26 Stephen K. Roberts, 'William Erbery', *ODNB*; Brian Ll. James, 'The evolution of a radical: the life and career of William Erbery (1604–54)', *Journal of Welsh Ecclesiastical History*, 3 (1986), pp. 34–6, 38–43; Richards, *Puritan Movement in Wales*, pp. 26–7; Christopher Love, *A Cleare and Necessary Vindication* (London, 1651), p. 36.

27 Moore, *Pilgrims*, p. 188; NLW, LL 1641/40; *GHNE*, p. 408; William Farrand Felch, *The Blynman Party* (Chicago, 1972), pp. 1–2; John J. Babson, *History of the Town of Gloucester, Cape Ann*, ed. Joseph E. Garland (Gloucester, MA, 1972), pp. 50–54, 189–90; 'Time of the arrival in New England of the following ministers', *NEHGR*, 1 (1847), p. 289.

28 MC, vol. 3, p. 2v. Pynchon said that Mary was his servant in Dorchester 'before she came to my son', but this can't have been while he was still living there: ibid., p. 2.

29 MC, vol. 3, p. 2. Her departure can be dated to 1640, as Alexander Edwards said in 1645 that he'd lived in Wales five years ago and knew ML at Wroth's ministry in Llanvaches. He also said that although ML departed on a later ship – he left Bristol in 1640 – she came in another ship six weeks later: Ebenezer Clapp Jr et al., *History of the Town of Dorchester, Massachusetts* (Boston, 1859), pp. 75–6. A 'Mary Doggett Lewis' arrived in Massachusetts in 1634, too

early to fit Edwards's account, but not for the start of Wroth's Llanvaches ministry: Robert C. Anderson et al., *The Great Migration: Immigrants to New England, 1634–1635*, 7 vols. (Boston, 1999–2011), iv, p. 281. Other unmarried MLs arrived in Maine in 1630 and Nantucket in 1630: C. E. Banks, *The Planters of the Commonwealth: A Study of the Emigrants and Emigration in Colonial Times* (Baltimore, 1961), p. 92; 'New England ship and passenger lists (continued)', *Boulder Genealogical Society Quarterly*, 4 (1972), p. 27.

30 David Cressy, *Coming Over: Migration and Communication Between England and New England in the Seventeenth Century* (Cambridge, 1987), p. 145; Samuel G. Drake, *Result of Some Researches Among the British Archives for Information Relative to the Founders of New England* (Boston, 1860), p. 62.

31 Henry Stevens, 'Passengers for New England, 1638', *NEHGR*, 2 (1848), pp. 108–10; Alison Games, *Migration and the Origins of the English Atlantic World* (Cambridge, MA, 1999), ch. 1, esp. pp. 65–7.

32 See Charles Boardman Jewson, *Transcript of Three Registers from Great Yarmouth to Holland and New England, 1637–1639* (Norwich, 1954). No Springfield names appear in Yarmouth passenger lists: TNA, E157/21–22; Bodl., Tanner MS 433.

33 Cressy, *Coming Over*, pp. 146–9, 152–9, 162–5, 169–73; Virginia DeJohn Anderson, *New England's Generation: The Great Migration and the Formation of Society and Culture in the Seventeenth Century* (Cambridge, 1991), pp. 57–9, 70–86.

34 Cressy, *Coming Over*, pp. 165–6; Josselyn, *Two Voyages*, p. 182.

35 Cressy, *Coming Over*, p. 174.

36 Clapp et al., *Dorchester*, pp. 28–31. David M. Powers suggests the Smiths married early in the 1630s; their first daughter Anna was born *c.* 1632. But if Anne Smith was born *c.* 1618, she would have been fourteen: *DH*, p. 75. Martha Smith was born 31 July 1641 and died in November: *VRS*, pp. 9, 60.

37 Earle, *Customs and Fashions*, pp. 82–3. For a typical Springfield indenture: HLAS, ESMC, ESM-04-04-03.

38 Sylvester, p. 32; Harral Ayres, *The Great Trail of New England* (Boston, 1940), pp. 308–12.

39 *LNL*, p. 465.

40 *VRS*, pp. 9, 60.

41 Edmund S. Morgan, *The Puritan Family: Religion and Domestic Relations in Seventeenth-Century New England* (New York, 1966), ch. 3; Earle, *Customs and Fashions*, pp. 11–13; Gerald F. Moran and Maris A. Vinovskis, *Religion, Family and the Life Course: Explorations in the Social History of Early America* (Ann Arbor, MI, 1992), ch. 4.

42 Fischer, *Albion's Seed*, p. 140; McIntyre, *Pynchon*, p. 26.

43 John Demos, *A Little Commonwealth: Family Life in Plymouth Colony*, 2nd edn (Oxford, 2000), ch. 3; Hawke, pp. 111–13; *WP*, v, p. 91; *Pynchons of Springfield*, pp. 23–4; Alice Morse Earle, *Child Life in Colonial Days* (New York, 1899), ch. 2.

44 Increase Mather, *Remarkable Providences Illustrative of the Earlier Days of American Colonisation*, ed. George Offor (London, 1856), p. 255; Morton, *New-Englands Memoriall*, pp. 94–5; *GHNE*, pp. 21, 199; Karen Ordahl Kupperman, 'Climate and mastery of the wilderness in seventeenth-century New England', in David D. Hall, David Grayson Allen and Philip Chadwick Foster Smith (eds.), *Seventeenth-Century New England* (Boston, 1984), p. 11.

45 Fischer, *Albion's Seed*, pp. 52–3; Allan Kulikoff, *From British Peasants to Colonial American Farmers* (Chapel Hill, NC, 2000), pp. 82–3; Kupperman, 'Climate', pp. 12–13; *GHNE*, pp. 19–21; *LNL*, pp. 7–8.

46 Howard, *Old Windsor*, pp. 53–4; quotation from a Connecticut man who lamented that in England people 'could sing and be merry': Franklin Bowditch Dexter (ed.), *Ancient Town Records*, vol. 1: *New Haven Town Records, 1649–1662* (New Haven, CT, 1917), p. 56.

47 Increase Mather, *A Testimony Against Several Prophane and Superstitious Customs, Now Practised by Some in New-England* (London, 1687), p. 5.

48 Thistlethwaite, p. 94; Mary Thomas Crane, 'Illicit privacy and outdoor spaces in early modern England', *Journal for Modern Cultural Studies*, 9 (2009), pp. 4–22, esp. p. 8; Oberholzer, *Delinquent Saints*, pp. 57–68; Earle, *Customs and Fashions*, pp. 238–9.

49 *GACW*, pp. 1, 11–12, 16–17; *FCHS*, p. 144; *DH*, p. 89; Green, p. 43; Morris, *First Church*, pp. 7, 11; Wright, *Meeting Houses*, p. 4; *TRSR*, pp. 15, 102. A son, Union Moxon, was born on 16 February 1642: *VRS*, p. 9.

50 *GACW*, pp. xi, 11, 19–21; *DH*, pp. 88–9; Wright, *Meeting Houses*, p. 10.

51 William Ames, *The Marrow of Sacred Divinity* (London, 1638); David D. Hall (ed.), *The Antinomian Controversy, 1636–1638: A Documentary History* (Middletown, CT, 1968), ch. 1; *DH*, pp. 92–3; *GACW*, pp. 21–3; 1 John 2:15.

52 *GACW*, pp. 45–88, quotation from David M. Powers's transcription of John Pynchon's sermon notes, 1640 (HLAS, ESMC, ESM-05-06-02), p. 30.

53 Thistlethwaite, p. 99; Michael P. Winship, *Godly Republicanism: Puritan, Pilgrims, and a City on a Hill* (Cambridge, MA, 2012), p. 178.

54 Alexander Gordon and Susan Hardman Moore, 'George Moxon', *ODNB*. Moxon was a near contemporary of Oliver Cromwell at Sidney Sussex College, who matriculated in 1616; Moxon arrived in 1620, by which time Cromwell had left.

55 Edmund Calamy, *An Account of the Ministers . . . Ejected or Silenced After the Restoration in 1660*, 2 vols. (London, 1713), ii, pp. 128–9; Gordon and Moore, 'Moxon'; *GACW*, p. 11.

56 Theo W. Ellis (ed.), *Manual of the First Church of Christ* (Springfield, MA, 1885), p. 8.

57 *GACW*, pp. 33–4, 45–88, quotations from David M. Powers's transcription of John Pynchon's sermon notes, 1640 (HLAS, ESMC, ESM-05-06-02), pp. 31, 45, 57.

58 TRSR, p. 9.

59 Elizabeth Reis, *Damned Women: Sinners and Witches in Puritan New England* (Ithaca, NY, 1997), chs. 1, 4; Mary Rhinelander McCarl, 'Thomas Shepard's record of relations of religious experience, 1648–1649', *WMQ*, 48 (1991), pp. 448, 460–61.

60 *DH*, pp. 85–7; *GHNE*, p. 423; 1 John 3:8.

61 Selement and Woolley (eds.), *Shepard's Confessions*, pp. 15–24, quotation at p. 19; Elizabeth Reis, 'The devil, the body, and the feminine soul in Puritan New England', *Journal of American History*, 82 (1995), p. 19; McCarl, 'Shepard's record', pp. 441–2, 446, 465–6.

62 John Davenport, *The Profession of the Faith* (London, 1642), p. 5. See also Susanna Bell, *The Legacy of a Dying Mother to her Mourning Children* (London, 1673), pp. 49–53.

63 *WP*, iv, pp. 495–6; Hosmer, ii, p. 220.

64 *Pynchons of Springfield*, pp. 27–9; Morison, 'Pynchon', p. 90.

65 *GACW*, p. 14; Thistlethwaite, p. 105.

66 Marty O'Shea, 'Springfield's Puritans and Indians: 1636–1655', *Historical Journal of Massachusetts*, 26 (1998), pp. 46–72; Wright, *Early Springfield*, p. 47 (quotation).

67 WPAB, p. iv.

68 *WP*, iv, pp. 432–4, 441–2; Carroll, *Puritanism and the Wilderness*, pp. 170–74.

69 Quoted in Louise A. Breen, *Transgressing the Bounds: Subversive Enterprises Among the Puritan Elite in Massachusetts, 1630–1692* (Oxford, 2001), p. 119.

70 *WP*, v, p. 115.

71 MHS, Ms. N-760 (iii), p. 7; *WP*, iv, pp. 495–6.

72 Michael Zuckerman, 'Identity in British America: unease in Eden', in Nicholas Canny and Anthony Pagden (eds.), *Colonial Identity in the Atlantic World, 1500–1800* (Princeton, NJ, 1987), pp. 115–57; Norman Pettit, 'God's Englishman in New England: his enduring ties to the motherland', *Proceedings of the MHS*, 101 (1989), pp. 56–70. On homesickness: Malcolm Gaskill, *Between Two Worlds: How the English Became Americans* (Oxford, 2014), pp. 123–4, 353–5; Susan J. Matt, *Homesickness: An American History* (Oxford, 2011), ch. 1.

73 Konig, *Law and Society*, pp. 69–70.

74 Cf. Daniel C. Beaver, 'Politics in the archives: records, property, and plantation politics in Massachusetts Bay, 1642–1650', *Journal of Early American History*, 1 (2011), pp. 3–25.

75 Keith Wrightson, 'Class', in David Armitage and Michael J. Braddick (eds.), *The British Atlantic World, 1500–1800* (Basingstoke, 2002), pp. 142–3.

76 TRSR, pp. 25, 26, 33, 34, 40, 43–4; *LNL*, p. 440; Wright, *Early Springfield*, pp. 26–8.

77 Morison, 'Pynchon', pp. 77–9; Selement and Woolley (eds.), *Shepard's Confessions*, pp. 43, 59, 61.

78 Alan Macfarlane, *Witchcraft in Tudor and Stuart England: A Regional and Comparative Study*, 2nd edn (London, 1999), chs. 10–16. On *maleficia*: Keith Thomas, *Religion and the Decline of Magic* (London, 1971), pp. 519–20, 540–43; John Putnam Demos, *Entertaining Satan: Witchcraft and the Culture of Early New England* (Oxford, 1982), pp. 171–2.

79 Ann Kibbey, 'Mutations of the supernatural: witchcraft, remarkable providences, and the power of puritan men', *American Quarterly*, 34 (1982), pp. 125–48. Robin Briggs interprets this aggression as a projection of accusers' self-loathing, which 'might endow their neighbour the witch with precisely those traits they most despised in themselves': *Witches and Neighbours: The Social and Cultural Context of European Witchcraft* (London, 1996), p. 168.

80 C. L'Estrange Ewen, *Witch Hunting and Witch Trials* (London, 1929), pp. 90–91, 207–9.

81 Ibid., p. 213.

82 On scepticism in the 1640s: Frederick Valletta, *Witchcraft, Magic and Superstition in England, 1640–70* (Aldershot, 2000), pp. 29–33.

83 Thomas Shepard, 1645, quoted in Andrew Delbanco, 'Looking homeward, going home: the lure of England for the founders of New England', *NEQ*, 59 (1986), pp. 376–7.

84 Richard Baxter, *The Certainty of the Worlds of Spirits* (London, 1691), p. 107; *WP*, iii, p. 298. For an Indian's dream of Satan, a man in black: Thomas Shepard, *The Clear Sun-shine of the Gospel Breaking Forth upon the Indians in New-England* (London, 1648), p. 10.

85 Sylvester, p. 22; *WP*, v, p. 38.

86 *The Country-mans New Common-wealth* (London, 1647), pp. 9–10. Francis Bacon thought envy the most dangerous emotion because it fed obsessively on body and soul: *Historie Naturall and Experimentall, of Life and Death* (London, 1638), p. 223.

87 Timothy Bright, *A Treatise of Melancholie* (London, 1586), p. 133. On the link between melancholy and witchcraft through 'awakened evil and dark wrath': Thomas Tryon, *A Way to Health, Long Life and Happiness* (London, 1691), p. 24.

88 *VRS*, pp. 9, 10; Natalie Zemon Davis, 'Boundaries and the sense of self in sixteenth-century France', in Thomas C. Heller et al. (eds.), *Reconstructing Individualism: Autonomy, Individuality, and the Self in Western Thought* (Stanford, CA, 1986), pp. 54–9, 61–2.

89 Made perhaps from Indian trading cloth or 'pennystone', a coarse woollen fabric from Yorkshire: McIntyre, *Pynchon*, p. 26; Dow, p. 79.

90 A writer imagined Hugh as 'blessed with a fine person and a genteel address', which made women love him and men hate him: Samuel Peters, *General History of Connecticut* (New York, 1877), p. 137. In contrast, an early twentieth-century children's book decided that he 'was not a very agreeable man and probably not good looking': Charles H. Barrows, *The History of Springfield in Massachusetts for the Young* (Springfield, MA, 1909), pp. 54–5. Henry Burt called him 'a roughspoken fellow', which he was – like almost everyone else: *FCHS*, p. 73.

3. Temptations of Desire

1 TRSR, pp. 26, 39; *CJWM*, pp. 116, 219, 228–9; Bridenbaugh, 'Use and abuse of the forest', p. 14; Cummings, *Framed Houses*, p. 119; Waters, *Ipswich*, i, pp. 18–19; George Francis Dow, 'The colonial village built at Salem, Massachusetts, in the spring of 1930', *Old-Time New England*, 22 (1931), p. 11.

2 Cummings, *Framed Houses*, pp. 29–30, 118–19; Bridenbaugh, 'Use and abuse of the forest', p. 13; Dow, p. 20; Wright, *Early Springfield*, p. 13.

3 Wright, *Early Springfield*, pp. 12–13. 'Most of the early Springfield people were drawn from Roxbury by Pynchon': Savage, i, p. 68.

4 Bridenbaugh, 'Use and abuse of the forest', p. 13; Dow, 'Colonial village', p. 12.

5 *DH*, p. 41 n.10. Roger Thompson says Hugh belonged to a 'scorned Welsh minority', but this is unproven, nor is Parsons a Welsh surname: 'Review: Jane Kamensky's *Governing the Tongue*', *NEQ*, 72 (1999), p. 139. See also T. J. Morgan and Prys Morgan, *Welsh Surnames* (Cardiff, 1985). C. E. Banks records an HP born Witham, Essex: *Topographical Dictionary of 2,885 English Emigrants to New England, 1620–1650* (Philadelphia, 1937), p. 53. But he probably died, Witham, 1655: TNA, PROB 11/248/718. Another HP was baptized, Babcary, Somerset, 31 January 1613 (http://search.findmypast.co.uk/record?id=r_947355133), but he was a witness in the 1650s: Somerset Heritage Centre, Q/SPET/1/D. 'Hughe Parson' was baptized, Boyton, Cornwall, 17 August 1610 (https://www.ancestry.co.uk/sharing/11531190?h=9137e7), but probably died, Boyton, 1673: Cornwall RO, AP/P/1271. A 'Hugo Parsons' was baptized in Ugborough, Devon, on 15 September 1613 (https://www.ancestry.co.uk/sharing/11379597?h=27e23e). For other HPs: Kingsbury, Warwickshire, 5 November 1612 (http://search.findmypast.co.uk/record?id=r_20848408500); Sandford-on-Thames, Oxford, 19 March 1615 (https://www.ancestry.co.uk/sharing/11379637?h=d9decf); and Bromyard, Hereford, on 2 June 1611 (https://www.ancestry.co.uk/sharing/11379607?h=b08980). The latter is possibly the 'Hugh Parsonns' who died Kington, Here-

ford, 16 December 1665 (https://www.ancestry.co.uk/sharing/11532110?h=b8f 4a4). A source claims he was born in Nether Stowey, Torrington, 11 March 1612, but there are no corresponding records: http://www.ogdensburg.info/geneal-ogy/getperson.php?personID=I7146&tree=tree1. Protestation Oath returns have two Devon HPs, at Highweek and Bridestowe: A. J. Howard (ed.), *The Devon Protestation Returns* (Bristol, 1973), pp. 305, 168. There is also a 'Hugh Parson' for St Germans, Cornwall: T. L. Stoate (ed.), *The Cornwall Protestation Returns, 1641* (Bristol, 1974), p. 242. The original Highweek, Bridestowe and St Germans returns lack signatures so cannot be compared to a Springfield example: House of Lords RO, HL/PO/JO/10/1/856/5, 86/81, 79/22. The Highweek HP can be ruled out, as he was registrar there, 23 January 1654: Charles Worthy, *Devonshire Parishes*, 2 vols. (Exeter, 1887), ii, p. 305. There is no evidence that HP of Springfield was related to Joseph Parsons: Burt et al., *Cornet Joseph Parsons*, esp. pp. 75–80.

6 TRSR, p. 37; Bridenbaugh, 'Use and abuse of the forest', p. 31; GACW, p. 17.
7 Records of Possessions, ff. 4v–5; Benton, *Warning Out in New England*, pp. 27–8; GACW, p. 16; Wright, *Early Springfield*, p. 28.
8 MC, vol. 3, pp. 2–2A; Matthew 2:16, 9:16.
9 CJWM, pp. 212–14; FCHS, p. 20; VRS, p. 19; DH, p. 69.
10 MC, vol. 3, pp. 2–2v.
11 CJWM, p. 91; Ayres, *Great Trail*, p. 304.
12 MC, vol. 3, pp. 2–2v; Clapp et al., *Dorchester*, pp. 75–7. In September Pynchon referred to a previous letter about her sent to John Winthrop Sr 'by quodnam's pinnace': WP, v, p. 45. Winthrop Jr had come via the Bay Path but returned by boat: Ayres, *Great Trail*, p. 304.
13 George Gardyner, *A Description of the New World* (London, 1651), p. 91; Alexander Young, *Chronicles of the First Planters of the Colony of Massachusetts Bay, from 1623 to 1636* (Boston, 1846), p. 400 (quotation).
14 JJW, pp. 246–7. See Noble and Cronin (eds.), *Court of Assistants*, ii, p. 89.
15 MC, vol. 3, pp. 2–2A.
16 Kupperman, 'Climate', p. 8.
17 Alan Gallay (ed.), *Colonial Wars of North America, 1512–1763: An Encyclopedia* (Oxford, 1996), p. 469; *Acts of the Commissioners of the United Colonies of New England*, 2 vols. (Boston, 1859), i, pp. 47–8.
18 WP, v, pp. 45–6. Her baby was born nine months and one week from her wedding date.
19 John Demos (ed.), *Remarkable Providences: Readings on Early American History*, 2nd edn (Boston, 1991), p. 449.
20 WPAB, p. 113.
21 VRS, p. 20.

22 Oberholzer, *Delinquent Saints*, pp. 113–14, 177; Earle, *Customs and Fashions*, pp. 70–71; Thomas Morton, *New English Canaan* (London, 1637), p. 178; Thomas Taylor, *A Good Husband and a Good Wife* (London, 1625), p. 26; Morgan, *Puritan Family*, ch. 2.

23 Ephesians 6:10–11; Henry R. Stiles, *The History of Ancient Windsor, Connecticut*, 2 vols. (1892; Somersworth, NH, 1976), i, p. x. See also Alexandra Shepard, *Meanings of Manhood in Early Modern England* (Cambridge, 2003), pp. 71–5.

24 VRS, p. 20. A nineteenth-century writer thought Hugh 'a queer stick', a bad match for Mary, 'a woman of a highly nervous organization', and that their marriage, 'the union of necessity with opportunity . . . promised no good either to them or to the village': Green, pp. 81–2.

25 VRS, p. 19; WP, v, p. 50.

26 *Hampden County*, pp. 45, 80, 117–18; Green, p. 102.

27 TRSR, p. 31; Wright, *Genesis*, pp. 16, 23.

28 Wright, *Early Springfield*, pp. 21, 26–7, 35.

29 James L. Garvin, 'Small-scale brickmaking in New Hampshire', *Journal of the Society for Industrial Archaeology*, 20 (1994), p. 24.

30 King (ed.), *Handbook*, pp. 30–31; Bridenbaugh, 'Use and abuse of the forest', pp. 12–13, 16.

31 Cummings, *Framed Houses*, pp. 29–30; Demos, *Little Commonwealth*, pp. 39–40; Earle, *Customs and Fashions*, pp. 130–31; *Hampden County*, pp. 247, 251, 270–71; Ulrich, pp. 19–21; WPAB, p. 113; Kupperman, 'Climate', p. 14; Sylvester, p. 22; Hawke, p. 38.

32 *Hampden County*, p. 77; LNL, p. 286; Ulrich, p. 23; Hawke, p. 80.

33 Hawke, p. 55; Waters, *Ipswich*, i, p. 24; *Hampden County*, p. 250; Dow, p. 44; Fischer, *Albion's Seed*, p. 144; Ulrich, pp. 27–8.

34 Dow, p. 53. A Springfield inventory of 1642 lists only a bed: CJWM, pp. 212–13.

35 Cummings, *Framed Houses*, p. 28; Demos, *Little Commonwealth*, pp. 31–3. A woman hung her waistcoat 'on a pin': WPDB, f. 14v.

36 JJW, p. 283.

37 LNL, pp. 10–11. Many were from South Wales, esp. Monmouthshire: Jacob L. Pritchard, *A Compilation of Some of the Descendants of Roger Pritchard c.1600–1671* (San Jose, CA, 1953), p. 1.

38 DH, p. 91; Jonathan Burt, baptized Harberton, Devon, 23 January 1624: http://search.findmypast.co.uk/record?id=gbprs%2fdev%2fbap%2f459053.

39 DH, p. 102; FCHS, p. 42; VRS, p. 9. Cooley was probably baptized in Tring, 25 February 1616: http://www.Cooleyfamilyassociation.com/benjamin_Cooley_position.html. See also http://search.findmypast.co.uk/record?id=gbprs%2fb%2f71248805%2f1, which shows that in 1669 Cooley was fifty-two, reinforcing the Tring theory: https://www.wikitree.com/wiki/Cooley-69.

40 Wright, *Early Springfield*, pp. 16–18.

41 *FCHS*, p. 20; *AWNE*, p. 224 n.3; *PP*, ii, p. 72n.

42 NEHGS, Mss A 1403 (Edward T. Jones, 'Griffith Jones of Springfield, Massachusetts, 1614–76', unpublished typescript, 1960), p. 2. See also: WPAB, p. 110; *LNL*, pp. xx, 89, 203, 447.

43 *VRS*, pp. 10, 60.

44 *AWNE*, p. 254 n.1; *VRS*, p. 19; *FCHS*, p. 42; *LNL*, p. 200; Savage, i, p. 238.

45 *FCHS*, p. 42; *LNL*, pp. 101–2, 204, 287; *AWNE*, p. 228 n.1; *VRS*, pp. 10, 19. On John and Pentecost Matthews: *LNL*, pp. 101–4, 121.

46 HLAS, ESMC, ESM-04-04-03; *VRS*, p. 20; *LNL*, pp. 110–11. Pepper moved in with Pynchon, spring 1649.

47 Edward J. Lane, 'The Morgans of Glamorgan', NLW, MS 5252A, f. 11; Green, p. 97; *LNL*, pp. 143, 391, 428, 430; *FCHS*, p. 42; WPAB, p. 28.

48 Bridenbaugh, 'Use and abuse of the forest', pp. 10–11.

49 WPAB, p. 113.

50 Garvin, 'Brickmaking', pp. 19–20, 23–6; *LNL*, pp. 96–7; Howard, *Old Windsor*, pp. 230–32; Cummings, *Framed Houses*, p. 119.

51 WPAB, p. 113; MS1649, p. 185; *LNL*, pp. 391–3.

52 *FCHS*, pp. 42–3; *WP*, iv, p. 254; *WP*, v, p. 50; *VRS*, p. 60.

53 Ulrich, ch. 2, esp. p. 37; Shepard, *Meanings of Manhood*, pp. 77–8, 83–4; Joanne Bailey, *Unquiet Lives: Marriage and Marriage Breakdown in England, 1660–1800* (Cambridge, 2009), chs. 3–4; William Whately, *A Bride-Bush, or A Direction for Married Persons* (London, 1619), p. 44 (quotation).

54 See WPAB, pp. 88, 113.

55 Anthony Fletcher, 'Manhood, the male body, courtship and the household in early modern England', *History*, 84 (1999), pp. 419–36; Elizabeth A. Foyster, *Manhood in Early Modern England: Honour, Sex and Marriage* (London, 1999), p. 31; Mark Breitenberg, *Anxious Masculinity in Early Modern England* (Cambridge, 1996), pp. 2, 3–6, 11.

56 Thomas Shepard, *The Sound Beleever* (London, 1645), p. 343; Alexandra Shepard, 'Manhood, credit and patriarchy in early modern England, *c.* 1580–1640', *Past & Present*, 167 (2000), pp. 76–7, 79, 87–8, 95.

57 Daniel Sennertus et al., *The Sixth Book of Practical Physick* (London, 1662), p. 96 (quotation); Lisa Wilson, *Ye Heart of a Man: The Domestic Life of Men in Colonial New England* (New Haven, CT, 1999), ch. 3, esp. p. 97.

58 Carroll, *Puritanism and the Wilderness*, pp. 93, 172–3.

59 LWP, p. 54.

60 TRSR, p. 102; *Hampden County*, p. 235; Chapin, *Deacon Samuel Chapin*, p. 20; *Hampden County*, p. 120. The accounts report the town 'much infested with wolves and foxes': TRSR, p. 67. For wolf hooks, see Pynchon's accounts, September 1636: 'Pincheon papers', pp. 228–30.

61 *RLCR*, pp. 188–9; Demos (ed.), *Remarkable Providences*, pp. 232–8, 450.

62 *JJW*, pp. 292, 293; WPAB, p. 113.

63 Nathanael Homes, *Daemonologie and Theologie* (London, 1650), p. 60.

64 Cressy, *Coming Over*, ch. 10.

65 John Davenport, *The Witches of Huntingdon* (London, 1646), p. 11; Jerome Friedman, *Miracles and the Pulp Press during the English Revolution* (London, 1993), ch. 3; *Signes and Wonders from Heaven* (London, 1645).

66 Lilian Handlin, 'Dissent in a small community', *NEQ*, 58 (1985), pp. 193–4, 196–7, 201; Cornelia Hughes Dayton, *Women Before the Bar: Gender, Law, and Society in Connecticut, 1639–1789* (Chapel Hill, NC, 1995), pp. 26–34.

67 Kupperman, 'Climate', p. 8; *GHNE*, pp. 324–5; Lockwood (ed.), *Western Massachusetts*, i, p. 100.

68 *VRS*, pp. 9, 10, 60. On the ravages of storm and flooding: 'Matthew Grant Record, 1639–1681', in *Some Early Records and Documents of and Relating to the Town of Windsor, Connecticut, 1639–1703* (Hartford, CT, 1930), pp. 78–9.

69 Davenport, *Witches of Huntingdon*, title page; MC, vol. 10, p. 210; *GHNE*, pp. 413–15; *JJW*, p. 288; David Loewenstein and John Marshall (eds.), *Heresy, Literature and Politics in Early Modern English Culture* (Cambridge, 2006), p. 5; *WP*, v, p. 91.

70 Christiaan G. F. de Jong, '"Christ's descent" in Massachusetts: the doctrine of justification according to William Pynchon (1590–1662)', in Christiaan G. F. de Jong and J. van Sluis (eds.), *Gericht Verleden: Kerkhistorische Opstellen* (Leiden, 1991), pp. 131–6, 140–46; Dewey D. Wallace, 'Puritan and Anglican: the interpretation of Christ's descent into hell in Elizabethan theology', *Archiv für Reformationsgeschichte*, 69 (1978), pp. 248–87; Philip Dixon, *'Nice and Hot Disputes': The Doctrine of the Trinity in the Seventeenth Century* (London, 2003), ch. 2.

71 Demos, *Entertaining Satan*, p. 177.

72 Hall, *Worlds of Wonder*, p. 44. On the desire for books, including the library of Archbishop Laud: Bodl., Clarendon MS 26, f. 110v.

73 *An Abstract of the Lawes of New England* (1641), in Force (ed.), *Tracts*, iii, no. 9, p. 12.

74 *WP*, v, p. 90; *JJW*, pp. 299–300; *RLCR*, p. 189.

75 *LNL*, p. 465; GACW, p. 19; WPAB, p. 94.

76 *FCHS*, p. 43. Lombard's birthplace was either Winsham in Somerset or Thorncombe in Dorset, probably in 1620s: http://www.my-roots.org/persons/UK/6252.php; http://www.maryandjohn1630.com/passengerlist_a.html.

77 *FCHS*, p. 43. Contenders come from Langton in Lincolnshire, Northamptonshire, Hertfordshire, Lancashire, Cumbria, Devon and London.

78 *FCHS*, pp. 20, 43, 62; *LNL*, pp. 200, 229; Savage, i, p. 438.

79 Paul R. Lucas, *Valley of Discord: Church and Society Along the Connecticut River, 1636–1725* (Hanover, NH, 1976), pp. 40–42, 59–61, 63–6; MC, vol. 2, p. 299; *WP*, v, pp. 90–92.

80 WPAB, pp. 113–14; HLSL, HLS MS 4344, f. 17r; Earle, *Customs and Fashions*, pp. 9; *VRS*, pp. 11, 60.
81 Norton, *Founding Mothers and Fathers*, pp. 222–6; Ulrich, pp. 127–38; *VRS*, pp. 11.

4. Sleeveless Errands

1 Josselyn, *Two Voyages*, p. 263; *WP*, v, pp. 114–15; John Gaule, *Select Cases of Conscience Touching Witches and Witchcrafts* (London, 1646), pp. 20–21.
2 Ulrich, pp. 28, 138–9, 158–9; WPAB, pp. 113–14.
3 *RLCR*, pp. 189, 190; Ross, *Before Salem*, p. 74.
4 *Pynchons of Springfield*, p. 29; TRSR, p. 52; Konig, *Law and Society*, p. 45; Bridenbaugh, 'Use and abuse of the forest', pp. 32–5; George Bliss, *An Address, Delivered at the Opening of the Town-Hall in Springfield* (Springfield, MA, 1828), p. 9.
5 WPAB, p. 114.
6 *WP*, v, pp. 136–7; Chapin, *Deacon Samuel Chapin*, pp. 16–17.
7 TRSR, p. 52; WPAB, p. 114.
8 *FCHS*, p. 195.
9 For a Welsh case from 1656, where witnesses were terrified by fiery lights on marshland and a vision of a witch: NLW, MS 4/985/2, f. 18.
10 *VRS*, pp. 9, 10, 11; Chapin, *Deacon Samuel Chapin*, p. 20.
11 Ross, *Before Salem*, pp. 73–4, 96; CSL, Matthew Grant diary, *c.* 1637–54, pp. 1–2; *RLCR*, p. 190; BPL, Ms. Am. 1502/1/4; Kupperman, 'Climate', p. 9.
12 CSL, Matthew Grant diary, *c.* 1637–54, p. 190; Ross, *Before Salem*, pp. 117–26.
13 *VRS*, p. 11; WPAB, pp. 114, 115, 147; *LNL*, p. 245. In Springfield, twenty-three householders had more land than Hugh; eighteen had less: *DH*, p. 96.
14 *FCHS*, pp. 20, 42; *LNL*, p. 202; TRSR, p. 37; WPAB, pp. 20–21; GACW, pp. 15–16; Agnes Thomson Cooper, *Beginnings: Thomas Cooper of Springfield and Some Allied Families* (Baltimore, 1987), p. 225.
15 William Drage, *A Physical Nosonomy* (London, 1665), p. 67; Savage, iii, p. 106; *VRS*, p. 20; *AWNE*, p. 221 n.2.
16 Kupperman, 'Climate', p. 9; Hawke, p. 90; Dow, p. 97.
17 MacDonald, *Mystical Bedlam*, p. 102; WPAB, p. 144. Alice Apsley of Saybrook (d. 1645) dispensed medicinal herbs: Lyle Koehler, *A Search for Power: The 'Weaker Sex' in Seventeenth-Century New England* (Urbana, IL, 1980), p. 115.
18 Anderson et al., *Great Migration . . . 1634–1635*, ii, pp. 210–12; *Hampden County*, p. 380; *A Book of Fruits and Flowers* (London, 1653), p. 32; *JJW*, p. 193; AAS, MSS Octavo vols. 'B' (John Barton, Account Book, 1662–76); Earle, *Customs and Fashions*, pp. 346–9; Dow, pp. 185–7. A sermon of George Moxon referred to using sheep's horn: MS1649, p. 185.

19 Dow, pp. 193, 197; Hosmer, ii, p. 225; LWP, p. 56.

20 LWP, p. 56; *PP*, ii, p. 23; WPAB, pp. 113–14; MacDonald, *Mystical Bedlam*, pp. 187–93.

21 Ann Marie Plane, 'Indian and English dreams: colonial hierarchy and manly restraint in seventeenth-century New England', in Thomas A. Foster (ed.), *New Men: Manliness in Early America* (New York, 2011), pp. 31–47.

22 MacDonald, *Mystical Bedlam*, p. 167. On emotional control: Anne S. Lombard, *Making Manhood: Growing Up Male in Colonial New England* (Cambridge, MA, 2003), pp. 10–11, 88–9.

23 A. B., *The Sick-Mans Rare Jewel* (London, 1674), pp. 16–17; Thomas Nashe, *The Terrors of the Night* (London, 1594), sig. C4v. On delusional dreams: Thomas Cooper, *The Mystery of Witch-Craft* (London, 1617), pp. 145–6; James Hart, *Klinike* (London, 1633), pp. 340–41; Thomas Brugis, *The Marrow of Physicke* (London, 1640), pp. 38–9, 66.

24 See e.g. *Troilus and Cressida*, Act 5, sc. 4, ll. 8–9. See also Anatoly Liberman, 'Sleeveless errand', *OUPBlog* (2017) – https://blog.oup.com/2017/04/sleeveless-errand-origins/.

25 WPDB, f. 7r (William Branch, 13 March 1651); Walter Charleton, *Natural History of the Passions* (London, 1674), p. 138.

26 Williston Walker, *The Creeds and Platforms of Congregationalism* (New York, 1893), pp. 154–6; Hawke, p. 36; Thistlethwaite, pp. 85–6; *RLCR*, p. 190.

27 *Englands Hazzard* (London, 1648), p. 2; *Englands New-Yeares Gift* (London, 1648), pp. 5–6; Henry Jessey, *The Exceeding Riches of Grace Advanced* (London, 1647), pp. 19, 56–9.

28 MacDonald, *Mystical Bedlam*, pp. 160, 165–9, 193–5; Ulinka Rublack, 'Interior states and sexuality in early modern Germany', in Scott Spector et al. (eds.), *After The History of Sexuality: German Genealogies With and Beyond Foucault* (New York, 2012), pp. 54–7.

29 Kupperman, 'Climate', p. 9; WPDB, f. 21v (Mary Parsons, 27 February 1651). On melancholy as exile from the self: MacDonald, *Mystical Bedlam*, p. 160.

30 WPDB, ff. 21v, 22v (Mary Parsons, 27 February and 18 March 1651).

31 Gaskill, *Witchfinders*, p. 221; *JJW*, p. 329; *VRS*, p. 60.

32 *VRS*, p. 12.

33 Frank Farnsworth Starr (ed.), *Various Ancestral Lines of James Goodwin and Lucy (Morgan) Goodwin of Hartford, Connecticut, Vol. II* (Hartford, CT, 1915), pp. 59–73; Savage, ii, p. 60; John J. Waters, 'Hingham, Massachusetts, 1631–1661: An East Anglian oligarchy in the New World', *Journal of Social History*, 1 (1968), pp. 351–70.

34 Demos, *Little Commonwealth*, pp. 29–31; Cummings, *Framed Houses*, p. 28; David H. Flaherty, *Privacy in Colonial New England* (Charlottesville, VA, 1972),

pp. 76–7, 79–83; WPDB, f. 14v; Waters, *Ipswich*, i, p. 29; Demos, *Little Common-wealth*, pp. 46–7.

35 Flaherty, *Privacy*, pp. 66–70.

36 Willingly believed supernatural stories were 'a remedy for the drudgery, dreariness and sheer misery of the daily grind', and can be seen as 'an extreme fiction, an offshoot of the fantastic': Marina Warner, 'Name the days', *London Review of Books*, 43 (February 2021), p. 38.

37 George L. Haskins, *Law and Authority in Early Massachusetts: A Study in Tradition and Design* (New York, 1968), pp. 139–40, 145–6.

38 GHNE, pp. 423, 530; John Hale, *A Modest Enquiry into the Nature of Witchcraft* (Boston, 1702), p. 17; Shurtleff, ii, p. 242; iii, p. 126; *JJW*, p. 341; Demos, *Entertaining Satan*, p. 92; Hosmer, ii, pp. 345–6.

39 *JJW*, p. 341; Hosmer, ii, p. 346. Witches were said to raise storms during their trials: Thomas Ady, *A Candle in the Dark* (London, 1656), p. 113.

40 VRS, pp. 11–12, 60.

41 VRS, p. 12; *JJW*, pp. 342–3.

42 MC, vol. 2, pp. 313–17, 320–26; GHNE, p. 530.

43 Essex RO, T/G 209/1, p. 1; WP, v, p. 271; Hutchinson, *History*, i, pp. 132–3.

44 Giovanni Torriano, *Piazza Universale* (London, 1666), p. 134.

45 George Webbe, *The Araignement of an Unruly Tongue* (London, 1619), pp. 6–7, 22–3, 75–6, 165–6; Perkins, *Government of the Tongue*, pp. 30–31.

46 The Marshfields probably relocated in 1648, the year Samuel opened an account at Pynchon's store: WPAB, p. 182; DH, p. 100; FCHS, p. 43. But Mary Parsons's insinuation that Widow Marshfield's 'grudging' was linked to the death of Pentecost Matthews's daughter, on 25 July 1646, suggests earlier: VRS, p. 60.

47 Ross, *Before Salem*, pp. 69–71, 92–3; Hosmer, i, pp. 140–41; Anderson, *Great Migration . . . 1620–1633*, iii, p. 2043; idem et al., *Great Migration . . . 1634–1635*, v, pp. 48–54; Douglas Richardson, 'Thomas Marshfield's wife Mercy: did their daughter marry John Dumbleton?', *American Genealogist*, 67 (1992), pp. 11–12; idem, 'The English origin of Thomas Marshfield . . . new light on his wife and children', *American Genealogist*, 63 (1988), pp. 161–3; LNL, pp. 70, 443; AWNE, p. 225 n.1; Trumbull and Hoadley (eds.), *Public Records*, i, pp. 76, 82, 87, 93, 96, 107, 115, 137.

48 Elizabeth Reis, 'Witches, sinners, and the underside of covenant theology', *Essex Institute Historical Collections*, 129 (1993), pp. 103–18; Hall, *Worlds of Wonder*, pp. 189–90, 192; David A. Weir, *Early New England: A Covenanted Society* (Grand Rapids, MI, 2005), chs. 3–6; Ross, *Before Salem*, pp. 54, 71, 97–8, 113–15.

49 Shepard, 'Wolcott shorthand notebook', p. 336 (John Wareham, 13 September 1640). Ephraim Huit said 'in Satan's buffetings, we are dogged with the foulest

of lusts, of atheism, idolatry, blasphemy, murder, or the like': *The Anatomy of Conscience* (London, 1626), p. 253.

50 Stiles, *Ancient Windsor*, i, pp. 444–5, 680–81; Demos, *Entertaining Satan*, ch. 11; *Records of the Particular Court of Connecticut, 1639–1663* (Hartford, CT, 1928), p. 43.

51 Ross, *Before Salem*, pp. 197–8; Richard Godbeer, 'Chaste and unchaste covenants: witchcraft and sex in early modern culture', in Peter Benes and Jane Montague Benes (eds.), *Wonders of the Invisible World, 1600–1900* (Boston, MA, 1995), pp. 53–72.

52 Mather, *Magnalia*, ii, p. 456; *Particular Court of Connecticut*, p. 56.

53 Hosmer, ii, pp. 354–5; Kupperman, 'Climate', pp. 9–11; *VRS*, pp. 11, 60.

54 *VRS*, p. 12; Willis, *Malevolent Nurture*, pp. 48, 79.

55 *CJWM*, p. 217.

56 WPDB, f. 14r (Blanche and Reece Bedortha, 27 March 1651); WPAB, p. 115.

57 WPDB, f. 14v (Blanche Bedortha, 1 March 1651).

58 WPDB, f. 15r (Blanche Bedortha, 1 March 1651 and Mercy Marshfield, 22 March 1651).

59 *VRS*, p. 12.

60 MC, vol. 9, pp. 6–14, quotation at p. 10.

61 WPDB, f. 18r (Griffith Jones, 25 February 1651). Drake supposed Jones was 'too drunk to know very precisely what he was about': *AWNE*, p. 233 n.1.

62 HLSL, HLS MS 4344, ff. 16v–17r; *CJWM*, pp. 219–20. On Pentecost Matthews as teacher: *LNL*, p. 121.

63 Mercy Marshfield married John Dumbleton *c.* 1645, then followed her mother and siblings to Springfield *c.* 1649–50, after the lease on her husband's land at Windsor expired: Richardson, 'Thomas Marshfield's wife', p. 13; Jacobus and Waterman, *Hale, House and Related Families*, pp. 521–2; *FCHS*, p. 43. This must have been the daughter Mary Parsons referred to, not Sarah, who did not marry until October 1649: *VRS*, p. 20. Mercy Dumbleton had her first child in 1648, in Windsor, suggesting she was indeed childless, 1645–7, which according to Parsons was why her mother 'did grudge at other women that had children': HLSL, HLS MS 4344, f. 16v.

64 Cf. the New England woman of whom it was said that 'the word devil had been so oft in her mouth as the very Indians had taken notice of it': Robert G. Pope (ed.), *The Notebook of the Reverend John Fiske, 1644–1675* (Boston, 1974), p. 207.

65 HLSL, HLS MS 4344, f. 17r. *CJWM*, p. 220, has Mary saying '*the* child died' when what she actually said to Pentecost Matthews was '*your* child died' (my italics).

66 HLSL, HLS MS 4344, f. 16v. Again *CJWM*, p. 219, mistranscribes 'your child' as 'their child', which has an entirely different meaning.

67 Morton, *New-Englands Memoriall*, p. 131.

68 Pynchon, *Meritorious Price*, sigs. A2r, A4v; McIntyre, *Pynchon*, p. 33; *CJWM*, p. 26. Pynchon later told Baxter, 'While I was in New England I had some intercourse with Mr Gataker by letters': DWL, Baxter Letters, 3.186 (1655), f. 186v.

69 *WP*, v, pp. 134–5; *CJWM*, pp. 19–20; *Hutchinson Papers*, 2 vols. (Albany, NY, 1865), i, pp. 214–23. Pynchon's sympathy came also from a desire that New England keep up with the expanding English economy: Margaret E. Newell, 'Robert Child and the entrepreneurial vision: economy and ideology in early New England', *NEQ*, 68 (1995), pp. 223–56.

70 C. H. Firth and R. S. Rait (eds.), *Acts and Ordinances of the Interregnum, 1642–60*, 3 vols. (London, 1911), i, pp. 1133–6; Thomas Hodges, *The Growth and Spreading of Haeresie* (London, 1647), pp. 5–8, 13–17, 20–25, 35–7, quotation at p. 13; John Ellyson, *Hereticks, Sectaries and Schismaticks* (London, 1647), pp. 13–15; *An Attestation to . . . the Truth of Jesus Christ, and to our Solemn League and Covenant* (London, 1648), pp. 14–15, 37–9.

71 Thomas Edwards, *Gangraena* (London, 1646); James Cranford, *Haereseomachia: or, The Mischiefe which Heresies Doe* (London, 1646), pp. 5, 16; Richard Vines, *The Authors, Nature and Danger of Haeresie* (London, 1647), pp. 64–6.

72 Edwards, *Gangraena*, pt 1, sig. A3, pp. 9–10; pt 2, p. 153; *GHNE*, pp. 533–4.

73 MS1649, pp. 1–22, 40, quotations at pp. 7, 22, 40. In the 1640s Moxon's sermons grew 'crankier, crustier, crabbier': *GACW*, pp. 36–7.

5. I Hear My Child Is Dead

1 WPDB, f. 7r (William Branch, 13 March 1651). For a case where a woman in bed saw visions of two children (one red, one white), surrounded by lights: BL, Add. MS 28223, f. 15.

2 WPDB, f. 23v (John Matthews, 27 Feb. 1651). Hugh's bad stomach may have been linked to his troubled mind and turbulent emotions: Michael Roper, 'The unconscious work of history', *Cultural and Social History*, 11 (2014), pp. 179–80.

3 *CJWM*, p. 219.

4 Ulrich, pp. 21–2.

5 William Pynchon, *The Jewes Synagogue* (London, 1652), p. 17.

6 Thistlethwaite, p. 87; WPDB, f. 16v (Hugh Parsons, 18 March 1651).

7 WPDB, f. 16v (Sarah Edwards, 27 Feb. 1651); Stanley Waters, 'Witchcraft in Springfield, Mass.', *NEHGR*, 35 (1881), p. 153.

8 Ibid.

9 WPDB, f. 16v (William Pynchon?, 18 March 1651).

10 Luke 12:48.

11 Hebrews 11:38; MS1649, pp. 40–47, quotations at pp. 45, 47.

12 WPDB, ff. 23r–23v (John Matthews, 27 February 1651); Jennifer Speake (ed.), *Oxford Dictionary of Proverbs*, 6th edn (Oxford, 2015), p. 87.

13 *CJWM*, p. 219; Hall, *Worlds of Wonder*, p. 45; Richard S. Dunn (ed.), *The Laws and Liberties of Massachusetts: Reprinted from the Unique Copy of the 1648 Edition in the Henry E. Huntington Library* (San Marino, CA, 1998).

14 *CJWM*, pp. 89–91, 116–18.

15 *CJWM*, pp. 219–20; HLSL, HLS MS 4344, ff. 16v–17r. The fine was fair, 40 bushels of maize being worth £5: WPAB, p. 14.

16 *CJWM*, p. 219.

17 Newcome, *Plaine Discourse*, pp. 10–12, 15–16, 22, 29, 30–31, 50, quotation at p. 29; Kristine Steenbergh, 'Emotions and gender: the case of anger in early modern English revenge tragedies', in Jonas Liliequist (ed.), *A History of Emotions, 1200–1800* (London, 2012), pp. 123, 124–30.

18 William Ramesey, *Helminthologia* (London, 1668), p. 346; Fay Bound, ' "An angry and malicious mind"? Narratives of slander at the church courts of York, *c.*1660–*c.*1760', *History Workshop Journal*, 56 (2003), pp. 59–77.

19 *CJWM*, p. 221.

20 *JJW*, p. 329; Morton, *New-Englands Memoriall*, pp. 131, 265.

21 Trumbull and Hoadley (eds.), *Public Records*, i, pp. 189–90; Shurtleff, iii, p. 158.

22 MS1649, pp. 47–120, quotations at p. 51.

23 *GACW*, pp. 26–7, 150–53; MS1649, pp. 93, 104–11, quotation at p. 105.

24 Ewen, *Witchcraft and Demonianism*, pp. 314–16.

25 Richard Baxter, *Aphorismes of Justification* (London, 1649); Winship, 'Contesting control', pp. 807–8; Selement and Woolley (eds.), *Shepard's Confessions*, p. 20. See also Pynchon's correspondence with Baxter in the mid-1650s: DWL, Baxter Letters, 4.173 (1654), 3.186–7 (1655); N. H. Keeble and Geoffrey F. Nuttall (eds.), *Calendar of the Correspondence of Richard Baxter*, 2 vols. (Oxford, 1991), i, pp. 158–9, 179–80.

26 *DH*, p. 93. Pynchon later told Baxter that he had heard his book 'so much preached against by Mr Wareham of Connecticut': DWL, Baxter Letters, 3.186 (1655), f. 186v.

27 Thomas Hooker, *The Covenant of Grace Opened* (London, 1649).

28 MS1649, pp. 111–20. Pynchon and Moxon were both influenced by Hugh Broughton, *A Treatise of Melchisedek* (London, 1591): *GACW*, pp. 35–6.

29 MS1649, pp. 120–30, quotations at pp. 127, 128; Matthew 5:1–12, 14; Romans 5:9.

30 *DH*, pp. 93–4.

31 Ross, *Before Salem*, pp. 43–5; Mark 3:25. On links between heresy and witch-craft: Gary K. Waite, *Heresy, Magic and Witchcraft in Early Modern Europe* (Basingstoke, 2003).

32 Cotton Mather recalled 'a notable story of a horrible witchcraft, wherein the devil got into a pulpit, and spoke strange things to his vassals there': *Optanda. Good Men Described, and Good Things Propounded* (Boston, 1692), p. 55.

33 E. J. Kent, 'Raiding the patriarch's toolbox: reading masculine governance in cases of male witchcraft, 1592–1692', in Susan Broomhall and Jacqueline Van Gent (eds.), *Governing Masculinities in the Early Modern Period: Regulating Selves and Others* (Farnham, 2011), pp. 173–88, esp. pp. 182–4 on Hugh Parsons.

34 WPDB, f. 7r (William Branch, 13 March 1651).

35 William B. Trask (ed.), 'Rev. Samuel Danforth's records of the First Church in Roxbury, Mass.', *NEHGR*, 34 (1880), p. 85; Starr (ed.), *Ancestral Lines*, p. 60; TRSR, p. 67; WPDB, f. 17r (Anthony Dorchester, 25 February 1651; Jonathan Taylor, 17 June 1651).

36 WPDB, f. 21v (Mary Parsons, 18 March 1651). New England's black-dog leg-ends originated in England: Hall, *Worlds of Wonder*, p. 88.

37 WPDB, f. 21v (Mary Parsons, 18 March 1651); f. 22r (Anthony Dorchester, 27 February 1651).

38 WPDB, ff. 21v, 22r (Mary Parsons, 18 March 1651; Anthony Dorchester, 27 February 1651); f. 19v (George Colton, 18 March 1651); f. 20r (Hugh Parsons, 18 March 1651).

39 WPDB, f. 5r (Jonathan Taylor, 22 March 1651); ff. 23r–23v (John Matthews, 27 February 1651).

40 MS1649, pp. 130–35, quotation at p. 131.

41 WPDB, f. 22r (Benjamin Cooley, 27 February 1651); Wilson, *Heart of a Man*, pp. 75–9; MS1649, p. 135.

42 WPDB, f. 19v (George Colton, 18 March 1651); *VRS*, p. 13 (Mary Colton, b. 22 September 1649).

43 WPDB, f. 21r (Hugh Parsons, 18 March 1651). Other sources help us to imag-ine the horror. In 1647 a man described how his child 'laid in a most grievous tormenting manner shrieking and crying out, tearing the flesh until it died': CUL, EDR 1647/10.

44 WPDB, f. 21r (Sarah Cooley, 18 March 1651). For evidence of this belief: Drage, *Physical Nosonomy*, p. 67; *The Triall of Maist. Dorrell* (London, 1599), p. 97.

45 WPDB, f. 21r (Mary Ashley and Sarah Leonard, 18 March 1651).

46 WPDB, f. 17r (Anthony Dorchester, 25 February 1651).

47 WPDB, f. 17r (Mary Parsons and Anthony Dorchester, 25 February 1651). On anger as 'a cruel tempest of the mind': Ramesey, *Helminthologia*, p. 265.

48 MS1649, pp. 138–42, quotations at pp. 139, 140, 142; Job 31:2–3. The incident with the beef-tongue broth took place late in September, and Moxon certainly gave this sermon on the 30th.

49 WPDB, f. 17r (Mary Parsons and Anthony Dorchester, 25 February 1651); MS1649, p. 145.

50 WPDB, f. 17v (Abigail Munn, 18 March 1651).

51 WPDB, f. 19v (William Pynchon, 18 March 1651); ff. 20r–20v (Jonathan Burt, 18 March 1651). Men expected other men to grieve, see e.g. the New Englander whose son lay sick: Michael McGiffert (ed.), *God's Plot: The Paradoxes of Puritan Piety* (Amherst, MA, 1972), p. 192.

52 VRS, pp. 11–13; WPDB, f. 20v (George Colton, 1 and 18 March 1651).

53 WPDB, f. 21r (Anthony Dorchester and Blanche Bedortha, 18 March 1651).

54 WPDB, f. 22r (Anthony Dorchester, 27 February 1651). Later Mary claimed she had accused him, but Dorchester and Parsons had no recollection of this: ibid., f. 19r (Hugh Parsons and Anthony Dorchester, 18 March 1651).

55 David E. Stannard, *The Puritan Way of Death: A Study in Religion, Culture, and Social Change* (New York, 1977), pp. 109–22; Earle, *Customs and Fashions*, pp. 364, 370, 374–5, 383; Fischer, *Albion's Seed*, pp. 114–16.

56 VRS, p. 60; MS1649, pp. 164–72.

57 VRS, p. 60; WPAB, p. 207.

58 GACW, pp. 12–13; TRSR, p. 65.

59 MS1649, pp. 173–9, quotation at p. 178; Winship, 'Contesting control', p. 809 n.7.

60 MS1649, pp. 179–83, quotations at pp. 179, 181.

61 Bridenbaugh, 'Use and abuse of the forest', p. 22; *Hampden County*, p. 261; Thistlethwaite, pp. 86–7.

62 In February 1651 Dorchester said he had left the Parsons household fifteen months earlier, i.e. November 1649, the month of his wife's burial: WPDB, f. 22r (Anthony Dorchester, 27 February 1651).

63 WPDB, f. 22v (Mary Parsons, 27 February 1651); CJWM, p. 221; MS1649, pp. 184–96, quotation at p. 195.

64 HLAS, ESMC, ESM-04-04-03; LNL, p. 407; VRS, p. 20; WPAB, p. 109.

65 RLCR, p. 197; Trask (ed.), 'Danforth's records', p. 85; WPDB, f. 2r (Mercy Marshfield, 22 March 1651; Samuel Marshfield, 12 March 1651). Cf. James 5:2–3, Job 13:28, and Isaiah 50:9. Jane Kamensky sees 'poetic flair' in Hugh's threat: 'Talk like a man: speech, power, and masculinity in early New England', *Gender & History*, 8 (1996), p. 36.

66 CJWM, p. 221.

67 WPDB, ff. 19r, 22r (Mary Parsons, 18 March 1651; Benjamin Cooley, 27 February 1651).

6. *Strange Dreams*

1 Carol F. Karlsen, *The Devil in the Shape of a Woman: Witchcraft in Colonial New England* (New York, 1987), pp. 22–3. Karlsen's source was John Hale, who mentioned a confessed witch at Springfield: *Modest Enquiry*, p. 19. George Lincoln Burr thought Hale confused Mary with Goodwife Lake of Dorchester: *Narratives of the Witchcraft Cases, 1648–1706* (New York, 1914), p. 408 n.4. Cf. Malcolm Gaskill, 'Witchcraft and power in early modern England: the case of Margaret Moore', in Jenny Kermode and Garthine Walker (eds.), *Women, Crime and the Courts in Early Modern England* (London, 1994), pp. 125–45.

2 Jane Kamensky, *Governing the Tongue: The Politics of Speech in Early New England* (Oxford, 1997), pp. 158–9. Elizabeth Kent sees Hugh as an 'unruly masculine agent': *Cases of Male Witchcraft in Old and New England, 1592–1692* (Turnhout, 2013), p. 105. Richard Godbeer stands between Kamensky and Kent: ' "Your wife will be your biggest accuser": reinforcing codes of manhood at New England witch trials', *Early American Studies*, 15 (2017), pp. 478–9, 481–3. On feminized male witches: Laura Apps and Andrew Gow, *Male Witches in Early Modern Europe* (Manchester, 2003), p. 7; Rolf Schulte, *Man as Witch: Male Witches in Central Europe* (Basingstoke, 2009). Erika Gasser argues that the male witch was 'undone as a proper man': 'Witchcraft, possession and the unmaking of women and men: a late sixteenth-century English case study', *Magic, Ritual and Witchcraft*, 11 (2016), p. 33.

3 WPDB, f. 19r (Mary Parsons, 18 March 1651).

4 *CJWM*, pp. 221–2; *WP*, vi, p. 19.

5 WPDB, f. 3r (Francis Pepper, 18 March 1651). Witnesses in 1622 described a victim's arms striking 'very fearfully', head shaking 'as though she were troubled with the palsy', foaming at the mouth, torso arched, legs 'stretched out . . . so stiff that her joints would not bend without breaking': TNA, STAC8/32/13. Another convulsing woman dislocated her limbs: Bodl., Tanner MS 28, ff. 161–2. A Connecticut woman fell 'into sounding fits, with her tongue flaring out of her mouth . . . and her eyes out of her head in a ghastly manner'; the smell of her breath was unbearable: Wyllys, Box 1, Folder 9, Ms. 344, f. 2v.

6 John Jeffries Martin, *Myths of Renaissance Individualism* (Basingstoke, 2004), ch. 3; Katharine Hodgkin, *Madness in Seventeenth-Century Autobiography* (Basingstoke, 2007), chs. 7–8.

7 This was probably Joseph Moxon, although he ceased printing in 1650, so perhaps his brother James Moxon. Their father, James Sr, was also a printer. Like George, these Moxons hailed from Wakefield in Yorkshire. The manuscript was sent in either late 1649 or early 1650, as the London bookseller George Thomason received his copy on 2 June 1650.

8 Morton, *New-Englands Memoriall*, pp. 133–4, 265, quotation at p. 134.

9 William DeLoss Love, *The Colonial History of Hartford* (Hartford, CT, 1914), p. 283; Mather, *Magnalia*, ii, p. 456. Payments to her gaoler ceased on 6 June 1650.

10 HLAS, ESMC, ESM-05-01-01, pp. 318–23.

11 Wright, *Genesis*, pp. 29–30; *LNL*, p. 215; *CJWM*, pp. 224, 226–7. The phrase was 'chafing his yard to provoke lust'.

12 *The Independents Dream, of a New-Nothing* (London, 1647), pp. 3–4.

13 George Walker, *Socinianisme in the Fundamentall Point of Justification Discovered, and Confuted* (London, 1641), pp. 11–13, 302. Walker was attacking Anthony Wotton, whose views on the Atonement were almost identical to Pynchon's: Samuel Wotton, *Mr Anthony Wotton's Defence Against Mr George Walker's Charge* (Cambridge, 1641), pp. 4, 12, 21.

14 *A True Relation of the Chiefe Passages between Mr. Anthony Wotton, and Mr. George Walker* (London, 1642), pp. 10–11.

15 De Jong, ' "Christ's descent" ', pp. 136–43, 146–7; *DH*, pp. 116–17.

16 Pynchon, *Meritorious Price*, pp. 74, 81, 102; Winship, 'Contesting control', pp. 809–11.

17 WPDB, f. 6v (Simon Beamon, 20 May 1651).

18 WPDB, f. 23r (John Lombard, 17 March 1651); Waters, 'Witchcraft', pp. 152–3.

19 Moore, *Pilgrims*, p. 79; John Norton, *A Discussion of That Great Point in Divinity, the Sufferings of Christ* (London, 1653), pp. 272–4.

20 *RLCR*, p. 73; *CJWM*, pp. 19–20; McIntyre, *Pynchon*, pp. 31–2; *DH*, pp. 160–62.

21 John Norton, *A Brief and Excellent Treatise Containing the Doctrine of Godliness* (London, 1648), sig. A2r ; Shurtleff, iii, pp. 215–16; *FCHS*, pp. 87–8.

22 John Eliot, 'A brief topographical description of the several towns in New England', MHS, Ms. S-565, f. 4; *WP*, vi, p. 76; Roger Williams, *The Bloody Tenent, of Persecution, for Cause of Conscience* (n.p., 1644); Firth and Rait (eds.), *Acts and Ordinances*, i, p. 1136.

23 Ruth E. Mayers, 'Sir Henry Vane the younger', *ODNB* ; John Lilburne, *Englands New Chains Discovered* (London, 1649). See also Nigel Smith, ' "And if God was one of us": Paul Best, John Biddle, and anti-Trinitarian heresy in seventeenth-century England', in Loewenstein and Marshall (eds.), *Heresy, Literature and Politics*, pp. 160–84.

24 Mayers, 'Vane'. See also: Ralph Cudworth, *A Sermon Preached Before the Honourable House of Commons* (London, 1647); *Christs Banner of Love* (London, 1648).

25 William Chillingworth, *The Religion of Protestants* (London, 1638), p. 199.

26 Henry Robinson, *John the Baptist, Forerunner of Christ Jesus: or, A Necessity for Liberty of Conscience* (n.p., n.d. [London, 1644]), sig. A3r; John Goodwin, *Some*

Modest and Humble Queries (London, 1646), pp. 2–4, quotation at p. 4; Williams, *Bloody Tenent*, p. 110.

27 *VRS*, p. 13.

28 WPDB, f. 5v (William Branch, 13 March 1651).

29 See e.g. WPDB, ff. 2r, 5v, 6r, 16r, 22r, 22v (various witnesses). For similarly furious male witches: John Demos, 'John Godfrey and his neighbors: witchcraft and the social web in colonial Massachusetts', *WMQ*, 33 (1976), pp. 242–65; Malcolm Gaskill, 'The devil in the shape of a man: witchcraft, conflict and belief in Jacobean England', *Historical Research*, 71 (1998), pp. 142–71; East Sussex RO, QR/E 18, ff. 26–31, 59–61.

30 Elizabeth Kent, 'Masculinity and male witches in old and New England, 1593–1680', *History Workshop Journal*, 60 (2005), pp. 81–2. According to Stephen Innes, 'people may have deflected their dissatisfactions with William Pynchon onto Parsons . . . a symbolic victim': *LNL*, pp. 137–8. Valerie Kivelson calls witchcraft 'a tool for ameliorating the harsh conditions of abusively enforced patriarchy, bondage, and social inequality': *Desperate Magic: The Moral Economy of Witchcraft in Seventeenth-Century Russia* (Ithaca, NY, 2013), p. 6. David M. Powers disputes Innes's 'symbolic scapegoat' theory, suggesting that accusers were unconscious of their emotions: *DH*, p. 96.

31 *Hampden County*, p. 381; *LNL*, pp. 110–11.

32 WPDB, f. 1v (Jonathan Taylor, c. 18–20 March 1651).

33 *LNL*, pp. 9–10, 210.

34 Brian P. Levack, *Witch-Hunting in Scotland: Law, Politics and Religion* (London, 2008), pp. 56–69; George Francis Dow (ed.), *Records and Files of the Quarterly Courts of Essex County, Massachusetts*, 8 vols. (Salem, MA, 1911–21), i, p. 108; Demos, *Entertaining Satan*, pp. 301–2; Hale, *Modest Enquiry*, p. 18.

35 *TRSR*, p. 102; *GACW*, pp. 12–13. See also John Matthews's comment from 1651, that Moxon 'will stay with us now', implying that he had intended to leave: WPDB, f. 16r.

36 *VRS*, p. 60.

37 WPDB, f. 21v (Mary Parsons, 18 March 1651).

38 On 20 May 1651 Beamon recalled this happening 'about February last': WPDB, f. 6r.

39 WPDB, f. 6r (Jonathan Taylor, 21 March 1651; Simon Beamon, 20 May 1651).

40 Ibid.

41 Ibid.

42 Virginia Bernhard, 'Religion, politics and witchcraft in Bermuda, 1651–55', *WMQ*, 67 (2010), pp. 677–708; Carla Gardina Pestana, *The English Atlantic in an Age of Revolution, 1640–1661* (Cambridge, MA, 2004), pp. 137–8.

43 Stiles, *Ancient Wethersfield*, i, pp. 29–30, 39, 257, 681–2; Demos, *Entertaining Satan*, pp. 348–9; Ross, *Before Salem*, pp. 149–51. For the Carringtons' indictments: Joseph Anderson, *The Town and City of Waterbury, Connecticut* (New Haven, CT, 1896), p. 164.

44 WPDB, f. 18v (William Pynchon and Mary Ashley, 1 March 1651); *DH*, p. 100.

45 Nelson, *Common Law*, p. 61.

46 Jane Kamensky, 'Words, witches, and woman trouble: witchcraft, disorderly speech, and gender boundaries in puritan New England', *Essex Institute Historical Collections*, 128 (1992), pp. 303–4; Martin Ingram, ' "Scolding women cucked or washed": a crisis in gender relations in early modern England?', in Kermode and Walker (eds.), *Women, Crime and the Courts*, pp. 48–80.

47 *Hic Mulier: Or, The Man-Woman* (London, 1620), sigs. A3r, B1v.

48 WPAB, pp. 209, 227; WPDB, f. 16r (Hugh Parsons and John Matthews, 18 March 1651).

49 WPDB, f. 16r (George Moxon, 18 March 1651); *GACW*, p. 27. We know it was late February 1651 from Mary's indictment and Beamon's evidence, 19 September 1656: *CJWM*, p. 29 n.76. The bewitchment occurred around when the witches were arrested, so February or March 1651.

50 Brian P. Levack, *The Devil Within: Possession and Exorcism in the Christian West* (New Haven, CT, 2013), chs. 4–8; Sarah Ferber, 'Demonic possession, exorcism and witchcraft', in Brian P. Levack (ed.), *The Oxford Handbook of Witchcraft in Early Modern Europe and Colonial America* (Oxford, 2013), pp. 575–92.

51 Demos, *Entertaining Satan*, pp. 128–31; Godbeer, *Devil's Dominion*, pp. 109, 114–15, 118–19. When an English girl was possessed, 'the whole neighbourhood and country round about were so alarmed at the strangeness of it that multitudes of people went to see her, and returned full of wonder and amazement': *Wonderful News from Buckinghamshire* (London, 1677), p. 4.

52 WPDB, f. 2r (Samuel Marshfield, 12 March 1651).

53 James Russell Trumbull, *History of Northampton, Massachusetts*, 2 vols. (Northampton, MA, 1898–1902), i, p. 49; David Harley, 'Explaining Salem: Calvinist psychology and the diagnosis of possession', *AHR*, 101 (1996), pp. 307–30, esp. p. 328.

54 Harvard University, Houghton Library, Autograph File, P, 1554–2005 (John Pynchon), testimony of Simon Beamon, 19 September 1656. Elizabeth Kent implies that the Moxon girls died: *Male Witchcraft*, p. 95.

55 Hutchinson, *History*, ii, p. 12; WPDB, f. 22v (Mary Ashley, 27 February 1651). Robert Ashley was licensed to run the alehouse (or 'ordinary') in September 1646: TRSR, p. 47.

56 WPDB, f. 23r (Francis Pepper, 27 February 1651); f. 18v (William Pynchon, Mary Ashley, 1 March 1651).

57 WPDB, f. 24r (Thomas Cooper, 3 April 1651).

58 Harvard University, Houghton Library, Autograph File, P, 1554–2005 (John Pynchon), testimony of Simon Beamon, 19 September 1656. Beamon says these events occurred 'about the time the witches were apprehended to be sent to Boston', but it was surely earlier.

59 Angus Gowland, *The Worlds of Renaissance Melancholy: Robert Burton in Context* (Cambridge, 2006), pp. 85–7. Cf. the carpenter's wife from Wapping who fell into raving fits after joining the Baptists: *The Snare of the Devil Discovered* (London, 1658), esp. pp. 8–9.

60 MacDonald, *Mystical Bedlam*, pp. 200–203.

61 WPDB, f. 22v (Benjamin Cooley, 18 March 1651); f. 21v (Mary Parsons, 18 March 1651); Reis, 'The devil, the body, and the feminine soul', pp. 20–23.

62 *VRS*, pp. 13, 20; *AWNE*, p. 219 n.1; WPDB, f. 12v (John Lombard, 1 March 1651).

63 WPDB, f. 12v (John Lombard, 1 March 1651).

64 WPDB, ff. 12r, 26r (Hannah and George Langton, 23 and 25 February and 18 [or 1st] March 1651); f. 12v (John Lombard, 1 March 1651); Weisman, *Witchcraft*, pp. 70–72. An English physician claimed a bewitched object, 'shall no sooner be on fire, but the witch will presently come running to behold it': BL, Add. MS 36,674, f. 148. For a New England case where rotten cheese was burned to find the woman who had bewitched it: Wyllys, Box 1, Folder 5, Ms. 340, f. 2r.

65 WPDB, f. 12r (Hannah and George Langton, 25 February 1651).

66 WPDB, f. 15r (Mercy Marshfield, 22 March 1651).

67 WPDB, ff. 26r–26v (George and Hannah Langton and Roger Pritchard, 23 February 1651). On the 'binding force' of 'shared anticipation' in accusations: Demos, *Entertaining Satan*, pp. 305–6.

68 WPDB, f. 13r (Thomas Miller and Thomas Cooper, 18 March 1651). Burnham does not appear in other Springfield records and was perhaps from Ipswich, MA: *AWNE*, p. 223 n.1.

69 'That any sensible man should have been silent at the repetition of such childish and contemptible nonsense is not at all strange': *AWNE*, p. 223 n.2.

70 WPDB, f. 13r (Thomas Miller and Thomas Cooper, 18 March 1651).

71 Starr (ed.), *Ancestral Lines*, pp. 60, 69; Records of Possessions, f. 41; WPDB, ff. 17r–17v (Anthony Dorchester, 25 February 1651); f. 18r (Griffith Jones, 25 February 1651).

72 Probably then; certainly between the incident in the woods and Mary's arrest.

73 *AWNE*, p. 224 n.2; *FCHS*, p. 43; *LNL*, p. 213; *VRS*, p. 20; WPDB, ff. 13r–13v (Thomas Burnham, 3 April 1651).

74 WPDB, ff. 5r, 24v (Jonathan Taylor, 22 March and 7 April 1651).

75 WPDB, ff. 22r–22v (Benjamin Cooley and Anthony Dorchester, 27 February 1651).

7. That Dumb Dog

1 Witches in Essex confessed that 'if any had angered them, they would go to their spirits and say: such a one hath angered me, go do them this mischief; and for their hire would give them a drop of their own blood, and presently the party was plagued by some lamentable casualty': *A Rehearsall Both Straung and True of . . . Fower Notorious Witches* (London, 1579), sigs. A8r–A8v.

2 Jim Sharpe, 'The witch's familiar in Elizabethan England', in G. W. Bernard and S. J. Gunn (eds.), *Authority and Consent in Tudor England: Essays Presented to C. S. L. Davies* (Farnham, 2002), pp. 219–32. In 1647 two mouse imps came to a man who had angered a witch, 'entered into his mouth and did torment him in his body': CUL, EDR 1647/19.

3 Gaskill, *Witchfinders*, pp. 50–51, 100–102; Philip Goodwin, *The Mystery of Dreames* (London, 1658), p. 61; Garthine Walker, 'The strangeness of the familiar: witchcraft and the law in early modern England', in Angela McShane and Garthine Walker (eds.), *The Extraordinary and the Everyday in Early Modern England* (Basingstoke, 2010), pp. 105–24.

4 WPDB, f. 22r (Benjamin Cooley and Anthony Dorchester, 27 February 1651); John Stearne, *A Confirmation and Discovery of Witch-Craft* (London, 1648), p. 26.

5 WPDB, ff. 22r–22v (Benjamin Cooley and Anthony Dorchester, 27 February 1651).

6 WPDB, f. 23r (John Matthews, 27 February 1651); f. 22v (Mary Ashley and Mary Parsons, 27 February 1651).

7 WPDB, f. 16v (Sarah Edwards, 27 February 1651); f. 22r (Benjamin Cooley, 27 February 1651); f. 22r (Anthony Dorchester, 27 February 1651); ff. 22r–22v (Benjamin Cooley and Anthony Dorchester, 27 February 1651).

8 According to Jonathan Taylor, Mary was arrested and examined on the same day, and Hugh the following day, which would have been the 27th: WPDB, f. 5r.

9 *VRS*, pp. 12, 19–20, 60; WPAB, p. 186; WPDB, f. 4r (William Brooks and John Stebbins, 18 March 1651).

10 This episode is undated but must have been then because the unnamed son has to be Joseph, born 15 March 1649; they had no other son who lived to the age of two.

11 WPDB, ff. 15r–15v (Blanche Bedortha, 22 March 1651).

12 Flaherty, *Privacy*, pp. 236–7.

13 See WPDB, f. 12v, which specifies Mary's presence at the second examination.

14 WPDB, ff. 14v–15r (Blanche and Reece Bedortha, Samuel Marshfield and Hugh Parsons, 1 and 18 March 1651); f. 14v (William Pynchon, 1 March 1651).

15 WPDB, f. 5r (Hugh Parsons, 1 March 1651); f. 16r (George Moxon, 18 March 1651).

16 WPDB, f. 12r (George and Hannah Langton, 1 March 1651); ff. 12v, 26v (Hugh Parsons, 1 March 1651; Roger Pritchard, 23 February 1651).

17 WPDB, ff. 12r–12v (Hugh Parsons, Simon Beamon, Reece Bedortha and George Langton, 1 March 1651).

18 WPDB, f. 16v (Hugh Parsons, 1 March 1651); James I, *Daemonologie* (London, 1603), pp. 29–30.

19 WPDB, f. 18r (Griffith Jones, Hugh Parsons and William Pynchon, 1 March 1651). Drake saw this as 'common sense against nonsense', but it proves Parsons knew something of the law: *AWNE*, p. 233 n.2.

20 McManus, *Law and Liberty*, pp. 35–6; Haskins, *Law and Authority*, ch. 10; Nelson, *Common Law*, pp. 74–5. The inquisitorial two-witness rule stressed confession, leading to 'strict examination': Gail Sussman Marcus, ' "Due execution of the generall rules of righteousnesse": criminal procedure in New Haven town and colony, 1638–1658', in David D. Hall, John M. Murrin and Thad W. Tate (eds.), *Saints and Revolutionaries: Essays on Early American History* (New York, 1984), pp. 102–3, 116–222.

21 WPDB, f. 18v (William Pynchon, Mary Ashley and Hugh Parsons, 1 March 1651).

22 WPDB, f. 20v (George Colton, 1 March 1651); f. 21r (Anthony Dorchester, 1 March 1651; Benjamin Cooley and Blanche Bedortha, 18 March 1651).

23 WPDB, f. 20v (Hugh Parsons, 1 March 1651).

24 WPDB, f. 23v (Thomas Merrick, 3 March 1651).

25 Ibid.

26 See Thomas Cooper's comment of 3 April, that by mid-March he had heard Hugh had no suspicious teats on his body: WPDB, f. 24r. According to Richard Weisman 'Hugh Parsons received some consolation when his Boston jailer swore that he could detect no witch's mark on the suspect': *Witchcraft*, p. 93. For Quakers in Boston searched as witches: Humphrey Norton, *New-England's Ensigne* (London, 1659), p. 7.

27 *VRS*, p. 61. The indictment against Mary Parsons specified that Joshua's murder took place 'in or near your own house': Shurtleff, iv (pt 1), p. 48.

28 WPDB, f. 2r (Samuel Marshfield, 12 March 1651).

29 WPDB, ff. 5v, 7r (William Branch, 13 March 1651).

30 Thomas Cooper said it was about mid-March, so probably the 14th; it was unlikely to have been Saturday night, owing to the Sabbath: WPDB, f. 24r.

31 ' 'Tis all one / To be a witch as to be counted one': Thomas Dekker et al., *The Witch of Edmonton* (London, 1621), Act 2, sc. 1, ll. 116–17.

32 WPDB, f. 24r (Thomas Cooper, 3 April 1651); David D. Hall, 'Witchcraft and the limits of interpretation', *NEQ*, 58 (1985), pp. 276–8; Laura Kounine, *Imagining the Witch: Emotions, Gender, and Selfhood in Early Modern Germany* (Oxford, 2018), ch. 3.

33 WPDB, f. 24r (Thomas Cooper, 3 April 1651).

34 WPDB, ff. 2r, 12v, 23r (John Lombard, 1 and 17 March 1651); f. 3r (Thomas Miller, 18 March 1651).

35 *LNL*, p. 137; *DH*, p. 100; WPDB, ff. 14v, 15v (Blanche and Reece Bedortha, and Hugh Parsons, 18 March 1651); f. 15r (Mercy Marshfield, 22 March 1651).

36 Thomas Ady, *The Doctrine of Devils* (London, 1676), p. 94.

37 Thomas Wright, *The Passions of the Minde*, 2nd edn (London, 1604), p. 108. Cf. Henry Newcome, *A Plain Discourse About Rash and Sinful Anger* (London, 1693), p. 8.

38 *CJWM*, p. 24; *DH*, p. 97; John Cotta, *The Triall of Witch-Craft* (London, 1616), p. 98; Michael Dalton, *The Countrey Justice* (London, 1618; 1630 edn), p. 302.

39 WPDB, ff. 15v, 16r (William Pynchon, 1 and 18 March 1651); f. 16r (Hugh Parsons and John Matthews, 18 March 1651).

40 WPDB, f. 16r (George Moxon, 18 March 1651). Such discrepancies exemplify the problem in legal cases of knowing what was actually said: Demos, *Entertaining Satan*, p. 190.

41 WPDB, f. 16v (Hugh Parsons and William Pynchon?, 18 March 1651).

42 WPDB, f. 18r (Griffith Jones, 18 March 1651); f. 18v (William Pynchon, Mary Ashley, 18 March 1651); ff. 18v–19r (Hugh Parsons, 18 March 1651).

43 WPDB, f. 19r (Mary Parsons, 18 March 1651). The source was 1 Corinthians 6: 19–20, though Mary may have heard it from Pynchon, who cited it when discussing the Atonement: William Pynchon, *The Meritorious Price of Mans Redemption* (London, 1655), pp. 256–7.

44 WPDB, f. 19r (William Pynchon, Mary Parsons, Hugh Parsons and Anthony Dorchester, 18 March 1651).

45 WPDB, f. 19v (William Pynchon and Hugh Parsons, 18 March 1651).

46 WPDB, f. 19v (George Moxon, Hugh Parsons and William Pynchon, 18 March 1651).

47 WPDB, ff. 19v–20r (George Colton, William Pynchon and Hugh Parsons, 18 March 1651).

48 WPDB, f. 20r (William Pynchon, Mary Parsons and Anthony Dorchester, George Colton and Jonathan Burt, 18 March 1651).

49 WPDB, f. 20v (George Colton and Hugh Parsons, 18 March 1651); Ulinka Rublack, 'Fluxes: the early modern body and the emotions', *History Workshop Journal*, 53 (2002), pp. 2, 6–7. According to Matthew Hopkins, witches 'never alter or change their countenances, nor let one tear fall': *The Discovery of Witches* (London, 1647), pp. 6–7.

50 WPDB, f. 21r (Benjamin and Sarah Cooley, Hugh and Mary Parsons, Mary Ashley and Sarah Leonard, 18 March 1651).

51 WPDB, f. 22v (Mary Ashley, 27 February 1651; Benjamin Cooley and Anthony Dorchester, 18 March 1651). For another case of a colonist dreaming about

fighting the devil: 'The diaries of John Hull', *Transactions of the AAS*, 3 (1857), p. 220.

52 WPDB, f. 23r (Francis Pepper, 27 February 1651; John Lombard, 17 March 1651; Hugh Parsons, 18 March 1651); f. 17v (Hugh Parsons and Abigail Munn, 18 March 1651).

53 WPDB, f. 21v (William Pynchon and Mary Parsons, 18 March 1651); ff. 12v–13r (Mary Parsons, Thomas Cooper and Thomas Miller, 18 March 1651).

54 WPDB, f. 3r (Thomas Miller, Miles Morgan and Francis Pepper, 18 March 1651).

55 WPDB, f. 4r (John Stebbins and Rowland Stebbins, 18 March 1651). A woman from Rowland Stebbins's village, Bocking, had been awaiting execution for bewitching a cow: Ewen, *Witch Hunting*, pp. 170–71.

56 WPDB, f. 4r (William Brooks, 18 March 1651); f. 23v (Thomas and Sarah Merrick and Hugh Parsons, 18 March 1651).

57 WPDB, ff. 1v, 5r, 6r (Jonathan Taylor, 18–20, 21–22 March 1651); f. 2r (Mercy Marshfield and John Lombard, 22 March 1651); f. 2v (Hugh Parsons, 22 March 1651).

58 WPDB, f. 2v (Mary Parsons, 22 March 1651).

59 We know it was Saturday 22 March, because Taylor said it was 'two nights before' Mary was taken to Boston, and we know this was Monday the 24th because Prudence Morgan said that HP 'was gone into the Bay the Monday before' 27 March, a Thursday: WPDB, f. 3r (Prudence Morgan, 27 March 1651); f. 25v (Jonathan Taylor, 7 April 1651).

8. Converse with the Devil

1 Trumbull, *History of Northampton*, i, p. 49; HLSL, Small Manuscript Collection (Special Collections), Papers in Cases Before the County Court of Middlesex Co., 1649–63, 4 vols.: ii, p. 302; Harvard University, Houghton Library, Autograph File, P, 1554–2005 (John Pynchon), testimony of Simon Beamon, 19 September 1656.

2 WPDB, ff. 3r–3v (Prudence Morgan and Samuel Marshfield, 27 March 1651?). For a 1656 case of a witch in the woods wearing a red waistcoat: Emerson W. Baker, *The Devil of Great Island: Witchcraft and Conflict in Early New England* (New York, 2007), pp. 82–3.

3 WPDB, f. 14r (Blanche and Reece Bedortha, 27 March 1651).

4 WPDB, f. 24r (Thomas Cooper, 3 April 1651). See also WPDB, f. 13v (Thomas Burnham, Joan Warrener and Abigail Munn, 3 April 1651).

5 Gura, *Glimpse of Sion's Glory*, pp. 308–9. 'Witchcraft and heresy seemed . . . to be walking hand in hand': Green, p. 119.

6 *VRS*, p. 13. Anna Taylor's sister Mary was born on 1 August 1649: ibid.

7 WPDB, f. 24v (Jonathan Taylor, 7 April 1651).

8 WPDB, ff. 24v–25r (Jonathan Taylor, 7 April 1651). For another witchcraft case involving snakes: HLSL, Small Manuscript Collection (Special Collections), Papers in Cases Before the County Court of Middlesex Co., 1649–63, 4 vols.: iii, pp. 600–609; Lucius R. Paige, *History of Cambridge, Massachusetts, 1630–1877* (Boston, 1877), pp. 356–64.

9 *VRS*, p. 61.

10 In October 1654 the Treasurer of Boston reimbursed several 'witnesses about witches': MC, vol. 100, p. 49. For expenses relating to a 1683 witch-trial, including transportation to Boston: Sylvester Judd, *History of Hadley* (Springfield, MA, 1905), p. 230.

11 See WPDB, ff. 2r, 3r.

12 Firth and Rait (eds.), *Acts and Ordinances*, i, p. 421.

13 George L. Haskins, 'Lay judges: magistrates and justices in early Massachusetts', in Daniel R. Coquillette et al. (eds.), *Law in Colonial Massachusetts, 1630–1800* (Boston, 1984), pp. 43–4.

14 McManus, *Law and Liberty*, p. 74. 'Whereas the inquisitorial mode aspires to establish the absolute truth of the matter, the accusatorial system is formalistic. It makes a fetish of the rules of the game, and arrives at a relative, synthetic truth sufficient for practical legal purposes': C. R. Unsworth, 'Witchcraft beliefs and criminal procedure in early modern England', in T. G. Watkin (ed.), *Legal Record and Historical Reality* (London, 1989), p. 88.

15 John M. Murrin, 'Magistrates, sinners, and a precarious liberty: trial by jury in seventeenth-century New England', in Hall, Murrin and Tate (eds.), *Saints and Revolutionaries*, pp. 164–5, 196.

16 Shurtleff, iv (pt 1), pp. 47–8.

17 John Cotton, *An Abstract of the Lawes of New England* (London, 1641), p. 10; *DH*, pp. 108–9; 'Hutchinson papers', *Collections of the MHS*, 1 (1825), p. 35.

18 Shurtleff, iv (pt 1), pp. 47–8.

19 Emerson W. Baker, *A Storm of Witchcraft: The Salem Trials and the American Experience* (Oxford, 2015), pp. 23–4, 28.

20 Shurtleff, iii, p. 229.

21 Shurtleff, iv (pt 1), p. 47.

22 Ibid.

23 Samuel Marshfield, Hannah Langton, Blanche Bedortha, Alexander Edwards, George Colton, Anthony Dorchester and Jonathan Taylor, all recorded as having sworn in court: WPDB, ff. 2r, 3r, 12r, 14r, 14v, 16v, 18v, 19v, 20v, 21r, 25v, 26r.

24 WPDB, ff. 12r, 26r (Hannah Langton, 1 and 18 March 1651, sworn in court 13 May 1651).

25 WPDB, f. 25v (Jonathan Taylor, 7 April 1651, sworn in court 13 March).

26 WPDB, f. 25v (Edward Rawson, 13 May 1651).

27 Mary Beth Norton, *In the Devil's Snare: The Salem Witchcraft Crisis of 1692* (New York, 2002), pp. 30–33, 41–2; Wyllys, Box 1, Ms. 372, 'Grounds for examination of a witch'. This document was derived from William Perkins: Ross, *Before Salem*, pp. 277–86.

28 Hoffer, *Sensory Worlds*, pp. 118, 122–4; Robert Malcolm Kerr (ed.), *Commentaries on the Laws of England of Sir William Blackstone*, 4 vols. (London, 1862), iii, p. 397; John H. Langbein, *Prosecuting Crime in the Renaissance: England, Germany, France* (Cambridge, MA, 1974), pp. 29–31.

29 Shurtleff, iv (pt 1), p. 47.

30 Ibid., p. 48.

31 *JJW*, p. 203; Hosmer, i, pp. 282–3.

32 Thomas Wright, *The Passions of the Minde in Generall* (London, 1604), pp. 330–31. See also: Alexander Roberts, *A Treatise of Witchcraft* (London, 1616), pp. 45–6; Richard Gilpin, *Demonologia Sacra* (London, 1677), pp. 72–3, 300–303; John Brinley, *A Discovery of the Impostures of Witches and Astrologers* (London, 1680), pp. 42–3, 108.

33 McManus, *Law and Liberty*, pp. 104–5; MacDonald, *Mystical Bedlam*, p. 83.

34 Shurtleff, iv (pt 1), p. 48. A witch formerly of witch-ridden Windsor had been executed at Stratford, Connecticut, in May 1651: Ross, *Before Salem*, pp. 154–6.

35 David D. Hall, *A Reforming People: Puritanism and the Transformation of Public Life in New England* (New York, 2011), p. 85; Hosmer, i, pp. 282–3.

36 *DH*, pp. 122–3; Shurtleff, iii, pp. 229–30; iv (pt 1), p. 48; *VRS*, pp. 13, 61.

37 Norton, *Discussion*, p. 273; Shurtleff, iii, p. 230; iv (pt 1), p. 49; Lockwood (ed.), *Western Massachusetts*, i, p. 106.

38 John Ashton, *The Devil in Britain and America* (London, 1896), pp. 321–2. It has been assumed that Mary was hanged, simply because she was condemned; others make a (weak) case for it: Daniel Allen Hearn, *Legal Execution in New England: A Comprehensive Reference, 1623–1960* (Jefferson, NC, 1999), p. 24. She may have been 'the malefactor, accused of witchcraft as well as murder' that Cotton Mather heard had been executed in Boston in the early 1650s: *The Wonders of the Invisible World* (London, 1693), p. 7. On this point: Justin Winsor (ed.), *The Memorial History of Boston*, 4 vols. (Boston, 1881), ii, pp. 137–8.

39 WPDB, f. 6r (Simon Beamon, 20 May 1651); Waters, 'Witchcraft', pp. 152–3.

40 Shurtleff, iii, p. 239.

41 *Second Report of the Record Commissioners of the City of Boston . . . Boston Records, 1634–1660*, 2nd edn (Boston, 1881), p. 70; George Fox, *Secret Workes of a Cruel People Made Manifest* (London, 1659), pp. 2–3.

42 Shurtleff, iv (pt 1), p. 96.

43 WPDB, f. 6r (Simon Beamon, 20 May 1651; Jonathan Taylor, 21 March 1651); WPDB, f. 17v (Jonathan Taylor, 17 June 1651).

44 *VRS*, p. 61.

45 WPDB, ff. 6r, 6v, 7r, 17v.

46 WPDB, f. 20v (George Colton, 1 and 18 March 1651).

47 WPDB, f. 10v (jury foreman?, 17 June 1651). This is a heavily crossed-out passage, suggesting that the court would not allow the verdict to stand.

48 Shurtleff, iii, p. 239; 'Hutchinson papers', p. 37.

49 Norton, *Discussion*, pp. 23–5, 37–8; Godbeer, *Devil's Dominion*, pp. 104–5; *DH*, pp. 119–22.

50 'Where precisely orthodoxy's boundaries were no one knew, for no one knew with finality what its contents were': Winship, 'Contesting control', p. 797.

51 Oberholzer, *Delinquent Saints*, pp. 42–4; Gura, *Glimpse of Sion's Glory*, pp. 315–21; Godbeer, *Devil's Dominion*, pp. 103–4; Valeri, *Heavenly Merchandize*, pp. 47–8.

52 Norton, *Discussion*, pp. 272–4.

53 Records of Possessions, f. 2; HLAS, ESMC, ESM-07-01-02; Wright, *Genesis*, pp. 28–9; *DH*, pp. 124–5.

54 *VRS*, pp. 13, 61.

55 Thomas Cobbett, *The Civil Magistrates Power in Matters of Religion Modestly Debated* (London, 1653), sigs. A2r–A2v. This lecture was given on 4 October 1652.

56 Shurtleff, iii, pp. 248, 257; iv (pt 1), p. 72; MC, vol. 48, p. 36. The order referred to more than one prisoner, possibly others implicated by Mary Parsons: *CJWM*, p. 23; David D. Hall (ed.), *Witch-Hunting in Seventeenth-Century New England: A Documentary History, 1638–1693*, 2nd edn (Boston, 1999), p. 31 n.1.

57 John Eliot, *Tears of Repentance* (London, 1653), p. 46; WPDB, ff. 2r, 31 (Samuel Marshfield, 12 and 27 March 1651).

58 WPDB, f. 8r; Shurtleff, iv (pt 1), p. 96; Marcus, 'Criminal procedure', pp. 122–5, 132.

59 WPDB, f. 8r.

60 She may even have retracted her evidence, thus saving Hugh's life under the two-witness rule: McManus, *Law and Liberty*, pp. 138, 142–3.

61 Shurtleff, iii, p. 273; iv (pt 1), p. 96; Hutchinson, *History*, i, p. 152.

9. New Witchland

1 Charles H. Levermore, 'Witchcraft in Connecticut, 1647–1697', *New Englander and Yale Review*, 44 (1885), p. 793.

2 Robert F. Oaks, '"Things fearfull to name": sodomy and buggery in seventeenth-century New England', *Journal of Social History*, 12 (1978), pp. 268–81; Dunn et al. (eds.), *Journal*, pp. 370–76, 629; Oaks, '"Things fearfull to name"', p. 273.

3 *GHNE*, pp. 551, 556–9, 573–4; Carla Gardina Pestana, *Quakers and Baptists in Colonial Massachusetts* (Cambridge, 1991), pp. 11–18, 123–4, 148–9.

4 MHS, Ms. N-1182, Carton 36: SH 114M U, Folder 35 (William Arnold, 1 September 1651). Dissidents had long compared the Massachusetts government to devilish necromancers and idolaters: Edward Winslow, *Hypocrisie Unmasked* (London, 1646), pp. 28, 42–3.

5 Bulstrode Whitelocke, *Memorials of the English Affairs*, 4 vols. (Oxford, 1853), iii, p. 221; John Sykes, *Local Records; or, Historical Register of Remarkable Events*, 2 vols. (Newcastle-upon-Tyne, 1866), i, pp. 103–5; Ewen, *Witch Hunting*, pp. 91, 237–8.

6 *Mercurius Politicus* (25 September 1651), p. 1091. The letter was anonymous, but the author was almost certainly Eliot: Winsor (ed.), *Memorial History*, ii, p. 137. Eliot wrote similar letters to Winslow in April and October that year: Bodl., Rawlinson MS C.934, ff. 9–11v.

7 Cotton Mather, *Late Memorable Providences Relating to Witchcrafts and Possessions* (London, 1691), sig. B3v; Alan Heimert and Andrew Delbanco (eds.), *The Puritans in America: A Narrative Anthology* (Cambridge, MA, 1985), p. 339.

8 Thomas Hobbes, *Leviathan* (London, 1651), pp. 63, 85, 107; Pat Moloney, 'Hobbes, savagery, and international anarchy', *American Political Science Review*, 105 (2011), pp. 189–204. See also Stuart Clark, *Thinking with Demons: The Idea of Witchcraft in Early Modern Europe* (Oxford, 1997), esp. chs. 33–44. On Hobbes, see ibid., pp. 303, 310, 599–600.

9 Thomas, *Religion and the Decline of Magic*, pp. 619, 625.

10 Johnson, *History*, p. 199 – Thomas Hutchinson's source in the 1760s: *History*, ii, p. 12.

11 John Seller, *A Description of New-England* (London, 1682), p. 2. Similarly enduring was the memory of the Carringtons of Wethersfield, executed for witchcraft in 1651, see testimony from 1669: Dow (ed.), *Quarterly Courts of Essex*, iv, p. 99.

12 BL, Lansdowne MS 93, ff. 185, 187, 189–215; Demos, *Entertaining Satan*, ch. 11, quotation (from Cotton Mather) on p. 341.

13 MC, vol. 3, pp. 7–10, 12–12B, quotation at p. 7.

14 'As night follows day, these seasons of moral fervor were succeeded by a sense of exhaustion and a slackening of rigor – to give way, at some point in time, to a fresh sense of crisis': Hall, *Puritans*, p. 157.

15 HLSL, Small Manuscript Collection (Special Collections), Testimony taken on behalf of Sarah the wife of James Bridgeman of Northampton, 11 August 1656, ff. 1–2, quotation at f. 1v; ibid., Papers in Cases Before the County Court of Middlesex Co., 1649–63, 4 vols.: i, pp. 290–92, 294–7, 298; ii, pp. 301–2; *CJWM*, pp. 24n, 29n; Trumbull, *History of Northampton*, i, pp. 42–52, 228–34. See also Hall (ed.), *Witch-Hunting*, ch. 6.

16 Harvard University, Houghton Library, Autograph File, P, 1554–2005 (John Pynchon), testimony of Simon Beamon, 19 September 1656.

17 *WP*, vi, pp. 383–4, 393–4, 410–11, 422–4, 456–8, quotation at p. 393; *VRS*, p. 61. Winthrop was sceptical about witchcraft: see his diagnosis of hysteria for a supposedly bewitched woman: *WP*, vi, pp. 300–302. See also Walter W. Woodward, *Prospero's America: John Winthrop Jr, Alchemy, and the Creation of New England Culture, 1606–1676* (Williamsburg, VA, 2010), ch. 7.

18 *PP*, i, pp. 16–17.

19 Stiles, *Ancient Windsor*, i, pp. 448–50; Ross, *Before Salem*, pp. 90, 103–5, 165–8; Demos, *Entertaining Satan*, pp. 4–6; Charles J. Hoadly (ed.), *Records of the Colony and Plantation of New Haven, from 1638 to 1649* (Hartford, CT, 1857), p. 77. See also Norton, *Founding Mothers and Fathers*, pp. 235–6.

20 CSL, Hartford County Court Minutes, vol. 2, 1649–62, pp. 160, 174–5; BPL, MS. Am. 1502/1/28r–28v; Mather, *Illustrious Providences*, pp. 135–9; *Particular Court of Connecticut*, p. 258; Stiles, *Ancient Wethersfield*, i, pp. 683–4; Trumbull and Hoadly (eds.), *Public Records*, ii, p. 132n; HLAS, ESMC, ESM-05-06-01, p. 69.

21 HLAS, ESMC, ESM-05-06-01, pp. 120, 122–3, 125, quotations at p. 123; HCRP, Probate Records, Hampshire County, 1660–1820, vol. 1 (1660–90), p. 59.

22 R. S. Greenlee and R. L. Greenlee (eds.), *The Stebbins Genealogy*, 2 vols. (Chicago, 1904) i, p. 77; Trumbull, *History of Northampton*, i, pp. 234–5. One source claims that Stebbins himself was accused as a witch, but this is surely a mistake: *CJWM*, p. 69 n.20.

23 Noble and Cronin (eds.), *Court of Assistants*, i, p. 228; Judd, *History of Hadley*, pp. 228–32; Mather, *Magnalia*, ii, pp. 454–6.

24 *VRS*, pp. 17, 21, 64; *FCHS*, p. 44; *LNL*, p. 209; Savage, i, p. 147; Judd, *History of Hadley*, p. 90. Thomas Beamon sued for libel and won damages of 40s.

25 Demos, *Entertaining Satan*, pp. 273–4.

26 WPDB, f. 25v (Jonathan Taylor, 7 April 1651).

27 Green, p. 123; Ruth A. McIntyre, 'John Pynchon and the New England fur trade 1652–1676', in *PP*, ii, pp. 3–70; Records of Possessions, ff. 2–2v; HRBD, pp. 20–22; HLAS, ESMC, ESM-04-03-04; ESM-04-02-10; *Hampden County*, p. 99; Wright, *Genesis*, pp. 31–3; *LNL*, pp. 30–34. John Pynchon's first slave, Peter Swinck, arrived in 1650: *Pynchons of Springfield*, p. 31.

28 Trumbull, *History of Northampton*, i, ch. 2; MC, vol. 112, pp. 403–9.

29 See e.g. Hampshire Book of Records for the Court of Pleas (from 1693 onwards), Massachusetts Quarterly Courts, 5 vols., i (1638–1738), Harvard University, Lamont Library, Harvard Depository, Microfilm M 442 (Barcode HNBVQ1).

30 MC, vol. 112, pp. 207–208; vol. 115, p. 27.

31 TRSR, preface page.

32 See Hampshire County land deeds in 1670s–80s: HRBD, *passim*, e.g. pp. 22–4, 39.

33 See exports to New England, 1651: London Metropolitan Archives, MS 7947. Also: John Pynchon's account books, 1651–66: HLAS, ESMC, ESM-05-01-01; 05-02-01; 05-02.02.

34 *LNL*, pp. 240, 242; *PP*, ii, p. 317; Bridenbaugh, 'Use and abuse of the forest', p. 20; George Ellis and John Morris, *King Philip's War* (New York, 1906), pp. 117–18; *Hampden County*, p. 98.

35 John Langdon Sibley, *Biographical Sketches of Graduates of Harvard University*, vol. 1: *1642–1658* (Cambridge, MA, 1873), pp. 296–7. Whether there was a connection between the Moxons and the Glovers is unknown. That Habakkuk Glover, Pelatiah Sr's brother, appears to have defended Pynchon's theology might be a clue: BPL, Ms. Am. 1502/2/20.

36 MC, vol. 11, p. 20; Thistlethwaite, p. 175. A disappointing preacher who came from Windsor soon returned to England: Moore, *Pilgrims*, p. 242 n.47.

37 See the 1687 letter from John Pynchon et al., to Increase Mather: BPL, Ms. Am. 1502/6/31.

38 Green, p. 81; MC, vol. 10, p. 98; vol. 11, pp. 11–12, 18–20.

39 *LNL*, pp. 132, 240–41; *FCHS*, p. 327; *CJWM*, p. 254. His wife was probably the Hannah Hackleton indicted (with a witch) for murder, adultery and saying 'there was as much mercy in the devil as in God': Helen Schatvet Ullmann (ed.), *Hartford County, Connecticut, County Court Minutes Volumes 3 and 4, 1663–1687, 1697* (Boston, 2005), pp. 47–8, 50, 62.

40 *LNL*, pp. 104, 147; *CJWM*, pp. 172, 317; *FCHS*, pp. 28–9. Burt died in 1715, aged ninety-one.

41 *CJWM*, pp. 231–2, 240, 243, 246–7, 256, 263, 317–18, 375, 387, 434; *FCHS*, pp. 243, 281; *LNL*, p. 78. Thomas Merrick died in 1704, aged eighty-four: *FCHS*, p. 41.

42 HLAS, ESMC, ESM-05-06-01, p. 31; *CJWM*, pp. 235–6.

43 *DH*, p. 124; HLAS, ESMC, ESM-07-01-02; ESM-05-02-01, pp. 136–7; ESM-05-01-01, p. 297; *LNL*, pp. 83, 210, 346–7; Starr (ed.), *Ancestral Lines*, pp. 60–61, 66, 68–72; *FCHS*, pp. 242, 383; *CJWM*, p. 112.

44 *LNL*, p. 201; *FCHS*, pp. 221, 233, 242, 255, 284, 293, 296, 320, 337, 338, 340, 386, 400; *LNL*, p. 90; *CJWM*, p. 375; Green, pp. 134, 176; Savage, i, p. 152.

45 H. Maria Bodurtha, *A Record of the Bodurtha Family, 1645–1896* (Agawam, MA, 1896), pp. 8, 9; *LNL*, p. 201; HCRP, Wills (George Colton, 1700).

46 Savage, iv, pp. 56–7; *VRS*, p. 13. Sarah Merrick was alive in February 1650, but died before October 1653, when her husband remarried: *VRS*, pp. 13, 20. See also Savage, iii, p. 198.

47 HRBD, p. 61; *VRS*, pp. 14, 15, 16, 17; *LNL*, p. 215; *FCHS*, p. 43; *AWNE*, p. 232 n.1. The Taylors lost another daughter, Rebecca, aged eight, in 1665: *VRS*, p. 62.

48 *LNL*, pp. 102–4, 121, 204; *VRS*, pp. 63, 65; *FCHS*, p. 42. In 1661 Matthews was fined for 'being found drunken and bereaved of his understanding': *CJWM*, p. 249.

49 *LNL*, pp. 70–71; *VRS*, p. 61.

50 Historical Records Survey, *Proclamations of Massachusetts Issued by Governors and Other Authorities, 1620–1936*, 2 vols. (Boston, 1937), i, pp. 54–8.

51 *TRSR*, pp. 1, 103; Records of Possessions, ff. 4v–5, 22; Anderson, *Great Migration . . . 1620–1633*, iii, p. 1692; *HRBD*, pp. 1–2, 12 (testimony from 1669).

52 Based on the probate inventories of John Searle (d. 1642) and Nathaniel Bliss (d. 1654): *CJWM*, pp. 212–13; *TRSR*, p. 67.

53 HLAS, ESMC, ESM-05-01-01, p. 32. Davis was married to Pynchon's sister Margaret: Pynchon, *Record of the Pynchon Family*, p. 5. Pynchon often used Davis's house for the purposes of commercial distribution: McIntyre, *Pynchon*, pp. 27–8.

54 Claimants for Watertown include *LNL*, p. 205, and *FCHS*, pp. 43, 77. See also: Henry Bond, *Genealogies of the Families and Descendants of the Early Settlers of Watertown*, 2nd edn (Boston, 1860), p. 869; Filby (ed.), *Passenger and Immigration Lists*, iii, p. 1616; Savage, iii, p. 362. Some argue against Rhode Island because the HP of Portsmouth came from London: www.geni.com/people/Hugh-Parsons-of-Portsmouth/6000000006579905362. But it seems Watertown HP was there by 1649. Samuel Drake said HP went to Rhode Island, via Narragansett: *AWNE*, p. 70. John Demos and Elizabeth Kent agree: *Entertaining Satan*, p. 302; *Male Witchcraft*, p. 92. This is supported by: Gerald J. Parsons, 'The early Parsons families of the Connecticut River valley', *NEHGR*, 149 (1995), pp. 69–70, as Rhode Island HP had a daughter named Hannah born at a similar time to the Springfield Hannah. According to C. E. Banks, Rhode Island HP came from Witham in Essex, near old Springfield, but he probably died there too: *Topographical Dictionary*, p. 53.

55 W. Keith Kavenagh (ed.), *Foundations of Colonial America: A Documentary History*, 3 vols. (New York, 1973), i, pp. 133–4; Wade C. Wightman, *The Wightman Ancestry*, 2 vols. (Chelsea, MI, 1994–7), i, pp. 1–2; Ian Atherton and David Como, 'The burning of Edward Wightman: puritanism, prelacy and the politics of heresy in early modern England', *English Historical Review*, 120 (2005), pp. 1215–50; Thomas, *Religion and the Decline of Magic*, pp. 160–61, 202–4.

56 This does, of course, assume that the Hugh Parsons of Portsmouth and the accused witch of Springfield were one and the same – see note 54, above.

57 Anderson, *Great Migration . . . 1620–1633*, i, p. 575; Parsons, 'Early Parsons families', pp. 69–70; John Russell Bartlett (ed.), *Records of the Colony of Rhode Island and Providence Plantations*, 10 vols. (Providence, RI, 1856–65), ii, p. 218; iii, p. 3; Burt et al., *Cornet Joseph Parsons*, p. 105.

58 Rhode Island Historical Society, Briggs Collection: Wills by Anthony Tarbox Briggs, vol. A, Will: FHL #0022302, will of Hugh Parsons, proved 14 January 1685. In due course, 'his family became extinct': Burt et al., *Cornet Joseph Parsons*, p. 105.

59 They definitely didn't sail in winter 1651 and were back before 27 May 1652.

60 *DH*, pp. 129–30, 173 n.9; Ross, *Before Salem*, pp. 44–5. Edward Holyoke wrote a book referring to Pynchon's work: *The Doctrine of Life* (London, 1658). Pynchon's daughter Mary married Holyoke's son Elizur: Pynchon, *Record of the Pynchon Family*, p. 5.

61 E. G., *A Prodigious and Tragicall History of the Arraignment, Tryall, Confession and Condemnation of Six Witches* (London, 1652), p. 4; Robert Filmer, *An Advertisement to the Jury-Men of England, Touching Witches* (London, 1653), sigs. A2r–A2v, pp. 5, 6–8.

62 West Suffolk RO, 613/909 (Nathaniel Barnardiston, 19 March 1647); Firth and Rait (eds.), *Acts and Ordinances*, ii, pp. 409–12; *The Ranters Monster* (London, 1652), pp. 4–5.

63 Roger Williams, *The Bloody Tenent Yet More Bloody* (London, 1652), esp. pp. 34–8, 306–9, quotation at p. 309.

64 'Hutchinson papers', pp. 35–7; Henry Vane, *Zeal Examined: or, A Discourse for Liberty of Conscience in Matters of Religion* (London, 1652), pp. 1, 5–9, 10–14, quotation at p. 7.

65 John Norton, *The Orthodox Evangelist* (London, 1654), quotation at sig. A2r; Waters, *Ipswich*, i, pp. 40–41, 287; Demos, *Entertaining Satan*, pp. 61–2.

66 'Hutchinson papers', pp. 35–7; Timothy J. Sehr, *Colony and Commonwealth: Massachusetts Bay, 1649–1660* (New York, 1989), pp. 45–6.

67 Thomas Clendon, *Justification Justified: or, The Doctrine of Justification Briefly and Clearly Explained* (London, 1653), sigs. A4r–A4v, pp. 13–15.

68 Pynchon, *Jewes Synagogue*, pp. 7–8, 76. The London bookseller George Thomason received his copy, 31 December 1652. See also Michael P. Winship, 'William Pynchon's *The Jewes Synagogue*', *NEQ*, 71 (1998), pp. 290–97.

69 *Scot's Discovery of Witchcraft* (London, 1651); Claire Bartram, ' "Melancholic imaginations": witchcraft and the politics of melancholia in Elizabethan Kent', *Journal of European Studies*, 33 (2003), pp. 203–11. The physician Thomas Ady thought that supposed witches were 'deeply gone by infirmity of body affecting the mind, whereby they conceit such things as never were, or can be': *Candle in the Dark*, pp. 124–5. Cf. Nicholas Gyer, *The English Phlebotomy* (London, 1592), sigs. A4v–A5r.

70 Philip C. Almond, 'King James I and the burning of Reginald Scot's *The Discoverie of Witchcraft*: the invention of a tradition', *Notes and Queries*, 56 (2009), pp. 209–13; Beinecke Library, Yale University, Osborn MS fb. 224.

71 Ewen, *Witch Hunting*, pp. 243–5.

72 Norton, *Discussion*, pp. 270, 272–4, quotation at p. 270.

73 Harvard University Archives, HUC 8662.300, pp. 8–9, 35, 46, 50, 53, 57, 103, quotation at p. 57; HLAS, ESMC, ESM-04-01-09; ESM-04-02-03; Wright, *Genesis*, p. 30; *DH*, pp. 130–31.

74 Gaskill, *Between Two Worlds*, pp. 6–7, 176–7, 192–4, 345–6, 348–51. The 1641 Massachusetts Body of Liberties has been called 'a New England Magna Charta': Wall, *Massachusetts Bay*, pp. 17–18.

75 Morris, *First Church*, p. 13; TRSR, p. 109; MC, vol. II, pp. 11–12, 18, 20, 170–170a, 180a–182; Records of Possessions, ff. 47v–48; HLAS, ESMC, ESM-05-01-01, p. 51.

76 *GACW*, pp. 38, 40; Morris, *First Church*, p. 13; Johnson, *History*, pp. 199–200; *CJWM*, p. 29. Some believe Moxon left in May 1653: Green, pp. 111–12, 122; *FCHS*, p. 22.

77 *DH*, p. 132; Wright, *Genesis*, p. 31; *CJWM*, pp. 226–7; HLAS, ESMC, ESM-04-03-04. Samuel Smith died on 14 June 1652: *VRS*, p. 61.

78 DWL, Baxter Letters, 3.186 (1655); Richard Baxter, *A Sermon of Judgement*, 11th edn (London, 1658), pp. 19–20, 120–23. Baxter called the crowd 'the greatest auditory that I ever saw': Keeble and Nuttall (eds.), *Correspondence*, i, p. 161.

79 William Pynchon, *A Farther Discussion of that Great Point in Divinity, the Sufferings of Christ* (London, 1655), sig. A2r; DWL, Baxter Letters, 3.186–7 (1655), quotations at f. 186r.

80 Henry Vane, *The Retired Mans Meditations* (London, 1655), esp. chs. 13–14.

81 John Towill Rutt (ed.), *Diary of Thomas Burton*, 4 vols. (London, 1828), i, p. 25; Paul H. Hardacre, 'William Boteler: a Cromwellian oligarch', *Huntington Library Quarterly*, 11 (1947), pp. 1–11.

82 Byington, *The Puritan*, p. 218.

83 Lambeth Palace Library, MS COMM. III/3, lib. 2, f. 20; Moore, *Pilgrims*, p. 259 n.125.

84 Gordon and Moore, 'Moxon'; Moore, *Pilgrims*, p. 121; Green, p. 112; *GACW*, pp. 38–40; Francis J. Bremer, *Congregational Communion: Clerical Friendship in the Anglo-American Puritan Community, 1610–1692* (Boston, 1994), p. 225. See also Congleton Library, Cheshire, CP/920/M (J. Micklethwaite, *Rev. George Moxon, 1602–1687*, 2001); Samuel Clarke, *The Lives of Sundry Eminent Persons* (London, 1683), pp. 83–92.

85 James, 'Evolution of a radical', pp. 41–2.

86 Roberts, 'Erbery'; McLachlan, *Socinianism*, p. 229; *Testimony of William Erbery*, pp. 43–7, 63, 211, 271, quotations at p. 63. See ibid., pp. 310–38, for 'The Honest Heretique, or, Orthodox Blasphemer', an account of Erbery's heresy trial.

87 Roberts, 'Erbery'; William Erbery, *A Mad Mans Plea* (London, 1653), pp. 2, 8–9; Anthony à Wood, *Athenae Oxonienses*, 2 vols. (London, 1691–2), ii, p. 105.

88 See e.g.: TNA, SP44/34, f. 47 (Ann Clarke, 1670); William Le Hardy (ed.), *County of Buckingham: Calendar to the Sessions Records, Volume 1, 1678 to 1694* (Aylesbury, 1933), pp. 328, 338, 347, 348, 393.

89 Pynchon became 'a man addressing his past, ominous in its silence as perhaps the past always is': Vella et al. (eds.), *Meritorious Price*, p. xxix. A copy of *A Farther Discussion of that Great Point in Divinity* (London, 1655), annotated by Pynchon, survives in the New York Public Library, shelfmark KC 1665 (Pynchon, Meritorious Price). He was surely dismayed to find Norton's printer had set the name 'Wotton' – Anthony Wotton, his mentor – as 'Norton', his nemesis: p. 118.

90 Ephraim Pagitt, *Heresiography, or, A Description of the Heretickes and Sectaries Sprang Up in These Latter Times* (London, 1654), sig. B4r, pp. 10, 19, 78–9, 93–4; Anthony Burgess, *The True Doctrine of Justification Asserted and Vindicated* (London, 1654), pp. 59, 69, 73; Nicholas Chewney, *Anti-Socinianism* (London, 1656), pp. 2–3.

91 *DH*, p. 148; *CJWM*, p. 30 n.72.

92 William Pynchon, *The Time When the Sabbath Was First Ordained* (London, 1654); HLAS, ESMC, ESM-06-02-01; *Priced Catalogue of a Remarkable Collection of Scarce and Out-of-Print Books* (New York, 1914), p. 987. Freud described conflict 'between what the drive demands and what reality forbids': *The Unconscious*, trans. Graham Frankland (London, 2005), p. 103.

93 BPL, Ms. Am. 1505/1/23 Pt 5.

94 William Pynchon, *The Covenant of Nature Made with Adam* (London, 1662), sigs. A2r, A3r–A4v; HLAS, ESMC, ESM-06-01-02; John Norton, *The Heart of N-England Rent at the Blasphemies of the Present Generation* (London, 1659), pp. 52–3.

95 Hutchinson, *History*, i, pp. 188, 190–91; Mayers, 'Vane'; Karlsen, *Devil*, p. 20.

96 TNA, PROB 11/309/551; J. H. Morrison, *Prerogative Court of Canterbury: Wills, Sentences and Probate Acts, 1661–1670* (London, 1935), p. 193; Waters, *Genealogical Gleanings*, ii, p. 859; HLAS, ESMC, ESM-04-02-04; ESM-04-04-02.

97 HLAS, ESMC, ESM-04-03-03; HCRP, Wills (John Pynchon, 1663).

98 TNA, CO 1/19 No. 104 (9 September 1665); *PP*, i, pp. 156–60; Wright, *Early Springfield*, p. 21; *LNL*, pp. 66–7, 202; Green, pp. 64, 157; *FCHS*, p. 42; *VRS*, p. 63; Ellis and Morris, *King Philip's War*, p. 119.

99 *News from New-England* (London, 1676), p. 5; HLAS, ESMC, ESM-05-06-05; ESM-05-06-01, p. 127; TRSR, pp. 124–7.

100 The classic statement on declension is Perry Miller, *The New England Mind: The Seventeenth Century* (New York, 1939). For critiques: Robert G. Pope, 'New England versus the New England mind: the myth of declension', *Journal of*

Social History, 3 (1969), pp. 95–108; Mark A. Peterson, *The Price of Redemption: The Spiritual Economy of Puritan New England* (Stanford, CA, 1997); Valeri, *Heavenly Merchandize*, ch. 2.

101 Quoted in Richard Middleton, *Colonial America: A History, 1565–1776*, 3rd edn (Oxford, 2002), p. 140. On the shift from godliness to commerce, and especially a growing obsession with land: Kenneth A. Lockridge, *A New England Town, The First Hundred Years: Dedham, Massachusetts, 1636–1736* (New York, 1970); Roger Thompson, *Divided We Stand: Watertown, Massachusetts, 1630–1680* (Amherst, MA, 2001); Richard P. Gildrie, *Salem, Massachusetts, 1626–1683: A Covenant Community* (Charlottesville, VA, 1975).

102 Moore, *Pilgrims*, p. 155; Felch, *Blynman Party*, p. 1; Babson, *Gloucester*, pp. 190–91; BPL, Ms. Am. 1502/1/74.

103 Norton, *Devil's Snare*, pp. 77–8, 87–93, 296–304. On 'invasion neurosis': James E. Kences, 'Some unexplored relationships of Essex County witchcraft to the Indian wars of 1675 and 1689', *Essex Institute Historical Collections*, 120 (1984), pp. 179–212. On the effects of the war: Jill Lepore, *In the Name of War: King Philip's War and the Origins of American Identity* (New York, 1998); Lisa Brooks, *Our Beloved Kin: A New History of King Philip's War* (New Haven, CT, 2018), esp. ch. 8.

104 Mather, *Illustrious Providences*, pp. 252–9; Cotton Mather, *Memorable Providences Relating to Witchcrafts and Possessions* (Boston, 1689), pp. 17–19. See also Stacy Schiff, *The Witches: Salem, 1692* (London, 2015), pp. 72, 267–8.

105 W. H. Whitmore (ed.), *Letters Written from New-England A.D. 1686. By John Dunton* (Boston, 1867), p. 72. Cf. Josselyn, *Two Voyages*, pp. 178, 182.

106 TNA, CO 5/857, No. 7; CO 5/905, pp. 414–17, 426–30; CO 5/751, Nos. 28–9.

107 The classic thesis is Paul Boyer and Stephen Nissenbaum, *Salem Possessed: The Social Origins of Witchcraft* (Cambridge, MA, 1974). For critiques: John Demos, *The Enemy Within: 2,000 Years of Witch-Hunting in the Western World* (New York, 2008), pp. 189–202; 'Forum: Salem repossessed', *WMQ*, 65 (2008), pp. 391–534.

108 Lawson, *Christ's Fidelity*, pp. 10, 26, 60–62, quotation at p. 61.

109 Joshua Scottow, *A Narrative of the Planting of the Massachusetts Colony* (Boston, 1694), pp. 48–51, quotations at pp. 49, 51.

110 HCRP, Wills (John Pynchon, 1703; Jonathan Burt, 1707); *LNL*, p. 465. Burt, who had bought the Parsons homelot in 1651, lived until 1715: *FCHS*, p. 42.

111 TNA, CO 5/788, pp. 281–4; CO 5/789, pp. 796–8; MC, vol. 11, pp. 214–217A; Wright, *Early Springfield*, pp. 54–5. Inhabitants included George Colton's descendants: Longmeadow Historical Society, Account Books, 1699–1910, Boxes 1–24 (Samuel Colton).

112 John Williams, *Warnings to the Unclean* (Boston, 1698), p. 12; King (ed.), *Handbook*, p. 317. See also Cotton Mather, *Pillars of Salt* (Boston, 1699), pp. 103–5.

113 Daniel Brewer, *God's Help Be Sought in Time of War* (Boston, 1724), p. 4; Joseph Lathrop, *A Sermon on the Dangers of the Times* (Springfield, MA, 1798), p. 5.

114 Demos, *Entertaining Satan*, p. 367; Byington, *The Puritan*, pp. 335–68; Steven Sarson, *British America, 1500–1800: Creating Colonies, Imagining an Empire* (London, 2005), pp. 143–6; Hugh Brogan, *The Penguin History of the United States of America*, 2nd edn (London, 1999), pp. 45–9; Joyce Appleby, 'Value and society', in Jack P. Greene and J. R. Pole (eds.), *Colonial British America: Essays in the New History of the Early Modern Era* (Baltimore, 1984), pp. 304–5, 307–9.

115 Murrin, 'Magistrates, sinners, and a precarious liberty', pp. 197–206; Carol Z. Stearns, ' "Lord help me walk humbly": anger and sadness in England and America, 1570–1750', in Carol Z. Stearns and Peter N. Stearns (eds.), *Emotion and Social Change: Toward a New Psychohistory* (New York, 1988), pp. 45–50, 57–9; Konig, *Law and Society*, pp. 65, 89, 115–18, 188–9; Richard Archer, *Fissures in the Rock: New England in the Seventeenth Century* (Hanover, NH, 2001), pp. 125–6, 148–50.

116 McLachlan, *Socinianism*, pp. 337–8; James, 'Evolution of a radical', pp. 42–3.

117 Hale, *Modest Enquiry*, pp. 20–21, 41–51, 52–7, 67–9, 71–7, quotation at p. 69.

118 'At the date when, in England, people gave up the practice of burning witches, they began to hang the forgers of banknotes': Karl Marx, *Capital*, 4th edn (London, 1928), p. 837.

119 Joseph Glanvill, *Saducismus Triumphatus* (London, 1681), pt II, pp. 308–9. The chief justice of South Carolina denounced sceptics in 1706: Jon Butler, 'Magic, astrology, and the early American religious heritage, 1600–1760', *AHR*, 84 (1979), pp. 335–8. In America more suspected witches were illegally killed after Salem than were legally killed before it: Owen Davies, *America Bewitched: The Story of Witchcraft After Salem* (Oxford, 2016), ch. 8.

120 'The tale of enchantment . . . have [sic] lost their hold on the minds of the great multitude . . . As for witches, the race is extinct': John G. Whittier, *Legends of New-England* (Hartford, CT, 1831), pp. 63–4. Belief in witches was like native 'savagery', viewed by colonists as both dangerous and absurd, as in John Cadwalader M'Call, *The Witch of New England: A Romance* (Philadelphia, 1824). On this point: Philip Gould, *Covenant and Republic: Historical Romance and the Politics of Puritanism* (Cambridge, 1996), p. 191. On the growing intellectual irrelevance of the devil: Jonathan Israel, *Radical Enlightenment: Philosophy and the Making of Modernity, 1650–1750* (Oxford, 2001), ch. 21.

Epilogue: An End to All Affection

1 Pynchon, *Record of the Pynchon Family*, pp. 6–16. The Pynchons' power depended on patron–client relationships, which waned after 1700: *LNL*, ch. 6.

2 *Hampden County*, pp. 344, 378–9, 380.

3 Vella et al. (eds.), *Meritorious Price*, pp. xlv–xlvi.

4 *LNL*, p. 137.

5 HCRP, Wills (John Pynchon, 1703; William Pynchon, 1740). 'The sea of opinion in England was too much roiled for another stone or two to add even a ripple': Morison, 'Pynchon', pp. 106–7. Pynchon's book 'seems to have exhaled its life in the flames in which it was burned upon Boston market place': Foster, *Genetic History*, p. 20.

6 HLAS, ESMC, ESM-06-01-03, p. 81. Another Salem judge, Samuel Sewall, owned Pynchon's 1655 book, *The Meritorious Price of Mans Redemption*, a copy offered for sale in New York in 2011.

7 Windsor Historical Society, Windsor, CT, Bedortha Family Collection, 1863–97, finding aid (boxes 2–3).

8 King (ed.), *Handbook*, pp. 15–16, 223–4; Henry Morris, *Early History of Springfield* (Springfield, MA, 1876), p. 17; Frank Bauer, *At the Crossroads: Springfield, Massachusetts, 1636–1975* (Springfield, MA, 1975), p. 9. The legend that Pynchon's house was moved and became a Swiss laundry is dubious: Wright, *Genesis*, pp. 18–19.

9 HCRP, Wills (Miles Morgan, 1700). Morgan's mark was a circle with an arrow, or sometimes a bow and arrow: MC, vol. 11, p. 19; HRBD, p. 48; WPAB, p. 23. Once someone wrote a beautiful signature for him: MC, vol. 112, p. 207.

10 Samuel Drake in *AWNE*, p. 72. For other nineteenth-century mentions of the case: Epaphras Hoyt, *Antiquarian Researches: Comprising a History of the Indian Wars* (Greenfield, MA, 1824), pp. 164–5; James Thacher, *An Essay on Demonology, Ghosts and Apparitions, and Popular Superstitions* (Boston, 1831), p. 101; Byington, *The Puritan*, pp. 196–7.

11 W. G. Sebald, *The Rings of Saturn*, trans. Michael Hulse (London, 1998), p. 125.

12 Thomas Pynchon, *Gravity's Rainbow* (London, 1973; 2013 edn), pp. 657–8. See also: Vella et al. (eds.), *Meritorious Price*, pp. xi, xvi–xvii; Deborah L. Madsen, 'Family legacies: identifying the traces of William Pynchon in *Gravity's Rainbow*', *Pynchon Notes*, 42–3 (1998), pp. 29–48.

13 J. G. Holland, *The Bay-Path: A Tale of New England Colonial Life* (New York, 1857), quotation at p. 227. See also Charles H. Barrows, *The History of Springfield in Massachusetts for the Young* (Springfield, MA, 1909), pp. 54–5. In her novel *Weave a Web of Witchcraft* (n.p., 2018) Jean M. Roberts sides with Hugh, echoing Samuel Drake, who called him 'an honest, sensible labouring man' beset

by his wife and witch-hunting Pynchon: *AWNE*, p. 66. Joseph H. Smith's critique of Drake is more sensitive: *CJWM*, pp. 20–25. Samuel Morison deemed Hugh a scapegoat and blamed Mary for killing their baby, 'an ill-favored, puling brat – a regular witch-child': 'Pynchon', pp. 97–8. Most writers pity Mary. 'Her character was so fair, that we must believe undoubtedly she was insane': Savage, iii, p. 362. David Powers calls her 'a hurt, fragile person . . . deeply distraught following the recent death of her second child': *DH*, p. 102. Regarding links between Mary's insanity and her faith, she resembles the 'Holy Sister' of St Ives, Huntingdonshire, 'a constant frequenter of godly meetings and religious exercises', who emigrated to New England and was hanged as a witch: John Nalson, *The Countermine* (London, 1677), pp. 93–4.

14 TRSR, p. 9.

15 In 2001 Massachusetts finally cleared the names of those executed at Salem in 1692: *New York Times* (2 November 2001), p. 12. Windsor, Connecticut, exonerated its executed witches, Alice Young and Lydia Gilbert, on 6 February 2017: Harlan Levy, 'Windsor "pardons" women hanged in 1600s', *Journal Inquirer* (14 February 2017), p. 3.

16 Marion Gibson, *Witchcraft Myths in American Culture* (New York, 2007), pp. 81–2. Mary Parsons was 'as much a martyr to be held in commiserating memory by us, as many others who fell by the way during the making of Springfield': Green, p. 109.

Sources and Methods

1 Bliss, *Address*, p. 19; Samuel G. Drake, *The History and Antiquities of Boston* (Boston, 1856), p. 323. Drake was, however, critical of past beliefs, dismissing the charges as 'childish nonsense' and the whole case as 'puerile, absurd and ridiculous': *AWNE*, pp. 70–71.

2 *AWNE*, p. 219; Gibson, *Witchcraft Myths*, p. 82. Since pages 1, 20, 21 and 52 are much dirtier than the rest, it's likely the depositions once formed two separate bundles (pp. 1–20 and 21–52) bound together later. The fact that p. 21 is a second title page supports the idea.

3 On historians as storytellers: Theodore Zeldin, 'Personal history and the history of the emotions', *Journal of Social History*, 15 (1982), pp. 339, 341–3; John Hatcher, *The Black Death: The Intimate Story of a Village in Crisis, 1345–1350* (London, 2008), preface; Rebekah Xanthe Taylor and Craig Jordan-Baker, '"Fictional biographies": creative writing and the archive', *Archives and Records*, 40 (2019), pp. 198–212.

4 Stephen Greenblatt, 'How it must have been', *New York Review of Books*, 56 (2009), pp. 22–5; John Higham, 'The limits of relativism: restatement and remembrance', *Journal of the History of Ideas*, 56 (1995), p. 673.

5 Morris, *First Church*, pp. 5–6.

6 Joyce Appleby, Lynn Hunt and Margaret Jacob, *Telling the Truth About History* (New York, 1994), p. 259.

7 Edward Muir and Guido Ruggiero (eds.), *Microhistory and the Lost Peoples of Europe* (Baltimore, 1991); Alf Lüdtke (ed.), *The History of Everyday Life: Reconstructing Historical Experiences and Ways of Life* (Princeton, 1995); Brad S. Gregory, 'Is small beautiful? Microhistory and the history of everyday life', *History and Theory*, 38 (1999), pp. 100–110; Richard D. Brown, 'Microhistory and the post-modern challenge', *Journal of the Early Republic*, 23 (2003), pp. 1–20; John Brewer, 'Microhistory and the histories of everyday life', *Cultural and Social History*, 7 (2010), pp. 87–109.

8 David Hopkin, 'Cinderella of the Breton polders: suffering and escape in the notebooks of a young, female farm-servant in the 1880s', *Past and Present*, 238 (2018), pp. 121–63. On modernization: Jack A. Goldstone, 'The problem of the "early modern" world', *Journal of the Economic and Social History of the Orient*, 41 (1998), pp. 249–84; J. G. A. Pocock, 'Perceptions of modernity in early modern historical thinking', *Intellectual History Review*, 17 (2007), pp. 55–63; Garthine Walker, 'Modernization', in *idem* (ed.), *Writing Early Modern History* (London, 2007), ch. 2; Jane Shaw, *Miracles in Enlightenment England* (New Haven, CT, 2006).

9 Katharine Hodgkin, 'Historians and witches', *History Workshop Journal*, 45 (1998), p. 272; Stuart Clark, 'Introduction', in Stuart Clark (ed.), *Languages of Witchcraft: Narrative, Ideology, and Meaning in Early Modern Culture* (Basingstoke, 2001), pp. 1–18.

10 David Levin, *In Defense of Historical Literature: Essays on American History, Autobiography, Drama, and Fiction* (New York, 1967), p. 90; Michel de Certeau, *The Writing of History*, trans. Tom Conley (New York, 1988), p. 250.

11 Lyndal Roper, 'Beyond discourse theory', *Women's History Review*, 19 (2010), pp. 307–19; Harley, 'Explaining Salem', pp. 329–30; Apps and Gow, *Male Witches*, pp. 10, 13–18; Edward Bever, *The Realities of Witchcraft and Popular Magic in Early Modern Europe: Culture, Cognition, and Everyday Life* (Basingstoke, 2008); Éva Pócs, *Between the Living and the Dead: A Perspective on Witches and Seers in the Early Modern Age* (Budapest, 1999), ch. 4. On witchcraft as 'witchcraft': Malcolm Gaskill, 'Masculinity and witchcraft in seventeenth-century England', in Alison Rowlands (ed.), *Witchcraft and Masculinities in Early Modern Europe* (Basingstoke, 2009), pp. 171–90.

12 Peter Laslett, *The World We Have Lost, Further Explored*, 3rd edn (London, 1983), ch. 12.

Index

Index

ary Parsons his wife saith that one Reason why
doth suspect you to be a witch is because you cannot
ide that any thing should be spoken against witches
saith that you told her that you were at a neighbo
house a little before Easter when there were speak
? Carrington & his wife that were now apprehended
or witches; she saith that when you came home &
spake these speeches to her: she said to you I
hope that god will find out all such wicked person
t. purge New England of all witches ere it
long be. To this she saith you gave her a naughty
look but never a word, but presently after upon a
slight occasion you took up a block & made
as if you would throw it at her head but yet
in the end you did not but threw it downe on t
hearth of the chimney. The expression of his anger
was because she wished the ruin of all witches

Hugh Parsons saith he doth not remember that ever
he took up a block to throw at her, but upon further
debate he said at last that he took up a block but
remembered not the occasion: at his 2d examination
he saith that he took up no block on that occasi
but it might well be on that occasion for
Mary Parsons saith that you said to her if ever an
trouble doe come unto you it will be by her meane
that she would be the meanes to hang you

Hugh Parsons saith that he might say so but mi
anger he is impatient & doth speak what he shoul
not: at his 2d examination he saith he might say
for she is the worst enemy that I have

he